Earl Proulx's

Earl Proulx's

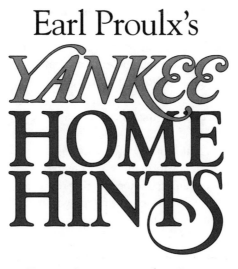

YANKEE HOME HINTS

From Stains on the Rug
to Squirrels in the Attic,
over 1,500 Ingenious Solutions
to Everyday Household Problems

By Earl Proulx
and the Editors of *YANKEE* Magazine

Printed in the United States of America on acid-free ∞, recycled ♲ paper

Library of Congress Cataloging-in-Publication Data

Proulx, Earl.
    [Yankee home hints]
    Earl Proulx's Yankee home hints: from stains on the rug to squirrels in the attic, over 1,500 ingenious solutions to everyday household problems / by Earl Proulx and the editors of Yankee magazine.
        p.   cm.
    Includes index.
    ISBN 0 – 89909 – 365 – 5 hardcover
    1. Dwellings — Maintenance and repair — Amateurs' manuals.   2. Home economics.
    I. Yankee (Dublin, N.H.)   II. Title.
    TH4817.3.P76 1993
    643'.7 — dc20   92–46642
                                      CIP

Distributed in the trade by St. Martin's Press

      8   10   9   hardcover

Earl Proulx's
YANKEE
HOME
HINTS

YANKEE BOOKS STAFF
Managing Editor: Edward Claflin
Associate Editor: Sarah Dunn
Art Director: Jane Knutila
Cover Designer: Vic Mazurkiewicz

YANKEE PUBLISHING STAFF
Book Editor: Sharon Smith
Associate Editor: Jamie Trowbridge
Contributing Writers: Richard Bacon, Ken Bibby, Jim
    Collins, Charles Davis, Steve Fowle, Martin Harris,
    Will Lange, Tim Matson, Steven Maviglio, Don
    Mitchell, H. Allan Mooney, Dave Nelson, Bill Novak,
    Georgia Orcutt, Gordon Peery, Susan Peery, Mike
    Peters, Paul Quinn, Steve Smith, Bob Trebilcock,
    Fran White, Dave Zilavy
Editorial Consultants: Andy Elder, George Lohmiller
Assistant Editor: Cynthia Schlosser
Book Designer: Jill Shaffer
Illustrators: Walter Carroll, Maryann Mattson,
    Jill Shaffer
Production Assistant: Linda Ottavi
Fact Checkers: Lori Baird, Gordon Bock, Gordon Peery
Researchers: Mica Cloutier, Isabel Clukay, Linda Clukay,
    Sue MacEwan
Copy Editor and Proofreader: Barbara Jatkola

To my mother,
who taught me
the importance of being honest.

And to my father,
who taught me
the importance of being clever.

Contents

Introducing Earl Proulx

HOW CAN YOU RESTORE a paint-hardened brush to usefulness? What's a homeowner to do about white rings on a mahogany desk? What's the best way to stack firewood? Just ask Earl Proulx. For 14 years, Earl has been answering questions like these in "Plain Talk," his popular monthly column in *Yankee* Magazine.

Earl was a handyman, builder and contractor before he became a columnist, and his practical solutions to everyday household problems come from years of experience. Earl is also a New Englander who holds to the Yankee notion that the old (and forgotten) way is usually the best. And thrift is his middle name.

Sometimes the problems Earl tackles in "Plain Talk" can be rather peculiar: How do you get a skunk out of the toolshed? (Earl's response: Remember that skunks hate smelly things.) How do you get moss to grow on a stone wall to make it look authentic? How can you get hardened concrete off your best shovel? For those desperately seeking the answers to unsolved household problems, the column has always offered ingenious and successful solutions. And readers who send in pictures of "Whatsits" — curious old objects they've picked up at yard sales or found in attics — have come to depend on Earl for expert identifications.

If it's in the home and it doesn't work, check with Earl.

1

Certainly the historical and quirky tips (along with solutions to the "Whatsits" mysteries) make "Plain Talk" fun to read, but *Yankee* readers also turn to the column every month for purely practical information. In a world where products are increasingly designed for obsolescence or even disposal, Earl's tips stand out. Got a run in your panty hose? Don't throw them away; you're going to need them to clean under the fridge. Break an old piece of china? With the proper adhesive, you can repair it. Water in your cellar? Don't spend money on expensive solutions without trying some simpler ideas first.

How did Earl come to know these secrets? You could argue that they're in his blood. Earl learned a good deal of what he knows about home repair from his father, a top-notch carpenter who worked all over New Hampshire's Monadnock Region. Earl apprenticed under his father from age 14 to 22, on projects ranging in difficulty from closing up summer cottages to building new homes. Then, in 1935, he bought a motorcycle, loaded his tools into a sidecar and went to work for himself laying linoleum. But Earl's skills were too wide-ranging for him to remain specialized for long, and he soon found himself working for a large general contractor.

For 30 years, Earl was a superintendent for large contractors, finding commonsense solutions to large-scale problems such as how to manufacture concrete blocks and how to divert a river long enough to repair a bridge abutment. His most impressive large-scale achievement came when he directed the activity of 50 carpenters during the construction of 27 stables at a racetrack — all in 27 days. But Earl also took on many smaller projects in his years with contractors. Large or small, he's done it all.

Earl has built homes for his family, doing the construction work himself on weekends and evenings, even when he held a full-time job. His first home was a model of frugal construction. He adapted a *Popular Mechanics* plan designed to use standard building materials to maximum efficiency. When he was finished, he had so little left over that he could fit the scrap lumber from the entire job in one small barrel. Extras on the house came cheap. He used old Burma-Shave signs for kitchen shelves ("nice 12" ponderosa pine") and lumber salvaged from old wooden chalkboards for shutters.

         EARL PROULX'S YANKEE HOME HINTS

In 1972, Yankee Publishing hired Earl to run its maintenance staff, and it wasn't long before Yankee employees came to depend on him to solve their home-related problems, too. After Earl had dispensed advice to staff members on topics as diverse as sagging rooflines and chair refinishing, the editors recognized that he was a valuable resource in more ways than one. If Earl could solve home problems for the editors, why not for *Yankee* readers? Thus "Plain Talk" was born.

Earl retired from Yankee's maintenance staff in 1985, but he continues to solve home-related problems in his current role as columnist. Every week he receives a fistful of letters from *Yankee* readers all around the country. He answers all their questions, takes on their challenges and gratefully accepts the occasional suggestions that come from his loyal audience. Working as hard on his "Plain Talk" correspondence as he has on any carpentry project, he still follows his father's advice: "Always do a little more work than you're being paid for, and you'll never have to worry about a job."

After 65 years, Earl's files are overflowing with notes and clippings. He's polished his best home repair stories, and we've helped him collect all the information on home maintenance and repair that we could fit between the covers of this book.

Earl's tips may inspire you to go to work right away, but before you do, there are a couple of things to keep in mind. Laws and regulations vary from one area to another, particularly between urban and rural areas. Where a tip notes that you should check with local authorities, please do so before you begin a major project.

It's also worth noting that some of the hints in this book call for products and materials that discount-store chains may not carry. We checked the availability of all the recommended items, so we know that you can find them at many hardware, paint and building supply stores, as well as at other retail outlets. For the more old-fashioned items, try small, independent stores.

But enough introduction. If you want a simple, surefire way to remove the black gunk from your cast-iron frying pan, turn to page 17 right away.

THE EDITORS OF *Yankee* MAGAZINE

Cleaning around the House

Be sure to stock up on baking soda and vinegar— not for cooking, but for cleaning.

THIS CHAPTER IS devoted to traditional, time-honored methods of cleaning that still work in the modern home. Need help with a greasy oven, a clogged steam iron, price stickers on your new glassware, tarnish on the best silver, yellowed piano keys or dead bugs stuck to the car windshield? Got a little extra baking soda, vinegar, mayonnaise, table salt, Worcestershire sauce or sour milk? This chapter tells you how to match each problem with the appropriate household solution—saving dollars on your household cleaning budget and, in many cases, saving the environment as well.

In choosing among the suggestions listed here, it's important to remember that when it comes to cleaning, there's often more than one right answer. For every cleaning tip I recommend in "Plain Talk," I receive a few letters from readers. They might have tried my technique and liked it, or maybe they want more details. Occasionally I receive letters from people who feel that there's only one way to skin a cat—like the man who wrote to tell me that to scour the inside of a garbage disposal, you should pour in very hot water and baking soda—not ice cubes and lemon rinds, as I had suggested. Both solutions are fine. Maybe he has some baking soda he needs to dispose of; maybe I have some lemon rinds sitting around. That's why you'll find a lot of alternatives listed here.

Some of these tips don't give specific measurements for cleaning solutions. There's a reason for that: The strength of your homemade cleanser will depend on your job. For a light cleaning, use a mild solution. Strengthen the solution if you're faced with a daunting task. But always test a cleaning solution before doing the full job. To be sure the cleanser is safe for the material you're working on, try it first on a spot that won't show.

GENERAL RULES

Cleaning Can Be Hazardous to Your Health
❏ If you see the word *caustic* on any of your cleaning agents, that means there's a danger of chemically burn-

---

IF YOU CAN'T FIND IT ...

... maybe you need to try another chapter. Check the index, or try these possibilities.

For Cleaning ...	*See the Chapters ...*
Barbecue grills	The Summer House
Carpets	Floors
Floors	Floors
Furniture	Furniture
Mildew	Maintaining the Exterior; Stains and Odors
Moss off roofs	Maintaining the Exterior
Stains on countertops	Stains and Odors

---

ing your skin. Wear rubber gloves when using caustic cleaners, and be especially careful to avoid splashing these chemicals.

❑ Do not mix chlorine bleach with toilet bowl cleaners, ammonia, lye, rust remover, vinegar or oven cleaner. You may inadvertently create chlorine gas, which is highly toxic—even lethal.

❑ Always store vinegar in a glass container. Combined with lead or copper, vinegar produces a deadly poison.

❑ When you're working with solvents (denatured alcohol, turpentine, paint thinner, kerosene or acetone, for instance), always seal containers tightly and store in a well-ventilated space. Keep the solvents away from an open flame while you are working with them, as they are extremely flammable.

❑ Oily cloths, such as those that have been used for cleaning, are also a fire hazard. As soon as you're through with them, spread them out to dry in an airy spot. Be sure they're completely dry before you throw them away.

❑ Always keep your work area well ventilated when you are working with solvents. Their strong odors can be dangerous unless accompanied by plenty of fresh air.

❑ Never leave cleaning agents in a spot where children can get at them. Swallowing them can be lethal, and they can be caustic to young skin. And just in case, be sure to keep the number of your local poison control center near the phone at all times.

Now for a Little Ragtime

❑ It's always a good idea to have cleaning rags around, but remember that not all fabrics make good rags. Cotton is very good, especially old diapers, men's undershirts or flannel pajamas. Linen is good, too, if you have any old

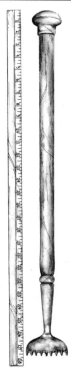

Whatsit?

THIS TOOL WAS found in an abandoned house. From the other objects found on the premises, I would guess that it dates to around the turn of this century. The house is located near a major river and farming community. Can you tell me the purpose of this implement?
— P.B., YANTIC, CONN.
This is an ice chisel for shaping large blocks of ice. It could still be used today in making ice sculptures.

napkins on hand. Stay away from synthetics, which don't absorb water or pick up dirt very well.

If It Doesn't Work Here, There's Always the Salad

❑ Mayonnaise is one of the best substances for cleaning pine pitch, grease or tar off your hands. Rub it on, let it sit for a few minutes and clean off the spot.

❑ Vegetable oil will also remove tar from your hands. Let it sit for a while, then rub it off.

De Grease! De Grease!

❑ Add a few drops of ammonia to soapy water to cut any grease in the water.

❑ To clean greasy hands, scrub them with soap, water and a little sawdust.

❑ Except when using chlorine bleach, add ¼ cup of vinegar to each gallon of rinse water whenever you're cleaning. The vinegar will help clean and eliminate streaking.

The Next Best Thing to Vinegar

❑ If—heaven forbid—you should run out of vinegar, you'll probably find some other potential cleaners in your kitchen. Tomato sauce, ketchup, Worcestershire sauce, mayonnaise and, of course, pickle juice all contain vinegar. In a pinch, substitute any of them for vinegar. Just remember that any of these will be weaker than vinegar, so it won't be quite as effective.

It's That Abrasive Personality

❑ Use a paste of baking soda and water as an inexpensive but effective scouring powder for all sorts of cleaning jobs, from countertops to rolling pins to gold-trimmed dishes.

MAJOR APPLIANCES

The Superstrength Cleaner: You

❑ Having trouble moving heavy objects like your refrigerator when you're doing spring cleaning? To solve the problem, you'll need a straw broom and a friend to help you. Push the bristles of the broom under the front of the refrigerator and, with the friend, tip the refrigerator onto

VINEGAR: THE BEST CLEANER OF ALL

IT SEEMS STRANGE to realize that a simple liquid in your kitchen cabinet could have so many uses in household cleaning. Vinegar cleans everything from garbage disposals to greasy pans to shower curtains. But the vinegar you buy in the supermarket is nothing more than acetic acid diluted with water to a strength of about 5 percent. It's one of the cheapest multiuse products you'll find on a grocery shelf.

Vinegar was the first substance to be officially labeled an acid, a term derived from the Latin *acidus*, meaning "sharp" or "sour." The term eventually was broadened to include all acidlike substances, and the word *acetic* was used to specify the acid in vinegar. Acetic acid is a powerful organic solvent and preservative commonly used in industry.

Vinegar is derived through a process that turns starches to sugars, which ferment into alcohol, which ferments a second time into vinegar. It can be made from grapes, wine, malt juice, beer or cider, among other things. From a cleaning perspective, the origins of the vinegar you buy (white or cider, for instance) do not matter. All varieties contain about 5 percent acetic acid.

You can buy stronger solutions of acetic acid at drugstores, but not without a prescription. If you don't want to go that far but would like a stronger solution than your bottled vinegar provides, you can boil your vinegar and evaporate the water in it to increase the percentage of acetic acid remaining. A 16-ounce bottle of vinegar evaporated down to 8 ounces, for instance, would result in an acetic acid solution of about 10 percent. Just remember, the stronger the solution, the more powerful the solvent—and the more dangerous it is to handle.

While you're stocking your cleaning closet, pick up an extra bottle of vinegar for the medicine cabinet. Vinegar is a great home remedy, too. When a customer comes in with a skin irritation, a local pharmacist suggests going home and sponging the area with vinegar. If the itching stops, the condition is on the outside of the skin and has been cured. If it persists, the condition is internal and it's time to call the doctor. This pharmacist also suggests vinegar sponge baths to treat sunburns and mixing equal parts vinegar and rubbing alcohol for drops that cure swimmer's ear. "People don't realize how many things vinegar can do," he says.

them. Then slide the appliance away from the wall. When you're through cleaning, use the same procedure to slide the appliance back into position. It works like a charm.

Refrigerators: Keep the Cold, Cure the Congestion

❏ Vacuum the condenser of your refrigerator occasionally. Otherwise, it will get clogged with dust, causing the unit to run more than it should. The condenser, which is located in the back or on the bottom of the refrigerator, looks like a large grill. If the condenser on your refrigerator is located underneath the appliance, get at it by removing the front bottom panel from the refrigerator. Then use the vacuum hose to reach underneath the unit.

Refrigerator Rust Prevention

❏ Coat metal refrigerator racks with floor wax to keep them from rusting.

Stoves: Get to the Grease

❏ To prevent grease buildup on oven walls, wipe them occasionally with a cloth dampened with a little vinegar and water.

❏ To clean grease buildup off oven racks, give the racks a bath. Put enough hot water in the bathtub to cover the racks, then mix in ¼ cup of dishwasher detergent and ¼ cup of white vinegar. Stir to dissolve the detergent. Wait for an hour or so, then rinse and dry the racks. Drain the water from your tub right away, or you'll get a nasty bathtub ring.

❏ To loosen the grime on an electric oven, try this: Make sure the oven is off. Heat 1½ to 2 quarts of water to a rolling boil. Keeping the water at arm's length, pour in ¼ to ½ cup of ammonia. Immediately place the pot in the oven and let it sit overnight. The steam will carry the ammonia through the oven, loosening the grease and dirt. The next morning, wipe the oven clean, scrubbing any heavily soiled areas.

❏ This method can also be used for gas ovens, but only after turning off the gas to extinguish the pilot light—an important procedure anytime you are doing heavy-duty cleaning on a gas stove. Turn the gas completely off so none is moving through the system. (This is equivalent to shutting off the water main to prevent water from flowing through the pipes.)

❑ To clean the reflector pans under the burners of your stove, wet them and sprinkle on some baking soda. Let sit for 5 minutes, then scrub the pans with a sponge. For particularly tough spills, try scrubbing with full-strength acetone (available in hardware stores and drugstores), then rinsing the pans off. If you use acetone, be sure you have plenty of ventilation.

❑ Clean the window in your oven or toaster oven only when the oven is cool. Spray on oven cleaner, wipe it off, then wash the window with glass cleaner. If you use only the oven cleaner, it will leave a stain when heated.

Chrome

❑ To clean chrome on appliances, rub with baby oil, club soda or a piece of lemon. Wash the chrome, then rub dry with a soft cloth.

❑ You can also clean chrome inexpensively by simply rubbing it with crumpled newspaper, a cloth rinsed in hot water and a little ammonia or a cloth soaked in vinegar.

❑ Another method for cleaning chrome is to rub on a thin paste of baking soda and water. Let it dry, then buff the chrome with a clean, dry rag.

❑ You can use a glass cleaner or automotive chrome cleaner on kitchen appliances. They're very effective.

❑ Sometimes you can clean chrome with a damp rag that's been dipped in wood ashes. The only way to find out whether this technique will work in a particular situation is to try it.

Deposit Insurance

❑ To clean chrome hardware that's beset with whitish lime deposits, cover

Whatsit?

WHAT WAS THIS wooden object used for? It's very well made, but I don't know what to do with it.
— P.H., LEXINGTON, MASS.

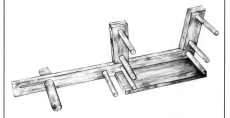

This is called a warping frame. When setting up a loom for weaving, you string up the warp first, then weave the woof between the threads of the warp. Rather than cut the warp threads individually, a weaver would wrap the yarn around this gadget and cut the threads all at once.

the chrome with a vinegar-soaked rag and leave the rag in place overnight. The next day, rub the chrome with the rag.

Washing Machines: Skip the Agitation

❑ Here's a way to clean the filter on your washing machine. First, use an old toothbrush to remove any lint. Soak the filter in white vinegar overnight, then rinse it with water.

❑ Don't wait for your washing machine to clog before you clean it. A heavily used washer should be cleaned once a year. First, fill it with hot water. Then make a solution of ½ cup of TSP (or another product containing trisodium phosphate), ½ cup of household (5 percent) bleach and 2 quarts of warm water. Pour this solution into the machine and run it through the wash and rinse cycles.

❑ You can also give a washing machine an annual cleaning by filling the machine with hot water, adding a quart of white vinegar and running the machine through the wash and rinse cycles.

Wash the Dishwasher

❑ To clean a dishwasher, place a bowl containing 2 to 3 cups of vinegar on the bottom rack. Leave all the racks in place, but don't put any dishes in them. Run the dishwasher through the wash and rinse cycles only, shutting the machine off before it goes into the drying cycle. The vinegar will splash about as the dishwasher runs, cleaning the whole thing.

Stick It to the Dust Bunnies

❑ You can clean lint and dirt from under large appliances without moving the appliances. Drape an old nylon stocking over a yardstick and slide the yardstick under the appliance.

❑ The nylon-on-a-yardstick technique is also good for cleaning cobwebs from the edges of hard-to-reach ceilings.

TRISODIUM WHAT?

Trisodium phosphate is a terrific multipurpose cleaner. One popular product with a trisodium phosphate base is TSP. Most automatic dishwasher detergents contain this cleaner, too. Check the label on your detergent. If trisodium phosphate is an active ingredient, you're in business. Just remember to wear rubber gloves when using any product containing trisodium phosphate, as it can be pretty rough on your hands.

THANK HEAVEN JOSEPHINE COULDN'T GET GOOD HELP

JOSEPHINE COCHRANE, when she invented the first automatic dishwasher, was no humble dishwasher looking for an easy way out. She was a blue blood from Chicago, a woman with wealth and servants and only so much patience. Her help, it seems, couldn't keep from breaking the occasional dish during cleanup after the frequent formal dinners Cochrane put on. So Cochrane, fed up with the expense, the time it took to replace her shattered dishes by mail order and the, well, plain *incompe-tence* of her help, headed out to the woodshed and rigged up a contraption in a large copper boiler. She fashioned wire compartments (sized to match her glasses, cups and saucers) in a wheel turned by a motor, and she figured out how to squirt soapy water over the whole works as it rotated. Lo and behold, the thing got the dishes clean.

Word spread in Cochrane's circle, and her circle being what it was, it spread to some pretty important places. Cochrane received her patent in 1886, then took the highest award at the 1893 Chicago World's Fair.

In the century since then, her invention has been a boon to hotel, restaurant and home owners alike.

SMALL APPLIANCES

When Plastic Melts on a Toaster Oven

❏ If plastic wrap melts on a warm toaster oven, unplug the oven, let it cool, then remove the plastic with acetone on a cloth pad. When working with acetone, be sure to allow plenty of ventilation; the fumes can be hazardous.

❏ You can also remove plastic that's melted onto a toaster oven by soaking a rag with ammonia and using it to cover the plastic. Leave the rag in place for a few minutes, then gently scrape off the plastic.

Air Conditioners: Clean That Filthy Filter

❏ To clean an air conditioner or humidifier filter, take the foam filter out of the grill and soak it in a solution of equal parts white vinegar and warm water. How often you need to do this depends on the conditions of use, such as whether there are smokers present. If you clean the filter regularly, an hour of soaking will be plenty. A dirtier filter will need to soak longer. Just squeeze the filter dry when it's clean.

Disposals: On the Rocks, with a Twist of Lemon

❏ To freshen a garbage disposal, dump in a tray of ice cubes and a handful of lemon rinds, then turn on the water and run the disposal as usual.

❏ You can use the same technique with a tray of ice cubes made from vinegar and water.

❏ To clean a garbage disposal—or any sink drain—pour in ½ cup of baking soda and flush with very hot water.

Steam Irons: Cleanup Time

❏ To clean gummed-up holes in a steam iron, mix ⅓ cup of white vinegar and 1 tablespoon of baking soda until well blended. Pour the solution into the iron. Heat the iron, leave it on for just a few minutes (until it begins to steam), and then turn it off and empty it. Fill it with warm water to rinse the well, then empty and rinse it again.

❏ If your iron leaves sticky black spots on your clothes, try this: Sprinkle a little salt on a piece of paper, then run the warm iron over the salt. The gentle abrasion will remove all the gunk.

❏ The salt-on-paper technique is also effective in cleaning starch buildup from the bottom of an iron.

❏ Another way to remove starch from the bottom of an iron is to rub a little toothpaste on the starch, then remove the paste with a clean, soft cloth.

❏ You can also clean the starch off the bottom of an iron by making a paste of baking soda and a little water, rubbing it on the iron with a soft cloth and wiping it off with a clean cloth.

COUNTERTOPS AND TABLETOPS

Quick Countermeasures

❏ To get a quick shine on countertops, wipe them down with vinegar.

❏ Plastic laminate countertops that have become dull with age can be brightened by applying a coat of a good automobile wax. Not much of the wax remains except the shine, so it's perfectly safe to put food on the counter afterward.

For Butchers and Bakers

❏ Coat new butcher-block counter sections with boiled linseed oil. Apply the oil with a paintbrush. Allow it to dry for 3 hours, then wipe it off. Wait 24 hours, then apply a second coat in the same manner. Wait another 24 hours, then wipe the second coat off by rubbing thoroughly with a clean rag.

❏ After the initial coat of boiled linseed oil, apply a light coat of vegetable or mineral oil to your butcher-block counters regularly to keep them clean and smelling good. Be sure to coat the sides occasionally to prevent the wood from drying out.

Tabletop Dust Prevention

❏ Apply silicone spray, available at hardware stores, to keep glass tabletops dust and lint free.

POTS AND PANS

Toward Cleaner Coffee

❏ To clean any kind of coffeepot (stove-top, glass or percolator), fill the pot with cold water, add a little baking soda, boil for a minute or so and rinse clean.

Clean Up Aluminum

❏ To clean burned food from the bottom of an aluminum pot or pan, wet the burned food, cover with baking soda and set aside for a couple of hours. Then scrape, wash and rinse the pan.

ONLY POPEYE WOULD ALWAYS STAND BY OLIVE

MANY TYPES OF OIL are commonly recommended for cleaning around the house. The source of olive oil is obvious, and many other vegetable and nut oils are named for the products from which they come. But the origins of certain other oils are more obscure. For instance:

Mineral oil is distilled petroleum. You can buy it at drugstores.

Castor oil comes from the seeds of the castor bean plant. You can get it at drugstores.

Boiled linseed oil, available at paint and hardware stores, is made from flax seed.

Neat's-foot oil is made from the hooves of cattle. ("Neat" is an archaic word for the common domestic bovine.) You can find it at leather stores and tack shops.

❏ If you're dealing with an aluminum pan that has food burned onto the bottom and is particularly greasy as well, cover the burned area with vinegar, then fill the pan with water and boil for about 10 minutes. Scrub and rinse. This is particularly effective with greasy frying pans because the vinegar cuts the grease.

❏ Wood ashes also can be used as a degreaser. Sprinkle 3 to 4 tablespoons of ashes on a greasy pot or grill, then scrub with a sponge or brush dipped in warm, soapy water.

❏ You can also clean a greasy aluminum frying pan by filling the pan with water and adding 1 tablespoon of cream of tartar. Boil the solution for a few minutes, then wash the pan and wipe it clean.

❏ The water-and-cream-of-tartar method can be used to clean a discolored aluminum pan, too. Fill the pan with water and add 1 tablespoon of cream of tartar. Boil for about 20 minutes. Wash and wipe clean.

Keep the "Stainless" in Stainless Steel

❏ To clean a stainless steel pan, first rinse it with white vinegar inside and out. Then shake on enough salt to cover. Rub lightly. This cleans the pan and keeps it shiny.

A Season for Every Cast-Iron Pot

❏ New cast-iron cooking pots can be seasoned by rubbing them with vegetable oil and placing them over low heat for 1 hour. This gets rid of any cast-iron taste that could otherwise permeate food, and it helps prevent sticking.

❏ Another way to season a cast-iron pot is by boiling potato peelings in it for 1 hour.

❏ To season a new or scrubbed cast-iron pan, coat it with mineral oil or

Whatsit?

Hope you can tell me what this iron item is and what it is used for. It is small, opens like a pair of ice tongs and has a center rod that is grooved partway up one side.
— E.G.C., Reading, Mass.

This is a lock pin for a Dutch yoke used on oxen. Before 1870, these locks were made of wood, so you can be pretty sure this one was made after that.

vegetable oil and place it in a warm (200°F) oven for a few hours. The oil will slowly soak into the pan.

❑ To get rid of any residual iron taste in a newly seasoned cast-iron pot, fill the pot with water, add a handful of hay and boil for a few minutes. This hay water can also be used to sweeten wooden or tin dishes. If you're working with wooden dishes, bring the water to a boil in another container, then pour it into the wooden dishes while it's still boiling hot.

Cast-Iron Cleanup: No Soap

❑ It's best not to clean cast-iron pots and pans with soap. Cast iron is porous, and it will absorb soap particles.

❑ To clean a cast-iron kettle, fill it with a solution of equal parts vinegar and water, then bring the solution to a boil. Turn off the heat and let the kettle sit for 2 to 3 hours. Rub the inside with steel wool before pouring out the solution. Season the kettle before using it again.

The Lady Who Burned Her Pots Clean

A N 86-YEAR-OLD WOMAN wrote to tell me how she converted a neighbor to her time-honored way of cleaning cast-iron pots and pans. It seems her folks had always given their pans a thorough cleaning by burying them in piles of leaves and setting the leaves on fire. This woman had been doing it for years; apparently it had turned into a fall ritual.

One day the elderly lady saw that her neighbor was getting ready to burn some leaves, so she went next door and asked if she could put her cast-iron pots and pans into the fire to clean them. Her neighbor laughed at the absurdity of the request but let

**A Word
from Earl**

her bury the pots in the leaves. She says he stopped laughing when the fire had died down and the pans shone like new. Since then, the elderly lady wrote, her neighbor always adds a few cast-iron pots and pans to the leaf pile before he sets it on fire each fall.

❑ Another way to clean a cast-iron pot is to fill it with warm water and drop in a couple of denture-cleaning tablets. Let sit for 1 hour, wash, rinse and air dry. No need to season.

❑ Burned food can be scoured off cast-iron pots and pans by mixing sand and vegetable oil in them and scrubbing with steel wool. Season afterward.

❑ The sand-and-vegetable-oil method also works for removing rust from cast iron.

WOOD

Clean Up without Cracking Up

❑ Clean wooden bowls with warm, soapy water, then rinse and wipe dry. If the inside of a bowl is worn, apply a coat of vegetable or mineral oil.

❑ Do not allow wooden objects to soak in water; they can crack.

❑ To clean wooden rolling pins, bowls and cutting boards, sprinkle on baking soda, dampen with a little water to make a paste and rub with a sponge. Then rinse well and dry with a cloth towel.

❑ To give wooden items a thorough cleaning, make a solution of equal parts household (5 percent) bleach and water, scrub it onto the surface of the wood and rinse well. Then apply a coat of mineral or vegetable oil. Allow the oil to penetrate for 1 hour, then wipe off any excess.

Polish It Off

❑ To restore a polished finish to wooden items, rub in a solution of 1 tablespoon of mineral oil and 1½ teaspoons of pumice (a fine abrasive available at paint and hardware stores) until the wood feels dry and smooth. Allow to dry for at least 12 hours. Repeat the process until the finish is restored. Then wipe off any excess with a damp cloth.

CRYSTAL AND GLASS

No More Cloudy Coatings

❑ To clean a glass bottle or decanter that's clouded by a calcium coating, fill the vessel with soapy water and add a splash of vinegar. Small bottles will need only a tablespoon or two of vinegar; large ones will need more.

❑ Film inside a wineglass or decanter may be removed by filling the glass with warm water and dropping in a crushed denture-cleaning tablet. Let the solution sit for a couple of hours, then wash and rinse.

❑ Another approach to removing the film from inside a wineglass is to fill the glass with a strong solution of ammonia and water. Wait a couple of hours, then wash and rinse.

Crystal Clear

❑ Clean crystal vases and glasses, or crystals from chandeliers, with a solution of 2 parts vinegar and 3 parts water. Use a paintbrush to apply the solution to tricky textured areas. Let sit, then scrub if necessary. Rinse and let dry.

Great Shakes

❑ To clean metal or glass saltshaker tops, soak them in boiling water with a teaspoon of cream of tartar (or use

The Bottle Wasn't Shipshape

SOMEONE ONCE asked me how to clean the inside of a bottle that contained a model ship. The bottle was not plugged, and dust had accumulated inside over the course of many years. Here are the instructions I gave him:

Make a wooden plug to fit the end of a vacuum cleaner hose, with an opening for a ¼" plastic hose in the plug. Attach a small piece of tubing or hose to the plug and test the suction. (If the vacuum motor is too strained or the suction is too strong, bore an extra hole in the plug.) Once you're satisfied with the suction, direct the small hose inside the bottle, being careful not to suck up parts of the model.

A Word from Earl

A rig like this will also work in other situations where you need to clean finely detailed pieces.

vinegar and water). Clean the holes with a cotton swab dipped in vinegar. (Don't try this with plastic shaker tops; they'll melt in the heat.)

Turn a Vase into a Saltshaker

❏ To clean a vase or a glass coffeepot, put in a few ice cubes and a spoonful or two of salt, shake gently for a minute or two, and then wash and rinse with cool water to avoid thermal shock. The salt and ice work as mild abrasives.

Deal with That Bottle Neck

❏ For vases or bottles with necks too narrow for ice cubes, you can create a mild abrasive from clean crushed raw eggshells mixed in water. Shake gently, pour out the eggshells, and then wash and rinse. The eggshells will not scratch the glass.

❏ Another mild abrasive for cleaning narrow-necked bottles and vases is uncooked rice. Mix a few tablespoons of rice with water in the bottle or vase. Shake gently, pour out the rice and water, wash and rinse.

Sticker Removal: Take It All Off

❏ Mayonnaise, vegetable oil or peanut butter will remove the residue from tape or stickers on glass. First, pull off as much tape as you can. Coat what's left with mayonnaise, oil or peanut butter until it is saturated. Then wash and rinse the glass.

❏ Coleman stove fuel or lighter fluid will also remove the residue from stickers or tape on glass. Rub on the fuel or fluid, let it sit for several minutes and wipe the glass clean.

❏ An alternative method for removing a decal from glass is to heat the decal with a blow dryer, then scrape off the decal.

Whatsit?

THE SMALL IRON PIECE pictured below has puzzled us for years. It resembles a stylized buffalo head or a small anvil with a strange bottom. Can you identify it?
— F.D., NORTH WALES, PA.

This is one blacksmith's idea of styling a tool appropriately for its intended use. This is a meat tenderizer shaped to represent a longhorn steer's head. To use it, place a hand between the horns, laying two fingers along the anvil and gripping the base of the horns with the other two. Then put a tough piece of beef on a block and pound it until it's tender.

❑ Other techniques for removing stickers from glass are to brush on vinegar or spray on a product such as WD-40. Then rinse thoroughly.

Get Paint Off That Glass

❑ Remove oil or latex paint from glass by wiping it with hot vinegar on a soft cloth. When the paint softens, scrape it off with a razor blade. (Or you can skip the vinegar and go straight to the razor blade. The vinegar just makes the process easier.) This technique is effective even after the paint has dried.

Clear Things Up

❑ Clean windows with a mixture of 1 part white vinegar and 10 parts warm water.

❑ When you use up the brand-name glass cleaner you bought in a spray bottle, don't throw away the bottle. Instead, refill it with car windshield washer fluid, which is inexpensive and available in large containers. Use this to wash the windows of your house.

❑ You can avoid streaked windows by drying the windows with crumpled newspaper.

The Butler Used BBs

IN "PLAIN TALK," I once recommended using warm water and a little sand to clean the inside of a decanter that had grown cloudy. I soon received a letter from a man whose father had been an English butler. His father had taught him that the proper abrasive in such a situation was BBs. I have no doubt BBs would work well, but I'm sticking with sand because I know from experience that fine sand cleans effectively without scratching.

A Word from Earl

If you remember to avoid products that scratch as well as clean, you'll probably discover lots of other fine abrasives around your house. Just use your common sense.

❏ Here's a time-honored technique for cleaning windows: Get in the habit of using vertical strokes on one side of the glass (say, the outside) and horizontal strokes on the other (say, the inside). That way, if you see streaks, you'll know which side they're on.

❏ Never wash windows on a bright, sunny day. Choose an overcast day instead. The windows will dry more slowly and will have fewer streaks.

❏ When nothing else seems to clean old, filthy glass, try scrubbing each pane with ammonia and a plastic scouring pad. Rinse with water to remove the grime. For a final wash, rub with a soft cloth soaked in a solution of 3 tablespoons of ammonia and 1 quart of water. Polish with old newspaper.

❏ Resist the temptation to use steel wool when cleaning grimy glass surfaces. Steel wool is an effective scourer and will clean the glass, but it will leave scratches, especially on older glass and especially with coarser grades of steel wool.

❏ The easiest way to clean kerosene lamp chimneys is to pour a little kerosene on newspaper and wipe the chimney. Be sure the chimney is completely dry before lighting the lamp.

❏ You can also clean a kerosene lamp chimney by putting a few drops of rubbing alcohol on a wet rag and rubbing the chimney with the rag.

❏ For a handy way to keep your eyeglasses clean, fill a spray bottle with a solution of ½ cup of vinegar and 5 pints of water. Spray on your glasses, then wipe off with a soft cloth or tissue.

Whatsit?

THE USE OF THIS LAMP is unknown to me. Can you help? The S-shaped tube is pinched to a small orifice at the wick end.

— C.A., REMSEN, N.Y.

This is an alcohol lamp that was used by jewelers and other craftsmen. Blowing into the tube would intensify the flame, which could be directed on the work at the right spot.

BRASS, BRONZE AND COPPER

Homemade Cleaners

❏ Always remember to test any cleaning agent on an inconspicuous part of the object you plan to clean.

The Navy Polishes Brass

A Word from Earl

I GOT A LOT OF LETTERS after I ran a tip in "Plain Talk" about cleaning your dishwasher with powdered fruit juice mix—some supporting the idea and others opposing it. One letter was from a man in the Navy. He cleaned with powdered juice mix all the time. In fact, he wrote, they didn't use any fancy brass cleaners aboard his ship. Instead they cleaned all their brass with powdered or canned fruit juice. I used that information to convince the naysayers that I wasn't crazy.

❏ You can clean brass, bronze and copper by rubbing on Worcestershire sauce or ketchup with a damp cloth.

❏ To make an inexpensive cleaner for brass, bronze and copper, mix equal parts salt and flour with enough vinegar to make a thick paste. Rub on vigorously with a damp cloth. Then wash, rinse and dry thoroughly.

❏ An alternative is to mix 1 tablespoon of salt and 2 tablespoons of vinegar in 1 pint of water. Heat until warm, then apply as above.

❏ Small brass, copper or bronze objects can be cleaned with a little toothpaste (not the gel type). Apply it with a soft, damp cloth or a toothbrush, then rinse and dry.

❏ To remove tarnish from brass, bronze or copper, dip a lemon slice or rind in a little salt and rub it on the object. Then clean and dry with paper towels.

❏ Add a little ammonia to a soap-and-water solution to clean these metals. Apply with a soft paintbrush or rag, then rinse and wipe dry.

Tarnish Deterrents

❏ Always dry metal objects carefully with a soft towel after cleaning. A damp item tarnishes quickly.

❏ For added protection, rub on olive oil or mineral oil to keep the metal shiny longer.

❏ Brass, bronze and copper objects that are not used for cooking can be protected from tarnishing with a coat of paste wax. Polish with a paper towel.

Special Treatments for Brass

❏ Before you decide how to clean your brass, use a magnet to tell plated brass from solid brass. The magnet will not be attracted to solid brass, but it will be attracted to the metal beneath brass plating.

❏ To remove paint from a solid brass object, such as an electrical outlet cover or door hardware, immerse the piece in water and boil for 15 minutes. Remove from the water and allow to cool. Then rub off the paint with a plastic scouring pad.

❏ To clean brass plating, apply silver polish with a soft rag. Or rub with a rag dipped in either ammonia and water or dishwashing liquid and water. Do not use steel wool or an abrasive cleanser; either of these will wear through the plating, and rust will develop.

Copper Cleanup

❏ The scale in a copper teakettle can be cleaned by boiling a solution of equal parts vinegar and water in the kettle once in a while. If stubborn scale remains, let the kettle soak after boiling.

PEWTER

Old Pewter: Handle with Care

❏ Old pewter was made of tin and lead. It is very soft and is prone to getting dents and scratches, which in turn collect dirt and dust. Clean an old pewter object gently with a steel wool soap pad dipped in silver polish. Be careful not to rub more than is neces-

Whatsit?

WE WOULD APPRECIATE your telling us for sure what this item is. We think we know, but how was it applied without causing injury?
— M.B., GRANBY, MASS.

This is a swamp shoe for a horse to wear when working on soft ground. These shoes would be put on the hooves and the bolts tightened to keep them on. As these shoes fit only on the hard part of the hoof, they would not cause the horse any pain.

sary. If you're not cautious, you can rub a hole right through the pewter.

❏ Here's another method for cleaning old pewter. Place the pewter in a pot of water with a little dishwasher detergent mixed in. Bring the water to a boil. Let it cool, then remove the object. Wash in soapy water, then polish. Sometimes it takes more than one boiling to get out all the marks.

New Pewter Is Less Persnickety

❏ Copper and antimony have replaced most of the lead in newer pewter, giving it a harder finish. There's no need to use steel wool when cleaning new pewter because there are generally no dents and scratches to wipe out. Just clean with soap and water.

❏ If your pewter tray is stained with marks from wine or beverage glasses, you can clean it easily. Sprinkle baking soda on the marks, then rub with a sponge moistened

The Great Tarnish Transfer

A WOMAN WROTE ME with a dilemma. She had left a sterling silver spoon standing in a cup of bleach, and the spoon had turned "black as an ace of spades." She'd tried cleaning it with silver polish, but with no luck.

I recommended she try an old trick for cleaning silverware. Mix 1 teaspoon of baking soda, 1 quart of warm water and 1 teaspoon of salt in a pot. Lay the tarnished silverware and a small piece of aluminum foil in the pot and put the pot on the stove. Boil for 3 minutes, then let the silverware soak for a few minutes more. When you're done, the tarnish will have transferred to the foil. Buff the silver with a soft cloth to shine.

**A Word
from Earl**

The woman wrote again to tell me how well this method had worked for her. Before she tried it, she thought the spoon was ruined.

with vegetable oil. Continue rubbing until the marks are gone. Wash as usual.

❏ A cream-type silver polish can also be used on pewter.

Pewter Should Live in a Glass House

❏ To slow tarnishing, store your pewter in a warm area and behind glass.

STAINLESS STEEL

Quick Fixes

❏ Baby oil and club soda are both good for cleaning smudges from stainless steel flatware, sinks or counter-tops. You don't need to rinse afterward.

Rust Removal

❏ To remove rust from knives or scissors, soak them in a mild solution of water and ammonia for 10 minutes. Then scrub off the rust with a steel wool soap pad. Rinse and dry.

SILVER

Tarnish Prevention

❏ Moisture causes your silver to tarnish. To prevent this, put a block of camphor, available at drugstores, in with the silver. Imitation camphor works as well.

❏ You can protect silverware from tarnish by wrapping each piece in plastic wrap. Be sure that the silver is completely dry before wrapping.

Tarnish Treatments

❏ Soak tarnished silverware in sour milk for half an hour. Then wash in soapy water to polish and brighten.

❏ To polish between the tines of a fork, dip a pipe cleaner in silver polish and run it in the problem areas.

Smooth Out the Scratches

❏ Use a paste of olive oil (or mineral oil) and dry putty to remove scratches in silverware. Dry putty (also called whiting) is the powder once mixed with linseed oil to make window glazing. Now you can buy premixed win-

dow glazing, but the dry putty is still available at some independent paint and hardware stores. After smoothing the paste on the silver, polish it thoroughly with a piece of chamois. The dry putty serves as a fine abrasive; the oil is a lubricant.

GILT AND GOLD LEAF

To Clean Gilt Picture Frames

❑ Clean gilt picture frames with a mixture of equal parts ammonia and rubbing alcohol. Apply the solution with a small brush, then pat dry.

Pure Gold Needs Protection

❑ Whereas gilt is gold paint, gold leaf is pure gold. Clean gold leaf with a solution of 9 parts rubbing alcohol and 1 part ammonia, applied very gently with cotton swabs. Be very careful; gold leaf is very thin. Have a professional clean the gold leaf on valuable heirlooms or antiques.

❑ Scrape gold-trimmed dishes with a rubber scraper and wash them with a mild dishwashing liquid. Never use an abrasive cleanser. If the mild dishwashing liquid isn't enough to remove food from gold trim, try rubbing the trim with a paste of baking soda and water applied with a soft cloth.

JEWELRY

Don't Forget to Brush

❑ To make a strong solution to clean gold jewelry, fill a small container with dishwashing liquid and 1 teaspoon of ammonia. Soak the jewelry in the solution for a few minutes, then clean with an old toothbrush. Rinse and pat dry.

❑ Clean costume jewelry by mixing together a small amount of dishwashing liquid and 1 teaspoon of ammonia, then brushing the mixture on with a toothbrush. Costume jewelry should not be soaked—stones will loosen, and imitation gold coatings may discolor.

Pearls of Wisdom
❏ Clean pearls only with clear, cold water, then dry them with a soft towel. Do not soak pearls, as this can loosen the string holding them together.

BATHROOMS

Erase the Film
❏ To clean soap film from tile, rub with lemon oil, white vinegar or household (5 percent) bleach, undiluted on a cloth. *Do not use vinegar and bleach together; the fumes from the combination can be lethal.*

❏ You can prevent the buildup of soap film in a shower by wiping down the shower wall after each use. A squeegee works well for this.

❏ Clean shower curtains without taking them down by wiping them with a sponge dampened with white vinegar.

❏ To help prevent a ring in the tub, add a few drops of baby oil to your bathwater.

❏ Use full-strength white vinegar to clean tubs, sinks and toilet bowls.

Get the Gray Out
❏ To whiten the grout between ceramic tiles, mix together fresh hydrogen peroxide and cleanser to form a

The Desperate Window Washer

A "DESPERATE" WOMAN wrote me about the water spots on her windows. She'd tried everything, she said: soap and water, Windex, Fantastik, Mr. Clean, 00 fine steel wool, alcohol, Glass Plus.

But she hadn't tried kerosene. I recommended that she apply it with crumpled newspaper. Newspaper costs less than paper towels, and it doesn't streak as much.

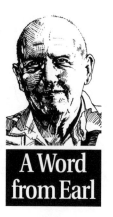

A Word from Earl

Those Nonslip Stickers Won't Quit

ONE OF THE MOST COMMON questions I'm asked is, How can I remove from my bathtub the adhesive flower stickers that are designed to prevent slipping?

In some cases, you can use a razor blade to scrape off the stickers, but not in a fiberglass tub. In this situation, I recommend using the edge of a block of wood to pry up the stickers; the wood won't scratch the tub.

A Word from Earl

Most people manage to get the stickers off, but they're left with a stubborn adhesive residue. Acetone rubbed on with a cloth is the best way to attack this. You need a lot because it evaporates quickly. Don't be discouraged if you only gum up the adhesive at first; you'll get it eventually. Make sure the room is well ventilated, or you'll end up tighter than the stickers.

thick paste. Scrub the mixture into the grout, using an old toothbrush. Let it sit for a few minutes, then rinse with a scrub brush and warm water. This method is just as effective as using commercial spray products made for this purpose—and much less expensive. Be sure to check the date on the label to be sure the peroxide is fresh, however, as it loses its effectiveness over time.

A New Use for Yesterday's Newspaper

❑ Water discoloration on chrome bathroom fixtures can be polished away. Rinse the fixtures with cool water, then polish with fresh newspaper or a soft cloth.

Don't Throw Your Money down the Drain

❑ If you've bought toilet-bowl cleaner in an automatic dispenser, don't throw the dispenser away when it's empty. Rinse it out thoroughly, fill it with household (5 percent) bleach and return it to the toilet tank. Substituting bleach for commercial toilet-bowl cleaner will save you money.

LAUNDRY

A Simple Softener

❏ As a softener for laundry, add 1 cup of vinegar during the rinse cycle.

Watch Out for Wool

❏ You can dry woven wool garments on hangers. Knitted wool clothing should be laid flat to dry; it will stretch if hung.

Lace Needs a Light Touch

❏ To clean light-colored old lace, try sodium perborate powder, a mild bleaching agent available at drugstores (they may need to order it for you). Soak the lace until clean in a mixture of 1 tablespoon of sodium perborate and 1 gallon of lukewarm distilled water. For heavily soiled items, change the water and continue soaking until clean.

Sock It to Those Socks

❏ Get grimy white cotton socks white again by boiling them in water with a slice of lemon.

Lint: We Have Lift-off!

❏ For a last-minute lint remover, wrap several strips of cellophane tape around your hand with the sticky side out. Press the tape against the lint, and the lint will lift right off. This works for animal hair, too.

CARS

For Tar on the Car

❏ Spray silicone or WD-40 will dissolve tar without harming your car's paint. Spray it on, let it sit for a few minutes and wipe with a soft rag.

SUBSTITUTIONAL LAW

A NUMBER OF common household products can be readily substituted for more expensive commercial cleaners. Here are some examples of cleaner substitutions.

For...	Substitute...
Brass polish	Worcestershire sauce, ketchup or toothpaste
Chrome cleaner	Baby oil, club soda, a piece of lemon, or baking soda and water
Glass cleaner	Ammonia, vinegar or alcohol
Shampoo	Dishwashing liquid diluted with water
Toilet-bowl cleaner	Household (5 percent) bleach or vinegar
Toothpaste	Baking soda mixed with a little salt, or baking soda mixed with hydrogen peroxide

❏ Mayonnaise will also remove tar from your car. Rub it on the tar and allow it to sit for a few minutes before wiping it off.

❏ Another way to remove tar or tree sap from your car's finish is to soak a rag in boiled linseed oil and leave it on the dirty spot for several minutes. Then wash as usual.

❏ You can remove pine pitch on your car top with rubbing alcohol on a rag.

Waxing Brilliant

❏ To repair minor scratches on a car, "color" the scratch with a wax crayon and buff with a soft cloth.

Streaking Went Out in the '70s

❏ To clean a car windshield that is streaked with heavy road film, make a solution of 2 tablespoons of cream of tartar and 1 cup of water. Smear it on the windshield, rinse off with water and wipe with newspaper or paper towels.

The Car That Really Sparkled (For a Day)

A FELLOW I WORKED WITH was going to trade in his car. He dropped by my shop and asked what I could do to help him make the car look as good as possible when he took it to the dealer that night.

I asked him, "Are you sure you're going to turn it in tonight?" He was certain. So at the end of the workday, I had one of my men wipe over the car quickly with a rag soaked in kerosene. The car gleamed as the man drove it off to trade it in.

**A Word
from Earl**

It was critical that he drive straight to the dealer, however. By the next morning, the kerosene on the car had probably collected so much dust that you couldn't tell what color the finish was. If we'd taken the time to buff the car before he left, the shine would have lasted longer.

❏ To remove stubborn streaks and film from a car windshield, try rubbing with kerosene and wiping with crumpled newspaper.

Debug Your Windshield

❏ To aid in cleaning dried bugs from your windshield and headlights, use a handful of old mesh onion bags as rags. Then polish off the job with a soft cloth or newspaper.

Bump the Bumper Stickers

❏ To remove bumper stickers from car chrome, paint on vinegar and let it soak in, then scrape off the stickers.

❏ Here's another way to remove bumper stickers: Brush on acetone or nail polish remover, let it sit and then scrape.

An Inside Job

❏ Clean vinyl upholstery with a damp cloth dipped in baking soda. Then wash with a mild solution of dishwashing liquid and water. Rinse thoroughly.

ODDS AND ENDS

Groom Your Broom

❏ A new broom will last longer if you soak the bristles in hot salt water before using it for the first time.

❏ To clean your broom and extend its life, dip it in warm water every few weeks.

Lemon Aid

❏ Before you start to vacuum, put a few drops of lemon juice in the dust bag. It will make the house smell fresh.

Make China Come Clean

❏ A mixture of lemon juice and salt cleans and shines china. Just rub it on with a damp cloth and rinse.

BRISTLING WITH OPPORTUNITY

WHEN THE YOUNG salesman for the Somerville (Massachusetts) Brush and Mop Company began to get requests for brushes that didn't exist, he heard opportunity knocking. His boss wouldn't listen, so young Albert Carl Fuller decided to knock on doors of his own, figuring any product that could be made as cheaply as those wire-twisted brushes, and could be sold as easily, must be a good thing.

Fuller set up shop in his sister's basement, selling brushes in the morning and making them in the afternoon. His innovative designs caught on, and at its peak in the 1950s, the Fuller Brush Co. employed a sales force of 30,000 and was the largest brush business in the world. The company still carries the widest line of brushes around.

Planning a Romantic Dinner? Freeze!

❑ Here's a tip that might save you time cleaning up wax drips from a candle: Put your candles in the freezer before you burn them. You'll find they won't drip as much.

The Brush-Off

❑ Clean hairbrushes with shampoo. Scrub it into the bristles, then rinse off. Rinse with white vinegar to remove soap residue.

❑ Hairbrushes and combs can also be cleaned by soaking them in water with a splash of ammonia. Let them sit for about 15 minutes, then rinse thoroughly before using.

SWEEPING THE NATION

Melville Bissell's allergies got the better of him. When the new carpet sweeper he'd bought didn't get up all the straw dust on the floor of his family's crockery store, he vowed he could do better. His prototype was made of dovetailed walnut and hog bristles and "sounded like a threshing machine, but effectively accomplished the work."

Within 4 years, Bissell was churning out 25 dozen sweepers a day—nothing to sneeze at. His innovation revolutionized carpet cleaning until the use of electric vacuum cleaners became widespread. Even today, carpet sweepers are a cheap alternative to vacuum cleaners—and they're good for places where you have a carpet but don't have electricity available.

Better Looks for Leather and Suede

❑ To clean leather luggage, use a solution of equal parts neat's-foot oil (available at leather and tack shops) and castor oil. Put the mixture on a soft cloth and rub it into the leather. The longer you rub, the better. Wipe off any excess with a clean rag.

❑ You can also clean leather by rubbing on a solution of equal parts white vinegar and boiled linseed oil.

❑ To clean suede, brush with a suede brush or steel wool, then wipe with a cloth dipped in white vinegar and wrung out almost dry.

The Thermos: Mix Your Own Cleaner

❑ To clean the inside of a thermos, mix lemon juice with equal parts cream of tartar and baking soda to make a thin paste. Fill the thermos one-third full with this mixture and shake. Let it sit for 15 to 20 minutes. Wrap a soft cloth around a small stick or wooden handle, holding it on with a rubber band. Use this to scrub the

FOR MEMBERS OF THE CLEAN PLATE CLUB

Some of the best cleaners, deodorizers and pest controls are stored in your refrigerator or kitchen cupboards—and it wouldn't do to run out. So that you can combine your other household needs and your grocery list, here's a quick summary of some of the food products recommended in these chapters for cleaning, fighting stains and odors, and controlling pests.

baking soda	cream of tartar	red pepper
bay leaves	eggshells	rice
black pepper	flour	salt
bread	ketchup	sugar
cinnamon	lemon	tomato sauce
cloves, powdered and whole	mayonnaise	vanilla extract
club soda	meat tenderizer	vegetable oil
coffee	milk	vinegar
cornstarch	onions	Worcestershire sauce
	peanut butter	yogurt

bottom of the thermos with the paste. Wash and rinse well.

Combination Cleaning

❏ Wash aluminum doors and combination windows with water and a household detergent. A soft-bristle brush should remove most dirt and mildew.

Toward Brighter Caulking

❏ You can clean some caulking compounds around storm windows and doors by applying a small amount of paint thinner with a rag, then rubbing it off. Rinse well with water. This method won't work in every case, but it won't hurt to try it.

Tickle Those Ivories

❏ To clean bone knife handles or any ivory object (such as piano keys), wipe on a solution of 1 tablespoon of hydrogen peroxide and 1 cup of water. No need to rinse.

❏ Bone and ivory can also be cleaned with yogurt. Apply plain yogurt with a cloth pad, then wipe it off.

❏ You can also clean bone and ivory with a paste of salt and lemon juice, applied with a damp cloth.

Brush Up That Basket

❏ To clean baskets and prevent drying, remove all dust with a soft brush, then apply a mixture of equal parts boiled linseed oil and turpentine. Rub this into the reeds and remove any excess with a dry cloth. If you rub it well, the basket will not be gummy or odorous.

❏ Here's another way to clean old baskets. Add a squirt of mild dishwashing liquid to lukewarm water. Dip a nail brush in this solution, then scrub the baskets with the brush.

❏ To protect old baskets, sponge on a mixture of 4 parts castor oil and 6 parts alcohol. Let it sit for half an hour, then wipe off the excess with a clean rag. Wipe dry.

Make Fake Flowers Bloom

❏ Plastic or silk artificial flowers aren't hard to clean. Place them in a large paper bag, adding about ¼ cup of salt. Close the bag and shake it to mix the salt through and around the flowers. Then take the flowers out of the bag and shake out the salt.

❏ You can also clean artificial flowers with mild dishwashing liquid and warm water. Make lots of suds and swish the flowers around in them. Then rinse the flowers and let them dry.

The Prodigy Who Spilled Yogurt

I ONCE HEARD ABOUT a woman whose young child spilled yogurt on the keys of her piano. The child, trying to clean up the yogurt, instead rubbed it all over the ivory. When the woman cleaned the yogurt off with a rag, the keys were polished and gleaming. Now this woman routinely cleans her piano keys with yogurt.

A Word from Earl

WHAT DID YOU DO IN THE WAR, DADDY?

HAD IT NOT BEEN for World War I, Tide might never have turned. It seems the Germans' supply of natural fats was being siphoned off for lubricants to be used in the war effort, making soap a scarce commodity. Then a couple of chemists suddenly remembered the work of one of their countrymen, a fellow named A. Krafft, who had observed in 1890 that certain short-chained molecules, when coupled with alcohol, lathered up like soap. Based on those findings, the chemists set out to make a wartime substitute for soap and in the process discovered that *detergents,* as the substances were known, were actually superior to soap in many ways. They cleaned better and more quickly, and they left no scum or residue. By 1930, the manufacture of synthetic detergents was widespread, and soon after the end of World War II, the world had its first laundry detergent for the automatic washing machine: Tide, created in the United States in 1946. It's been getting out the dirt ever since.

No More Dirty Words

❏ To clean an old typewriter, first place rags around the outside of the machine to protect it from spatters. To clean the gum out of the works (the apparatus that moves the keys), apply rubbing alcohol with an old toothbrush. Then clean the surface of the keys with a soft cloth dipped in detergent and water. Wipe dry with a clean cloth.

For a Clean TV Screen

❏ To clean a dirty television screen, wipe the screen with alcohol on a clean rag.

❏ You can also clean a dirty television screen with vinegar and water. Combine 1 part white vinegar with 10 parts water and wipe the mixture over the screen with a clean rag.

Soapstone: Here's the Rub

❏ Give old soapstone sinks a thorough cleaning by rubbing lightly with extra-fine sandpaper or steel wool.

A Clean Slate

❏ Clean a slate sink by scrubbing it with a mild solution of household ammonia and warm water, then letting it dry.

❑ You can also clean a slate sink with a solution of equal parts white vinegar and water.

Woodwork: Getting a Scrubdown

❑ Clean painted woodwork with a solution of ½ cup of white vinegar, 1 cup of ammonia, ¼ cup of baking soda and 1 gallon of lukewarm water. No rinsing is necessary with this solution.

❑ To remove a decal from a painted wood surface, dampen a piece of blotter paper and place it over the decal for a few hours. The decal will loosen enough so that you can remove it safely with a dull table knife.

Ditch the Dog Hair

❑ To remove dog hair from upholstery without damaging the furniture, dampen a chamois cloth with water, then rub the cloth over the upholstery.

The Minister's Sticky Situation

I ONCE RECEIVED a letter from a minister who was having a problem during a hot, humid summer. He complained that the old pews in his church had become extremely tacky—to the point that the varnish was coming off on the clothes of his parishioners.

I wrote back that I doubted the varnish was coming off. I thought the problem was a layer of old polish and grime that had built up after years of use and was being loosened by the hot weather. To clean off this layer, I suggested he mix ¼ cup of turpentine and ¾ cup of boiled linseed oil into 1 gallon of hot water, then scrub the pews with this solution and a soft rag.

**A Word
from Earl**

This solution works for any old, dirty woodwork. After the wood is clean, you can apply a fresh coat of varnish if you want.

Spruce Up Fireplaces and Wood Stoves

❏ Before cleaning fireplace brickwork, cover the floor nearby with newspaper to protect it from spatters. With a stiff brush or sponge, apply a solution of ¼ cup of TSP (or another product containing trisodium phosphate) and 2 gallons of warm water. (Wear rubber gloves for this.) Rinse well.

❏ The standard method of cleaning fireplace glass doors is to wipe on ammonia with a clean cloth, then polish with another clean cloth. Open the damper when cleaning with ammonia to help dissipate the odor.

❏ You can also clean fireplace glass doors with a mixture of wood ashes and a little water. Apply this mixture with a sponge and rinse off.

❏ To clean rust from a wood stove, give it a good scrubbing with a dry wire brush.

THERE'S A NEW MOVEMENT CALLED CHILDREN FOR DISARMAMENT

YOU MAY HAVE heard a parent or grandparent, speaking to a fractious child, threaten to "battle your rear end." In the old days, farm women doing wash by hand alternately soaked their clothes in hot water and "battled" (beat) them with a short wooden paddle called a battling stick. The paddle obviously had some other applications as well.

Stains and Odors

Inventiveness is the key to success.

IDISCOVERED a clear stain on the top of my washing machine recently. I can only guess what made it. The stain was 1½" wide and 2½" long with round corners. It looked to me as though a bottle had been set there and some liquid had run down the outside and hardened.

First I tried an all-purpose cleaner that was advertised as being able to remove soap scum, grease, heel marks, crayon and food stains. It did nothing. Next I tried lacquer thinner, again without results. Then I tried rubbing with a cloth and vinegar. That seemed to soften the spot somewhat, so I coated the area with vinegar and let it sit for a few minutes. When I rubbed the area again with the cloth, the stain came off without a trace.

Stain removal is a process of trial and error. You can never be sure what will remove a stain, so experimentation is important. I start with the easiest and most obvious solution and branch out from there. Maybe I need to try something different.

Maybe the method I'm using is the right one, but I need to apply a stronger solution or leave it on longer. As mentioned in the previous chapter, it's important always to test the cleaning agent on an inconspicuous part of the stained item before you go to work on the entire piece.

This chapter offers plenty of options for getting rid of everything from bloodstains to tobacco odors. After your next dinner party, turn to these pages to find out how to rid the tablecloth of beer, chocolate, coffee and tea stains—even candle wax. When the kids come in from play, you'll find more help in this chapter. Look here for ways to get gum, tar, crayon and grass stains out of play clothes (or any other fabric). You'll also find treatments for rust on the countertop, green stains on porcelain bathroom fixtures, water marks on leather and mildew on just about anything.

The second part of this chapter offers hints for freshening up musty closets and suitcases, eliminating bad food odors and salvaging smelly sneakers. (Hint: Even if you never cook outdoors and don't

IF YOU CAN'T FIND IT . . .

. . . maybe you need to try another chapter. Check the index, or try these possibilities.

For Eliminating . . .	*See the Chapter . . .*
Carpet stains	Floors
Odor in a cat's litter box	Pets and Pests
Odors in carpets and hardwood floors	Floors
Odors in closed-up houses	The Summer House
Skunk odor on dogs	Pets and Pests
Stains on wooden furniture	Furniture

own a cat, now's the time to stock up on charcoal briquettes and kitty litter.) By the time you finish this chapter, your house will be cleaner and sweeter smelling than ever before—and you may never go back to expensive commercial products again.

FABRICS

For Rust-Free Fabric

❏ Rust stains on fabric sometimes can be removed with lemon juice and salt. Put the mixture on the stain and let it sit for a few minutes. Next, stretch the area of the stain over the sink and pour boiling water through it until the stain is gone. (This is best done by two people—one to stretch the fabric and one to pour the boiling water. If you're working alone, stretch the material over a craft hoop before pouring the water through it.) Then wash normally.

Coffee and Tea Stains

❏ To remove coffee and tea stains from fabric, spread the fabric over the sink and pour boiling water slowly through the stain.

Place the stained area of the fabric in a craft hoop, then pour boiling water on the stain.

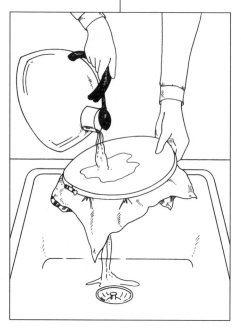

Berry Good Stain Removers

❏ Stains from fruits, berries and juices should be sponged immediately with cold water. Then, if it's safe for the fabric, hold the garment over the sink and pour boiling water through the stain. Follow up by working laundry detergent into the stain, then rinsing.

Cut the Chocolate

❏ To remove cocoa and chocolate stains, scrub the stained area immediately with ammonia.

Blood, Sweat and No Tears

❏ To remove bloodstains from a washable fabric, soak the piece in a strong solution of laundry detergent and cold water. To determine whether the garment can be washed or whether it must be dry-cleaned, check the care label.

❑ To remove a fresh bloodstain from a washable fabric, try a solution of ½ teaspoon of salt and 1 cup of water.

❑ To remove a bloodstain from any white fabric that you'd be afraid to wash in your washing machine, soak the stain in hydrogen peroxide.

❑ An easy way to remove bloodstains from white cotton fabrics is to soak the stained area in cold water with a generous splash of ammonia. This works best if it's done while the stain is still fresh.

❑ Sponge deodorant and perspiration stains with detergent, then launder the stained garments at the water temperature and with the bleach recommended for the fabric. Sometimes fabric color can be restored by sponging a fresh stain with ammonia, then rinsing.

❑ To restore the fabric color after removing an older perspiration stain, try sponging with vinegar, then rinsing.

Grease Removal

❑ To remove grease from washable fabrics, scrub with distilled water and soap. Distilled water is "soft," so it helps cut the grease.

The Lady Wanted a Brownout

A WOMAN WROTE to ask for a way to remove a brown stain of unknown origin from the floor of her colonial home. I told her to try equal parts milk, water and household (5 percent) bleach.

She wrote back that the solution had worked so well on her floor that she'd gone on to other brown stains in her house. She even removed a 3-year-old barbecue sauce stain from a white sweater. I haven't had occasion to use this solution much myself, but it clearly worked for her.

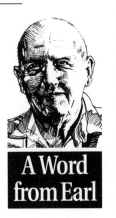

A Word from Earl

AMMONIA: TO THINK IT ALL STARTED WITH A CAMEL

AMMONIA IS a colorless, pungent gas composed of nitrogen and hydrogen. It is readily absorbed by water, and the combination of water and ammonia gas is what makes up the liquid ammonia you buy in the store. Today ammonia is usually obtained as a by-product of the coal industry, but in earlier times it was prepared in commercial quantities by heating the antlers of deer. The word *ammonia* comes from the Greek name for the god Amen. It was near the temple of Amen in Egypt that ammonia was first prepared from the dung of camels. How ironic that ammonia is now popular as a deodorizer.

Extinguish the Stains

❏ To remove ugly stains on clothing from fire extinguishers or car batteries, make a paste of dry starch and cold water, apply the paste to the stain and let the fabric sit for a while. Then rinse with water.

Hair Dye in Clothing

❏ To rid clothing of hair dye stains, wash the item in very sudsy water with a generous splash of vinegar. If the item is white, you can then bleach it with hydrogen peroxide and launder as usual. If it's not white, skip the peroxide.

It's My Party, and I'll Rinse If I Want To

❏ To remove dried-on beer stains from fabric, sponge on a solution of equal parts vinegar and dishwashing liquid, then rinse with warm water.

After the Party's Over . . .

❏ To remove candle wax from table linens, rub the spots generously with vegetable oil. Gently wipe off any excess oil with a paper towel, then wash as usual.

❏ To remove a lot of candle wax, scrape the excess wax off the fabric. Place the fabric between several layers of paper towels or brown paper bags and press with a warm iron. If the fabric is one you would normally iron at a very low temperature, be careful to avoid burning it while removing the wax. In that case, simply hold the iron just above the paper and move it back and forth. It doesn't take much heat to soften the wax and transfer it to the paper. Remove any remaining stain with a cleaning fluid such as Energine, available from hardware stores.

❏ You can remove dried fruit stains from linen by rubbing the spot on each side of the fabric with a bar of soap such as Ivory, then applying a very thick mixture of cornstarch and cold water. Rub this in well, then leave the linen exposed to the sun and air until the stain comes out. If the stain is not gone in 3 days, repeat the process.

Tablecloths Shouldn't Have Yellow Polka Dots

❏ Yellow spots on table linens may be caused by soap remaining in the fabric after laundering. When the linens are ironed, the heat turns the soap spots yellow. To remove these spots, put fresh lemon juice on them, then sprinkle the juice with salt. Stretch the area tightly over a pan and pour hot water through the stains.

❏ Denture-cleaning tablets will remove yellow stains from fabric. Find a container big enough to hold the stained fabric. Fill the container with warm water and throw in the tablets according to the ratio prescribed on the package. After the tablets dissolve, add the stained item to the solution and soak until the spots are gone.

Give Lipstick the Kiss-Off— with Hair Spray

❏ You can use hair spray to remove lipstick stains from clothing. Spray it on, let it sit for a minute or two and wipe carefully.

Make a Note: Ballpoint Ink Removal

❏ Aerosol hair sprays will remove some ballpoint ink stains from clothing. Try this technique: Hold a rag under the fabric to blot the ink that comes through on the other side, then aim and spray.

❏ Hair spray will sometimes work in removing a ballpoint ink stain from your hands, leather or plastic. Just spray it on the stain, rub it in with your hands and rinse right away.

❏ You can also remove ballpoint ink stains by sponging them with alcohol or a cleaning fluid such as Energine, available from hardware stores.

Whatsit?

THIS OBJECT was found in my mother's house. It's metal, 11" long and 5" wide. The center knob appears to be a thumb rest and is riveted to the main part. Stamped on the back is "Happy Thought, PAT. Mar 25 02, Shepard Novelty Co., Springfield, Mass." Can you tell me what it is?

— R.W., MELROSE, MASS.

I'm guessing about this. After the turn of the century, the bottoms of petticoats were pleated. I think this was used to hold the cloth at the correct spacing to sew the pleats.

One Stain Led to Another

A LOYAL "PLAIN TALK" READER wrote saying that he had tried my tip for cleaning a teakettle. He'd boiled a solution of white vinegar and water in it, and the process had cleaned the scale out nicely. There had been a catch, though. Before he could turn down the heat, his kettle had boiled over, spilling the boiling vinegar and water onto his stainless steel stove top and creating a stain there.

A Word from Earl

It turned out that the stain was not a problem to remove. I advised him that a little fine steel wool and elbow grease would do the job.

In the process of eliminating a stain, it sometimes happens that you create a new one. For instance, you can remove lipstick from fabric by rubbing the stain with peanut butter. But you must be sure to wash the fabric with warm water and dishwashing liquid before the peanut butter dries. Otherwise, you'll just be replacing one stain with another.

You can get almost any stain out if you experiment—and persist.

Get Rid of Baby Formula Stains

❑ Unflavored meat tenderizer will remove some milk and baby formula stains from fabric. Make a paste of the tenderizer and cool water, rub on the spots, allow to sit and wash as usual. The meat tenderizer contains an enzyme (extracted from a palm tree) that breaks down protein. Since there is protein in milk and baby formula, the enzyme helps remove those stains.

When the Bubble Bursts

❑ If soft chewing gum is stuck in fabric, harden it with ice before you try to remove it. Or you can place the item in a plastic bag and put it in your freezer. Then scrape off the residue and remove any leftover grease stain with dishwashing liquid or lighter fluid.

One for the Road

❑ Sponge tar stains immediately with a cleaning fluid such as Energine, available from hardware stores. Repeat as necessary until the stains are gone.

Scribble Stains

❑ To remove marks on fabric from carbon paper or pencil, sponge the stains with cold water, then leave the fabric to soak in more cold water. After half an hour, rub dishwashing liquid into the affected area, then rinse. If the stain remains, apply a few drops of ammonia and repeat the dishwashing liquid treatment.

❑ To remove lead pencil from fabric, try rubbing with a clean, soft eraser.

❑ To remove crayon from fabric, first scrape off any excess. Sponge detergent onto the stain, then rinse and dry. If the stain remains, sponge with a cleaning fluid such as Energine, available from hardware stores.

An Easy Way to Polish It Off

❑ Fingernail polish can be removed from certain fabrics, such as linen, the same way you get it off your nails: Apply polish remover. Remover with or without an acetone base will work. Sponge it on, then rinse with water. (This technique is not recommended for polyester or cotton fabrics.)

How to Drive the Green Away

❑ To remove grass stains, work laundry detergent into the stained area and rinse.

❑ If a grass-stained garment can't be washed, moisten the stain with alcohol, then rinse.

What You Can Do About Mildew

❑ Mildew on fabric can sometimes be removed by moistening it with lemon juice and salt, then leaving the item to dry in the sun. To be sure this is safe for

Whatsit?

WOULD YOU PLEASE identify this object for me? I've had it for 20 years or more, and no one can tell me what it is or its use. On the reverse side are the words "Pat'd May."
— R.J., ESMOND, R.I.

This is a pie lifter, used to take hot pies out of the bake oven. It was usually kept hanging near the fireplace.

THE FUNGUS AMONG US

MILDEW IS a visible fungus that attacks in warm, humid, damp or shady conditions. Look for spots or splotches of black, brown or purple. Since mildew often looks like dirt spots, it's best to test a small area to make sure it *is* mildew before taking further action. Place a few drops of household (5 percent) bleach on the area in question. If the area loses color, there is good reason to suspect mildew. If the bleach leaves the area brownish, the problem is most likely dirt or grime, washable with warm, soapy water.

the fabric you're dealing with, it's a good idea to test the solution on an inconspicuous area before proceeding.

❑ Mildew on fabric can also be removed by sponging with hydrogen peroxide, then leaving the item in the sun to dry.

❑ Don't assume that an air conditioner will eliminate problems with mildew. If it's damp outdoors, you need to close the outside air intake on your air conditioner. Otherwise, it can actually bring in damp air, contributing to the dampness that encourages mildew.

Treatment for Paint and Varnish Stains

❑ Oil paint or varnish on fabric should be treated before the stain dries. Sponge with the solvent recommended on the paint or varnish label or with turpentine. While the material is still wet with solvent, soak it in a concentrated solution of dishwashing liquid and water. Wash with laundry detergent. Repeat if necessary.

❑ Latex paint can be washed out of fabric with soap and water if you get to it before it dries.

Hot Stuff

❑ Scorched fabrics may not be repairable, but try working laundry detergent into the scorched area immediately, then rinsing. If the stain remains, apply hydrogen peroxide and rinse again.

A Step in Time

❑ To treat a shoe polish stain, work laundry detergent into the fabric immediately and rinse. If the stain remains, sponge with alcohol and rinse again.

❑ You may need turpentine or a cleaning fluid such as Energine (available from hardware stores) to remove some types of shoe polish stains. To be sure the product you choose is safe for your fabric, test it on an inconspicuous area first.

❑ An alternative way to remove shoe polish stains from fabric is to make up a solution of ¼ cup of ammonia, 2 to 3 drops of dishwashing liquid and 2 quarts of warm water. Apply the solution to the stain, then brush it out and pat dry with a towel.

Urine Stains

❑ To get rid of urine stains, soak the item in clear water for 30 minutes. If the item will stand up to heat, use hot water. Work in detergent, then rinse. Launder in a bleach that's safe for the fabric. If the fabric color has changed, sponge with ammonia. If the stain remains, sponge with white vinegar. Then launder again.

❑ Cats, like many other animals, tend to urinate repeatedly in the same places. When cleaning or removing urine stains, you must neutralize the odor—not just mask it— or the cat will likely return to the spot and dampen it again. A mixture of equal parts white vinegar and baking soda is a good neutralizer. Apply it as you would any cleaning solution. Soak the fabric in it or sponge it onto a problem area of the carpet or wall.

SODA: THE MARKET IS RISING

BAKING SODA, or sodium bicarbonate, was originally produced through a chemical reaction that combined salt and carbon dioxide. It was used primarily by bakers as a substitute for yeast, to which some people are allergic. In the early 1950s, the discovery of trona—a crude sodium bicarbonate mineral deposit—revolutionized the process of producing baking soda and made it readily available to all consumers.

Today consumers use more baking soda for cleaning and deodorizing than they do for baking. It's cheaper and less abrasive than most cleansers. Other uses also have been discovered over the years, from deodorizing refrigerators to brushing teeth.

The largest users of baking soda today are not humans, though, but dairy cows. To help them digest their acidic diets, cows are often given up to 4 ounces of sodium bicarbonate per day. People, of course, use baking soda for the same purpose—but not in those quantities.

SUEDE AND LEATHER

Help for Suede

❑ To get rid of stains on suede, rub them out with an art gum eraser.

❑ Rubbing with a nail file will remove small spots from suede.

On-the-Spot Treatments for Leather

❑ To remove white water spots on leather, cover them with a thick coat of petroleum jelly. Leave the petroleum jelly in place for a day or so, then wipe it off with a soft cloth.

❑ You can also use petroleum jelly to remove ballpoint ink from leather. Either rub it directly on the spot or put a gob of it on and leave it for several days, then wipe it off.

❑ Another way to get ballpoint ink out of leather is to saturate the spot with hair spray, allow it to dry and brush lightly with a solution of equal parts white vinegar and water.

❑ Oily stains on leather sometimes can be removed by applying a cleaning fluid such as Energine (available from hardware stores) with a soft cloth. To be sure it's safe for the particular leather you're dealing with, test the cleaning fluid on an inconspicuous area first.

❑ To remove surface mildew from leather goods, wipe the leather with a solution of equal parts alcohol and water.

❑ To clean scuff marks off shoes, wipe with toothpaste on a damp rag.

❑ To polish patent leather, wipe the object with a cloth pad dampened with vinegar. Then wipe it dry with a clean, soft cloth.

Whatsit?

WE HAVE MOVED this item from Massachusetts, and we still don't know what it is. It is 16" high and cast iron, I think. How do we remove the black paint—or do we leave it? Hope you can identify it.
— M.O., SAN JOSE, CALIF.

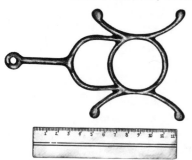

This is a trivet used to hold a pot or spider on a fireplace hearth. You can remove the black paint by placing the trivet in the fireplace and letting the paint burn off, but I would leave it on, since it doesn't hurt the value.

❑ To clean salt marks off boots and shoes, try a mixture of 1 part white vinegar and 3 parts water.

❑ At times a cat will use a leather bag or shoes as a litter box. To clean up after such an incident, sponge the item inside and out with a solution of equal parts vinegar and water, then blot as dry as possible with thick cloth towels or paper towels. To attack the odor, place a couple of cups of coffee grounds in the bag or shoe and close it up in a paper bag along with crumpled newspaper. Change the newspaper as needed until the smell is gone.

COUNTERTOPS

Rust Removal

❑ Clean rust spots from countertops with lemon juice and salt.

❑ You can also get rust spots off a countertop by rubbing in toothpaste (not the gel type) with your finger. Rub until the stain is gone, then rinse and wipe dry.

Counteraction

❑ When a store package leaves a purple ink stain on a counter, remove the stain by rubbing the spot with lemon juice and then wiping it off.

❑ Use silicone spray, available in hardware stores, to remove crayon from counters.

❑ To remove a mustard stain from a counter, rub in a sprinkling of baking soda with a damp cloth or sponge.

KITCHEN AND BATH FIXTURES

Porcelain Problems

❑ If standard cleansers don't work to remove dark marks on porcelain, mix a thick paste of fresh hydrogen peroxide and a scratchless cleanser such as Bon Ami. Then add a pinch of cream of tartar. Cover the stains with the paste and let it sit for at least 20 minutes. Rub the marks off with a plastic dish scrubber, then rinse. Repeat as needed.

❑ You can remove the green stains that water from copper pipes sometimes leaves on porcelain. Combine equal parts scratchless cleanser and cream of tartar, then add

The Tub Needed a Bleach Bath

A Word from Earl

A WOMAN WHO HAD brown stains from a nonskid mat in the bottom of her bathtub wrote for help. She had tried to remove the stains with a number of cleaning agents, including household (5 percent) bleach.

Bleach is a good idea, but bleach needs time to work. If you pour it in the tub, it won't necessarily stay where you want it. So I recommend this: Lay several paper towels on top of the stain and soak them with bleach. Leave the paper towels in place for about 45 minutes. Then remove them and rinse out the tub. Repeat if necessary.

enough fresh hydrogen peroxide to make a thick paste. Scrub the mixture on the stain and allow it to sit for half an hour before rinsing. Repeat if necessary.

If You Want a Clean Slate

❑ To get rid of rust stains in a slate sink, scrub with full-strength vinegar.

❑ To remove grease spots from soapstone, sprinkle on cornstarch and let it sit for 15 minutes. Then rub it off with fine steel wool.

CHINA

New Life for the China Cabinet

❑ To remove coffee or tea stains from a cup, wet the cup with vinegar. Then dampen a rag with water, dip it in baking soda or salt and swab out the stain.

❑ Denture-cleaning tablets will remove coffee or tea stains from a cup. Fill the cup with water, drop in a tablet and let it soak for 3 to 4 hours.

Resurrecting Old China

❑ Brown stains found on old china may be removed by soaking the china in a mild solution of household (5 percent) bleach and water. Soak for an hour or so, then wash and rinse. This works for rust stains either on or under the glaze. In severe cases, the stains may show up again. If they do, repeat the process.

❏ To remove stubborn brown stains on old china, rub on a solution of equal parts vinegar and salt, then rinse.

MARBLE

Marble Marvels

❏ Use a cream-type silver polish to remove stains and water marks from marble tabletops.

❏ You can also remove stains on marble tabletops by scrubbing with a paste of salt and lemon juice, then wiping clean with a damp cloth.

A Tough Treatment for Tough Stains

❏ Stains in marble that resist other cleaning methods will usually give in to a treatment of fresh hydrogen peroxide and a couple of drops of ammonia. (To make sure the peroxide is fresh—it loses strength as it ages—check the expiration date on the label.) Pour the mixture on the stains and let sit for a couple of minutes. Then wash, rinse and wipe dry.

GLASS

Don't Disown Discolored Glass

❏ To clean severely discolored glass or crystal, soak the item in a solution of ammonia and water for several hours, then wash and rinse.

❏ Another way to clean badly discolored glass is to soak it in vinegar with the contents of a tea bag, then wash and rinse.

❏ Sometimes badly discolored glass can be restored by soaking it in acetone (in a well-ventilated area) for a few hours. Wash and rinse before using.

❏ A glass cruet or decanter that has been used to store vinegar or wine for years will discolor from the chemicals in the liquid. If you can't remove the discoloration, you can at least hide it and still use the container for decorative purposes. Place the container in a 140°F oven for a few minutes. (This heat is less than what you subject your dishes to when you wash them, so it's safe, but don't let the oven get any hotter than that, or the glass will break.) Remove the container with an oven mitt, put a couple of tablespoons of vegetable oil in it and shake to coat. Place the container upside down and leave for 2 to 3 days until all the oil has drained out except for a thin film on the inside of the glass. Wipe off the neck with a paper towel. The glass will look like new.

Inside the Bottle Neck

❏ To remove stains inside vases, pitchers and bottles, apply acetone with a rag. (When using acetone, always be sure your work area is well ventilated.) If the neck of the object is too narrow to reach inside with a rag, pour in the

The Glassware Wouldn't Come Clean

A WOMAN WROTE to say that she had stored some newspaper-wrapped glassware in cardboard boxes in a damp cellar for 5 years. When she unpacked the glasses, she discovered white marks on them similar to the water marks left after using a dishwasher. None of the things she'd tried—dishwasher detergent and a soft brush, Lestoil, nail polish remover, scouring pads—had removed the spots.

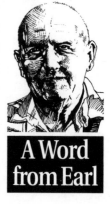

A Word from Earl

If you store something in a damp place for a long time, you're just asking for stains. In this case, the newspaper that was protecting the glassware from breaking absorbed the moisture in the cellar and stained the glass.

A simple way to clean spots from glass is to rub the glass with a cut lemon, rinse and dry with a soft cloth. In more extreme cases such as this one, I recommend polishing the glass with a cream silver polish. The ultrafine abrasive in the polish will remove almost anything from glass.

acetone, add a little sand and swish the mixture around. Empty out the acetone and sand, then wash and rinse.

OTHER STAINS

Bubble, Bubble, Pots Are No Trouble

❑ To get rid of whitish lime deposits in a pot or wood stove steamer, fill the pot with water, a little vinegar and raw lemon slices or rhubarb. Boil for 15 minutes. Then scrub the pot, rinse and wipe dry.

New Life for the Library

❑ Rub any grease spots on old books with an art gum eraser or fresh white bread. Dust on talcum powder or borax, leave it on for 1 hour and then dust off.

❑ A thin paste of cornstarch and a cleaning fluid such as Energine (available from hardware stores) may be used to clean grease, mold or mildew from some cloth bookbindings, but test it first on a spot that doesn't show too much, because it may change the color.

Out, Out, Wallpaper Spot!

❑ To remove a spot of grease on wallpaper, try rubbing it with a piece of rye bread. Work the bread into a ball and put a drop or two of kerosene on the area of the bread that you'll use for wiping the wallpaper. Rub gently. (No need to rinse.) If the pattern on the paper starts to wear off, use a crayon to touch it up. The crayon won't be noticeable unless someone really looks for it.

❑ To remove crayon from wallpaper or paint, rub with a damp cloth and a dab of toothpaste. Then rinse with a clean, damp cloth.

MUSTINESS

A Must-Win Solution: Dry It Out

❑ Do anything you can to dry out that musty basement or closet: Open the doors and windows wide, take bureaus and drawers outside into the sun, turn on a closet light and keep it on for a couple of days or place an electric fan on the floor for added air circulation. Anything you can do to dry out the offending space is probably time well spent. A few precautions now will ward off everything from mildew to insect infestations. And if you don't stop the problem at its source, you'll end up dealing with must and mildew over and over again.

Get Rid of the Mustiness

❏ Use unwrapped bars of soap in place of expensive scented sachets. They're just as effective in scenting drawers.

❏ Get rid of musty odors in drawers, closets or rooms by placing a small container of scented cat litter in the affected area. Refresh the litter every few days until the odor is gone.

❏ Relatively small items with musty odors should be placed in plastic bags with cat litter. Seal the bags tightly with tape or clothespins and let them sit for a few days. Then dump out the litter and repeat if necessary.

❏ To get rid of a musty odor in upholstered furniture, spray a deodorant or sprinkle cat litter over the piece. Let it sit for a while, then vacuum. Repeat if necessary.

Restore a Musty Suitcase

❏ To get rid of a musty smell in suitcases that have been stored, vacuum the luggage, then rub the lining with a solution of equal parts rubbing alcohol and water (or use a solution of lemon juice and salt in water). Try these solutions first on an area that won't show, in case they change the color of the material.

❏ Another way to save a musty suitcase is to fill it with crumpled newspaper, then close it up. Change the paper every 2 or 3 days until the odor is gone.

❏ A musty suitcase can also be treated by placing containers of cat litter inside and closing the suitcase for a few days. Repeat with fresh litter if necessary.

It's Those Old College Textbooks . . .

❏ To get rid of a musty odor in books, fill a large brown bag with crumpled

GROW-IT-YOURSELF AIR FRESHENER

THE WORLD'S BEST home air fresheners might be green plants. One study done by NASA found that one plant for about every 100 square feet of floor space can remove up to 87 percent of toxic organic pollutants such as benzene and formaldehyde. Plants produce oxygen, too.

newspaper, put the books in the bag and seal it tight. Leave the books in the bag for a day or so. Change the paper and repeat the treatment each day until the odor is gone.

Other Must Removers

❑ Parched rice will eliminate must and mildew in an enclosed space such as a metal cabinet or safe. Parch the dry rice by cooking it over high heat, stirring constantly, until it starts to show scorch marks. Then place a shallow pan of the rice in the musty space.

❑ To prevent musty odors from developing in a closed cottage, place pans of charcoal briquettes in several rooms. The charcoal will absorb moisture. You can burn these briquettes in your barbecue later.

❑ Musty odors can also be treated with household (5 percent) bleach. Place shallow pans of bleach in a closet and leave them until the musty odor is gone.

Whatsit?

I INHERITED THE TOOL shown here from my father-in-law some 35 years ago. The chisel portion is offset from the handle by about 6". The chisel is 2⅛" long x ⅝" wide x ⅝" high. I have never found a use for it. Can you tell me its purpose?
— S.S., COLUMBUS, OHIO

This appears to be an iron used to melt wax sticks to fill furniture scratches. It was heated enough to melt the wax and let it flow into the scratch. Then it was used to smooth the surface.

CLOSETS, DRAWERS AND TRUNKS

Bad Smells: Coming Out of the Closet

❑ To reduce mustiness and moisture in closets, place a few charcoal briquettes in a shallow pan on the floor. Replace the briquettes every few months to keep the closets fresh.

❑ To remove unpleasant odors from a closet, wash the walls, ceiling and floor thoroughly with a mixture of 1 cup of ammonia, 1 cup of white vinegar and ¼ cup of baking soda for every 1 gallon of water. Repeat if necessary.

❑ If closet odors persist, place a shallow pan of cat litter in the closet. Keep the door closed. Refresh the litter every few days until the odor is gone.

Get Rid of the Mothball Smell

❑ Mothball odor can be removed from a chest of drawers by scrubbing with a solution of equal parts white vinegar (or lemon juice) and rubbing alcohol. Remove the drawers from the chest. Dampen a sponge in the vinegar-alcohol mixture and scrub the interior of the chest, including the boards at the back and under the top. Scrub all unfinished parts of the drawers inside and out, then put them outside in the sun to dry. You may have to repeat this if the odor is very strong. This method works on trunks, too.

❏ Another method of removing mothball odor from a chest of drawers or trunk is to line the drawers or trunk with a large sheet of paper, sprinkle with coffee grounds and close the drawers or trunk tightly. Leave overnight,

The Fur-Store Owner Was Fuming

A LOCAL STORE WAS having its fur vault fumigated, as it did every year after all the furs had been moved into storage for the summer. Something went wrong during the process, and the vault was overloaded with fumes. No one knew what to do to clear out the room. There were no windows, and the vault's only opening was the door. If the employees set a fan in the doorway, it would blow the fumes out into the rest of the store.

The store called the contractor I was working for at the time to see what we could do. We had a couple of army surplus oil-fired heaters that had

A Word from Earl

originally been used to warm airplane motors in cold weather. These were complete with cloth ducts 1' in diameter—once used to distribute the heat anywhere it was needed on the airplane. We set one of the heaters in the vault, connected enough cloth duct to reach up the stairs and outdoors, and ran just the fan on the heater to expel the polluted air from the room. As the fumes were sucked out, they were automatically replaced with fresh air.

Never underestimate the power of fresh air to eliminate even the strongest odors. You just have to figure out a way to get the air to the odor.

then remove the paper with the grounds. Repeat with fresh coffee grounds if needed.

❏ If you're removing the mothball smell from a cedar chest, you'll want to get the cedar fragrance back after the mothball odor is gone. To do this, scrub the interior with sandpaper.

❏ To remove mothball odor in clothing that has been stored, place the clothing in the dryer with scented fabric softener sheets and run on the air-only setting for 15 minutes.

❏ You can also get the mothball smell out of clothing by placing the clothes in a large plastic bag, adding scented fabric softener sheets, closing the bag tightly and leaving it for 3 to 4 days.

KITCHEN ODORS

Extract That Fridge Scent
❏ Refrigerator or freezer smells can be eliminated by wiping the entire interior of the appliance with pure vanilla extract on a cloth, rubbing it on hard. Wipe again with a clean cloth.

❏ To kill the awful smell in a refrigerator that was left closed when the power was turned off (as in a summer cabin), leave a dish of charcoal in the fridge for a few days. For a particularly bad case, renew the briquettes periodically until the smell disappears.

❏ To eliminate freezer odors, place a cup of coffee grounds inside, close the door and leave overnight. In the morning, remove the coffee. If the odor is not completely gone, repeat the process with fresh coffee grounds.

❏ Another way to rid a refrigerator or freezer of bad odors is to clean the inside with a solution of equal parts vinegar and water, then wipe dry.

Cover Up That Burned-Food Smell
❏ To rid the air of the smell of burned food in the oven, sprinkle cinnamon in a shallow pan and place the pan inside the oven while it's still warm but not hot.

Kill Those Kitchen Odors

❏ Pouring vinegar down the drain is an effective means of eliminating odors.

❏ Simmer a cup of white vinegar on top of the stove to rid the air of strong onion, garlic or other unpleasant cooking odors.

❏ To remove a lingering odor in your microwave oven, wet a cloth with warm water, wring it out and dip it in baking soda. Lightly scrub down the inside of the oven.

❏ Another way to eliminate unpleasant odors in a microwave oven is to place in the oven 1 cup of water mixed with 1 tablespoon of lemon juice. Heat at full power for 1 minute, and the oven will smell much better.

❏ To get rid of fish odor in a frying pan, fill the pan with water, add vinegar and bring to a boil. Then wash and rinse as usual.

Clean-Smelling Hands

❏ Fish or onion odor on hands can be removed by washing with baking soda or by rubbing with fresh lemon.

❏ You can also kill onion odor on hands by rubbing your fingers with salt water.

Make Old Wooden Bowls Smell Better

❏ To get odors out of wooden rolling pins, bowls or cutting boards, rub with a piece of lemon. This process will also remove the taint of onions. There's no need to rinse; the wood will absorb the lemon juice.

Look for the Wooden Lining

❏ Some bread boxes are lined with wood. To remove the odor of the wood, put a few drops of vanilla extract in a cup of water and apply to the interior of the box with a rag. Rub hard.

ANIMALS

Eau de Dog

❏ Dog odor can be eliminated by sprinkling baking soda on the dog's coat, working it into the fur with your hands and then brushing well. The dirt in the dog's fur will come out along with the soda.

❏ To rid a room of pet odors, pulverize a heaping table-spoon of coffee grounds. Scatter the coffee in a frying pan and warm over low heat until the coffee odor is strong, then place the pan in the room until the coffee cools.

Fire Those Mouse Scents

❏ If mice or other rodents have made a nest in a box of stored china or other ceramics, you may have a hard-to-correct odor problem. One potential solution is to have the ceramic refired at a professional ceramic shop. The high temperature will burn off any trace of organic matter. The danger is that, in some cases, the firing might also alter the finish or pattern on the china, so try one piece and see how that comes out before you have the whole lot refired.

The Scent Was Roast Mouse

A FELLOW I WORKED WITH came to work one day in the winter complaining about a terrific odor in his house. He owned an old two-story colonial in the country. He said the odor was just as strong on the second floor as it was on the first.

Now, a dead mouse will smell pretty strong, but it usually affects only one room. I went to his house that night to try to find the source of the smell.

When I saw that he had a hot-air heating system, I realized the smell had to be coming from the heating ducts. On top of every hot-air furnace is the

A Word from Earl

plenum, a large sheet-metal chamber from which a pipe leads to each room. I reached inside the plenum. Sure enough, I found a large mouse in there. The furnace was cooking it slowly and efficiently, distributing the odor all through the house.

OTHER ODORS

Coffee around the Sofa

❏ To treat upholstered furniture that smells of smoke from a fire, sprinkle coffee grounds over the furniture, then enclose each piece in a large sheet of plastic to make it airtight. Let it sit overnight or longer, vacuum up the coffee, and shampoo.

Give Leather Odors the Boot

❏ New leather boots, bags or shoes sometimes have an odor left from curing the leather. To get rid of this odor, sprinkle coffee grounds in the item and enclose it in a plastic bag. Keep it in the bag for a day or so, then repeat with fresh coffee grounds if necessary.

Kitchen Aid for Smelly Shoes

❏ To keep shoes and boots from developing an unpleasant odor, make your own odor-eating balls. For each ball, pour a few teaspoons of baking soda on a small cotton rag. Tie the ends of the rag together and secure them with a rubber band. Set one ball in each shoe overnight. The balls can be used again and again.

❏ To freshen smelly sneakers (or any canvas shoes), sprinkle the insides with salt. Wait 24 hours for the salt to absorb the odor, then shake it out. Repeat if necessary.

Drive Away the Smell

❏ To rid a car of odors, clean all the upholstery and carpeting with a mixture of vinegar and water. Sponge the solution into the carpeting and blot it with an old towel. Clean all the interior surfaces with the same solution and dry thoroughly.

❏ To kill the smell of stale cigarette or cigar smoke in a car, leave a shallow pan of ammonia in the vehicle overnight or all day. After removing the pan, roll down the windows and allow the car to air out before driving.

LOCKING IN STALENESS

ONE LAST-RESORT solution applies to many odor-related problems, especially those involving floors or walls. Remove as much of the surface as possible, then cover it with a layer that seals the lingering odors in. For wood floors, this might mean sanding and then finishing with polyurethane. It might mean pouring a concrete floor in an old dirt cellar or tiling over an old bathroom wall. These are usually drastic measures taken only after everything else fails.

❏ You can also get rid of stale smoke odor in a car by leaving shallow containers of coffee grounds in the car. Ventilate the car thoroughly by opening all the windows and let the wind blow through for several hours.

Two-Holers Need a Little More

❏ For outhouse odors, sprinkle wood ashes in the hole after each use. Occasionally add a few handfuls of grass, hay or ferns—the greener the better—and a thin layer of dirt over all.

Other Odor Eaters

❏ If you spill oil and an odor persists after you have cleaned it up, try one of the commercial products that can quickly dispel the odor. Consider using Odors Away (available from hardware stores) or Sid Harvey's Odor Neutralizer (available from oil companies). Follow the package instructions.

❏ To treat tobacco odor in a room, put 1 pint of hot water in a bowl and add 3 tablespoons of ammonia. Leave the bowl in the closed room overnight.

Pets and Pests

Cats don't like lemon, pigeons avoid mirrors, and skunks hate strong smells.

FIFTY YEARS AGO, someone told me this method of getting fleas off your dog: Have your dog take a short stick in his mouth and back slowly into the water. As the dog backs into the water, the fleas will work up his body toward his head. When the dog is entirely in the water, all the fleas will be on the stick. Then simply take the stick from the dog's mouth and throw it away.

I've never known this to work, and nobody's ever explained to me how you get the dog to back into the water, but I've certainly had fun recommending it to people. The rest of the ideas in this chapter, however, are more than just fun; they really work. You can learn new tricks for coping with the family pet—how to break a dog from digging holes, remove burrs from a dog's coat and get a cat to stick to the litter box. You'll discover ideas for keeping raccoons out of the garbage, skunks out of the woodshed and squirrels out of the bird feeder. Smaller pests are covered, too. Find out how you can catch slugs with beer, use whole cloves to discourage silverfish and soothe a bee sting with a cut onion. There's even an idea for a better mousetrap.

DOGS

Let Your Dog Keep His Coat

❏ A dog's coat is his natural protection against heat, sun and insects. Don't trim or shave the coat just because it's summer.

Get Rid of Fido's Burr-den

❏ To remove burrs from a dog's hair, soften them by applying a few drops of a light oil or shampoo, then comb them out.

❏ Another way to remove burrs from your dog's coat is to crush them first with a pair of pliers. Be careful not to pinch your dog's hide in the crushing operation.

Tick Attack

❏ To help loosen a tick attached to a dog, place a drop of vegetable oil or mineral oil on the tick. Then pull gently but steadily. The point in loosening the tick first is to allow it to be removed intact. Just pulling with tweezers often leaves the jaws or head behind.

IF YOU CAN'T FIND IT . . .

. . . maybe you need to try another chapter. Check the index, or try these possibilities.

For Getting Rid Of . . .	See the Chapter . . .
Leeches	The Summer House
Mice in a summer house	The Summer House
Pet odors	Stains and Odors
Pet urine stains	Stains and Odors

Teach a Dog New Tricks

❑ To cure a dog of chewing on his paws when he gets bored, paint the spot he likes to chew with oil of cloves (available at drugstores).

❑ Dogs also chew on wood when they are bored. To cure a young dog of this habit, sprinkle oil of cloves or red pepper on the woodwork you prize.

❑ To cure a dog of digging holes, crumble a toilet freshener cake and spread the pieces where the dog likes to dig. The smell will drive him away.

❑ Here's another way to train a dog not to dig. The next time your dog digs a hole, drive a stake into the hole and tie him to it on a 2-foot rope or chain. Leave him there for

HERE'S HOW TO SLOW FIDO

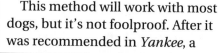

IF YOU WANT to break a dog of chasing cars, cut a piece of broom handle the width of the dog and drill a hole in the center of the wood. Tie a short cord through the hole, and attach the other end to the dog's collar so that the stick hangs at knee level. The dog will be able to walk without trouble, but when he runs, the stick will get between his legs and trip him.

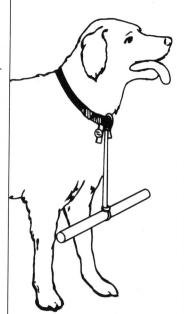

To deter a car chaser, make sure the stick falls at knee level.

This method will work with most dogs, but it's not foolproof. After it was recommended in *Yankee*, a reader wrote to say he had tried it on his fox terrier. He said that for two days the stick had kept his dog from chasing cars. "On the third day," he wrote, "I was sitting on the porch when suddenly my dog perked up his ears. Hearing a car coming up the road, he picked up the broom handle in his mouth and after the car he went."

For clever dogs, you'll need to find another remedy.

The Husky That Loved the Vacuum Cleaner

I HAVE HAD HUSKIES for 45 years now. I always dread spring, when they begin to shed their winter coats. I work on them with a wire-bristled comb, but even after combing, a lot of loose hair remains on the dogs. I've tried brushes and even a broom to get off this hair, always with poor results.

A Word from Earl

I had one husky that, after I had combed him, watched me use the vacuum cleaner to get loose hairs off my pants. I motioned with the hose, hoping he'd let me use it on him. Nothing doing. He ran off.

The next time I combed him, I took the attachment off the vacuum hose and let him get a look at it. He let me rub the disconnected attachment over his back. The next day I did not start the vacuum cleaner but let him watch me rub my pants with the attachment on the hose. Then I approached him with the hose and got him to stand still while I rubbed it over his back. Finally, I switched on the motor, and he let me vacuum off all the loose hair. He came to like it, so I used the vacuum cleaner to suck up loose hair all spring.

I'm trying to train the husky that I have now to let me use the vacuum cleaner on him, but so far it's no go.

2 hours to think about his misdeeds. Repeat this procedure the next time he digs a hole. After three holes and three chain-ups, he should get the idea.

Dogs for Fussy Housekeepers

❏ If shedding is a factor in deciding what kind of dog to have, remember that not all breeds shed equally. Consult a local veterinarian or pet shop owner before you buy.

Dog Meets Skunk

❏ A bath of tomato juice is the traditional cure for a dog that's had a run-in with a skunk, but that's messy and ex-

The Dogs That Wouldn't Stop Digging

AFTER A "PLAIN TALK" READER asked how to stop his dog from digging, a woman wrote me with a creative suggestion. She claimed it had worked with two of her dogs.

First, dig a hole where the dog likes to dig. Blow up some small balloons and tie them. Put the balloons in the hole and cover them with dirt. When the dog starts to dig in the loose dirt, he will pop a balloon or two with his toenails. The noise will scare the dog, and he'll dig no more.

pensive. Instead, give the dog a bath with a solution of equal parts vinegar and water.

❏ An alternative way to free a dog of skunk odor is to make up a solution of two packets of Massengill Douche Powder (available at drugstores and grocery stores), following the directions on the package, and bathe the victim. This works on human victims of skunks, too.

CATS

Try a Little Cat Cologne

❏ Before filling a cat's litter box, sprinkle the bottom with baking soda to keep down the odor.

Cats Aren't into "Hot and Spicy"

❏ To keep a cat from scratching the wooden legs of chairs or woodwork, rub the wood with chili sauce, then buff.

Assign Him to a New Post

❏ To discourage a cat from scratching upholstered furniture, give him a scratching post—about 2' high and covered with carpet on a base large enough so that the cat won't tip it over.

Use a scratching post to keep your cat's claws off the furniture; ½" plywood makes a good base.

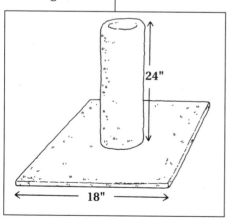

24"

18"

It's easy to make a scratching post yourself, or you can buy one at a pet or discount store.

The Well-Groomed Cat

❏ Keep a cat's claws trimmed. If you trim the claws yourself rather than having the vet do it, make sure you don't cut back into the vein in the cat's nail. This vein runs about three-fourths of the length of the nail. Always file the nail afterward.

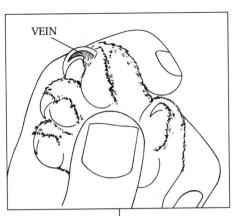

VEIN

Pinch a cat's toe between your fingers to force the claw to extend. Then you can clip the nail more easily.

❏ A cat will usually keep himself clean. Give your pet a bath only if he has grease or grime on his coat that he cannot clean off by himself.

Direct Your Cat Back to the Litter Box

❏ If your cat is urinating in the house, here's a way to break the habit. Dip a cotton ball in lemon extract, squeeze out

The Cat That Needed a Cleaning

IT'S NOT A GOOD IDEA to bathe a cat often, but sometimes it's necessary. A woman who lives in a city wrote me that her cat occasionally gets grimy enough to warrant a bath. Here's her method of cleaning the cat without getting scratched to death.

Fold a terry towel in half and sew up two of the three open sides. Put your cat inside the towel, leaving his head outside the opening. Secure the towel around the cat's neck with a drawstring or safety pins. Now dip the protected cat into warm water that has a little shampoo mixed in and rub gently. After you release the cat from the towel, dry him as best you can with a dry towel.

A Word from Earl

This woman admitted in her letter that her cat won't speak to her for some time after being subjected to this procedure. But at least the cat is clean.

Whatsit?

I BOUGHT THIS ITEM from an auctioneer knowledgeable about old tools, but even he didn't know what it is. Can you inform us? It has a sharp point, a loop on each side and a square head.

— D.T., HAMBURG, N.J.

This is an anvil used by farmers to straighten out blades in scythes, sickles and other tools that got bent during use. It was easily carried and could be driven into the ground or a tree stump. The rings on the side prevented the anvil from sinking into the ground when the bent blade was being hammered.

Secure your garbage can with a bungee cord to keep raccoons out.

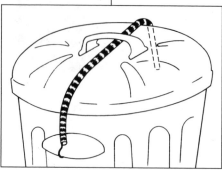

the excess and place it in an aluminum tea ball (designed to hold loose tea). Hang the tea ball by its hook in the spot where your cat is urinating. The smell should keep the cat away. Refresh the lemon once a week until the cat is trained.

FLEAS

Let There Be Light

❏ To catch fleas, place a shallow pan filled with water and a little dishwashing liquid in the room that's infested. At night, turn on a lamp and focus it right over the pan. Turn off all the other lights in the room. The fleas will jump at the light and fall into the dish. You'll be amazed at the number of fleas you'll catch the first night. Change the solution as needed. Although there will be some nights when you won't catch any fleas, continue the treatment for at least 2 weeks to get the next generation of fleas after they hatch.

A Flea-Free Diet

❏ Get fleas off your dog or cat by sprinkling ½ to 1 teaspoon of brewer's yeast on the animal's food daily or by crushing a tablet of 25 milligrams of vitamin B_1 (thiamine) on the food. Brewer's yeast is available at health food stores and pet stores; vitamin B_1 is sold in drugstores.

❏ To help keep a pet free of fleas and ticks, add 1 teaspoon of vinegar to each quart of the animal's drinking water.

RACCOONS

A Garbage Proposal

❏ To keep raccoons out of your garbage, use heavy-duty cans with locking tops and store them so they can't be tipped over. A rubber bungee cord can be used for a can with a lid that doesn't lock on securely. Stretch the cord tight from one handle over the top of the lid to the other handle.

❑ To keep persistent and clever raccoons out of your trash, sprinkle a little ammonia on each trash bag you put in the can. This will keep dogs out, too.

Corny Suggestions

❑ To prevent raccoons from eating your corn, paint vegetable oil on the outside of the ears with a small paintbrush, then sprinkle on some red pepper. This can be a lot of work, but if you're desperate enough, it could be worth it.

Those Rockin' and Rollin' Raccoons

A READER WROTE to tell me that raccoons raided his garbage cans three nights in a row. He wondered whether I had a solution, short of staying up all night with a gun or keeping the garbage cans indoors. My advice was to place a small radio near the cans and leave it playing all night.

I got a letter from him later saying that my recommendation had worked. The raccoons had left his garbage alone, but there had been some complications. It seems that the radio had not been well anchored, and the raccoons had walked off with it. "Somehow in the process of transporting

A Word from Earl

the radio, the raccoons turned it up very loud, and the whole woods radiated with music," he wrote. "The coons placed the radio in a hollow of a high tree, so all we could do was let the batteries wear out—which took two days and two nights. The raccoons seem to like disco music best, but we don't."

I wrote back to suggest that if he liked country music better, he should try leaving a banjo out by the trash.

❏ Wood ashes will also discourage raccoons from eating corn. Sprinkle the ashes on the outside of the ears in the early morning so that the dew will help them stick on, or mix the ashes with water and brush the mixture on the ears. Also spread some on the ground around the stalks.

❏ Set dog hair around corn and other crops threatened by raccoons. The smell keeps the coons away.

❏ Plant butternut squash around the perimeter of your garden to keep out raccoons. They don't like to scratch their bellies on the prickly squash vines and won't cross the area.

Whatsit?

WHILE DOING some repair work on my old barn (c. 1825) this spring, I came across this oddity. Can you tell me what it is and how my ancestors used it?
— J.H.C., BARNSTABLE, MASS.

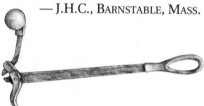

This is a nail and spike puller. By taking the long handle in one hand and the ball in the other, you could drive one jaw of the instrument into the wood alongside a spike. As you put pressure on the ball, the other jaw would grab the head of the spike from that side. Then, as you forced the handle down toward the floor, the pressure on the curved piece against the floor would hold the jaws tight, pulling the spike out enough so that it could be removed entirely with a bar or hammer.

SQUIRRELS

High Wire Acts

❏ Here's one way to hang a bird feeder so that the squirrels won't get into it. Slip the feeder onto a long wire and hang it between two trees, but away from any low branches.

Fool with Spools

❏ Particularly agile squirrels may try to scamper along the wire to reach your bird feeder. To deter these acrobats, string empty thread spools on the wire.

A Taste for Fine Furniture

❏ Squirrels will sometimes chew on outdoor redwood furniture. To discourage this, try rubbing the legs of the furniture with chili sauce, then buffing.

Keep Your Attic Off-Limits

❏ To keep squirrels out, check for holes in your attic. Use wire mesh to close all openings under the roof edge where it joins the sidewalls.

❑ Get rid of any tree branches that hang over your house and outbuildings so that squirrels can't use them as ladders.

Extra! House Exposed

❑ Squirrels will sometimes chew holes in unfinished wooden siding or exposed wood. To prevent this, brush a wood preservative such as Cuprinol on the siding or wood. If one coat does not stop the squirrels, brush on a second coat. Apply lots of preservative in areas where the squirrels have already started chewing.

They Won't Like the Sound of This

❑ It's worth trying ultra-high-frequency sound devices to repel squirrels and other small animals.

SKUNKS

Pests on the Run

❑ To get rid of skunks, put some pieces of a solid laxative such as Ex-Lax where the skunks can find them. They will eat the laxative and leave. They won't come back.

Trust Me on This One

A NATURALIST ONCE told me how a skunk goes about spraying a target. First, while facing the target, the skunk plants its front feet firmly on the ground. It then lifts its tail and its whole hind end into the air. It swivels its rear end around and points its spray straight over its head at the intruder. The entire act takes only a few seconds, according to the naturalist.

I can confirm from my own experience the naturalist's first observation. But whenever I've been confronted by a skunk that's facing me with his front paws in position, I haven't stuck around to verify the rest.

A Word from Earl

SKUNKS

Talk About Low Self-Esteem

❏ Believe it or not, skunks hate strong odors. You can discourage a skunk from moving into a woodshed or other small building by hanging a bar of strong disinfectant or room deodorizer in the space.

WOODPECKERS

Send Woody Wandering

❏ Woodpeckers will peck holes in wooden siding or stucco when looking for insects. To discourage them, caulk any cracks where insects might enter. Consider consulting a pest inspector/exterminator if the woodpeckers persist.

❏ If you have trouble with birds pecking holes in the eaves and wooden shingles of your house, try fastening some toy snakes around where the birds are bothering you. Hang them so that they move in the breeze.

DILEMMA IN BLACK-AND-WHITE

A *YANKEE* READER once sent in this story.

"A skunk snuck into the garage one rainy day and sat holed up in the corner amongst the shovels and rakes, wishing that I—a Big, Loud, Annoying Person—would leave him alone. Banging on pots and pans didn't faze him, and though I'd heard they don't like mothballs, I was pretty certain I didn't have enough on hand to significantly fill the garage, it being a two-bay. I was reluctant to leave the doors open all night for fear the critter's in-laws were over in the rhododendrons, waiting to move in. And I knew that *I* sure as heck wouldn't leave a nice dry spot to go back out in the rain—which got me to thinking.

"I hooked up the garden hose, stood a good distance away, and directed a private little downpour on Mr. Black-and-White. He shuffled. He budged. He hid by the lawn mower. No good. I kept it on him. Then, like a disgruntled picnicker, he high-speed-waddled out the open door to where I'm sure it seemed to him like the rain was letting up a good deal."

All of which suggests that one of the best ways to get rid of any unwanted animal is simply to make its life darned uncomfortable.

The Skunk That Walked Away

ONCE WHEN I WAS running the maintenance department at Yankee, a skunk holed up in the small utility shed behind one of the office buildings. Everyone got pretty worked up. How were we going to get it out?

Believe it or not, skunks hate strong odors. They don't even like their own odor, so they are not likely to spray in a confined space. Leaving the front door of the shed open, I took a can of insect repellent and sprayed it into the shed from the back. The skunk didn't like the smell of the spray and soon sauntered out.

And everyone else breathed a sigh of relief.

A Word from Earl

❏ To keep woodpeckers from pecking holes in wooden shingles or siding, brush a coat or two of a wood preservative such as Cuprinol on the siding.

PIGEONS

The Answer Is Blowing in the Wind

❏ To repel pigeons and other birds, hang colorful strips of cloth or plastic in areas where they'll blow in the breeze. Wind socks work nicely for this.

Nobody Ever Said They Were Vain

❏ A common place for a pigeon to roost is on decorative molding along the gable end of the house where the roof returns. If you install small mirrors in those places (either standing against the wall or lying on top of the return), the pigeon will be startled by its own reflection when it lands and will be scared off.

Place a mirror in a strategic spot to scare away pigeons.

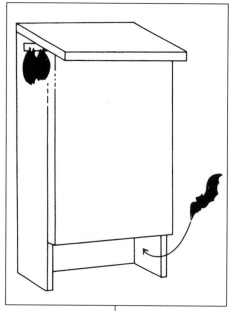

The bottom of a bat house is open, allowing the bats to fly inside and hang from the walls and ceiling.

BATS

Consider a Bat as a Tenant

❏ Long considered pests, bats are now appreciated for the amount of bugs they consume. You can encourage their presence by providing them with a proper bat house. These are available from mail-order suppliers such as L.L. Bean.

Get Rid of the Old Bat

❏ To help keep bats out of your house, press hardware cloth (available from hardware stores) into any cracks in the walls and ceiling of your attic.

❏ In getting bats out of an attic, remember one basic principle: You must evict all the bats before sealing the building against their reentry. Otherwise, trapped animals—especially flightless young—will die and rot in hidden parts of the house, creating an unpleasant odor. Bats feed at night, so this is a logical time to work on keeping them out.

Even the Babies Don't Like Night-lights

❏ To remove bats from your attic, seal all cracks except the one the bats are using to enter the attic. (A bat can get through a very small opening, but you can tell where the creatures are getting in by the droppings around the opening.) Get more light into the attic. If necessary, for a few days leave a 25-watt bulb on all the time at the peak of the roof in the attic. Then one night after dark, when all the bats should be out, seal their entrance holes. Any bats left in the morning can be caught and put outside.

FLYING ACES

NEXT TIME you start to wonder what you can do to rid your property of bats, remember this: A single bat can catch and kill 900 insects an hour—as many as 3,000 in a night.

SNAKES

Get Rid of Mice, and You'll Get Rid of Snakes

❏ Snakes feed on mice. You can take advantage of them to control the mouse population—in a barn, for example. Conversely, if you can get rid of mice in a house, you will automatically get rid of snakes, because the snakes come there for the food.

Call Them Social Climbers

❏ Snakes will climb the hollow walls of a house and have been known to spend the winter in the attic. To keep them out, close all openings that a snake might use to get in.

Stick to the Subject

❏ To catch a snake in your house, try one of the glue boards usually used for catching mice and rats. A glue board is a piece of cardboard coated with a sticky material—just like flypaper, only heavier. You can find these boards in hardware stores and other places where flypaper is sold.

A glue board less than a foot square will hold a large snake. In addition to the glue board itself, you'll need a piece of plywood about 18" square. Bore a ¼" hole near one edge of the plywood. Then nail the glue board to the plywood with the sticky side up. The additional weight will prevent the snake from dragging the glue board off.

In the cellar or wherever snakes are a problem, place the glue board flat on the floor next to the wall (a snake hugs the wall as it travels). When the snake crosses the glue board, it will wiggle around and become stuck.

Once you catch a snake, you'll need to get rid of it. Drive a nail into the end of a 3' wooden pole and hook the nail into the hole you drilled in the plywood. Drag the snake out into the open and destroy or release it.

❏ If you prefer to release the snake once it's outside, pour vegetable oil on the glue board to soften the glue, and the snake can go on its way.

Whatsit?

WE HAVE A PUZZLING item illustrated herewith. It's about 3½" long, and the screw eye is an additional 1⅜". It's metal, but we don't know what kind of metal. We're sure it's not tin. The screw shows evidence of having been screwed into painted wood. It may not be an antique.
— R.L., ROCKVILLE, MD.

At first I thought this was a tieback for a curtain. However, after consulting with others, I learned that the fixture was used to hold a bartender's towel. How was I to know that? I've never been behind bars of any kind. One person I consulted said that in Alaska, they used to have these holders fastened to the front of the bar to hold a towel that would allow the men to wipe their mustaches after getting them soaked with beer.

SNAKES

If Only They'd Had This in the Garden of Eden

❏ Snakes love the warmth of stone steps or a stone wall in a sunny spot. To deter them, sprinkle a bag of dried sulfur, available at farm and garden stores, around the house. This will keep ants away, too.

GARDEN PESTS

Bulb Protection

❏ Old tin cans will deter rodents from attacking your bulbs. Remove both ends from each can, punch several holes in its side for drainage, and push it down into the ground so that it forms a cylinder around a bulb.

Garden Concert

❏ Is your garden loud enough? Foil pie pans, wind chimes and windmills will generate noises that will frighten would-be invaders. If all else fails, try piping in some accordion music.

The Best Defense Is a Fence

❏ If you are putting a fence around your garden to keep out animals, give special attention to the top and bottom. The fencing material should be buried a few inches in the ground. Otherwise, ambitious raiders will simply dig under it. Keep it loose at the top, perhaps by extending the fencing above the fence posts. Animals can't climb up a wobbly fence.

Woodchucks Don't Like Mirrors

SOMEONE ONCE told me that a good way to keep a woodchuck out of the garden is to get some glass gallon jugs and fill them three-quarters full with water. Put the jugs along the edge of the garden. The theory is that when the woodchuck sees its reflection in the jug, it will think it's another animal and run away.

I've never done this myself, but some people swear by it, so it's worth a try.

A Word from Earl

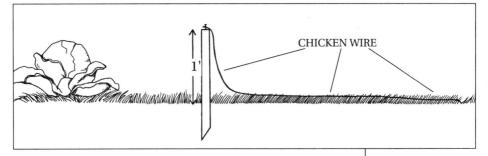

CHICKEN WIRE

1'

❏ Horizontal fencing can be effective, too. Animals that might dig under or leap over an upright fence won't walk over 3 or 4 feet of chicken wire lying on the ground. To make this protection most effective, prop up the end of the fence closest to the garden (a foot or so should do it).

Horizontal fencing keeps small animals out of the garden. Prop up the end so the chicken wire continues about a foot off the ground.

Save the Citrus

❏ Save orange and lemon rinds to deter squirrels and cats from digging in the garden. During the winter, store the rinds in the freezer. In the spring and periodically throughout the summer, bury the rinds here and there just under the surface of the garden.

RATS AND MICE

Build a Better Mousetrap

❏ Use peanut butter as bait for your mousetraps. You can reset the traps and catch several mice before you need to add bait.

Just Stamp Your Feet, and They'll Go Away

❏ In the winter, check the trunks of young fruit and ornamental trees for damage from mice. Stomping the snow around the trunks after each snowfall will inhibit mice from tunneling.

Drive Mice Out of Your Car

❏ If mice are getting into your car's insulation, sew on some cotton balls soaked in pure peppermint extract. (Common locations for car insulation are under the hood and on the fire wall that separates the engine from the cab.)

How to In-Pail a Mouse

❏ Here's an efficient way to trap mice. Punch two holes opposite each other near the top of a pail. Run a wire the

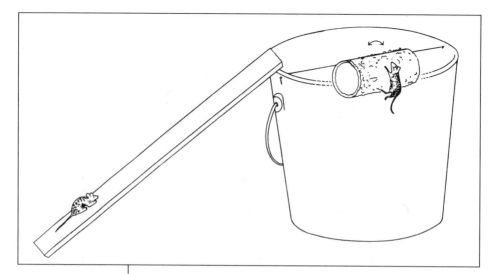

Build a better mousetrap. The mice fall in, and they can't climb out.

long way through a baking powder can from which both ends have been removed. Spread cooking grease on the outside of the can and cover it with bread crumbs. Hang the can so that it can spin freely suspended over the pail. Place a board or a mailing tube at a gentle incline leading up to the pail. Mice will be attracted to the bread crumbs and fall into the pail; they will not be able to climb out. You can release the mice at a distance from your house.

Pause Before You Poison

❑ You may want to avoid chemical rat and mouse poisons. These products typically work by dehydrating rodents,

She Sent the Moles on the Run

A WOMAN FROM OHIO wrote me with a simple way to get rid of moles. Make a hole in one end of a mole tunnel and drop in a chocolate-flavored Ex-Lax tablet. Then cover the hole with a little dirt.

I'd heard this remedy before, but I'd never realized how popular it was. The woman told me that her pharmacist sells more Ex-Lax in the spring, when moles are a real nuisance, than at any other time of year.

A Word from Earl

sending them in search of water. Usually they find the water and drown in it; sometimes they end up in your toilet. *Never leave these products out where children or pets can get into them.*

MOLES

A Change of Diet

❏ To drive away moles, dip an ear of corn in roofing tar (available at roofing supply stores) and place it in the animals' tunnel. They don't like the smell of tar, and you'll block their run.

❏ You can also try getting rid of moles by sprinkling red pepper in their tunnel entrances.

Ring around the Tulips

❏ Place a ring of gravel around your bulbs. This will discourage moles from eating the bulbs.

SILVERFISH

At Least They're Well Educated

❏ Silverfish eat glue, books, papers, artwork and clothing. You can discourage them by wiping bookshelves, both top and bottom, with turpentine.

Plan a One-Way Trip

❏ To get rid of silverfish, put about ¼" of flour in a small, straight-sided glass. Run a strip of adhesive tape from bottom to top on the outside. Silverfish will travel up the tape and drop into the glass, but they won't be able to get back out. Place a glass or two in each room where you've seen silverfish.

Add Sugar and Spice

❏ You can also eliminate silverfish by sprinkling a solution of boric acid and sugar around a room. The acid is poisonous; *never put it in spots where children or pets can get at it.*

WHO SAID MIGHTY MOUSE WAS JUST A CARTOON?

THE LATIN NAME for the common house mouse, *Mus musculus,* means "muscular thief." A mouse can squeeze through a ¾"-diameter hole, has a range of up to a mile and lives for about 1 year, during which time it leaves behind about 18,000 droppings.

☐ Add whole cloves to bags of stored clothing to keep out moths and silverfish.

ANTS

Help from the Kitchen Cupboard

☐ Wipe cabinets, shelves, countertops and baseboards with a solution of equal parts white vinegar and water to help keep away ants.

☐ Squirt lemon juice on windowsills and the bottoms of doors to keep ants from coming into the house.

☐ You can discourage those small sugar ants from getting into your kitchen by sprinkling a little red pepper around the baseboards and at the rear of the counters.

☐ If you don't have red pepper on hand and you need to get rid of sugar ants, try ground cloves or even black pepper.

IDENTITY CRISIS

CARPENTER ANTS and subterranean termites are both notorious wood destroyers, but there are important differences between them. Carpenter ants, unlike termites, do not eat or digest the cellulose in the wood they remove. Their sole purpose in removing the wood is to create space for their colonies. Termites are very messy eaters. They leave their tunnels clogged with organic grit, dead termite bodies and fecal matter. By comparison, carpenter ants are fussy housekeepers. They leave their tunnels looking as if

Carpenter ant.

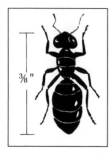

⅜"

they've been sandpapered. (You know they are there because of the little piles of sawdust they leave beneath their holes.)

The insects themselves are easy to tell apart. Most termites—if you ever see them—are tiny, white and thick-waisted. They look like grains of rice with legs, mandibles and straight antennae composed of strings of tiny beads. Since exposure to open air rapidly evaporates their body liquids and causes death, you will rarely, if ever, see them working above ground. In contrast, carpenter ants do work above ground. A carpenter ant is much larger than a termite and black in color. It has a wasp-like waist and bent "elbowed" antennae. The queens of both species are black and

Termite.

¼"

□ Another way to get rid of ants is to mix equal parts borax and confectioners' sugar with enough water to make a syrup. Put this mixture in flat pans or jar lids and place them under counters and behind appliances, but *out of the reach of children and pets*. Ants are cannibals. One ant will eat the syrup and die. Another will eat the dead ant and die. Eventually you'll get the whole nest.

They Never Developed a Taste for It

□ To get rid of ants in the lawn, mix about 1 pound of coffee grounds in 1 quart of hot water and pour this on anthills. Red ants, which make big hills, will require a big dousing.

Aw, Dry Up!

□ Carpenter ants are usually attracted by a water source (such as a roof or plumbing leak). As a first step in elimi-

have wings, but even here the differences in the waists and antennae are still apparent.

You can identify a termite problem in another way, too. Look for mud tunnels on the foundation walls—in the cellar, outside or under your porch. Subterranean termites, which live underground in colonies, come up through these tunnels during the day to feed. The tunnels are about ½" wide, semicircular and built from the ground up to woodwork. They can be inside the house—on posts in the cellar, for instance—as well as out-side. If you find any tunnels, check with a local exterminator about treating the foundation area.

Subterranean termites are found throughout the United States, but homeowners also commonly encounter two other varieties of these pests. Damp-wood termites, named for the moist wood in which they build their nests, are found in the Southwest, on the West Coast and in southern Florida. Dry-wood termites live in totally dry wood. They're a concern mostly in California, Nevada and New Mexico, as well as along the Gulf Coast.

Termite queen.

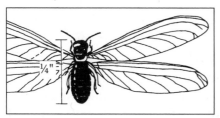

Carpenter ant queen.

The House with the Terminal Termites

A CUSTOMER CALLED one day and asked me to stop by his house, a stucco building that he had just had treated for termites by a company from out of state. The company had told him that he would have no more trouble, since they had drilled all around his house, inside and out, injecting pesticide and eliminating the termites. Now he wanted me to replace all the damaged woodwork in his house.

I went into his cellar through the bulkhead. He went into the house to put on the cellar lights. As he came down the cellar stairs to show me what he wanted replaced, the three bottom steps collapsed under him, and termites ran in every direction. He was one angry man.

A Word from Earl

You have to be careful when dealing with pest control companies. Get bids from at least three companies, as their estimates will vary a lot. Check their references carefully. Some will guarantee that their method will completely rid your house of the pests, but it has been my experience that the best anyone can do is slow the insects' progress. Once you have a termite problem, you will have it for a long while.

nating the ants, be sure to eliminate the moisture. This is very important—and sometimes all that is needed.

Don't Sweat the Small Stuff

❏ If you're not sure whether the ants you see in your house are of the carpenter variety, follow this simple rule of thumb: If it's big and it's black, it's a carpenter ant.

TERMITES

They Need Support

❏ Subterranean termites are a common problem throughout the United States, but they're tropical in origin and need a moist, relatively warm environment. You can discourage subterranean termites by caulking and painting around porch supports and applying creosote to the supports. This will minimize the amount of water the wood will absorb.

❏ To minimize soil dampness near your house's foundation and thus discourage termites, be sure to direct rainwater away from the foundation and porch area. Install gutters and downspouts, and make sure the ground around the foundation is sloping away from the house.

❏ Be on-site the day any backfilling is done to be sure the contractor doesn't leave any scrap wood underground. It can attract termites to your house.

How Firm a Foundation

❏ To avoid termite infestation, make sure that wooden siding and other wooden structural elements do not come into contact with the soil. A distance of 18" between soil and house parts is fairly standard today. Dirt tends to build up around the foundation, so you'll need to lower the soil level periodically where it contacts the foundation.

A TERMITE'S FAVORITE MEAL

JUST AS A DOCTOR can describe the type of person most likely to suffer a heart attack, it's possible to draw a profile of the structure most likely to attract structural pests. The structure is, of course, made of wood and placed on a stone or concrete foundation. It is located in a moist, shady yard near a surrounding forest. There are several dead trees still standing nearby. The woodpile in the yard is slowly decaying, and the area where the householder cuts and splits firewood is covered with sawdust. Several live trees stand very close to the house, their branches touching the roof and siding.

The siding of the house is of vertical pine boards, their end grain within a few inches of the soil. The sill, which rests on top of the foundation just behind the boards, is of untreated spruce nested in fiberglass "sill sealer," which keeps out the wind but keeps the sill moist. Behind the sill in one part of the house is a damp, unventilated crawl space with an earth floor. A leaky gutter has been dripping onto a flat rock, and the water has been splashing up against the siding.

This is a lovely sight to structural pests. It's very much like a tethered goat in lion country: Visitors are practically guaranteed.

The Terror of Termites

JUST ABOUT THE WORST termite damage I've ever seen started in a house where I was called in to repair the floor. The termites had eaten the floor out from under the linoleum but had not touched the floor covering. A few weeks later, I was called to replace a wooden rail fence they had chewed up—about 60' from the house I had repaired earlier. The next fall I was called to repair termite damage to the house next door. The ground between the houses was saturated with the pesky bugs. When I dug a trench along the foundation of the second house to put in pesticides, I uncovered termite colonies as big as 6" in diameter.

A Word from Earl

The moral is that it's important to catch termite problems early. Once they get on a roll, it's almost impossible to stop them.

POWDER-POST BEETLES

Sawdust without a Saw Is Not a Good Sign

❏ Powder-post beetles are small insects that can eat and destroy the wood in a home. They tunnel into wood and live there for most of their lives. People usually learn of these intruders by the telltale dust that rains down from the beetles' tunnels when a beam is tapped with a hammer. To find out whether your beams have an active infestation, knock all the powder you can from the beam and then clean it up. If you observe new powder in the cleaned-up area over the next couple of weeks, call an exterminator.

Furniture Infestations

❏ Furniture, as well as the structural elements of houses, can be infested with powder-post beetles. Small piles of sawdust around a chair leg show that the beetles are alive and working. To treat a piece of furniture, spray kerosene in any holes that are evident and wipe the furniture with boiled linseed oil. It takes many years for beetles to eat enough to seriously damage a piece of furniture, so it's likely that you can catch the problem in time if you are observant.

❏ Another method of treating powder-post beetles in furniture is to enclose the affected area in plastic. Cut a small slit in the plastic just large enough to accept the nozzle of a spray insecticide. Spray the chemical inside the plastic bag, filling the area with the fumes. Close the slit with tape and keep it closed overnight. Repeat the process the next day. Let the closed bag sit one more day. By then the fumes should have penetrated the beetles' holes.

COCKROACHES

Clean the Bugs to Death
❏ Cockroaches eat bookbinding, paper and starched clothing. They also contaminate food. To rid the house of cockroaches, sprinkle boric acid powder under appliances, behind the refrigerator, under counters and in any other places that are *out of the reach of children and pets.* The cockroaches will step in it and ingest it when they groom themselves.

There's No Place Like the Drip Pan
❏ Roaches love the area under the refrigerator—especially the drip pan and motor. Vacuum up all dirt and dust from around these areas, and wash out the drip pan often. Any area that is warm and dark or that is the least bit damp will be a home for them.

The Bugs Crawl In; They Don't Crawl Out
❏ Another way to get rid of cockroaches is to make a trap with a glass jar that's about 4" high. Put some bacon grease and a small chunk of banana in the bottom of the jar. Smear a band of petroleum jelly about ¾" wide

Whatsit?

I NEED HELP identifying this object. One chain has a ring on it. The other chain is like a needle. What is it? Does it have anything to do with wine?
— J.P., WHITEHOUSE STATION, N.J.

This appears to be a holder for a bride's bouquet. The pin was pushed through the bouquet to keep it in the holder, and a finger through the ring helped the bride hold on to it.

around the inside of the jar, about ½" from the top. Stand the jar in the area where the roaches are a problem. The bugs can crawl in, but they can't get out.

Plug the Passageways

❏ A common passageway for cockroaches is through the holes for the plumbing under the kitchen sink. Plug these tightly with rags, and you'll stop roach traffic.

STINGING INSECTS

At Least You'll Be Crying for a Different Reason

❏ Stung by a bee? Apply a slice of onion to the spot and hold it on for a minute or so.

Try a Mud Pack

❏ One of the simplest old-time treatments for bee stings is a handful of mud. If no other treatment is available, just scoop up the mud and hold it on the sting until the mud dries.

The Hole Story

❏ Bees will bore holes in your house's siding and leave a sticky yellowish discharge. If you plug a hole with the bees in it, they'll bore their way out—possibly into your living area—so it's best to get rid of the bees before you plug any of their holes.

Beauticians Take Note

❏ To get rid of bees, try spraying them with hair spray. The hair spray will stiffen their wings, and the bees will drop to the ground. It won't kill them, though, so be careful when picking them up.

Getting Sucked In

❏ Another method of collecting bees from the outside of your house is to mount the suction hose of a vacuum cleaner next to their entrance and leave it running all day. As the bees come out, they'll be sucked into the vacuum cleaner. Take care when you're emptying the bag. Place it in a plastic bag and seal the whole thing.

SOME PEOPLE ARE NEVER SATISFIED

GROUND HORNETS can be a serious problem because they're likely to sting you every time your lawn mower gets near them. If you happen to live in a neighborhood that attracts skunks or raccoons, you may be able to solve the problem easily. Just leave a few bits of garbage near the nest. A skunk or raccoon will be attracted by the garbage and discover the hornets, which it will eat—adults, nest and larvae. Of course, you'll still have the problem with the skunks.

They Had the Table for Lunch

I WAS CALLED ONE TIME to a fairly new house, where the owner had been moving her dining room table and had found a small hole in the floor where one of the table legs had been. She had heard about termites and wanted the house checked out.

I examined the cellar timbers and found that termites had entered the foundation from sand fill under the steps, gone along a carrying beam and somehow determined that the table leg sat on that spot. The owner was lucky that she found it before the pests had gone farther. Termites have been known to eat the whole inside of a table without coming out into the light.

A Word from Earl

Since the house was small, we were able to jack it up off its foundation and install aluminum termite shields all around. A termite shield is just a piece of aluminum flashing fashioned to fit between the concrete foundation wall and the wood sill above it. I'd recommend that anyone building a new house in a forested area—especially a pine forest—install termite shields.

A Good Soak in the Tub

❏ For outdoor wasp traps, make a solution of sugar and water and put it in a small margarine tub with a cover. Make a small hole in the lid, place it on top of the tub and hang the tub in a tree. The wasps will crawl in and won't be able to escape. To dispose of the wasp-filled tub, place it in a plastic bag and seal the bag carefully before throwing it out.

Hit Them Where They Live

❏ Wasps build their nests in hedges and shrubbery. About the only way to get rid of them is to spray the nests, when they start building them, with an insecticide made for wasps or with a carbon dioxide fire extinguisher. Spray at dusk, when the occupants are lazing, and walk away rapidly. Don't wait until it's so dark that you have to use a flashlight, because some of the angry wasps may be at-tracted to the light.

Yellow Jackets: There Goes the Neighborhood

❑ Yellow jackets sometimes crawl into the empty area above a porch ceiling and build their nests there. You can stop this problem before it starts by caulking any open-ings in the ceiling to keep the yellow jackets out.

❑ If you have access to the empty area above the porch ceiling, place a commercial product such as a Pest STRIP or another stationary insecticide there each spring. It will keep that space free of insects for the entire summer.

SPIDERS

Charlotte Doesn't Live Here Anymore

❑ To get rid of spiders, put cedar chips in the toes of old panty hose. Hang the hose from the porch ceiling or other areas where spiders build their webs.

❑ To discourage spiders, spray rubbing alcohol on win-dowsills or leave perfumed soap chips scattered about.

THE BATTLE OF
THE BOTTLE

BLUEBOTTLE and greenbottle flies are also called blowflies. They lay eggs, which hatch into maggots that feed on dead animals. If you have a sudden influx of blowflies in the house, a squirrel or bird proba-bly died in the attic, chimney or basement. The flies, finding it quickly, covered it with eggs. The dead animal may have been con-sumed so fast by the hatching maggots that there was lit-tle smell.

When the fly maggots mature, they generally move away to pupate (change into adults). At this stage, they're likely to crawl into a conve-nient fireplace. It's only when the adults emerge into the house, rather than outdoors, that the fly problem be-comes apparent. To get rid of these insects, hang the brand-name product Pest STRIPs or spray the infested area with insecticide, follow-ing the product direc-tions carefully.

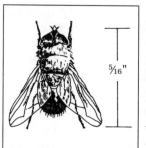

Bottle fly.

5⁄16"

FLIES AND MOSQUITOES

A Buzz in the Attic

❏ Cluster flies are mainly a nuisance; they do not bite. They enter buildings in the fall for warmth and gather by the dozens in attic windows. It is impossible to keep them out of older houses, as they can get through very small openings. The easiest way to deal with them is to let them die and vacuum them up.

❏ If you're determined to get rid of cluster flies as soon as possible, you can hang the brand-name product Pest STRIPs. Or mix together 1 teaspoon of brown sugar, ½ teaspoon of black pepper and 1 teaspoon of milk. Put this mixture in shallow dishes on the floor of the room where the flies are gathering.

Natural Pest Control

❏ Swallows consume tremendous numbers of flying insects. If you have surface water nearby—a lake, pond or stream—you may want to erect swallow houses on your property to encourage these birds to settle. Check for building plans at your local library.

Undercover Agents

❏ Blackflies bite most fiercely under cover—up sleeves and trouser legs. To discourage them, wear rubber bands over clothing at these openings. If you're really pestered by these little buggers, wear a head net over a brimmed hat.

Maybe They Prefer Chocolate

❏ Rubbing the skin with baby oil or imitation vanilla extract repels biting insects such as mosquitoes and blackflies.

Be a Soft Touch

❏ Avon's Skin-So-Soft makes a good nontoxic insect repellent. Rub a liberal amount on exposed parts of your

THE BLOOD DRIVE

CHEER UP! Even though there are 2,500 species of mosquitoes in the world, there are only 200 or so here in the United States. You know that annoying, high-pitched sound that some nights makes you wish the mosquito would just bite and be gone? Most often it is created by the female to attract a male. Mosquitoes mate in midair, and then the female goes off in search of blood to mature her eggs. One study found that a single mosquito bit 44 times in 100 days. (Don't you wish you could have helped research that one?) The only places there aren't any of these wonderful insects are the open sea, the North and South poles, dry deserts and areas above 12,000 feet. Plan your vacation accordingly.

body. It's especially good for people with sensitive skin and for very small children.

❏ Rub cider vinegar on your skin to repel insects. If you take in enough cider vinegar by putting it on foods you eat, you'll develop a body odor that will repel insects, including blackflies. They will swarm around but won't bite.

Itching for a Cure

❏ To eliminate the itch of insect bites, rub on meat tenderizer or lemon juice.

❏ White vinegar is another remedy for relieving the itch of insect bites. Apply it full strength. Don't use vinegar if the area is raw, however.

BZZ CRACKLE POW ZZZTT!

EVER EXAMINE the pile of charred remains under your bug zapper? The few mosquitoes you'll find are hardly worth the mound of beneficial insects fried by the noisy contraption. (A Canadian study once found that less than 4 percent of the bugs killed by zappers were mosquitoes.)

To keep mosquitoes from carrying you off, a better strategy is to eliminate their breeding sites on your property. These bugs need standing water to lay their eggs in, and they will use any water they can find. They'll go for puddles, old cans, plant pots—how about the old boat out back that usually has some rainwater in the bottom? If you have an ornamental pool, throw in some guppies to gobble up the bugs' youngsters before they get a chance to nibble on you.

SLUGS

A Beer Trap for Slugs

❏ To keep slugs out of your garden, fill shallow pans with beer and place them in the garden with the rims flush to the ground. When the slugs go to drink the beer, they'll drown.

Ashes, Ashes, They All Fall Off

❏ Spread a 6"-wide band of wood ashes around your garden to keep out slugs and crawling worms. If slugs are a problem in just one part of your garden, place the band of ashes around that section only.

❏ As a protection from slugs, cover delphinium crowns with the ashes from a coal-burning stove. Don't put coal ashes on a vegetable garden, however, as they are toxic.

Seashells by the Seashore

❏ If you have access to quantities of seashells, try crushing them and spreading them around plants as a deterrent to slugs. The shells will also add nutrients to the soil.

Bugs Are Such Fussy Eaters

❏ To get rid of bugs in houseplants, push a clove of garlic into the plant's soil. If the garlic sprouts and grows, just cut it back.

❏ It also pays to grow garlic in outdoor flower beds; it's a natural bug deterrent.

❏ To keep bugs out of flour and cereal without leaving any telltale flavor, place a few bay leaves in your bag or box.

Playing Cricket

❏ If crickets are a problem, fill a plastic squeeze bottle—such as the kind talcum powder comes in—with borax. Sprinkle borax in any cracks, as well as along the baseboards, in the area where the crickets are gathering—*but only in areas that are out of the reach of children and pets.*

Light a Fire under Earwigs

❏ Earwigs are attracted to damp wood and are often found in firewood stored in the house. (Luckily, earwigs don't damage the house the way termites or carpenter ants do.) Don't bring in any wood that's damp or starting to rot unless you put it on the fire right away.

❏ If you have an infestation of earwigs around firewood, sprinkle borax around the woodpile. Keep borax away from pets and children, however.

Let Us Spray

❏ A very small amount of dishwashing liquid mixed with water makes a spray that will debug many house and garden plants. Soaps vary, so it's best to start with a weak mixture and experiment with one or two plants until you're sure the solution is gentle enough.

❏ Another effective homemade bug killer is nicotine spray. Soak cigarette butts in water and spray the mixture on the bugs.

BUG DEALS

IF YOU'RE LOOKING for alternatives to spraying chemicals all over your garden, you might be tempted to buy beneficial bugs such as praying mantises and ladybugs to control garden pests. It sounds like a pretty good idea, but many of these bugs are raised in warm climates. If you live in a colder area, they either won't survive or won't stick around your garden for long. Instead, encourage beneficial native bugs to come to your yard by planting (and allowing to bloom) members of the mint, cabbage and carrot families.

Get to the Root of the Problem

❏ Place a mixture of lime and wood ashes around cabbage, beets and onions to discourage root maggots. Use equal parts lime and wood ashes. Moisten the roots of transplants, then dunk them in the mixture before setting them in the soil.

❏ If lime is not available, dipping the roots of transplants in wood ashes alone will deter root maggots.

If Only Mr. McGregor Had Known

❏ To keep out rabbits, try placing dried sulfur, available at farm and garden supply stores, around the edge of your garden.

❏ To discourage deer and rabbits, sprinkle blood meal around your crops after each rainfall. Blood meal will also benefit the soil by adding nitrogen. (Don't use this technique if you have dogs that roam in the garden. They may be attracted to the scent of the blood meal and start digging.)

A Coffee Break

❏ If your garden is infested with ants or cutworms, sprinkle used coffee grounds on the infested area.

Before You Start on the Maple Sugaring . . .

❏ On a relatively warm (40°F) day in February or March, spray fruit trees with dormant oil to smother insect masses. You can buy the spray at a farm supply store and rent a sprayer there if necessary.

A Time to Plow

❏ Plow or till the garden in the fall to expose both hibernating insects and weed seeds, which will then perish.

Oh, Deer

❏ The tender branches of small fruit trees are a temptation for deer. Try

---

Whatsit?

My son found this in a field near our house. It's made of iron and weighs about ½ pound. Do you know its use?

— B.S., Galloway, Ohio

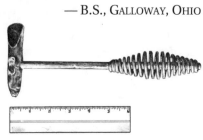

This is a welder's chipping hammer. When you weld two pieces of metal together, you use a torch to melt a bead of welding material (weld) into the crack between the pieces. The excess melted metal that accumulates around the joint is called the slag. This hammer could be used to knock the slag off while it's still red-hot and not solid. The coil on the hammer handle keeps it from getting too hot to hold.

IF IT DRIES, IT DIES

THOSE LITTLE, oval-shaped creatures that occasionally show up in homes along the coast are sow bugs. Often found congregating under kitchen sinks, in basements or bathrooms, or along foundations, they aren't really bugs at all. Instead, they're crustaceans, more closely related to lobsters and crabs than to flies or roaches. Although you might think the difference is significant only to trivia experts, it's the key to getting rid of these critters.

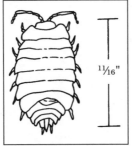

Sow bug.

Most crustaceans live in the water and "breathe" with gills. While sow bugs are terrestrial, as true crustaceans they use gills, which lose water to the air much faster than do the internal breathing tubes of true insects. This means that sow bugs need very damp conditions to survive. (They even carry their young in pouches, like kangaroos, to ensure that the young start life under ideal moisture conditions.) If the area they're living in gets too dry, sow bugs have to find another water source. But their sense organs don't allow them to determine which way to go to find water. They move about randomly, their speed related to the humidity. If they move into areas with higher humidity, they slow down, eventually stopping at about 100 percent humidity. Those moving into drier conditions run faster and faster, either getting into more acceptable surroundings or drying out—and dying.

hanging some strongly scented soap on the branches to discourage them.

❏ To keep deer away, spread human hair around your crops. Get the hair at your local beauty parlor or barbershop.

Some Like It Wet

❏ Sow bugs congregate in damp areas as long as food is available. Eliminate the sources of moisture in your house, and the sow bugs will disappear. Repair the flashing around the chimney, fix that leaky faucet and insulate sweating pipes. Consider a dehumidifier if overall humidity is high.

The Home Workshop

From creative organization to building tools, there's a lot you can do yourself.

I HAVE SET UP EIGHT FULL SHOPS in my life at various jobs and residences. I put together my first shop when I was 12. My parents let me use a 4' x 8' space in the cellar of our house.

Right away I began collecting tools and materials that my father cast off. My older brother and I put them to use building playhouses in our backyard. The playhouses grew increasingly complicated as we scavenged more tools and materials and as we grew more experienced. In the end, we had a four-house village—one for each kid in my family—complete with sleeping bunks, electricity, running water, a fire hydrant and speaking tubes. I even built a wood stove for my house, using an old 5-gallon gas can for the stove and an old toilet vent pipe for the chimney.

I learned at an early age that you don't need a large shop full of expensive tools and materials to be productive. If you're imaginative and resourceful, you can make the most of any shop.

This chapter contains tips for saving space and organizing everything in your workshop, adapting old tools to new uses and preventing rust from forming on your best equipment. You'll learn how to store twine, garden hoses and long extension cords without tangling. You'll discover new ways to recycle scraps of inner tube and wire screening, old dishwashing liquid bottles, even the little plastic squares that come on your bread bags. And you'll find out how to turn an old piece of glass into the best tool you've ever used for stripping furniture.

SAFETY

Stand by Your Saw—Not in Front of It

❏ Never stand directly in line with a rotating saw blade or grinding wheel. Always stand to the side. You can't tell when a saw might throw a piece of wood or when a grinding stone might shatter.

Avoid Aftershocks

❏ Never work with electrically powered tools while barefoot or standing on a wet surface. Always stand on a board, mat or some other dry surface.

Pay Attention to the Dress Code

❏ Most people are aware that you should wear eye protection whenever you use a power tool. Another thing to watch for is appropriate dress. Loose clothing is a serious hazard; caught in operating machinery, it can instantly pull in and trap the operator, with serious results. Roll up

---

IF YOU CAN'T FIND IT ...

... maybe you need to try another chapter. Check the index, or try these possibilities.

For Tips On ...	See the Chapter ...
Gluing	Furniture
Masonry	Maintaining the Exterior

THE SHAKER IN THE SAWMILL

ACCORDING TO Greek legend, when a fellow named Talus was using a serpent's jawbone to cut a tree limb, he suddenly had a bright idea. He rushed home, hammered the toothed profile on a sheet of iron and made sawing much easier for everyone, especially snakes. Archaeology shows that the ancient Egyptians had well-refined saw technology and the early Romans made their saw teeth with "set," just as modern saw makers do.

Later, the English used pit saws to create paneling for their manors. The sawyer stood atop the logs, lifting the heavy saw all day. His pitman held the other end of the saw and dragged it back down in a flurry of sawdust. At the end of a day at the sawpit, both men tended to have a notorious thirst.

By colonial days, waterpower was replacing muscle, but the saw blade still rose and fell, leaving straight marks on the wood, perpendicular to the length of the piece. In the more powerful mills, a number of saws were ganged together in a frame, cutting out many planks simultaneously.

Then someone with a spark of genius saw that the blade was cutting only half the time, as the blade came down, while a circular blade would cut continuously. We can thank Sister Tabitha Babbitt, a Shaker, for that insight, which revolutionized sawmill production. When steam power was coupled to the circular saw, production rose and trees fell. And with the advent of railroads came a way to transport all the wood that was cut, setting in motion the first mass-production processes of the building industry and eliminating the need for a sawmill in every town forever.

long shirt sleeves above the elbow or wear short-sleeved shirts, and tuck in shirt tails. Don't wear jewelry while operating power tools; it, too, can get caught in the equipment and cause serious injury. And recognize that long hair is a threat around machinery. When working with power tools, always tie back long hair in a ponytail and wear a cap.

SHOP ORGANIZATION

A Space for Everything
❏ Storage space in a shop is always at a premium, so be sure to take advantage of any space you have overhead.

EARL PROULX'S YANKEE HOME HINTS

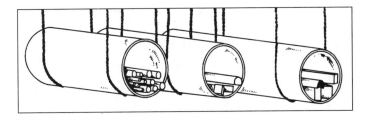

To save shop space, hang cardboard tubes from the ceiling and store lightweight building materials in the tubes.

Start with wide cardboard tubes. (Fiber tube forms, typically used for pouring concrete footings, work nicely.) Hang them horizontally from the ceiling by lightweight chains or ropes. These tubes are ideal for storing dowels, moldings, thin scrap stock and other long, lightweight materials. You can cut the tubes to different lengths and then sort the materials into tubes of appropriate lengths.

❏ Why invest in hardware such as Peg-Board systems to organize your tools, when you can make simple tool organizers yourself? Mount chisels and screwdrivers, for instance, in a piece of wood with the appropriate-size holes drilled in it.

❏ To store small, heavy stock, lean an old ladder against a wall at a low angle, with the rungs parallel to the floor. Then place your small stock in the bays created by the ladder rungs. This takes more floor space than ceiling or wall storage, but it's a good way to store heavier objects.

Organize your stock by propping a ladder against a wall and using the rungs as storage dividers.

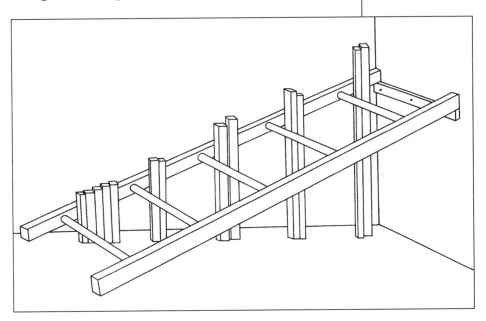

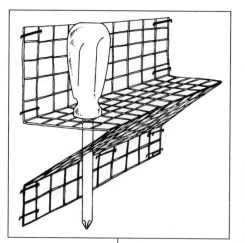

A simple shelf of hardware cloth.

❑ Another simple way to store small tools is to make a shelf out of ½" hardware cloth (heavy-duty wire screen with a ½" x ½" mesh). The hardware cloth is pretty strong and can hold most tools you might otherwise put on a Peg-Board.

Detangle the Twine

❑ To keep twine untangled, hang a large kitchen funnel on the workshop wall and put the ball of twine inside, feeding one end of it through the small end of the funnel.

Perfect Containers

❑ One-gallon metal paint thinner cans are good containers for storing hardware and other small objects. Cut the top off each can with a can opener and pour out any remaining thinner. There's no need to wash the cans; the last traces of the thinner will evaporate. These rectangular cans are especially good for storage because they fit

The Well-Planned Workshop

Like most people, I find that space is at a premium in my shop, so I've laid out my equipment as efficiently as possible. My workbenches run around the perimeter of the room. Instead of taking up space on those benches, my miter box and many of my power tools—a lathe, planer, drill press, band saw and grinding wheel—are organized on a 30"-high island in its center. My island is 6' x 9', but the principle will work for an island of any size. A lot of the space taken up by power tools is in the stands and motors. I've saved space where possible by mounting the tools to the island and hiding the motors underneath it.

A Word from Earl

If you try this setup in your workshop, you'll find it saves a lot of space.

neatly on a shelf—like volumes of an encyclopedia.

❑ Use baby-food jars and coffee cans to store screws, nails and small hardware items. To save space, use screws to secure the lids of baby-food jars under a convenient shelf, fill the jars with small hardware and then screw the jars onto the lids. The jars will be handy and their contents easy to identify.

Loop-the-Loop

❑ Does it seem that your long extension cord never uncoils smoothly no matter how carefully you loop it up? Here's a solution. Take a 5-gallon bucket, such as the ones used for drywall joint compound, and cut a 1½" hole in the side, near the bottom. Pass one end of the cord through the hole from the inside, so the plug is on the outside of the bucket. Then feed the rest of the cord into the bucket from the top—it should loop in fairly neatly by itself. Cut a notch in the lip of the bucket, and hook the other end of the cord in the notch, so it's always handy. Now you have both ends where you can get to them, and you can reel out all you need without tangling.

❑ To hang up a big coil of rope, wire or garden hose, nail a loop of inner tube to the wall, pull the lower end of the

Tired of untangling extension cords? Solve the problem with a 5-gallon bucket.

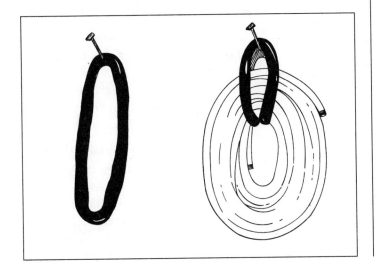

To hang a coil of garden hose, first nail a strip of inner tube to the wall. Then loop the loose end of the inner tube through the coil and hang it on the nail.

Low-Tech, Low-Mess Painting

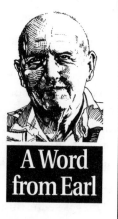

A Word from Earl

A PAINT STATION LIKE THE ONE I have in my workshop is a feature I'd recommend to anyone who paints small objects frequently. All you have to do is install a dispenser of brown shipping paper at the base of a bench that's about 30" high. Whenever you want to paint something, you just pull out enough paper to cover the bench. When you're done, you can throw away the paper.

loop through your coil and hang that end on the nail—effectively doubling the loop.

Put Your Glass on Edge

❏ To avoid breakage, always store glass windowpanes on edge, as you would phonograph records. Lean the stack against an upright surface.

The Magnetic Approach

❏ Keep magnets handy in your toolbox and your shop. They make it easy to pick up hardware that you spread out or spill.

ITEMS OF MANY USES

Don't Kick the Bucket

❏ Never throw away a 5-gallon bucket after you've emptied it. These buckets are heavy-duty and can be used to hold or carry anything. You'll be glad you saved them if a pipe springs a leak.

❏ Need to do some work on the ceiling? Five-gallon buckets make good, stable stilts. Remove or tape down the wire handle on each bucket, turn the bucket upside down, make a foot stirrup out of duct tape and off you go. (You don't want the tape to stick to

SAY WHAT?

BY NOW, YOU'VE probably gotten into the habit of wearing earmuffs or earplugs when you start up your ferociously loud table saw, but take heed: What determines hearing loss is not just how loud the noise is but also how long it lasts. Even that relatively quiet new lawn mower can cause damage when you spend most of the day mowing the back field. Hang your ear protectors in a convenient spot, carry them with you or even splurge and hang an extra pair right on your noisiest tools to make sure they're handy when you need them.

your shoes, so double it—sticky side to sticky side—on the part that your foot slides under.) You'll be surprised how much time this saves over moving a stepladder, and there's no need to worry about safety. If you secure the duct tape carefully, it will *never* let go.

Old Brooms: Salvage the Spare Parts

❏ Never throw away a mop or broom before you salvage the handle. These can be used to replace broken handles on other tools or as garden stakes.

Let Your Fingers Do the Caulking

❏ Sometimes your fingers are the best tools for smoothing roofing cement or auto body putty, but those materials are awful to get on you and worse to get off. Pick up a box of latex exam gloves at your drugstore and put a pair on before getting into the goo. You can get your hands right into the mess and then just peel off the gloves, goo and all. Be careful using this trick with thinners and solvents, though; some of them eat right through the gloves.

You can make great stilts out of old 5-gallon buckets. Secure duct tape to the bucket to serve as a stirrup.

DUCT TAPE: THE QUICK FIX NO HOME SHOULD BE WITHOUT

DUCT TAPE IS a fibered tape known for its strength and durability. Sold in different grades (including one that is sunlight resistant), duct tape was originally used on heating and air-conditioning ducts but is now a quick fix for everything from leaky canoes to ripped seat covers to torn cardboard boxes. It's water resistant, and its glue works well under a wide range of temperatures—so it can be used both indoors and out. Once distinguished by its silver color, duct tape has recently become available in other colors, including black, white, red, blue and orange. Appropriate for solving a wide range of home repair problems, it requires no special skills or equipment—and it's therefore one of the first items that should be added to any home repair kit.

Recycle That Old Inner Tube

❏ A long strip of inner tube makes a versatile clamp even on odd-shaped objects. Just stretch it, wrap it tightly around the piece and tie it off.

❏ To keep the latch and padlock on a shed door from rusting, place a scrap of old inner tube over them. Nail the inner tube along the top edge to secure it. Simply lift up the flap when you want access to the lock.

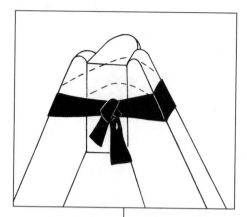

A strip of inner tube makes a versatile clamp for odd-shaped objects.

Your Bread Bag Has a Bonus Scraper

❏ Don't throw away those little plastic squares that close your bread bags. When you're gluing a project, you'll find they make fine little scrapers to clean up glue that has been squeezed out.

Cushion Comfort for Your Ladder

❏ When you're hauling large, heavy items such as ladders and staging on top of your car, protect the roof with one of those blue foam pads designed for carrying canoes. The pads, available at sporting goods stores, are lightweight, small and easily maneuvered, so they're perfect for this purpose.

Whatsit?

Cᴀɴ ʏᴏᴜ ᴛᴇʟʟ ᴍᴇ what this tool is? The cylinder is made of iron and weighs 9 pounds.
— G.H., Dᴏʏʟᴇsᴛᴏᴡɴ, Pᴀ.

This is a mason's tool used to indent fresh concrete and thus create a nonskid surface on steps and the edges of landings.

HARDWARE

A Penny Saved

❏ As a rule of thumb, when you're working with lumber made of softwood, the penny of the nail you use should be the same, in eighths of an inch, as the board you're nailing. For a ½" (⁴⁄₈") board, a 4d nail is fine.

❏ Also as a rule of thumb, when you're working with hardwood, select nails one penny smaller than the thickness of the nailed piece. For a ¾" (⁶⁄₈") board, use a 5d nail.

NAILS: COUNTING THE PENNIES

WHEN YOU ASK to be tossed a ten-penny nail, you're hitting on one of the great mysteries of the construction world. It's common knowledge that the penny indicates both the length and diameter of a particular nail, but no one knows why we designate nails in the penny system. There are, however, two popular explanations of how this system came to be.

One idea is that nails got their names because 100 six-penny nails originally cost 6 pence, 100 four-penny nails cost 4 pence, and so on. A more likely explanation comes from the fact that 1,000 six-penny nails weigh 6 pounds, 1,000 four-penny nails weigh 4 pounds, and so on.

Throughout history, the abbreviation for penny has been the letter *d*, the first letter of denarius, a Roman coin. So a ten-penny nail is also referred to as a 10d nail. Got that?

In the American colonies, nails were hammered one at a time from red-hot iron. This became a huge cottage industry, as nearly all farmers needed a few nails. By 1800, nail-cutting machines existed for the mass production of cut nails (chopped off from bars of iron with a guillotinelike knife). It wasn't until 1851 that William Hersel of New York invented the first machine for making nails out of wire, and wire nails were not common in house construction until about the 1880s. Today nails are made at rates of up to 500 pieces per minute. They're most often stamped from wire rolls of low-carbon Bessemer steel. There has been a nail made for just about every situation possible. One manufacturer claims production of more than 10,000 types of nails.

Break Away

❏ Before pulling out a rusted nail or spike, hit it to drive it in just a little. This breaks the rust and makes removal easier.

❏ You can loosen a rusted screw by spraying on a loosening agent such as WD-4.

❏ Another way to attack a stubborn rusted screw is to brush it with kerosene. Wait a few minutes, then unscrew it.

❏ To loosen a rusted nut or bolt when you have no penetrating oil, soak a rag in a cola drink, club soda, ammo-

NAILED AGAIN!

NAILS OF DIFFERent penny calibrations may vary in diameter, style of head, style of point and coating, among other things, but they are always consistent in their length. A six-penny nail, no matter what the type, is always 2" long. Here's a handy chart for penny sizes:

2d = 1"
3d = 1¼"
4d = 1½"
5d = 1¾"
6d = 2"
10d = 3"
20d = 4"
40d = 5"

Nails measuring 4" or longer are commonly called *spikes.* Small, short, sharp-pointed nails with broad, flat heads are called *tacks.* Thin, flat or round nails with a slight projection rather than a pronounced head are called *brads.*

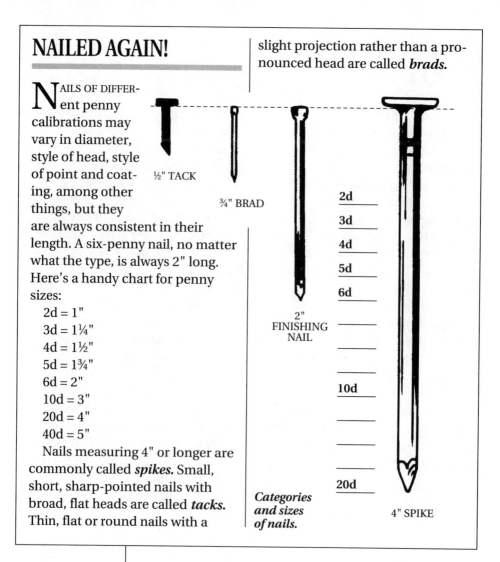

½" TACK
¾" BRAD
2"
FINISHING
NAIL
4" SPIKE

2d
3d
4d
5d
6d
10d
20d

Categories and sizes of nails.

nia or cider vinegar, then leave the wet rag on the nut for about 1 hour, or until the nut can be loosened. Repeat if necessary.

❑ To loosen a screw that is stuck, insert your screwdriver in the screw head and tap the handle of the screwdriver with a hammer while you try to turn the screw with the screwdriver.

❑ Another way to loosen a rusted screw is to press a hot soldering iron against it for a few seconds.

BUYING TOOLS

Better Tools Make a Better Handyman

❏ Always buy the best tools you can afford and keep them sharp and properly adjusted. Better tools and a little experience are all that separates most amateurs from the professionals.

Buying Power

❏ Purchase your power tools the same way you would buy a car: from a reliable and honest dealer. Remember a crit-

---

My Basic Toolbox

A Word from Earl

N̲O ONE OUTFITS A SHOP all at once. You accumulate tools as you need them, and all homeowners' needs are different. But if I were just starting to set up a shop—and not ready to spend a fortune on power tools—here are some tools that I'd put at the top of my list:

Nail hammer, 16 ounces with curved claw
8-tpi (tooth per inch) hand crosscut saw for most work
12-tpi hand crosscut saw for fine work
½" wood chisel
1" wood chisel
Electric drill
Small set of drill bits
Standard-blade (slotted) screwdrivers (large and small)
Phillips-head screwdrivers (large and small)
Adjustable pliers
8" mill bastard file
Smooth plane
Try square

2' framing square
Retractable steel ruler
Small pipe wrench
Adjustable wrench (about 10" long)
Small wrecking bar
Combination sharpening stone
Fine (1⁄16") nail set
Oilcan
Putty knife
Hatchet or half-ax
Hacksaw with coarse and fine blades
Coping saw and blades
18" spirit level
Bevel square
Mason's trowel

---

ical question: Where will you get parts and service when you need them?

Made in Japan

❏ If you find yourself doing a lot of projects that require very precise cuts, one tool you might consider getting is a Japanese woodworking saw. Japanese saws are designed to cut on the upstroke (as opposed to American saws, which cut on the downstroke), a direction that causes slower but much more controlled cutting. If your local woodworking supply store doesn't have them, try to find a mail-order supplier by asking some local woodworkers or checking the back of a woodworking magazine.

The Tools Were Battle Tested

AFTER WORLD WAR II, I WENT to work for a contractor. I was setting up my shop when the boss came in and asked what equipment I needed. He was going to a Navy auction where some used power tools were for sale.

I told him I wanted a table saw, a jointer, a band saw and a few other things, but I warned him not to spend more than $100 on a single machine. I was skeptical about what he'd find at the auction, and he didn't know much about power tools.

To my amazement, he returned from the auction with one power tool that performed almost all the tasks I had in mind, and he'd paid only $150

A Word from Earl

for it. It was a table saw, jointer, band saw and drill press—all run off one 5-horsepower motor. It stood 4½' square and 3' high. It turned out that this tool had been built to outfit the shop on board a Navy battleship. That was why it was so compact. I had to repair a loose bearing in the table saw, but it ran wonderfully after that.

It's rare to come across a find like that, but auctions are a great place to look for bargains on shop equipment in general.

WOOD SAWS: MAKING THE CUT

UNDERSTANDING wood saws requires understanding wood. Wood is made up of long fibers that are stronger than the bonds holding them together. You can split a piece of wood with one blow, but only Paul Bunyan could fell a tree with one swipe of an ax. Two basic types of wood saws reflect the different ways of cutting through those fibers.

Crosscut saw teeth are little triangles. Their bases are attached to the body of the saw blade, and the other two sides are filed so that

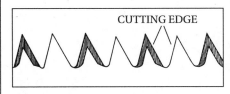

Crosscut saw.

both of the two triangle sides are sharp. They cut on both the forward and backward strokes, cutting across the fibers and making two short boards out of one long one.

The teeth of *ripsaws* are little chisels, their sharp edges running

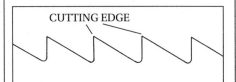

Ripsaw.

perpendicular to the length of the saw. A ripsaw chops off the ends of wood fibers, making two narrow boards out of one wide one.

Both types of saws need to have *set:* Alternate teeth are bent slightly in opposite directions so that the cut the saw makes, called the *kerf,* is wide enough to allow the saw to move freely without binding.

Get a Grip

❑ A good handsaw has a comfortable grip, so you can grasp the saw all day without getting cramps in your hand. It's hard to find a new saw with a decent grip, so it's worth looking for good old saws at flea markets or in places that sell used tools. The ornamental work you find on old handsaws is a plus.

USING TOOLS

The Plane Truth

❑ When starting to plane, put more pressure on the toe (front) of the plane. As you reach the end, put more pressure on the heel (back). This will give a true cut.

❏ End grain is tough to plane. You can get good results by holding the plane firmly on the end grain so the blade is at an angle relative to the board. Make sure your blade is very sharp. Work alternately from each side to the middle, or you may tear out one side when you're pushing out on it.

Chisel Away

❏ If you're working with a wood chisel, learn to watch the cutting edge, not the handle, when you strike the chisel with the hammer or mallet. This will give you a greater awareness of exactly what you're accomplishing.

Hit the Nail on the Head

❏ Having trouble hitting the nail straight on the head? Try pretending there's a pinpoint in the exact center of the head and concentrate on hitting that. The extra mental focus this exercise requires may improve your average.

The Hammer Always Strikes Twice

I F A GARDENER has a green thumb, as they say, then a carpenter has a purple thumb.

I was shingling once with a helper who was new at the job. He hit his thumb with the hammer and took off a large piece of skin. I bandaged it with a thick layer of gauze and tape. He said a Band-Aid would have been sufficient, but I assured him that a large bandage was in order. I didn't tell him why he needed the extra treatment, but he soon found out. It wasn't long before he clobbered his thumb again. Without the added padding of the bandage, his hammer would have claimed a second chunk of flesh.

A Word from Earl

Once someone has hammered his or her hand, he or she always manages to hit it again. I've seen it happen a thousand times. So it's smart to cover up your wounds well before you proceed.

HAMMERING: SLING BEFORE YOU SWING

SWINGING A HAMMER all day is tiring for your arm, but it's even more fatiguing for your hand, which has to grip hard on the hammer just as it strikes the nail. That's a lot of exertion, and a lot of shock that has to be absorbed.

Although you don't see it much in these days of automatic nail guns, there's an old-time trick that has saved many arms from going numb. Make a figure eight of strong cloth or belt webbing, making one loop of the eight to fit your wrist and the other loop to fit the

Use strong cloth or belt webbing to make a "hammer handle."

hammer handle. Slip your wrist through one loop and the hammer handle through the other, then grab the handle above the loop. Now when you swing the hammer, the loops will pull tight and grip the hammer handle. This will allow your hand to relax and merely guide the hammer, saving a lot of wear and tear on your most important tool: you.

❏ It's a challenge to hammer in a small brad without hammering the fingers that hold it. Next time, poke the brad through the edge of a piece of cardboard. The cardboard gives you something to hold on to while you tap the brad in most of the way. Then pull the cardboard free and pound the nail flush.

❏ Another solution, if you find yourself banging your fingers when starting small nails in wood, is to try using a piece of putty or clay to hold the nail upright. Once the nail is started, pull away the putty or clay and use it for starting the next nail. Be aware, however, that clay can leave oil on bare wood that can interfere with the subsequent finish. Choose your spots accordingly.

❏ Knotty or tough wood tends to bend nails driven into it. To lessen the problem, lubricate your nails with beeswax, paraffin or soap. A ¼" hole drilled into the wooden butt of your hammer is a handy place to store the lubricant. Before you use a nail, you can easily insert it in the wax.

❏ An alternative for dealing with tough wood is to predrill it (drill a hole slightly smaller in diameter than the nail) before inserting the nail. In some areas, this predrilled hole is called a pilot hole.

Don't Split Up

❏ To avoid splitting wood when driving a finish nail near the end of a plank, flatten the chisel point of the nail with a couple of hammer blows. This allows the nail to tear through the wood fibers rather than splitting them apart.

A Turn of the Screw

❏ When you have to get a screw into a tight place and don't have a magnetic screwdriver on hand, push the screw through from the sticky side of a piece of masking tape, then tape the screw to the screwdriver. When you get the screw well seated, pull the tape and screwdriver free.

❏ If you're having a tough time driving a screw, smear some paste wax on the threads. This lubricates the hole and helps dissipate heat, reducing the chance of screw breakage.

FAST(ENER) FRIENDS

WHAT'S YOUR FAVORITE fastener? Ask any home handyman or weekend woodworker, and you'll probably get an impassioned encomium on one favorite: drywall screws. Old-style wood screws require that you drill a guide hole, or they'll split the wood. And you have to countersink the top of the hole, or the screw head won't be flush. The screws take forever to crank in by hand, and the screwdriver always wanders off the slotted head, causing some interesting decoration on the workpiece.

Not so with drywall screws. They tap their own holes, neatly countersink their own heads and are made for power driving with a Phillips head in a drill. And they have another use most people aren't aware of: Drywall screws were designed in the 1960s when commercial structures were first required to use metal studs. Metal studs? These screws work in metal? Sure enough, those needle-sharp points drill and tap right through thin metal.

Keep your jars of old-style screws around the shop, but as time goes by, they may become historical relics.

❏ Soap is also an effective lubricant for screws that are hard to drive. Just scrape the threads of the screw across a dry bar of soap.

File This Way

❏ If you look at a file under a magnifying glass, you can see on the ridges of the file the teeth that do the actual filing. Always direct the file so that it is cutting. If you draw the file along wood or metal in the opposite direction, you'll clog the file.

❏ When breaking in a new metal file, use it with only a little pressure at first until the needlelike teeth are worn down. Then you can apply more pressure without danger of breaking the teeth.

❏ Rub the teeth of a file with a piece of chalk to fill in the gaps between the teeth. Otherwise, iron filings will clog the file.

Go Straight

❏ The best way to get something perfectly vertical is to begin the project by hanging a plumb line. A plumb line is essentially a heavy object on a string. When the object is at rest, the string is perfectly vertical. For the most accurate readings, use a tool called a plumb bob—a toplike object on a string. The tip of the plumb bob points to the spot directly below the top of the string.

❏ Here's a way to stop your plumb line from tangling: Wind it onto the reel of an old chalk-line holder. If you have a chalk line that is broken or worn-out, save the holder for just such a use. Dump out the old chalk before winding the plumb line onto the reel. (It's okay if a little chalk remains.)

Glass: Cut the Friction

❏ Before cutting glass, dip the cutter in light oil to lessen the friction. Repeat the dipping process before each cut.

Whatsit?

THE RELIC ILLUSTRATED here has me puzzled. Can you tell me what it is and what it was used for?
— S.A., DAYVILLE, CONN.

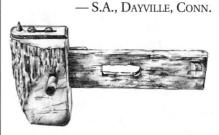

This is a marking gauge for timbers. It was used to mark a hole to be bored at a certain point or to scribe a long distance on a timber.

The board at left is not plumb.

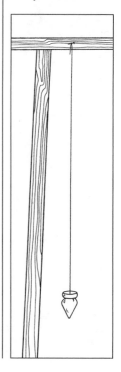

WOULD YOU please identify this item, which someone gave my mother? — B.H., AMBOY, WASH.

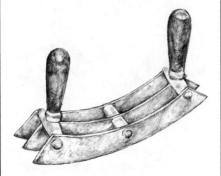

This is a triple-bladed chopping knife used in cooking. It can be used to chop beef, plain or corned; cabbage, cold or boiled; spinach; brussels sprouts; and other foods.

This lubricates the bearing and the cutting point, which receive tremendous stress.

❏ It's also a good idea to brush kerosene lightly over the surface of glass that you're about to cut. This will make the cutting easier.

❏ Always pull a glass cutter swiftly and continuously along the line to be cut. Never go over the same cut twice; that dulls the cutting wheel and blunts the taper on the inside of the first cut.

The Simple Sort

❏ Sorting through old screws for the ones you want is best done on a flat surface. Pour all the screws out onto a piece of flexible cardboard or a section of newspaper. When you're done, roll the cardboard or newspaper into a U shape and pour the screws back into their container.

On the Level

❏ One way to get a straight line is to use a line level. The string must be tight for the level to read accurately. Don't position the level in the middle of the string. If it is sagging at all, the line level will read level. Instead, place the

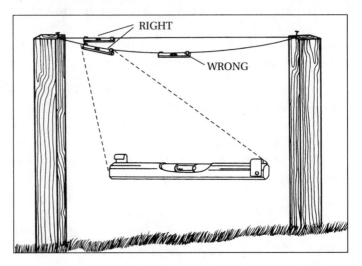

Always place a line level near one end of the line, not in the center.

level near one end. Then if the line sags, you know it and can stretch the string tighter.

MAINTAINING TOOLS

Aye, There's the Rub

❏ To ease the use of a handsaw—especially when sawing green wood—and to keep the saw from rusting, rub both sides of the blade with wax. (Don't bother to wax the teeth. The wax won't last a moment on them while they are cutting.) An old candle is handy for this. Don't worry if some of the wax gets on the wood you're working with; it will come off in the sanding process before you finish the piece.

How I Learned to Sharpen a Handsaw

WHEN I WAS 15, MY FATHER sat me down with a fine panel saw and said, "A carpenter's no damn good if he can't file his own saw." He showed me how to "breast" the tips of the teeth first, filing them until they were all the same height. Then he showed me how to set the teeth to either side and file each one. It takes a lot of patience and practice to sharpen each tooth of a saw, and I found it hard at first. I sharpened that panel saw until there was almost nothing left of it. But I soon got the hang of it, and before long I was sharpening saws for my father, my brothers and all the men on the crew.

A Word from Earl

Sharpening every tooth of a handsaw is more than most home carpenters care to undertake, but it's good to know that these saws do need to be sharpened occasionally and that the tooth-by-tooth technique is the only way to do it. If you're not inclined to sharpen your handsaws yourself, your local hardware store should be able to recommend someone to do the job. Or look in the yellow pages under Saws.

Whatsit?

THE TOOL ILLUSTRATED here was found by a friend in an old barn. We have no idea what it is. The short extension is solid, like the head of a hammer. Can you identify this for me?

— R.C., MAUSTON, WIS.

This is a saw set, used to bend the teeth of a saw. It would bend the teeth slightly in alternate directions, one left and the other right, so that the saw cut a slot in the wood a little wider than the blade itself. This allowed the saw to move through the wood without rubbing.

Don't Get Rusty

❏ You can take the rust off tools by wiping them with kerosene and then scrubbing with steel wool. You may need to soak them in kerosene for a while if the rust is heavy. In that case, it's fine to immerse the handles, too.

❏ Another option for cleaning rusty tools is to use a rust dissolver, such as a product called Naval Jelly, available at hardware stores. Keep it away from painted surfaces, however.

❏ A wood bit with clean, smooth flutes will easily eject the wood chips it creates. A rusty bit will bind and clog when boring deep holes. You can keep the flutes in good shape by rubbing them lightly with steel wool whenever you detect a bit of rust.

❏ Don't oil your tools to prevent rust. Some finishes do funny things (like scab or fisheye) in the presence of even a drop of oil. If you oil a tool and then try to use it on wood with one of these finishes, you could have problems. Instead, leave a charcoal briquette in the toolbox. This will reduce moisture and help keep tools from rusting.

Swell Ideas

❏ To clean wood from a rasp or file, dip the tool in hot water for a few seconds. The wood will quickly swell as it soaks up the water and will pop out of the pockets it's filling. Remove the tool from the water, brush the wood out of the teeth and let the tool dry.

❏ If a wooden handle on a hammer or ax is loose, place the tool in a bucket of cold water, making sure the head is immersed. (The handle can stick out the top of the bucket.) Leave it to soak overnight. In the morning, remove the tool from the water and dry off the head to prevent rust. Then immerse the head and handle again— this time for 12 hours in a solution of equal parts turpentine and boiled linseed oil. The water makes the handle swell, securing it tightly in the head. The oil traps the moisture in the handle, so the handle *stays* tight.

Adjust the Tool, Not Yourself

❏ It's common for a tool—whether it's a new electric power saw or an old hand plane—to need just a bit of tailoring for each new user. After you use a tool for a bit and discover its quirks, don't be afraid to tinker with it to get it feeling just right for you. You might want to sand a wooden handle to make it thinner and more comfortable for your grip, for instance, or wrap a handle in foam tape to soften the vibrations as you use it.

It's Nonbinding

❏ If you're having a tough time pushing wood over the metal of your machines, rub the metal machine surface with beeswax. The wax will lubricate the sticky area and remove some of the wood resins that are causing the binding. Don't worry if some of the wax gets on the wood you're working with. It will come off in the sanding process before you finish the piece, so it will not interfere with the finish.

Be Square

❏ To check the squareness of any square, find a board, table or piece of plywood with one straight edge. Put the body of the square up to that edge. Mark a line along one side of the square's tongue, in the same way that you

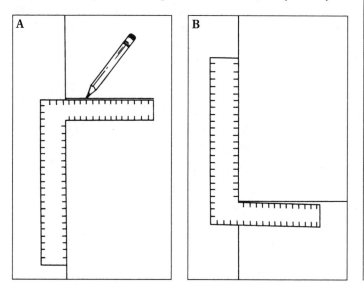

Mark along the tongue of your square (A), then flip the squqare (B). The pencil mark should still be in line with the tongue of the square. If it's not, as at right, your square is out of square.

would normally use it. Now flip the square over, keeping the body of the square in line with the edge. Now that the square has been flipped, if the line is not perfectly parallel with the other side of the tongue, your square is out of square.

PROTECTING TOOLS

Lend Money, Not Tools

❏ If you value your tools, never loan them out. They are easily absorbed into another person's collection, even when the borrower has the best of intentions.

❏ If you can't bring yourself to turn down a neighbor's request to borrow a tool, try an alternative approach. Paint a brightly colored stripe around the handle of each of your hand tools. This will be a reminder to the borrower that the tool belongs to you, and it will also help in spotting tools dropped in the grass or garden.

❏ Prevent unauthorized use of your power tools by fitting a tiny padlock through the small hole in one of the prongs of the tool's electrical plug.

SHARPENING TOOLS

Dig In

❏ Most people never sharpen their garden tools, but doing so can make a difference in how well they work. Sharpen a shovel by filing the top (inside) edge—the one that holds the soil. File in the direction that's away from

To sharpen a shovel, start by holding the handle toward you and filing the inside edge away from you (A). Next, lightly file the burr off the other side (B). To sharpen a hoe (C), file the inside edge first, working the file away from the hoe's handle.

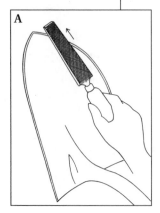

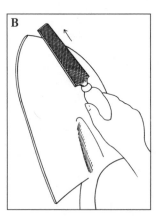

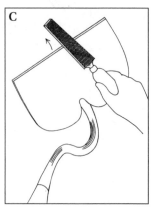

HONING YOUR TOOLS: SHARPS AND FLATS

Sharpening edged tools such as axes, chisels and shovels is less difficult and more important than many people realize. Sharp tools are faster and safer than dull ones, since they're easier to control and less likely to slip. Sharpening is a matter of removing as little metal as possible as quickly as possible to get the edge correctly shaped, then polishing the two faces that make up the edge. Typically, you need a coarse stone and a fine stone (or a combination stone) to do this. Any light oil will do for a lubricant.

First rub the blades of the tools against the coarse stone to take the edge of each tool back to the bottom of the deepest nicks, to flatten the rounded-off faces of the edge and to bring the two faces back to the correct angle. Then rub each tool against the fine stone, which takes out the scratches left by its coarser cousin. The job is properly finished by stropping (sharpening) the blade on a scrap of leather. That will remove the wire edge left by the earlier stages. The edge isn't really sharp until it won't reflect any light.

the handle. Then turn it over and lightly file the feathered edge off the back.

❏ Sharpen a hoe by filing the inside edge—the one that faces you in use—and working away from the handle. Then take the feathered edge off the outside.

Sharp Knife Tricks

❏ If your knife goes dull and the whetstone is nowhere in sight, sharpen the knife on the edge of a clay flowerpot.

❏ When sharpening a knife, always position the knife so that when you stroke the stone, the edge of the knife is leading. If you stroke it with the edge trailing, it will leave

If you stroke a knife blade in the wrong direction when sharpening it, you'll get a feathered edge (A) that will fold over (B) when you use the knife. To avoid this, stroke the knife blade with the edge of the knife leading (C).

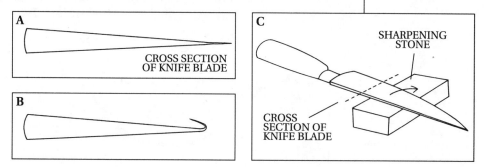

A — CROSS SECTION OF KNIFE BLADE

B

C — SHARPENING STONE — CROSS SECTION OF KNIFE BLADE

When I Needed a Tool That Didn't Exist

I'VE SPENT A LOT OF TIME pulling large nails and spikes from old timbers so they can be reused. This process requires two tools: a hammer to drive the nail back through the timber

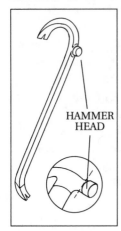

HAMMER HEAD

For the ultimate wrecking tool, weld the striking end of a hammer head to a wrecking bar.

A Word from Earl

and a wrecking bar to grip the nail head and pull it out. Switching back and forth between the hammer and the wrecking bar is very time-consuming, so I invented a solution: I sawed off the striking end of a hammer head with a power hacksaw. Then I had that part of the hammer head welded onto my wrecking bar. This made it easy to both drive and pull the nails with the same tool, and my wrecking bar is still easy to use for other projects.

If you reuse a lot of old timbers, you might want to have a similar tool made.

a fine feather edge that will not stand up when you use the knife. It will feel sharp—until you use it.

MAKING TOOLS

Your Level Best

❏ If you need to level something over a span greater than the length of your longest level, try making your own water level: a ¼"-diameter clear plastic tube nearly full of wa-

Make your homemade water level any length that's convenient. In fact, it can be very long, to level items some distance apart.

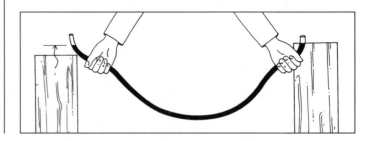

ter. You'll need a piece of tubing at least as long as the span. Position the tubing so the water level at one end is even with the desired height. Raise the other end of the tube to approximately the same height, then note the exact point to which the water rises at the far end of the tube. That's the point that's level with the water at the other end.

Check Your Depth Perception

❏ If you need a hole in a piece of wood and don't have a drill bit handy, put a nail in the drill's chuck (the part of the drill that tightens around the bit). It will work nearly as well as a drill bit.

❏ You can make a simple drill depth guide by wrapping a flag of tape around the drill bit. Just place the tape at the depth where you want the drilled hole to stop.

❏ You can make a more secure and long-lasting drill depth guide by cutting a dowel to the desired length, chamfering its end and drilling through it lengthwise down its bore, leaving the dowel on the bit. The dowel will keep your bit from going in too deep. Don't push too hard on it, or the dowel will mar the wood you are drilling.

Whatsit?

I FOUND THIS object in my backyard in the Adirondacks. Can you tell me what it is?
— G.M., RAQUETTE LAKE, N.Y.

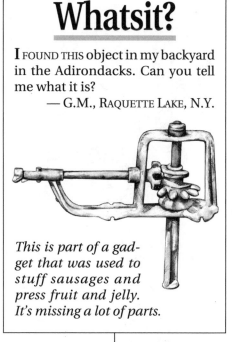

This is part of a gadget that was used to stuff sausages and press fruit and jelly. It's missing a lot of parts.

To drill a 1"-deep hole (A) with a 3"-long drill bit (B), use a 2"-long dowel. Drill a hole through the length of the dowel (C), leaving the dowel on the bit. Then drill the hole (D).

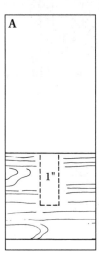

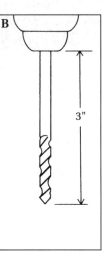

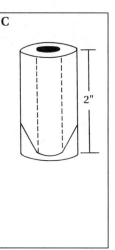

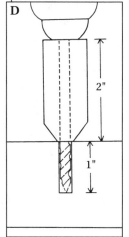

Make your own wire wheels out of window screening.

Useful Tools from Spare Parts

❏ Once an old metal file has grown too dull for further use, use an electric grinding wheel to grind down the end and make it into a chisel. You can buy a handle for the file if you don't already have one. Or you can fashion a handle out of a 6" length of broomstick.

❏ A wire wheel spun by an electric drill is a good mechanism for removing rust and scouring metal. If you're tired of buying and wearing these out, you can make your own. Cut about a dozen 5"-diameter circles out of spare metal window screening. Drill a ¼" hole in the center of each and slip all the circles onto a bolt with washers on either side. Lock them on with a nut, then insert the end of the bolt into the chuck of your electric drill and tighten it. As with any wire wheel, wear eye protection when using this device and watch out for flying wire.

Old Blades Can Still Hack It

❏ If you break a hacksaw blade that is still sharp, don't throw it away. Make a handle for it and use it to get into tight places where a regular hacksaw is too large.

❏ Old or broken hacksaw blades make good, flexible tools for applying glue, crack filler or cement. Using an electric grinding wheel or a hand file, grind down the teeth a bit, then grind the end to any shape desired. To store a broken blade, hang each piece by its hole. (There's a hole in each end of an unbroken blade.)

A New Role for Cut Glass

❏ You can turn a pane of glass into a fantastic scraper for refinishing projects. The edge of a piece of glass does

Whatsit?

CAN YOU HELP ME identify this item? It is made of iron and measures 4¼" long, 2" wide and 1⅜" high. The patch on the handle says October 31, 1876. Even the handle is metal. What was it used for?
— E.H., STOUGHTON, MASS.

This is called a fluting iron. It was heated on the stove, then run over a garment to put fluted crimps in the cloth. The handle on the fluting iron could be turned over to make smaller or larger crimps.

a good job of scraping—it cuts well, but not too deep—when you draw it toward you at an angle. A piece that is approximately 1" x 3" is easy to handle, but the nice thing about scraping with glass is that your scraper can be any size. If you're scraping a flat surface, cut the glass pieces with a slight arc so that the corners of the glass won't gouge the wood. If you're scraping something curved, such as a table leg, straight pieces of glass are fine. In either case, you may want to cover the noncutting edge of the glass with tape as a safety precaution. When one edge of the glass gets dull, flip it over and use the other.

Fill 'er Up

❏ A bottle with a pull-top valve—the kind that dishwashing liquid comes in—makes a great oilcan. It's especially good for putting bar and chain oil in the small filler hole on your chain saw.

You Can Handle It

❏ You can make most wooden handles more quickly than you can go buy one. Just cut a rectangle of any appropriate wood (ash, which is light and strong, is a good choice) and shape the handle with a drawknife. Sand the shaped handle to the desired smoothness. This allows you to custom-make any tool handle.

❏ If your wood-splitting maul handle is continually getting chewed up when you miss your target, don't bother buying the black rubber sleeves sold at hardware stores. One of these will protect the handle for a while, but over time it, too, will get torn up. Instead, take a 6" piece of 1½" black plastic water pipe, slit one side, slip it over the handle up by the head and clamp it down with a couple of hose clamps. The hard plastic will protect the wood for many seasons.

OLD PLANES: A GLIMPSE OF PERFECTION

A LOT OF HANDYMEN have acquired, somewhere along the line, one or more of those old-time molding planes—the kind with the hardwood body and the wedge-fitted metal blade. But how many have successfully used one?

Old molding planes don't refuse to work just because they're in the hands of new owners; they refuse because they can't deal with modern, uneven, coarse-grained lumber. They work to perfection with lumber as old as they are: tight and straight-grained climax forest pine and spruce, even hemlock. If you ever get a chance, try one of those planes on a scrap of really old pine and see if you can't produce an edge-bead as fine as ever came off the hand of a nineteenth-century craftsman.

STEEL WOOL
IS OFTEN SUPERIOR

STEEL WOOL IS a versatile and useful abrasive. It's better than sandpaper for some applications because it is pliable and can be worked around curves and other hard-to-sand places. It's also less likely to scratch finishes, so it can be used on surfaces such as chrome and enamel. Like sandpaper, steel wool is sold in grades ranging from coarse (4) to superfine (0000).

Steel wool was invented in Germany in the late nineteenth century. The best machines for making it still come from there, and the technique hasn't changed much in the past hundred years. Great rolls of low-carbon steel wire about ⅛" thick are rapidly pulled through a 30'-long machine, where a series of four hardened steel knives shave off thick filaments with a triangular cross section. The most commonly used steel wool ranges from about 0.003" thick down to about 0.0005" thick. Common uses of steel wool include smoothing wood, polishing chrome, removing rust from iron and cleaning pipe threads.

SANDPAPER AND STEEL WOOL

Preserve Your Sandpaper

Tuck the ends of the sandpaper inside the slit in the section of hose or plastic pipe, and you'll have an instant cylindrical sanding pad.

❏ Sandpaper stored on a shelf or workbench tends to curl and harden. Prevent this by storing it between two pieces of ¼" plywood fastened together with a piano hinge or large rubber bands.

❏ Keep sandpaper as dry as possible. If your shop is moist, store sandpaper in a metal box or plastic bag.

Get around a Problem

❏ To sand moldings or other curved surfaces, wrap sandpaper around a piece of molding, a dowel or a few layers of corrugated cardboard bent to the desired contour.

❏ Another simple way to make a cylindrical sanding pad is to slit a short length of hose or plastic pipe, then wrap the sandpaper around the hose and tuck the ends in the slit.

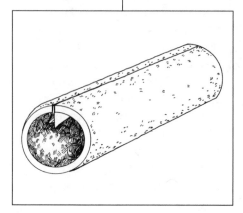

Steel Wool, Step by Step

❏ Many people don't realize that steel wool comes in a number of different grades. When polishing or smoothing a surface with steel wool, you should work as you would with sandpaper: Start with a coarse grade and gradually proceed through finer and finer grades.

❏ After you polish an object with sandpaper or steel wool, always wipe the surface with a clean cloth to pick up the dust that the scouring has left behind.

Avoid the Rust

❏ If you're planning to use steel wool on a project where rusting is a concern, choose bronze wool instead. Available at marine supply stores, it costs a little more, but it holds up better under heavy use. Bronze wool doesn't rust, so you don't have to worry about the small slivers that invariably stick to the surface you're working on.

Whatsit?

NEITHER I NOR ANY of my friends has the slightest idea what this is. Could you possibly identify it?
— W.J.M., RIDLEY PARK, PA.

This tool was used by goldsmiths and silversmiths to make chains. When clamped to a table, it gave the craftsman a small anvil on which to make links of the same size. The hand vise on top held the chain and closed the links.

PLYWOOD: MAKING THE GRADE

PLYWOOD IS GRADED A, B, C or D based on the defects in the surface of the wood. Grades C and D have knotholes, but the knots are larger in D. In A and B, knotholes and other defects are patched and the surface of the sheet is sanded. Only an occasional patch will appear in an A sheet.

Both sides of a sheet of plywood are graded. An A-A sheet would be used for furniture making. If you were paneling a wall, you might use B-D plywood and put the D side against the studs. D-D plywood is used to sheath the outsides of new homes, where neither surface of the plywood will be seen.

For wet conditions—exterior use or in bathrooms—it's advisable to use marine plywood, which is available at lumberyards. The layers of marine plywood will not delaminate when wet.

GARDEN TOOLS

Mr. Sandman, Bring Me a Bucket

❏ Keep a bucket of sand, sprinkled lightly with kerosene or oil, in the shed or garage where you store your garden tools. When you're through using the tools, scour them with the sand to keep them clean and rust free. (Do not use this technique if you store your tools inside the house, however; in a living area, the fumes would be a health hazard.)

A Little Oil Will Help Your Garden

❏ To maintain the wooden handles on your garden tools, occasionally apply boiled linseed oil with a cloth. Use just enough so the wood absorbs the oil.

A Reel Idea for Your Garden Hose

❏ A garden hose will last longer if you roll it up after each use. To make a reel, attach an old bucket or metal wastebasket to the garage or barn wall by nailing it securely through the bottom. Coil your hose around the bucket, then store your nozzles and sprinklers inside.

WORKBENCHES

Pocket Change

❏ Some workbench designs call for recessed pockets for storage at the back of the bench. The idea is to keep your tools and hardware handy and still maximize your work area. If you're going to make a bench like this, make the bottom of the storage pockets from wire mesh. Otherwise, as you use the bench, they will fill up with sawdust and require constant cleaning.

Top That!

❏ If you have some extra vinyl or linoleum tiles left over from a flooring job, use them to make a hard, smooth work surface on a workbench.

It's a Holdup!

❏ To help hold small shop projects in place while you're working on them, and to protect your workbench from wear, consider making yourself a

A bench hook consists of three pieces of wood: one for the base, one to hold the bench hook against the workbench and one to hold your work in place.

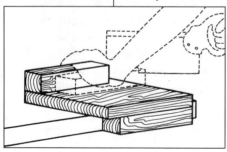

bench hook. The illustration on the facing page shows the basic format, but you can make this device in any size and to any proportions that are comfortable for you. Use scrap lumber for your hook. When it gets beat up from sawing or chiseling, make a new one.

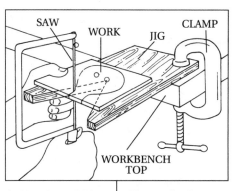

❏ To secure the board you're cutting with a scroll or coping saw, and to keep from having to adjust a vise as you turn the piece you are cutting, make this handy jig. Cut a V in a block of wood. Secure the block of wood to your workbench so that the V extends outward from the edge. (If you don't want to attach the block permanently, you can clamp it on.) Rest your work on top of the block, with your saw cutting in the V. The jig will support your work as you cut downward, and you're free to adjust the positioning of your work as you move along. The saw does not cut on its upward motion.

Clamp the jig to the workbench to provide support when cutting with a scroll saw or coping saw.

SAWHORSES

Steady and Sturdy

❏ A good height for a sawhorse is 2'. Use a 2 x 6 for the top piece. A shelf built into the sawhorse 1' from the ground is optional but recommended. It gives you a place to put tools, works as a step and makes the whole thing sturdier.

A practical design for a sawhorse.

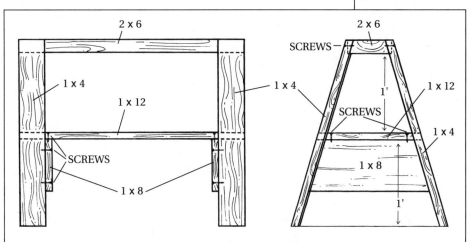

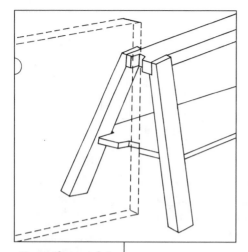

Taper the notch in the end of your sawhorse so that it can hold doors of varying widths.

❏ You can cut a notch in the end of your sawhorse to grip the end of a door when you are working on it. This works best when you have a shelf on your sawhorse with a matching notch. If your notch is 2" wide at its outer edge and tapers down to 1", it should hold most doors.

LUMBER

In Dry Dock

❏ It is usually a good idea to store boards and other lumber up high, where they will be warmer, less damp and out of the way. Many people stack lumber on the rafters of the garage. That's okay, as long as the garage is dry. Make sure boards are supported at frequent intervals to prevent warping.

MEASURE FOR MEASURE

TERMINOLOGY FOR LUMBER measurements is not self-explanatory. A dressed 2 x 4 from a lumberyard, for instance, does not measure 2" x 4"—that would take all the fun out of it. In that instance, 2" x 4" is the *nominal* size of the wood —the size to which the sawmill cuts each piece. Shrinkage and planing make it somewhat smaller, so its *dressed* size —1½" x 3½" —is the actual measurement of the piece you buy at the lumberyard.

Here's a basic translation table for the widths and thicknesses of standard sizes of lumber. The left column lists what you ask for when shopping at a lumberyard; the right column gives the actual dimensions of the finished lumber. (At a sawmill, unlike a lumberyard, you can expect your wood to be full measure. There, a 2 x 6 will measure a full 2" thick and a full 6" wide.)

ROUGH OR NOMINAL SIZE	DRESSED OR SURFACE SIZE
1" x 3"	¾" x 2½ "
1" x 4"	¾" x 3½"
1" x 6"	¾" x 5½"
1" x 8"	¾" x 7¼"
1" x 10"	¾" x 9¼"
1" x 12"	¾" x 11¼"
2" x 3"	1½" x 2½"
2" x 4"	1½" x 3½"
2" x 6"	1 ½" x 5½"
2" x 8"	1½" x 7¼"
2" x 10"	1½" x 9¼"
2" x 12"	1½" x 11¼"

EARL PROULX'S YANKEE HOME HINTS

A LUMBER BUYER'S DICTIONARY

D ON'T CONFUSE your lumber. When you're working with softwood, distinctions in materials are based partly on the nominal size of the pieces (the size as the pieces are cut at the mill, before shrinkage and planing make them somewhat smaller). A **board** is a dressed (finished) piece with a nominal thickness of less than 2" and a nominal width of more than 2"; it has two squared edges. **Dimension lumber** is material used for framing; each piece has a nominal width of 2' or more and a nominal thickness from 2" up to (but not including) 5". **Timbers** are 5" or larger in both nominal thickness and width.

Generally, softwood boards are classified as **select** or **common.** Select boards (finish lumber) are graded in three categories, in descending order of quality: B and better, C select and D select. Common boards are graded, in descending order of quality, from #1 common through #5 common.

Select structural is the best grade for timbers and dimension lumber, followed by grades #1, #2 and #3. Smaller pieces of dimension lumber may also be graded, in descending order, as standard, utility and stud material.

Armed with this information, you ought to be able to go to the lumberyard and get yourself some attractive pine boards for that bookshelf you want to build. Or you can slap together the doghouse with inexpensive stud material.

Twisting and Turning

❏ When a board cups, moisture is usually the culprit. Try using moisture to bend it back into shape. Lay the cupped board concave side down in wet grass, in an area that's exposed to the sun. When the sun hits the convex surface, that side of the board will contract faster than the wet side. Watch the board closely; it could take 4 hours or as long as 4 days to undo the cupping. Store the board inside again as soon as it has straightened out, or it will start cupping in the other direction.

❏ Want to know if a timber is "winding" (warped) or slightly twisted? Take

DETERMINING LENGTH: SOMETIMES IT'S SIMPLE

C ERTAIN APPLICATIONS of wood are not typically sold in terms of board feet. Clapboards, moldings and millwork, which are all thin, are more often sold by lineal feet. The price is arrived at by multiplying the price per lineal foot by the length of the piece you need.

HOW MANY BOARD FEET IN A BOARD?

LUMBER IS commonly sold by the *board foot,* a unit of measure corresponding to a block of wood 12" long x 12" wide x 1" thick. Board feet calculations are based on *actual* measurements when the boards are being sold that way (at sawmills, for example) and on *nominal* measurements when they're being sold *that* way (as at most commercial dealers and lumberyards).

Following is a chart of board foot calculations for various lengths of popular dimension lumber. To use the chart when you're estimating the cost of the project, first figure out the dimensions and lengths of boards you need. Look down the left column to find the dimensions you want in the boards you're buying. Then look across the top row for the total length you need. At the intersection of those two measurements, you'll find the appropriate board foot value. Then multiply your total board feet by the price per board foot to arrive at your total cost.

Example: Let's say you need 24' of 1" x 8" cherry to finish a project, and that cherry is going for $4 a board foot at the local building supply store. According to the chart, 12' of 1" x 8" stock equals 8 board feet, so 24' will equal twice that, or 16 board feet. 16 x $4 = $64. Good luck with the project.

CALCULATING BOARD FEET

DIMENSIONS	12' LONG	14' LONG	16' LONG	18' LONG	20' LONG
1" x 4"	4	4⅔	5⅓	6	6⅔
1" x 6"	6	7	8	9	10
1" x 8"	8	9⅓	10⅔	12	13⅓
1" x 10"	10	11⅔	13⅓	15	16⅔
1" x 12"	12	14	16	18	20
2" x 3"	6	7	8	9	10
2" x 4"	8	9⅓	10⅔	12	13⅓
2" x 6"	12	14	16	18	20
2" x 8"	16	18⅔	21⅓	24	26⅔
2" x 10"	20	23⅓	26⅔	30	33⅓
2" x 12"	24	28	32	36	40
4" x 4"	16	18⅔	21⅓	24	26⅔
6" x 6"	36	42	48	54	60
8" x 8"	64	74⅔	85⅓	96	106⅔
10" x 10"	100	116⅔	133⅓	150	166⅔
12" x 12"	144	168	192	216	240

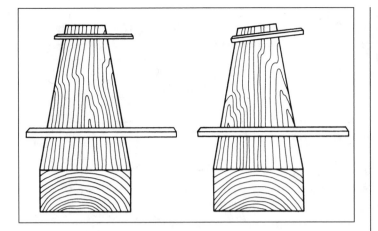

two narrow boards, each 2' long and of the same width. Lay them on top of the timber, perpendicular to it, about 2' in from each end. Then stand at one end of the timber and sight along the tops of the boards. If the timber is straight, the boards will be parallel. If the timber is winding at all, the boards will be tipped in different directions.

❏ If a board is twisted, follow the same procedure for straightening it as for correcting cupping, only weight the corner of the board that sticks up. This method doesn't

LUMBER: DENOTING THE DEFECTS

BUYING A BOARD from the lumberyard is not the simplest of tasks. How can you possibly remember all the details, when more than 100 different factors are involved in the uniform system for grading wood?

In grading for natural defects alone, there are 11 conditions of decay, 16 of knots and 12 of pitch pockets. It's unlikely that you'll need to memorize them all before you buy the wood for your next home project. But it's useful to know the general sources of these defects.

Decay, called *dote* or *rot,* usually comes from a fungus. Knots are the result of branches growing off the trunk of the tree. A pitch pocket is created when sap is trapped between the tree's growth rings.

Then there are 20 man-made blemishes, called *mismanufactures.* In this category, a grader looks for planer scars and burns, torn grain, intact bark and uneven width or thickness.

PROBLEM WOOD: WATCH OUT FOR SPLIT ENDS

HERE ARE SOME common lumber problems—and what you can do about them.

Checking: Small (and sometimes not so small) splits. End checking, the most common form, occurs because the ends, exposed to the air, dry faster than the rest of the board. Prevent this by sealing the end grain. You can use wax, shellac or paint. You'll notice when you buy a 2 x 4 from a lumberyard that all the ends have been painted to prevent checking. Sometimes end checking can be trimmed off. Serious checking

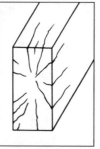

Splits, particularly in the end grain of a board, are called checking. End checking sometimes can be trimmed off.

seems to occur more frequently in hardwoods.

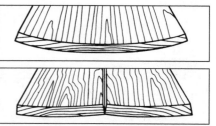

Cupping leaves a board slightly U-shaped. To lessen the impact of this problem, rip a cupped board in two.

Cupping: Like warping (see end of box), this usually occurs when the board dries unevenly or is exposed to moisture. In cross section, the board is dished or U-shaped. In extreme cases, the board can be ripped in half (with the grain, along the length of the board) and used as two separate (narrower) pieces.

Knots: A knot marks the spot where a branch was attached to a tree trunk. There are sound knots and dead knots. If you shut your eyes and run your hand over a board, you won't be able to feel the sound knots; ignore them. If you

always solve the problem, but it's certainly worth a try. Otherwise, you can try cutting the board into two or more shorter lengths—or, better yet, avoid using it altogether.

❏ Boards bow because of the natural curve in their grain. There is little you can do to straighten a board that's bowed, but you can still use it in rough construction.

METALWORK

Close the Door on This One

❏ If you want to put a 90-degree bend in a thin piece of sheet metal but don't have a sheet-metal brake, try clos-

can wiggle the knot with your fingers or if it's soft to the touch, you have a dead knot; eventually it will fall out. Occasionally, you'll get a stud or rafter with too many knots to bear the load safely. Cut it up for blocking (extra supports between large timbers for added strength and rigidity) or use it to support an existing stud. For wainscoting, paneling, cabinets and the like, more knots mean more rustic, so match the material to the job.

Shake: Separation of the wood lengthwise along the growth rings. (Cut an onion into slices, top to bottom, and you'll see how it happens.) The tree that produces lumber of this quality should never have been sent to the sawmill; it was probably dead before it was

cut. Shake is bad news; it's impossible to correct.

Wane: Bark and/or rounded edges remaining on the piece after it's sawed out. Some wane can be hidden by simply flipping a board over before nailing.

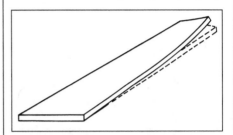

A warped board does not lie perfectly flat. To restore a warped board to its original flatness, try leaving it in damp grass.

Warp: Twisting of a board or dimensioned (not rough) lumber as it dries. Sometimes you can rehabilitate a board with heavy nailing or by leaving the board in wet grass. Cutting the board into two or more shorter lengths can help minimize the impact of the warping. Better yet, leave it at the lumberyard.

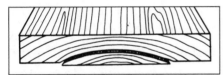

Shake, the separation of the grain along the growth rings, is impossible to correct.

ing the metal between a door and doorjamb. This works well with thin pieces of metal; just don't get carried away and try it with really thick stock.

Saw a Thin Sheet

❏ To saw thin sheet metal without distorting the edge, clamp the metal between two pieces of scrap wood and saw the whole thing—wood and all.

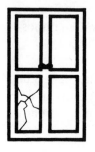

Basic Household Repairs and Maintenance

ONE TIME I HAD JUST ABOUT finished building a new house when I heard the owner in the next room cursing her brand-new vacuum cleaner. Apparently the motor ran fine, but the machine would not pick up dirt. I told her that the problem couldn't be too serious and took the cover off the works. I discovered that the belt between the motor and the beater brush was missing, so the vacuum could not pick up anything. She went back to the store and got a belt. I installed it for her, and the vacuum worked well after that.

Even if you're not mechanically inclined, it pays to give a broken machine a thorough inspection before you have it serviced. (This does not mean disassembling it to the point where you void the warranty.) With a little probing, you can sometimes diagnose the problem yourself—and maybe even fix it. You'll find that even very simple repairs, like the ones that follow, can be both satisfying and rewarding.

You don't have to be a home repair expert to take advantage of the advice in this chapter. Here you'll find simple solutions for everything from stuck jar lids to drawers and windows that stick in their tracks. You'll also find an old-fashioned way to *make* things stick together—when you need to mount one piece of paper on another. Other suggestions include using a pencil to make a door latch more easily, fixing a window shade that rolls to one side and trying a handy technique for storing all those gallon jugs on their way to the recycling center. You'll even discover a quick way to make your new copper weather vane look like a valuable antique. (Hint: It helps if you have a farm animal nearby.)

STUCK STUFF

Get the Lid Off
❏ To loosen a stuck jar lid, hold the jar upside down and pour warm vinegar around the neck at the joint between the glass and the top.

IF YOU CAN'T FIND IT . . .

. . . maybe you need to try another chapter. Check the index, or try these possibilities.

❏ If you don't have one of those rubber jar openers, try substituting a wide rubber band. This will give you the grip you need to unscrew a stubborn jar lid.

BASIC ADHESIVES

An Old-Fashioned Way to Mount Paper or Cardboard

❏ Need an adhesive for cardboard or paper that will create a joint with almost no thickness? Try using fresh egg white. This old-fashioned technique will hold securely and not stain either material.

The Soft Touch

❏ To soften water-based glue that's hardened in the container, add a few drops of vinegar. This will not work with super glue, however.

Keep Rolling Along

❏ Use an old paint roller to spread glue quickly over large surfaces.

ODD JOBS

Tighten Your Own Glasses

❏ Sometimes the tiny screws on your glasses won't stay tight. Take them off and dab them with a drop of shellac or super glue, available at hardware stores. Put the screws back in and tighten them firmly. The screws shouldn't come loose again—unless you *try* to loosen them with a screwdriver.

Brass: Instant Antiques

❏ If you want to make a shiny new brass object look like antique brass, add a small amount of burnt umber (available from art supply stores and good paint stores) to urethane varnish, then coat the new brass with this mix-

UNITED THEY STAND

GLUES AND ADHESIVES work either by welding—dissolving the surfaces to be joined and mating them chemically—or by penetrating surface fibers and holding them together by the strength of the hardened glue. A product such as PVC (polyvinyl chloride) works by welding, so it's most effective when the surfaces being joined are free of all foreign material. Penetrating glues (like aliphatic resin carpenter's wood glue, available at hardware stores) work best on a slightly roughened surface. In either case, the glue joint should be as tight as possible. Use just enough glue so that a thin bead oozes out around the crack, clamp the joint tightly after gluing and be sure to allow the glue to dry completely.

ture. Experiment first on an inconspicuous area to get just the right color.

Antique in Two Weeks

❏ Anxious to give your new copper weather vane the green tint characteristic of antique copper that's been outside for years? Bury it in a manure pile for 2 weeks, and you'll have the effect you want.

Take a Stab at Finding an Antique

❏ You can tell real antique ivory from reproduction varieties by using this method. Heat the end of a needle with a match, then try to insert the needle into a spot that will not show. The heated needle will not pierce real ivory, but it will sink into any imitation.

Effective Countermeasures

❏ To salvage a Formica countertop with a chipped edge, cover it with stainless steel edging (available at lumber-

---

The Power to Heal

I HAD A CUSTOMER who locked all his keys inside a big rolltop desk. He called me on a Sunday to see if I could help. How could he get his keys without damaging the desk?

Opening the desk was easy. With a sharp knife, I slit the tambour—the "rolltop"—between two of the slats and let it slide back into the rear of the desk. My customer got his keys. But then I had to put the tambour back together. I released the lock, lifted off the top section of the desk and removed the two pieces of the tambour. An application of duct tape to the tambour's backing held the two pieces together nicely. When I installed the tam-

A Word from Earl

bour back in the desk, no sign of entry could be seen. The duct tape also was concealed as the tambour rolled back.

There's no limit to the uses of duct tape. From fixing pipes to repairing furniture, it's one of the basic necessities for any homeowner.

WHAT A CAN CAN DO

Recycling an aluminum can saves the energy equivalent of half that can's volume in gasoline. In fact, for the amount of energy it takes to make 1 ton of new aluminum, you can recycle 20 tons of aluminum from scrap.

yards or home centers). This edging fits over the counter edge and covers the chips. Do not get aluminum edging; it's likely to make a black streak across the front of any clothing that touches it.

❑ Before cutting out a space for a sink in a laminate countertop, mark your cutting line on the laminate and run masking tape around the outside of the line. The tape will prevent the laminate from chipping.

❑ Buy narrow T-shaped hardware to cover the gap between your kitchen counter and stove. This will seal a gap up to ¼" wide and prevent food from collecting there.

Hang in There

❑ If the bars of your wooden clothes-drying rack leave brown stripes on your clothes, you can solve the problem easily by wrapping strips of aluminum foil around each bar.

❑ Another cure for a drying rack that leaves stains on clothing is to coat the bars with polyurethane.

WEIGHT REDUCTION

The average person in the United States throws out his or her own weight in packaging materials each month—an expensive prospect, considering that packaging accounts for $1 out of every $10 we spend. A good strategy to counter this trend is to buy a product in the easy-to-use size once and thereafter buy the jumbo bottle. Just keep refilling the smaller one from the bigger one.

RECYCLING

Save Space
While You Save the Earth

❑ To save space in your recycling bin, open the bottoms of tin cans as well as the tops. Then step on the sides of the cans to squash them flat.

❑ To store those unwieldy plastic gallon jugs on their way to being recycled (or on their way to the spring down the road), tie a length of string to the handle of one jug and thread the remaining jugs on the string. Make a loop in the other end and hang it on a nail.

A Comforting Idea

❏ If you want to salvage the down from a worn-out comforter, try this. Put a new bag in your vacuum cleaner. As you open the seams in the comforter, hold the end of the vacuum hose close and vacuum the down into the bag. You may have to replace the bag more than once to gather all the down. Open the bags when you are ready to put the down in the new comforter.

WINDOWS AND SHADES

Stuck on You

❏ Drawers, sliding doors and double-hung windows are notorious for getting stuck. To lubricate them, you can rub their tracks with a bar of soap or a candle stub, or spray them with a product such as WD-40.

Window Shades: Nonreturnables

❏ Here's a way to repair a window shade that won't roll up. Remove the shade from its hangers and place an old-fashioned clothespin (the kind without any wire) over the pin at the end of the roller. Use the clothespin to rewind the pin of the roller in a clockwise direction until the spring is tight. Then replace the shade in its hanger.

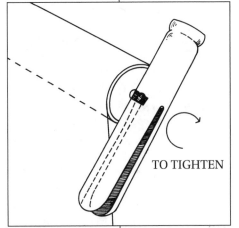

TO TIGHTEN

Use a clothespin to fix a shade that won't return. With the clothespin, grasp the pin on the end of the roller and rewind it.

Many Happy Returns

❏ If a shade returns to the top too fast, remove the shade, unroll it a few turns and replace it in its hangers.

Going Straight

❏ To fix a shade that runs to one side instead of returning straight, try this tip. Unroll the shade until it is fully extended, but be careful not to pull the shade off the wooden roll. Place a piece of paper about 1" wide and 3" long inside the edge of the roll on the side that the shade is running away from. Be sure to place the paper at the very top of the roll so it won't fall out the next time you pull down

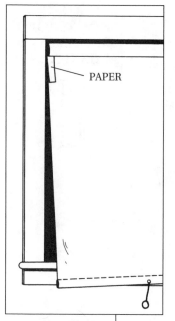

PAPER

If the shade is running away from the roller on the left, correct the problem by positioning the paper as shown.

the shade. Hold it there for a second while you release the shade, then let the shade roll up with the paper inside. The shade should roll straight. If it still rolls to the same side, unroll it again, insert another piece of paper on top of the first one and release the shade again. The principle is that adding paper makes that side of the roll larger, and the shade will always climb toward the larger side.

DOORS

Don't Leave Bare Wood

❏ Since you don't see the top and bottom edges of a door, it's easy to forget to paint them. But those edges, especially on an exterior door, are the ones most exposed to moisture. Don't leave bare wood on any edge of a door, interior or exterior. Moisture will seep into any unfinished surface and cause the door to swell.

❏ It's easy enough to check whether the top of a door has been painted; just stand on a chair and look. But how can you check the bottom of a hanging door without taking it off its hinges? Simply slide a small mirror under the door. You can examine the paint job in the reflection.

A Square Deal

❏ If any door, window, drawer or its casing isn't square, the structure will bind. To check the squareness of the structure, measure the two diagonals of the rectangle, from corner to corner. If you can't hook your tape over an edge, set the tab the same way into each corner for accurate measures. Equal measurements mean squareness.

A Prescription to Relieve Swelling

❏ If a door has become too wide because of swelling, always plane the hinge side of the door rather than the side where the lock is. Any imperfections in the planing will be less visible there. Also, you'll need to reset some hardware after the planing, and it's easier to chisel out the hinge pockets than to reset the lock.

❏ When adjusting a door that rubs, plane off only enough wood to let the door shut properly. If you plane off too much wood, you'll be left with a bad fit when the door shrinks.

It All Hinges on This

❏ Changing the depth at which the hinges are set is usually the easiest way to fix a door that sticks or won't close properly. An obviously loose hinge is the one to attack first. Where the problem is less obvious, use simple logic. If the bottom outer corner of a door is dragging on the threshold, tighten the top hinge. If the door is already fitting tightly at the top hinge, put a shim in the bottom hinge.

PARTS OF A DOOR

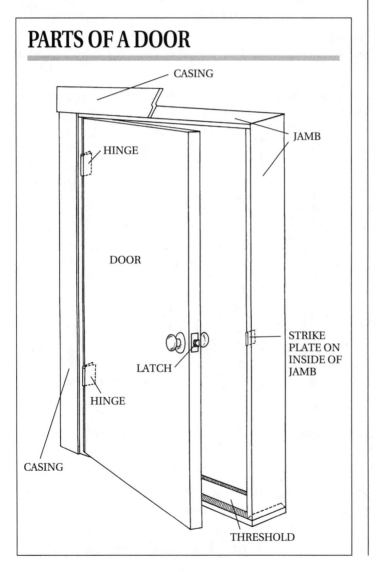

❑ To set a hinge more deeply, loosen the hinge from either the door or the jamb, chisel away the wood underneath and reinstall the hinge.

❑ If a hinge is set too deep, remove the hinge, insert a piece of paper or cardboard and reinstall the hinge plate over the paper.

❑ The top hinge bears most of the weight of a door, and sometimes it will become so worn that the door will sag on the hinge and rub on the threshold. You could buy a new hinge or adjust the setting of the old one, but there's an easier way. Take the door off, remove the bottom hinge plate (which won't be so worn) and switch it with the top one.

❑ If you have a problem with hinge screw holes that are too loose to hold the screws, try inserting a sliver of wood with each screw. A wooden matchstick or toothpick works well. Put the matchstick in butt first, then break off the head.

❑ You can also deal with loose hinge screw holes by stuffing a little steel wool in the holes before inserting the screws.

Keep Your Balance

❑ A door that swings shut from its own weight is off balance. Moving the bottom hinge on the doorjamb away from the stop will make it stay open. You needn't move the hinge much; usually 1/16" will do it. If the door has three hinges, you'll need to adjust the middle hinge accordingly. Plug the old screw holes with wood slivers before replacing the hinge plate(s).

Door Latches: A Penciled Correction

❑ You can adjust any door so that it latches more easily if you rub a soft pen-

Whatsit?

I PURCHASED THIS item, made of copper, at a flea market. It's about 5" in diameter. Can you tell me what it is?
— S.M., SOUTH WINDSOR, CONN.

This is a tuning cone, a hollow metal cone used for tuning the smaller pipes of pipe organs. One way for an organ tuner to alter a note is to slightly open the top of the appropriate pipe and make it wider. To do this, the organ tuner holds the pointed end of the tuning cone down into the pipe and lightly taps the base of the cone, thus forcing the soft metal slightly outward. For a different result, the tuner places the open end of the tuning cone over the top of the pipe like a hat and taps the pipe lightly with it.

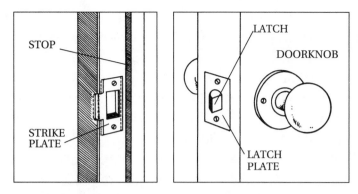

STOP

STRIKE
PLATE

LATCH

DOORKNOB

LATCH
PLATE

cil over the entire surface of the strike plate (the piece the latch goes into). The graphite in the lead reduces the friction between the latch and the strike plate.

Strike Two!

❏ If a door doesn't latch at all, check the positioning of the strike plate. Within the doorjamb, adjust the strike plate up or down, in or (with a shim) out, until the door latches.

Rattles Are for Babies

❏ A door that rattles has too much play between the strike plate on the jamb and the back of the stop (the strip of wood that protrudes from the casing behind the strike plate). Remove and reset the strike plate closer to the stop.

Doorknobs: A Touch of Glass

❏ To tighten a glass doorknob that is loose and spins freely in its metal mounting, force a drop of super glue into the joint between the metal and glass in at least two places. If the glue won't go in this way, remove the knob from the door, drill a hole in the metal from the back and force the glue in between the metal and glass that way.

The Squeaky Door Gets the Oil

❏ Squeaky doors are a nuisance that can be fixed by lightly lubricating the hinge pins. Remove one pin at a time and coat it lightly with any all-purpose oil such as 3-In-One Household Oil or WD-40. (You can also use graphite or even petroleum jelly.) Replace the pin. If the door still squeaks, repeat the process with the next hinge. The top hinge of a door is more likely to squeak, so lubricating it first can save you time.

My Brief Career in Breaking and Entering

I ONCE INSTALLED a new front door for a security-minded customer. She had to leave the house before I finished, so I gave her a key to the new lock. I kept the other key until I finished checking the fit of the door, then dropped the key through her mail slot.

The next morning, I got a call from my customer, who was locked out of her house. Without thinking, she'd left her key with her son while visiting him the night before. I told her that I no longer had a key to her door but I could get into her house.

I met her at the house and asked her to sit on the front step while I went around back. I didn't want her to know how I got in, because I knew it would make her

A Word from Earl

worry. The house had double-hung windows on the ground floor that locked with a simple clasp between the two sash. I found one window that had a little play in it. By working the window up and down for a while, I was able to loosen the clasp and then open the window. I climbed in and opened the door.

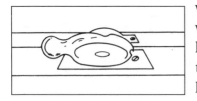

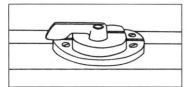

An old-fashioned clasp (top) creates pressure between the two sash. A more modern clasp (bottom) actually locks.

About a week later, the woman drove up to my job site and said, "Earl, you've got to tell me how you broke in. I've been so worried that I haven't been able to sleep." When I told her how I'd done it, she asked me to fix the windows so it couldn't be done again. I installed clasps that lock on all her ground-floor windows.

If you're particularly security conscious, you might want to have such clasps installed on your ground-floor windows to prevent someone from breaking in the way I did.

DOOR LOCKS

Give It a Shot

❏ If a door lock doesn't turn smoothly or easily, it may need lubrication. To lubricate the works of a lock, give the keyhole a shot of a spray such as WD-40 and turn the key back and forth in the lock a few times. You may need to spray again.

Get a Broken Key out of a Lock

❏ How do you get a broken key out of a lock? Hunt down a narrow saber saw blade that has good-size teeth. Insert the blade into the keyhole beside the broken key as far as you can. Twist the blade so that a tooth or two dig into the side of the key, then slowly draw the key out. If you don't hook the key at first, keep trying.

Instant Burglarproofing

❏ An entrance door that opens out is vulnerable because a burglar need only remove your hinge pins to take off the door. You can secure such a door by inserting dowels between the hinge side of the door and the casing—a technique used in some safes and vaults. In the edge of the door, drill two ⅜" holes about 1" deep. One hole should be just below the top hinge and the other just above the bottom hinge. Cut a couple of ⅜" wood dowels to about 1½" long and glue them into the holes in the door, leaving them projecting about ½". Then drill a pair of ⁷⁄₁₆" holes ⅝" deep in the jamb directly opposite the holes in the door. (Use dowel centers to locate the precise spot.) Round the ends of the dowels just enough so that when the door closes, the dowels will slide into the ⁷⁄₁₆" holes. A burglar can still take out your hinge pins, but he won't be able to remove your door. The lock will be holding one side and the dowels the other.

The dowel protrudes from the door and nests in the hole in the jamb, creating a more burglar-resistant door.

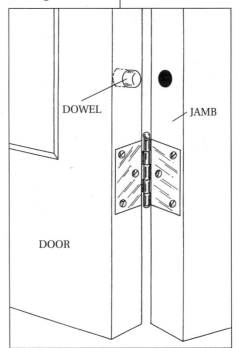

DOWEL

JAMB

DOOR

Painting Inside and Out

Picking up the brush is the last thing you should do.

RIGHT AFTER HIGH SCHOOL, I worked for a doctor and his wife at their summer place, an old farm with an ell that they used as a game room. I painted for them all summer, so by fall I had lots of odds and ends of paint left over. The doctor's wife suggested that I mix all the paint together and use it up on the game room. When I tackled the job after she'd gone to the city one day, the mixture turned out to be a nice gray color, but I ran out of paint with one door to go. She came back that night and said she loved the color. Then she asked me to mix some more paint and give it another coat!

I didn't have any more paint left, so I asked my father what I should do. He said, "Nothing to it. Just buy some paint as near to the gray color as possible. Then wait until she goes to the city again and paint the room over. Be sure to get the first coat entirely covered before she gets back, and she won't notice the difference."

It worked like a charm.

You probably won't run into quite this dilemma, but here are some tips to keep in mind for your own painting jobs. This chapter offers hints on removing old paint and wallpaper, mending cracks in plaster and painting radiators. Also included are ideas for making your paintbrushes last and cutting your cleanup time, as well as tips for working with siding and stucco. Perhaps best of all, you'll find some very simple but effective ways to reduce the fumes in indoor painting and to keep the bugs out of the paint when you're working outdoors. (Any painter will tell you that the job will go much more quickly when nobody's bugging you.)

Some of the hints in this chapter tell how to create special effects in your paint jobs—mixing paints that shine like gold, silver or copper, for instance. The large chain stores don't always carry the products required for these special treatments, but don't despair. You can find these items at art supply stores and independent paint stores.

IF YOU CAN'T FIND IT . . .

. . . maybe you need to try another chapter. Check the index, or try these possibilities.

For Information On . . .	See the Chapter . . .
Penetrating and surface finishes	Floors
Removing paint from fabric	Stains and Odors
Removing paint from glass	Cleaning around the House
Repainting wood stoves	Heating and Cooling
Vapor barriers	Heating and Cooling
Varnish	Furniture
Wall and ceiling surfaces	Walls, Ceilings and Trim

REMOVING OLD INTERIOR PAINT

First You Strip

❑ If you need to remove casein paint, try a combination of household ammonia, steel wool and elbow grease. It's a good idea to wear rubber gloves for this. First, apply the ammonia with a sponge. As soon as the paint is loosened, wipe the surface with a paper towel, then scrub hard with steel wool. You'll need to repeat the entire process several times.

❑ To remove old calcimine, add a cup of vinegar to a pail of warm water. Sponge the mixture onto the calcimined

WHAT'S THAT WHITE STUFF ON YOUR WALLS?

I F YOU LIVE IN an older house, most of the old paint inside is probably a mixture of oil and lead. But some old houses still sport hand-mixed milk- and water-based interior paints. These were naturally white, but they could be tinted. They were also slightly transparent. *Do not try to paint over these substances.* New paint will not adhere to their powdery surfaces, so it is essential that they be removed before repainting.

How do you know what you're dealing with? Here are some of the most likely possibilities.

Casein paint was a milk-based paint commonly used on furniture and outbuildings before the Civil War. It has a low sheen, a pastel color and a hard finish, and it's not easily removed. If you suspect you may be dealing with casein, try removing it with commercial paint stripper. If that doesn't work, the paint is probably casein.

Calcimine was a mixture of zinc oxide, glue and water. Its surface, when dry, is so powdery that it rubs off on anything that brushes against it. It was commonly applied to ceilings, where it would never be touched. One of the best giveaways in identifying calcimine is that if you scrub its surface with water or vinegar, the paint will begin to come off.

Whitewash was a liquid plaster made from slaked lime; it sometimes contained milk or animal products as a binder. A very inexpensive paint, it was used to brighten up dark, unfinished spaces such as attics and cellars— the places where you're most likely to find it today. Whitewash is easy to identify from its thick, plaster-like appearance.

GET THE LEAD OUT

BEFORE THE health hazards of lead paint became generally recognized, most paint was lead based. That means the paint found in most homes built prior to 1950, and in many built before 1976, is lead based. That's bad news. Ingesting lead paint—whether in the form of chips from peeling paint or as fine dust particles—causes lead poisoning, which can lead to brain damage.

If you live in an older house—and particularly if you have young children, for whom lead poisoning is a particularly dangerous threat—have the paint in your house tested to determine what's lead paint and what's not. Look in the yellow pages under Lead Paint Detection and Removal Services for help in testing.

What to do about lead paint once it's identified is a very controversial subject, and guidelines seem to keep changing. If lead paint *is* found in your house, check with your state health officials for guidelines on what to do about it.

surface, wetting the area thoroughly. Wait a few minutes, then add 1 cup of a cleaner that contains trisodium phosphate to another pail of water. While wearing rubber gloves, dip a scrub brush in this solution and go over the prepared area with the brush. This is a good job for two people—one to prepare the surface and the other to follow with the scrub brush. It's easier if you work on one small area at a time. Let the surface dry thoroughly before repainting.

Hyde molding scrapers have interchangeable triangular and teardrop-shaped blades.

❑ If you have a ceiling that was originally painted with calcimine, remove the old paint entirely before applying something new. Paint won't stick to calcimine directly.

❑ Whitewash is best removed with a combination of vinegar and elbow grease. Brush on the vinegar, then scrape with a putty knife.

❑ The one tool that every person stripping paint should have is a Hyde molding scraper; it can be resharpened and lasts forever. The blades on these scrapers are interchangeable. A triangular blade can handle almost every surface, and a teardrop blade will get you into the few places that the triangle won't reach.

Brick: Where There's a Wall, There's a Way

❏ To remove paint from standard, smooth bricks, use a water-soluble paint remover such as Bix Tuff-Job Remover. By checking the container label, you can find out whether another brand you're considering is easily cleaned up with water. (Paint remover works well on standard bricks but is not very effective on tapestry bricks, which have a lot of little grooves in which old paint sticks.)

❏ If you don't want to use a chemical stripper to remove paint spatters from brick, you may be able to cover them up. Try rubbing the spattered area with other bricks of the same color. The brick dust will act like chalk to conceal the spatters.

Sandblasting Cons and Pros

❏ Some people recommend sandblasting to remove old paint from a brick house, but don't listen to them. The process turns the old paint into particles that can be inhaled, so it's a potential health hazard. Besides, the process, no matter how gentle, removes the brick's outer hard finish, changing its look and its weather resistance.

❏ Though not recommended for your walls, sandblasting *is* the easiest way to remove paint from old bathtubs and

---

PEELING WALLS: THE SOLUTION MAY BE SIZING

I F YOU HAVE a problem with relatively new plaster walls that do not take paint well or that peel easily, the problem may be that they were never properly sealed. If that's the case, you'll need to remove all the paint, seal the plaster and apply a good primer before painting.

You can buy a premixed sealer or use sizing instead. Traditionally, sizing was an animal glue bought as a powder. Mixed with water and applied with a wide wallpaper brush, sizing was the cheap and easy way to seal a surface before painting. Powdered synthetic sizing is still available. It's less expensive than premixed sealers and just as good for sealing plaster. However, it should be used with caution. Sizing is extremely toxic when inhaled and especially dangerous to unborn babies. *Avoid inhaling the fumes from sizing, and do not use it at all if you are pregnant.*

---

radiators. But don't do it inside the house. Remove the fixtures and take them to a professional who has the necessary equipment for the job. Tubs and radiators are difficult to move (rent a refrigerator dolly from a rental store and use that), but the procedure is not nearly so difficult as cleaning up your house—and your health—after a sandblasting operation.

REMOVING WALLPAPER

Off with the Old

❏ To simplify the process of removing old wallpaper that doesn't have a water-resistant surface, mix up a solution of equal parts warm water and white vinegar. Use a sponge to sop a section of wall with the solution, continuing until the wallpaper won't absorb any more water. Let it sit for 15 minutes or so, sop the wallpaper again and then peel it off with a broad-bladed putty knife. It should come off easily; if it doesn't, repeat the process and try again. (This process doesn't work with vinyl-coated wallpaper, which doesn't absorb moisture.)

❏ To remove vinyl wallpaper, sand lightly with 60-grit sandpaper. Be careful not to cut through the paper; just scour the surface. Mix liquid wallpaper remover (available at hardware stores) and hot water according to the directions on the remover. Apply it to the paper with a brush or roller. Let it soak until the bubbling stops, then scrape off all the paper. Be forewarned, though: If the paper was applied over drywall without a primer or sealer, you won't be able to get it off without pulling off the outer paper layer of the drywall.

❏ Wallpaper that has been painted over can be difficult to soften and remove. Try scoring the paper with a ra-

Whatsit?

PLEASE HELP US identify this box. The drawer and box are about 8" x 10", and the brass-colored arch appears to be a handle when it is folded up. It forms legs when the piece is opened. What is it?
— R.S., CORNISH FLAT, N.H.

This is an old photo album. Before you went to visit Aunt Minnie, you would put photos of Cousin Willie and his children in the drawer and fold it up. Then you'd just carry the album by the handle to her house, where you would set the thing up as an easel and use it to display the pictures.

zor knife and spraying the scores with liquid wallpaper remover (available at hardware stores).

A Last Resort

❏ If you're dealing with wallpaper that was applied directly over drywall and find it impossible to remove, sand off all the ridges and pull off any loose paper. Spackle areas of bare drywall to fill them level with the surrounding paper. Fill any nail holes or dents and sand these repairs by hand. Apply a latex sealer. When it's dry, check to make sure everything is filled and sanded. Reseal if necessary, then apply new wallpaper or a finish coat of latex paint.

PREPARING THE SURFACE

Clean Up Those Walls

❏ Always wash the surfaces you plan to paint—preferably with a product such as TSP or another substance containing trisodium phosphate. A solution of ½ cup of TSP dissolved in 2 gallons of warm water can be used for washing walls, stripped woodwork and trim. Be sure to wear rubber gloves when working with TSP, and rinse the surface before painting.

Old Plaster: Fill the Cracks

❏ To fill hairline cracks in plaster, dip your finger in spackling compound and draw it along the crack. Dampen larger cracks with water before filling them with compound. This prevents the plaster from sucking the moisture out of the spackle and causing it to shrink.

❏ Drywall joint compound is best for filling relatively small cracks and holes in old plaster and in woodwork. Use latex caulk in cracks that are going to expand and contract, such as miter joints on door casings.

To Match a Patch

❏ To help match a patch on a textured wall, try dragging a paintbrush over the wet joint or spackling compound. The bristles of the brush will leave tracks in the patch.

❏ To match a stipple effect with a patch, try lightly touching the brush to the wet compound and pulling it back rather than brushing.

❑ To match a pebbled wall, add sand to the patching compound. You may need to experiment with proportions to be sure the texture of the patch matches the existing wall.

Meddling with Metal

❑ Before painting aluminum, wipe it down with a solution of equal parts vinegar and water to remove oxidation (the white substance on the surface of the aluminum) and oil. Paint bonds best to a clean surface, and a thorough cleaning such as this reduces the chances of peeling. The mixture will evaporate, so there's no need to rinse it off before painting.

❑ Wipe other metals with turpentine or paint thinner before painting. Apply a metal primer, then a finish coat of good metal paint.

Before You Paint, Ventilate

O NCE WHEN I WAS in high school, I had the job of building some new bookshelves in a room of the high school library. It was a small room, and there was no window. The building part went fine, but then I had to paint what I'd built, and all the old shelves, too. I took the books down from the old shelves and stacked them in a big pile in the center of the room. There were an awful lot of books for so small a room. There were an awful lot of shelves, too, and it seemed to take forever to paint them all. Then I passed out.

A Word from Earl

I came to when the industrial arts teacher who was supervising the project came in to see how I was doing. I was lying on top of the pile of books, flat on my back, staring straight up at the ceiling. I looked around. My brush was in the paint can, and all the shelves were painted. Somehow I'd managed to finish the job before losing consciousness.

Since then, I've always made sure I've had a window open wherever I've been painting.

❏ To clean ironwork before painting, apply a coat of white vinegar and let it dry. The mixture will evaporate, so you don't need to rinse it off.

Stains and Other Knotty Problems

❏ If you want to paint wood that was previously stained, you can avoid removing the old stain before applying the paint. Apply a coat of a white shellac stain-kill product such as B-I-N. (If stains are still visible through the first coat, apply another.) This will also cover knots on new woodwork—or ones that are bleeding through old paint. Let the shellac dry (this doesn't take long) and then paint over it with any color. Take care to ventilate the room well. Fumes from any shellac-based product are ferocious.

THE RIGHT PRODUCTS

Colors: The Perfect Match

❏ When matching a paint color that's already on your walls, always bring home samples of the actual paint you're considering; don't try to match paint chips, which aren't always true representations of the colors you'll get in your home. Ask the store to mix a small amount of a shade that seems appealing, then take it home and paint a section of wall with it. (Some paint stores will mix as little as a pint for you. Even if you have to buy a quart, it's a lot better to check out that amount than to invest in gallons and find out you hate the result.) Then you can see your chosen shade in bright or dim natural light and lamplight.

❏ One way to keep track of the paints you've used is to write the information on the back of a light switch plate in each room as you paint the room. Then the manufacturer's name and the color will be there when you need them.

❏ If you're trying to stain new woodwork to match what you already have but can't find a stain that matches, try mixing two stains. Be sure to experiment first on scraps of the same type of wood. Then mix enough stain for the whole job. Try to use two stains that are the same brand; different brands don't always mix well.

Special Effects Department

❏ If you want to add texture to the surface you're painting, consider using sand paint (paint mixed with sand). You can achieve the look of rough plaster, for instance, in the pattern of your sand-paint brush marks on walls or ceilings. An application of sand paint can also hide defects in the surface of the walls or ceilings you are painting. It's

---

The Color Had to Be Right

O NCE I BUILT AN ADDITION on a woman's home, with a big picture window in one room. When it was time to paint that room, I asked her what color walls she wanted. She looked out the window and said, "Paint it the same color as the trees outside." Then she left for the day.

When the painter came in, he complained, "Gee whiz, just like the trees outside. Which branch? This one or that one? How am I going to know which color to paint it?" I told him to paint three shades of green on the wall. So he painted the swatches on the wall, and I picked one out. He was used to people picking their colors off the store  **A Word from Earl** paint cards, and he wasn't very happy with my technique. "Supposing she doesn't like it," he said. "Then I'll have to paint the whole thing over again." I crossed my fingers and assured him that she'd love the paint I picked out.

Fortunately, she did.

I never could have made up my mind from a little paint chip. But when I saw the swatches, I knew what I wanted. You don't always have to work from those tiny paint chips they give you in the store.

QUICK-AND-DIRTY PAINT RESEARCH

RESTORING A HOUSE'S interior to an exact earlier color can be tricky business. The pigment in the paint has a tendency to change over time, whether fading from sunlight or darkening with age. And the medium in the paint—usually a drying oil of some kind—can alter the color as well. Linseed oil, for example, yellows and darkens over time.

It is possible to get an idea of early or original paint colors without spending money on a professional analysis. Pick a protected spot on the wall—one where the paint is intact, unweathered and away from direct sunlight and dark corners. This will give you the best representative sample for analysis. With a razor blade or X-Acto knife, cut a ½" scallop-shaped crater through all the layers of paint. This exposes as much of the paint strata as possible. Using 220-grit wet/dry sandpaper and mineral oil, sand the sides of the cut. Do a final polishing with 600-grit paper, then wipe the area clean and rub it with mineral oil.

This process helps to bring out the colors and also reveals particularly thin layers and subtle differences between layers. Use a magnifying glass and a good source of white light to examine the area, and remember that the colors you're looking at are the aged colors, probably a bit yellower or browner than the originals.

possible to mix sand into ordinary paint, but it's easier to buy prepared sand paint from a good paint or hardware store. Keep stirring this mixture as you apply it; otherwise, the sand tends to sink to the bottom of the can. Sand paint comes with grits of various sizes; which one you choose depends on the effect you desire.

❑ Enamel finish paint, which you can buy in either oil or latex, is especially good for kitchens, baths and laundry rooms. It provides an excellent seal against dirt penetration and can be washed repeatedly. But its high gloss shows off every little imperfection in the walls, so don't use it on rough, old plaster. It looks good only on smooth surfaces.

All That Glitters Isn't Gilt

❑ You can mix a paint that shines like gold but lasts longer than gilt paint. Buy a yellow oil paint in the shade you want and add bronze powder to it until the mix is the color you desire. (You can get the bronze powder at art supply stores.) Use turpentine to thin it, and stir the paint often as you apply it.

❏ To get the appearance of gold on a sign, paint on a coat of flat white, then rub on burnt umber oil color (available at art supply stores and good paint stores) with a rag to get a variation of color. Be sure to buy burnt umber that's already mixed in oil—not the powdered kind.

❏ To achieve a polished silver look, mix aluminum powder #242 (available at art supply stores) with a clear lacquer until you get the color you want. Again, stir frequently while applying. Finish the job with a coat of clear lacquer.

❏ For a copper color, mix chrome yellow paint and a little burnt sienna in oil. The latter is one of a number of dry pigments that are premixed in oil (to make blending easier) and are available at art supply stores. These pigments are used primarily by sign painters and traditional trade painters.

Doing Right by Radiators

❏ Don't use true gold or silver paint on a radiator. These paints have an insulating effect, so a radiator painted with

COLOR CODING, VICTORIAN STYLE

V ICTORIANS FOLLOWED an interesting set of guidelines in choosing their interior color schemes. It was believed that furniture and costume "showed" better against a dark background, while artwork looked better against a lighter one. It became customary to paint or cover the lowest 3' of a Victorian wall (the dado) in a rich, dark color such as maroon or brown, then shift to a light or neutral color for the remainder of the wall. The dark section also gave the illusion of strength, as if holding up the larger wall above it. For cornices and moldings, bright colors were preferred. Blue was especially popular because it enhanced the perception of distance—making ceilings look higher than they actually were.

If you own a Victorian home, you might be lucky enough to see this in your interior color schemes, especially in formal rooms. If those rooms have been painted over in different colors, you might keep these Victorian principles in mind next time a room needs painting.

OIL OR LATEX?

Paints come in two general kinds, oil and latex. In the old days, oil paints were of vegetable origin; today they combine alkyd resins with a petroleum base. Some people prefer oil paints, which are often considered more durable—especially in areas of high traffic and moisture. Also, oil paints will not rust metal (such as screws or nail heads) with which they come in contact.

Latex paints, which are water soluble, have a more rapid drying time—which sounds like an advantage, except it means they also tend to "set up" (start to harden) in the brush even while in constant use. On a hot, dry day, you will likely have to flush your brush several times to keep it workable. (Just hold it under running water and shake out the excess water.)

Latex paints are generally less expensive than oil paints, and cleaning up after using them involves only water. For those reasons, as well as environmental concerns about the toxins released over the years by the older oil paints and even the modern alkyd ones—and by the solvents used in cleaning them up—oil paints are now being phased out of the market. By the time you make up your mind, you may no longer have a choice.

them will give off less heat. The recommended paint for maximum heat transfer is nonmetallic flat black paint. A flat finish radiates better than a glossy one, and black is slightly better than other colors.

❏ If you know what kind of paint was used on your radiator the last time, you can paint directly over it. Use nonmetallic latex if the old paint was latex and nonmetallic oil if the earlier coat was oil.

❏ If you want to paint over existing paint on a radiator but are uncertain about what kind of paint was used for that earlier coat, apply an oil-based primer. Then for your finish coat, use either oil or latex.

BRUSHES

Buying the Right Brush
❏ Always use natural-bristle brushes with oil-based paint and synthetic brushes with latex.

❑ When buying a new paintbrush, whether it's a natural-hair or synthetic brush, always look for one that has flagged (frayed) bristles, because they hold more paint. An old brush will hold less paint than a new one because the flagged ends will have worn off.

❑ Tapered brushes in small sizes are best for painting a window sash. The exact size is a matter of personal preference, but a 1½" or 2" brush is comfortable for most people.

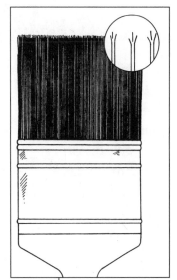

New Brushes: Avoid Hair Loss

❑ If you're going to use a new brush on a finicky job, wash the brush once before you begin, and you'll avoid getting loose hairs in the finish. To be on the safe side, use the brush only on under-coats until it's broken in. Of course, the more expensive the brush, the less likely it is to shed.

Flagged (frayed) bristles hold more paint.

Longer Life for New Brushes

❑ If you buy a top-quality, natural-bristle brush for painting with varnish, soak it in a can of boiled linseed oil for 12 hours before you use it the first time. Just squeeze the linseed oil out of the bristles before you paint. This will make the brush easier to clean and will extend its life in general.

Paint and Varnish Brushes: Equal but Separate

❑ It's a good idea to reserve one brush exclusively for use with varnish. Once you've used a brush to apply paint, you'll never get it completely clean again, so don't apply varnish with it.

It takes some practice, but if you leave a slight bead of paint on windowpanes, you'll do a better job of keeping out water.

GETTING READY TO PAINT

Cover Up with Care

❑ When spreading drop cloths to protect your floors from paint spatters, avoid using plastic. It's too slippery and can cause accidents.

❑ When you paint a window sash, avoid masking the glass with tape or scraping along the glass-wood con-

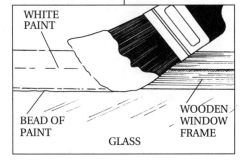

WHITE PAINT

BEAD OF PAINT

GLASS

WOODEN WINDOW FRAME

My Stirring Experience

IN THE EARLY 1930S, when I worked on a painting crew, we used to mix the paint in an old washtub. The ingredients were boiled linseed oil, turpentine, white lead, colors in oil and a little bit of drying agent. One painter in the group—usually the oldest—knew how much paint to make to cover the entire house. He had to be right. If we ran out of paint, it was impossible to mix more of the identical color.

A Word from Earl

My job was stirring the tub of paint with a 3' paddle as the paint mixer added the various materials. Overnight, a skin of the drying agent and linseed oil would form on the surface of the paint in the tub, so more of those ingredients had to be stirred in each morning. I spent more hours than I care to recall standing over a paint tub, stirring.

Today's premixed paint is a lot less seat-of-the-pants. You don't have to reconstitute it each day, and the label on the paint can gives the manufacturer's recommendations as to the amount of paint it will take to cover a certain area. So if you know the square footage of the surfaces you're planning to paint, it's easy to calculate how much paint you'll need.

nection with a razor blade. Instead, allow a slight bead of paint to come over onto the glass, covering the window putty. This ensures keeping water out. It takes a little practice to do this effectively, but it's worth it.

❏ If you do use masking tape to mask around woodwork, affix it on the day you are going to paint and remove it immediately after you finish. When masking tape dries on a surface, it can be hard to remove. (It can also pull off other paint, so be careful where you use it.)

Mix It Up

❏ When you're in the middle of a job and one can of paint is running low, pour in some paint from a new can and mix the two together. That will ease the transition to the next can of paint, the color of which will not precisely match the paint of the first can.

❑ Here's an alternative to the awkward job of mixing a full gallon of oil-based paint all at once. Before you start stirring, pour the thinner liquid at the top of the can into an empty can. Stir the remaining sediment well, then slowly add back the liquid while you continue stirring.

❑ To stir latex paint, you can use a bent rod or an old beater from a kitchen mixer in an electric drill. Don't use this method on an oil-based paint, though; a spark from the drill could ignite the paint.

❑ Whitewash is still a practical, inexpensive way to brighten up your attic or cellar. To make your own, pick

COLONIALS WEREN'T ALWAYS DULL

TODAY MANY PEOPLE think of brown, light blue or gray walls as "the colonial look." But that's not the look with which the colonists lived. Colonial interiors featured new pine paneling that was a light honey color and remained so for many years. When this was first painted, it was with brilliant milk paints. Often these paints were so thin that the grain of the underlying wood showed through. The paint surface was smooth and soft, often accented with fine brushstrokes. Never was the molding detail obliterated, as it sometimes has been in recent times, by layer after layer of thick, hard enamel.

Plaster also had a pronounced texture of its own. It was porous and soft to the touch, in contrast to the hard plasters of today. The entire surface also carried the texture of the irregular lath beneath it. Although frequently the plaster walls were whitewashed, just as often they were painted instead with pastels.

With the beginning of the Greek Revival period, the pastels of earlier times often gave way to more solid greens, yellows, roses and oranges, with woodwork painted lighter colors for contrast. In some cases, the walls were stenciled or painted with imaginative freehand designs or landscapes.

So what happened to all those light, bright walls? Time and age have given the impression that muted colors were the original ones. Put together a lot of creosote from a lot of fires, a good number of dirty fingers and plenty of general aging, and you get the dirty picture.

up a jar of hydrated mason's lime—not agricultural lime—in powder form at a masonry supply store. Add enough lime to 1 gallon of whole milk to make the mixture the consistency of cream. Add 1 cup of turpentine for hardener. Stir until well mixed; paint at once. (If you wait, the turpentine and milk will separate.) Don't worry; your walls won't smell like sour milk after the whitewash has dried.

Stop Fuming

❑ To eliminate paint odor, stir 1 tablespoon of vanilla extract into each pint of paint. This has no effect on the paint.

❑ Here's another way to absorb odor in a room being painted. Roughly chop a large, unpeeled onion into big

Filling the Lady's Darker Desires

W HEN PREMIXED PAINTS were first developed, only one shade of white was available. I was painting the inside of a house for a woman who didn't like that standard, off-the-shelf white. It was too bright for her. Feeling that something a little darker would be more appropriate for her old colonial home, she asked me to mix a white paint for her that didn't look so new. I wasn't sure she was right about what was authentic, but she was the boss, and I got the effect she wanted by adding drops of lampblack to the gallons of premixed paint we bought. (Lampblack, a pigment made from soot, was commonly used to tint paint before any mixed paint was available.)

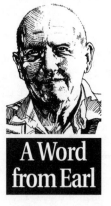

**A Word
from Earl**

Although you have the choice of hundreds of premixed whites today, you can save money by buying base white paint (which is less expensive than a tinted paint) and tinting it yourself with lampblack (available at hardware stores). Use an eyedropper and add only 1 drop at a time, stirring continuously. The paint can get dark quickly, so be careful and take your time when adding drops. Keep a good record of the mixture you decide on, in case you want to duplicate it later.

pieces and place it in a pan of cold water in the appropriate room.

Dump the Drips

❑ If you're dabbing your brush against the rim of the can, here's a way to prevent paint from dripping down the outside of the paint can (and being wasted). Try attaching a wire across the middle of the can opening and dabbing your brush on it rather than on the sides of the can.

❑ An alternative is to cut an old paint can lid in half, put it on the new paint can and use the cut edge for dabbing.

❑ You can also avoid paint dripping down the outside of a can if you use a nail to punch a series of holes in the bottom of the groove around the edge of the can. (Since the lid is sealed by the pressure against the sides of the groove, you'll still get a tight seal when you put the lid back on.) Reducing drips means saving paint, mess and cleanup time.

Whatsit?

CAN YOU HELP identify this object? We're mystified by it.
— J.T.G., LEWISTON, N.Y.

This is a hackle. Linen makers used a series of hackles ranging from coarse to fine; the one shown is a coarse one. Bundles of flax fibers were drawn through the spikes to separate out the coarse fibers and dirt. The coarse fibers were used to make work shirts and bags, and the fine fibers were used for the best linen.

APPLYING INTERIOR PAINT

He Who Hesitates Is Saved Some Work

❑ If you're refinishing a floor *and* painting the room, setting priorities will save you time and aggravation. As you (or someone you hire) sand the edges of the floor, the edge sander will scuff up the baseboards. There's no way to avoid it, so it's best to hold off on painting the baseboards until the floor has been sanded. Your final coat of paint on the baseboards will cover the scuff marks from the sander.

The Right Place at the Right Time

❑ Paint a room from the top down. Start with the ceiling, do the walls next and then work on doors, windows and other trim. If you're going to paint the floors, do them last.

❑ When you're painting stairs, paint every other one. Wait until those are completely dry, then paint the oth-

Whatsit?

I HAVE NO IDEA what this tool was used for. It's 16" long overall and not particularly sharp. What is it?
— H.B., MONTAGUE, MASS.

Back in the 1880s, certain products—sugar, flour, fruit, etc.— came in wooden barrels. These staples would get packed down because of their weight and the moisture they had absorbed. This tool, called a sugar auger, was used to bore into the food to break it up. Then some of the food could be removed for use.

ers. That way, you can use the steps more easily without injury before the whole job is dry.

❑ If you're painting the walls of a room and can't complete the job in one pass, be sure to stop at the end of a wall rather than in the middle. Paint dries differently at different times, so you risk leaving a visible line if you stop midwall. It's especially important to keep this in mind if it appears you are going to run out of paint.

Reach Out—With a Broomstick

❑ When you need to paint in places that are not easily accessible, try strapping a broomstick to the handle of your paint brush to extend your reach. It's hard to do fine work with this kind of contraption, but often the work doesn't need to be precise in a spot that's hard to reach.

The Roller Derby

❑ It's not worth using a roller to paint very small rooms such as bathrooms and closets. You have to paint around the trim and into the corners with a brush anyway, so the roller doesn't offer a real time saving in such small spaces.

❑ For larger surfaces, a roller with a heavy nap does have an advantage over a brush: You can apply more paint with the roller. In some instances, you can cover a wall in one coat with a roller, whereas it might take two coats with a brush.

❑ You can paint over a pebble-finish ceiling with a heavy-nap roller. The pebble effect will be lessened slightly, but the paint will adhere to the old surface.

❑ Put a plastic bag over the roller pan before pouring in the paint. When the job is finished, just throw away the bag; the pan needs no cleaning.

❑ Can't get around that radiator to paint behind it? Check with your local paint store; you'll probably find it stocks paint rollers about 1" thick and 7" long, with 24" handles, for just such predicaments.

BASICS OF EXTERIOR PAINTING

Timing Is Everything

❏ Spread out your painting chores. Give the house one coat of paint now; wait 2 or 3 years before applying another. This method is better than applying two coats in the same year because it gives the paint a chance to set and makes it less apt to peel.

❏ Although you should avoid working in bright, direct sun, the best time to paint is during a run of decent weather—usually a time when it's so hot out that you would rather be doing anything but painting. The heat dries out the wood, which is the way you want it for painting. Don't wait for the cool days of fall to start your outside paint job. There may be too much rain then, and painting the exterior of a house takes so long that it may not be finished before winter. You don't want to start an exterior paint job one season and finish it the next.

How to Paint a Fence in a Hurry

WHEN I WAS STILL NEW at painting, my father set me and another painter on opposite sides of a wrought-iron fence and told us to paint it black. When you paint a fence, you really flip your brush around, and if you happen to wear glasses (or are wearing sunglasses), pretty soon you're looking through polka-dot glasses. That's if you're painting it alone. Of course, the two of us, being right opposite each other, were really spattering each other. So I started trying to paint faster and get ahead of the other fellow to avoid being spattered. Then he tried to paint faster so he could catch up and pepper me. We finished that fence in a hurry—which is exactly what my father had intended.

A Word from Earl

❏ When painting on a hot day, stay in the shade as much as possible. It's better for your paint job and easier on you.

The Perils of Peeling

❏ To determine the cause of paint blistering on the outside of a house, cut open a blister. If there is still a coat of paint or primer on the siding underneath, either the surface wasn't prepared properly before the paint was applied or the two layers of paint were incompatible. If the siding under the blister is bare wood, the cause of the blistering is moisture in the walls. One of the most common sources of this kind of moisture is the absence of a vapor barrier in the walls.

❏ In older houses, you can provide a vapor barrier by applying a paint specifically made for this purpose. (Ask your paint store for vapor barrier paint.) In each room, apply at least one coat on the inside of each exterior wall.

PREPARING THE EXTERIOR

A Chalky Complexion Is Not a Good Symptom

❏ Your exterior paint has a problem if you run your fingers over it and they look as if you have dipped them in talcum powder. This can happen if your paint is of poor quality or is aging. Some paints were designed to "chalk" as a way of continually repelling dirt. These paints eventually rubbed away to nothing, and they're no longer made. No matter what the cause, you can fix a chalky area by rubbing it with a stiff bristle brush, priming with a product made for this purpose and repainting.

Scraping and Stripping: The Bare Facts

❏ Sharpen your hand scraper frequently throughout a paint scraping project. It's the rough edge left on the scraper after you file it that removes the paint.

❏ Do you have a serious peeling problem? For the initial scraping, consider using a heavy-duty paint scraper from your garden shed. If you sharpen your hoe, you can use it to scrape a large area in a short time. The hoe's long handle makes it easy to reach more of the surface without moving your ladder. After the initial scraping with the hoe, follow up by going over the surface more carefully with a paint scraper.

Washing: The High-Pressure Approach

❏ Some people recommend pressure washing as a method for removing old paint. The major advantage to this approach is that it can clean off a lot of peeling paint in a short time. But is also blows paint chips everywhere, and it can tear up any trim that's not secure. You need to consider all these factors when deciding whether to go the pressure washing route.

❏ If you rent pressure washing equipment or hire a contractor to remove old paint in this way, you'll need 1,200 to 1,500 pounds per square inch of water pressure for the spray to remove loose paint effectively. If your house has wood siding, the washing nozzle must be kept at least a foot away from the siding to avoid digging into the wood.

❏ After pressure washing, wait a day or so for the exterior to dry. (The exact timing depends on the weather.) Then follow up with a little scraping by hand.

PAINTING VS. STAINING

SHOULD YOU USE paint or stain on the outside of your house? There's no one correct answer, but here are two (or three) sides of the question.

Paints and stains both protect wood from weather, but they do it in different ways. Paints harden into a protective coating on a wood surface. Stains penetrate, then harden. Both are available in your choice of oil- and water-based formulas.

Paints generally provide better and longer-lasting protection from the elements than do penetrating stains. They cover the grain of the wood, whereas most stains, though changing the color of the wood, leave the grain visible to some degree—a feature that you may or may not consider desirable. Color choices in stains are somewhat limited, but you can paint a house any color you can imagine.

On the other hand, stains require much lower maintenance (just adding another coat every few years—no stripping needed), and they allow a house to "breathe" out moisture rather than trap it inside. It's also easier for an amateur to get good results with stains than with paints.

If you want to protect your siding but like how it looks now, you might want to consider clear wood finishes. They have many of the same characteristics as stains, but they don't significantly change the color of the wood.

Don't Let Your Neighbors Push You Around

O NCE I WAS BUILDING three new houses for a contractor. We painted the first one tan and the second one green. When it came time for the third one, we decided to paint it barn red.

Whenever I painted a house red, I'd put on a base of white paint tinted with red. Or I'd put on gray, which is a neutral color that you can paint over with a finish coat of any color. I had some red left over from another job, so I poured a little into some cans of white and had my men start painting the house pink.

A Word from Earl

Pink houses do not go over well with New Englanders. Soon the doctor's wife across the road came over and said that she would not stand for that color on a house near her gray one. Within a few days, she had other neighbors upset, too.

By the time the entire first coat was on, however, the color was more of a dusty rose. The neighbors' attitude also had changed. Gradually, they came to like the color so much they asked me to leave it on the house, and I ended up mixing more of the same for the second coat.

The house was sold, and a year or so later, the owner wanted to paint it again. She called her painter to arrange for the paint job, but he had to call me to okay the color. It turned out she loved that dusty rose and wanted him to match it.

No Balking; Start Caulking

❑ Before painting, you need to caulk all cracks and openings in the siding less than ⅜" wide. Before caulking, fill large cracks with scraps of wood or backer rod (a spongy, plastic, noodlelike material made for this purpose and available from hardware stores and masonry supply stores). Use acrylic latex caulk; you can paint over it afterward.

❏ If you're caulking a crack and don't intend to paint over it, use silicone acrylic caulk. It's more durable than acrylic latex caulk, but it can't be painted over.

❏ If you push the caulking gun over the crack you are sealing, you will fill the crack and smooth the caulking in one operation. If you have to pull the caulking gun along the crack, you will need to smooth out the caulking with your finger.

A Primer on Primers

❏ If you are painting on metal, use a rust-inhibiting primer for the first coat. You can then use any good house paint or enamel for the finish coats.

❏ If the instructions on the can of primer specify a coverage of 1 gallon per 400 square feet, don't try to stretch the coverage to 450 square feet. Your primer coat will be too thin, and the finish coat may not adhere properly.

❏ Be sure to apply both primer and a top coat within 2 weeks of each other. Do not prime in the fall and wait until spring to apply a top coat. If you wait too long, one coat of paint is likely to peel away from the other.

❏ Radially sawn clapboards are sawn with the grain running tangentially to the board. They accept paint and stain exceptionally well. They are the best kind of clapboard you can buy, but they are also the most expensive. If you're using flat-sawn clapboards—in which the grain runs parallel or any other way but tangentially to the board—you should prime or stain the backs of the new clapboards before attaching them to the house. (Prime them if you're painting the fronts; stain them if you're staining the fronts.)

When the lumber is sawn so that all the pieces radiate out from the center (A), the resulting, radially sawn clapboard looks like this (B). When the lumber is sawn with the grain of the board (C), a resulting pair of flat-sawn clapboards looks like this (D).

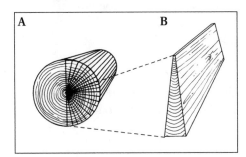

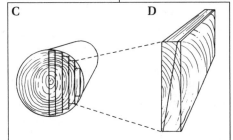

PAINTING INSIDE AND OUT

❏ Priming is especially important if you're working with red cedar clapboards. If the clapboards are not properly primed before painting, the oil in them will bleed through and stain your paint job. There are special primers for red cedar. If you have red cedar clapboards, use one of these primers.

OTHER EXTERIOR IDEAS

A Debugging Device

❏ Add a few drops of citronella to 1 gallon of paint to keep away flying insects such as blackflies and mosqui-

---

JUST HOW BRIGHT WERE THE VICTORIANS?

BEFORE THE VICTORIANS, people left the exteriors of their homes unpainted or covered the broad surfaces with one of the few available colors (usually white or a pastel), generally imitating building materials such as brick or stone. Sometimes they used more vivid tones to accent the details.

Then along came A.J. Downing, an aesthetic philosopher of the 1840s and 1850s. As part of his campaign to make Gothic Revival the nationally preferred style of architecture, Downing also encouraged the notion that white buildings were contrary to nature —or, at the very least, a boring alternative.

Downing's push for Gothic Revival never succeeded, but his theories on color did resurface in the 1880s and 1890s, when they were exploited by the *late* Victorians and an infant ready-made paint industry. These manufacturers revived the philosophy of natural colors and packaged it as "exterior decoration." They promoted new colors in new combinations and displayed the results in slick new product literature. Such brochures illustrated ways to decorate older homes in the new, brighter styles.

The result? A late nineteenth-century epidemic of brightly colored houses—and the vivid illusion that all Victorian and Edwardian homes (those ornate structures of virtually the entire nineteenth century) were originally painted in the style of the 1880s. Don't believe it. If your house was built prior to 1880, it's just as likely that it was originally painted in more subdued tones. Never assume that the paint for your Victorian home has to be bright to be authentic.

---

toes. The citronella won't affect the paint, but it will keep the bugs from messing up your fresh paint job.

Don't Drip

❏ When painting the outside of a house, here's a simple way to keep paint from dripping down the outside of the can. After you dip your brush in the paint, simply dab each side of the brush lightly against the inside wall of the can. This prevents drips but keeps most of the paint on your brush, so you don't have to go back to the paint can as often.

Ladders: Playing It Safe

❏ If you can, always place the top of your ladder against a still-to-be-painted surface. If you must lean it against new paint, wrap the ends of the ladder with rags and cover them with old socks. This will prevent the ladder from damaging your paint job.

❏ When placing a ladder against a wall, the safest angle is about 1' away from the wall for every 4' up the wall.

APPLYING EXTERIOR PAINT

First Things First

❏ Start painting a house at its highest point, beginning with the trim. When all the trim on one side is finished, paint the window and door frames. For windows, start at the glass and work outward. This gives you more control so you can avoid getting more than a bead of paint on the glass. When the detail work is done, paint the body of the house, working from the top down to avoid dripping on already-painted surfaces.

❏ When painting clapboard siding, work on a section of five or six clapboards at a time. For each section, draw the edge of the brush along under the edge of each clapboard. With the flat of the brush, finish painting the face of the clapboard. It's impor-

SEEING RED

FOR MANY YEARS, red paint was the cheapest paint made. That's why all schoolhouses used to be red and why barns, when they were painted at all, were also red. When pride began to replace utility, the three sides of a house that could be seen from the road would be painted white, and the rear would be painted red.

tant to make a good seal in the cracks, and this way you won't forget to paint the underside of the clapboards.

❏ For the final coat on clapboards, start at the top of a wall and paint a band about 4' high across the entire side. Then paint another complete band below the first and repeat the process until that side of the house is done. If you overlap new paint onto dry paint, the line may be visible, but when you use this technique, the shadows of the clapboards hide that line.

Window Wisdom

❏ Put a coat of boiled linseed oil on window sash and sills before puttying. Putty on dry wood will lose its strength because the oil will be sucked out of the putty and into the wood. The coating of boiled linseed oil will prevent this, and the sash will last longer. Let the oil soak into the wood for about half an hour after applying it. Then wipe off any excess and apply the putty.

The Day I Learned from the Pros

WHEN I FIRST BEGAN painting for my father, he had me start with the part that experienced painters don't like to work on: the shutters. I was trying to learn, so I asked the head painter, "How many pairs of shutters does a good painter do in a day?" He replied, "Fourteen pair." So I started in, working like crazy to get that many done.

When my father came by the job site, he asked me how many pairs I'd completed that day. I told him fourteen, and he looked surprised. "You did well," he said. "I don't know a painter who can do more than eleven pairs in a day."

A Word from Earl

That day I learned two things from the professionals. First, having an ambitious goal can help you get through a boring job. And second, don't believe everything people tell you!

❏ An alternative to applying boiled linseed oil to window sash and sills is to apply a coat of paint before you start puttying. Let the paint dry, then apply the putty.

❏ Always paint window sash white or another light color. This will make them last longer. Wood that's painted a dark color absorbs more heat from the sun and dries out much faster than wood painted a light color.

NONWOOD SURFACES

Siding Is Simple

❏ Before painting aluminum siding, wash it with a solution of 2 gallons of warm water, 1 cup of TSP (or any product containing trisodium phosphate) and 1 cup of household (5 percent) bleach. Apply the solution with a soft scrub brush, then rinse the area thoroughly with the garden hose. After letting the siding dry, apply latex paint.

Stuck on Stucco?

❏ When working with stucco, be sure that you purchase a paint that is made for masonry application. It's fine to use a latex paint designed specifically for exterior masonry surfaces, but don't use ordinary latex paint. This prevents the house from breathing, so the stucco hardens, causing it to chip and crumble.

❏ Another way to "paint" stucco is to apply a skim coat of new stucco over your old stucco. Mix 1 part portland cement, 3 parts aggregate (such as silica sand) and enough water to make a stucco mixture that is the consistency of paint. Apply a thin coat of the mixture to the stucco. This method works especially well on very rough stucco surfaces—as long as you like the natural color of the stucco.

Whatsit?

WE HAVE THIS ITEM displayed at our local museum, but we don't know what it is. Can you tell us?
— M.S., MARTINEZ, CALIF.

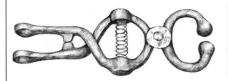

This tool was used by a veterinarian to restrain a bull, ox or even an unruly cow when performing dental work or minor surgery on the animal's head. After the ball ends were clamped into the animal's nose, a rope would be put through the holes in the other end and tied to a ceiling beam to hold the head in position while the vet worked on the animal.

CLEANUP

Paintbrush Hang-Ups

❏ There's no need to wash your brush between coats of varnish or paint. Hanging it in a can of water or solvent will prevent bent bristles. To hang a brush, insert a piece of rigid wire (from a coat hanger, for instance) through the hole in the brush handle. Lower the brush into the container with the water or solvent until the wire is supported on the rim of the container. Avoid immersing the ferrule in the liquid.

❏ Here's another way to hang a brush in water or solvent—offering more control over the height of the brush in the liquid and thus a better way to avoid bent bristles. Put the water or solvent in a coffee can. Cut an X in the center of the can lid, and push the brush handle through the X from the inside. Snap the brush and lid back on the can, and the lid will suspend the brush in the liquid.

Don't Toss That Old Brush

❏ You can restore a brush that has hardened after use with latex paint. Hang the brush in a 1-gallon pail with 1 cup of liquid laundry detergent. Fill the pail with hot water until the bristles are covered (don't immerse the ferrule). Agitate with the brush until the detergent is dissolved. Leave the brush to soak for 3 days, agitating the bristles occasionally, then remove it from the solution and rinse thoroughly. When the brush is almost dry, wrap newspaper around it, leaving 2" of paper beyond the bristles. Fold the excess paper back over the brush head and secure it with rubber bands. When the brush is dry, it will be clean, soft and restored to its original condition.

❏ A paintbrush that's hardened after use in oil paint or varnish can be soft-

---

Whatsit?

THE OBJECT SHOWN here appears to be made of cast iron and was found in a shed in Maine. Do you have any idea what it is and how it was used?

— W.H.B., ROWE, MASS.

This was a boon to housewives. The only thing it couldn't do was burp the baby. Held one way, the four prongs could be used to tenderize meat. If held in other ways, the small hooks could

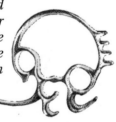

be used to remove hot pots from the stove or the long prong could be used to remove stove lids. Placed on the table, it served as a trivet. I suppose that when all else failed, you could put your fingers through the holes and use it as a good set of brass knuckles for protection.

---

ened in hot vinegar. Place the brush in a pan, cover it with vinegar and simmer on the stove for 5 to 10 minutes. Rinse the brush thoroughly, then follow the procedure in the preceding tip to recondition the bristles.

❏ To straighten a clean, dry brush that's been bent from standing too long in thinner, soak the brush in warm water for an hour or so. (This makes the bristles more flexible.) Then bind pieces of scrap wood on either side of the bristles, securing them with a stout cord or elastic band. Leave the wood on until the bristles stay straight.

Paintbrush Handles: A Prescription to Avoid Swelling

❏ If you're using latex paint, when you've finished with a particular brush, you can leave it in water until you're ready to clean up. But if the brush has a wooden handle, avoid leaving it too long. Prolonged soaking in water will swell the wood, which in turn will stretch the metal ferrule. When the wooden handle dries out and contracts again, the metal will retain its enlarged size, so the handle will be loose in the ferrule.

Latex Cleanup: It Couldn't Be Easier

❏ When you're using a brush with latex paint, you'll need to clean it off once in a while, even when you're not yet through with a job. Doing this is easy. Just hold the brush under an open faucet and rinse out the paint. Then shake all the water out of the brush.

Try a Couple of Shortcuts

❏ If you're painting with the same latex paint for 2 days in a row, save yourself some cleanup time. At the end of the first day, wrap your brushes and rollers in aluminum foil and place them in the freezer overnight. The next day, remove them from the freezer about half an hour before you wish to resume painting so they have time to warm up. (This method doesn't work indefinitely; always clean brushes and rollers properly if you don't plan to use them again the next day.)

❏ If you're using oil paint and can't stand the thought of pouring out a whole jarful of expensive thinner just to soak one brush, here's an alternative. Choose an empty white glue bottle that's the appropriate size for your brush.

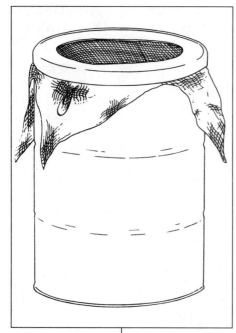

Make a handy paint strainer out of cheesecloth and a coffee can.

Cut the top off and clean the bottle thoroughly, then pour in the paint thinner and insert the brush. The flattened shape allows you to use a small amount of thinner to cover the bristles.

Strain to Save Your Paint

❏ Sometimes your paint or thinner will get contaminated with debris, but you can still save it. To make a strainer for paints and thinners, cut out the center of a coffee can lid, leaving about ½" of lid around the edge. Place a square of cheesecloth under the lid and snap the lid and cloth on the can. Pour the paint into the can through the cheesecloth.

Good Painters Aren't Polluters

❏ Because paint can contaminate the environment if carelessly dumped in a landfill, it is classified as hazardous waste. Rather than tossing it in with other garbage, set your leftover paint aside until your town or city announces a time and place for collecting hazardous waste. Bring it to the collection site then so it can be disposed of properly.

STORAGE

No More Clogged Nozzles

❏ To prevent a clogged nozzle on an aerosol paint can, store the nozzle in a small jar filled with paint thinner. Take the nozzle off right after you finish spraying. (These nozzles pop off and on easily.) It's smart to save good nozzles from empty cans as spares.

Save That Paint Can

❏ Sometimes the water in latex paint rusts a hole in a paint can; then the water slowly leaks from the can and evaporates. To prevent this, tap the lids of your paint cans with a hammer to be sure they're tightly sealed, then turn over the cans periodically. This is actually a good practice for all your paint cans; it keeps the paint ingredients from separating entirely.

❏ Always cover a paint can with a rag before tapping it shut. This prevents spatters.

❏ It's safe to store both latex and oil paints inside, but not flammable materials such as paint thinner, contact cement and lacquer thinner. These have vapors that ignite easily when exposed to a flame, and they could explode in case of a fire. They're best stored in a well-ventilated garage or other outbuilding. It's fine to keep them in an unheated area; they won't freeze.

❏ Don't store latex paint in an area where it's likely to freeze. Once frozen, it will no longer be usable.

Oil Paint: Skip the Skin

❏ To prevent a skin from forming on oil paint, try this. Before storing a partially used can of paint, cut a piece of wax paper to size and set it directly on the surface of the paint in the can.

❏ Another way to keep oil paint from skinning over is to pour a little thinner on top of the paint, then close the lid tight. The fumes from the thinner leave no air in the can to cause the paint to dry out.

Walls, Ceilings and Trim

Don't cut corners on construction. But for finishing touches, shortcuts can make all the difference.

I N THE WINTER OF 1939, I had been out of high school 8 years and was a finish carpenter on a job for a composer. The man wanted to transform a large room in his house into a library with deep bookcases built into all the walls. We had to remove all the original finish work in the room—the door and window casings, fireplace mantel, ceiling moldings and baseboards—and build it out 10" to match the depth of the bookshelves. The work was very complicated, but the library was beautiful when we finished.

All the woodwork was of basswood, and it was beautiful. I can remember marking cuts with a jackknife on that job. A pencil point was not precise enough for the work we did. I think I enjoyed that job as much as any that I've ever done. Today work like that is unaffordable—unless, of course, you do it yourself.

Even if that kind of project is more than you care to undertake, here are some ideas that will save you both time and money on your inside finish work.

Included in this chapter are tips for repairing old plaster, laying drywall and patching holes in walls and wallpaper. You'll also find ingenious stains for barn boards and a simple trick that will hide the truth when the paneling shrinks. And if you don't have a partner for a project that typically requires two people (installing a new ceiling or putting up awkward lengths of molding), be sure to take advantage of the tips that tell you how to do the whole thing on your own.

PLASTER

Off with the Old

❏ A lightweight wrecking bar with at least a 2"-wide blade is a good tool for removing old plaster and lath (the narrow wooden support strips under the plaster).

❏ There is such a thing as proper dress for tearing down old plaster. Wear a dust mask and a long-sleeved shirt buttoned tight at the neck. If you're removing plaster from a ceiling, an old wide-brimmed hat and eye protection are essential equipment.

❏ No matter how careful you are, plaster dust will get into everything. But it does help to haul away the plaster and lath as you tear it off the wall. After you finish, vacuum down the studs and the boards behind them, and

---

IF YOU CAN'T FIND IT ...

. . . maybe you need to try another chapter. Check the index, or try these possibilities.

For Tips On ...	*See the Chapter ...*
Removing old wallpaper	Painting Inside and Out
Removing wallpaper stains	Stains and Odors
Staining wood	Painting Inside and Out

HOW THE OLD-TIMERS GOT PLASTERED

EARLY PLASTER was made by combining clay with hay or hair, or sand with shell lime. Because the plaster was of such poor quality, it was applied sparingly: in nooks and crannies, usually from the waist up. (Chair rails were developed to prevent chairs from chipping plaster.) As more limestone was quarried toward the mid-1700s, improved lime kilns made fine white lime, which produced better plaster. By the turn of the century, entire walls and ceilings were regularly covered with plaster.

vacuum the floor. Let the dust settle, then vacuum the floor again.

DRYWALL

Proper Planning

❑ Plan ahead when you're laying drywall. It's best to minimize the number of joints you'll need to tape and to position those joints in places where they will be least noticeable. The standard dimensions of a sheet of drywall are 4' x 8', but the sheets come in longer lengths as well. If you're working on a wall that's just short of 12' long, for instance, you may want to buy 4' x 12' drywall and lay it horizontally.

❑ Longer sheets of drywall laid vertically are good for the walls of rooms with high ceilings. Keep in mind, however, that larger sheets of drywall are more awkward to handle.

Nail It Down

❑ Avoid using smooth-shank nails to put up drywall; gypsum drywall nails are stronger and are rosin coated to improve anchoring. Better yet are drywall screws, which can be driven with an electric drill and won't pop out later.

❑ If you drive a nail and it misses a stud, pull it out; if you don't, it will pop out later and come through paint or wallpaper. To hit the stud, try again 1" to the right or left of the place you tried first.

❑ When nailing drywall, hit the nail just hard enough so that the hammer drives in the nail and creates a dimple in the paper (the top surface of the drywall) without cutting through it. This makes a place for the joint compound to fill.

Stud Location: The Measured Approach

❑ Whether nailing or screwing drywall in place, you'll need to anchor it to the studs underneath. That's hard to do if you're laying the drywall over an existing wall surface, such as plaster. To locate the studs, start by measuring 16" (or some multiple of 16") from the nearest major framing member—like the corner of a room or a door frame. Then keep measuring in 16" intervals. Studs are almost always laid 16" on center in new construction, and that's been the standard for some time.

Stud Location: The School of Hard Knocks

❑ Another tactic for locating studs is to tap the wall with your knuckle and listen to the sound. As you tap along the wall, you'll notice that the sound goes from hollow to solid to hollow. The less resonant, higher-pitched solid

THE DATING GAME

I F YOU'RE TRYING to date your house, you may be able to find a clue in its plastering job. Although it's difficult to determine the age of plaster itself, you can come up with an approximate date by examining the lath behind the plaster.

The earliest lath was hand-split with a hatchet, resulting in an irregular board that expanded like an accordion. Wet plaster pressed against the lath would ooze between the splits before hardening, forming a permanent "key," or attachment.

After the use of circular saws became widespread around 1830, split lath was still used in rural areas, but elsewhere the fastest, cheap-est way of producing lath became sawing boards into thin, regular strips. This process, distinguished by the regularity of the lath and the saw marks, remained standard into the twentieth century, when drywall began replacing plaster as the wall covering of choice.

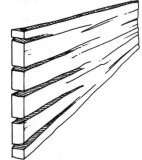

LEFT: *Hand-split lath was irregular, allowing the plaster to ooze between the splits before hardening.*

BELOW: *Sawn lath is characterized by its consistent size and shape and by saw marks.*

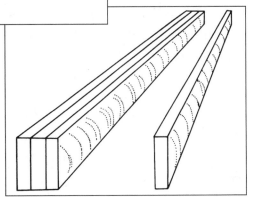

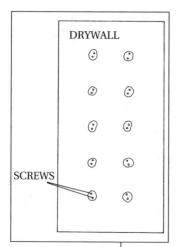

DRYWALL

SCREWS

Doubling up on drywall screws will add strength to your drywall job and cut down on the time it takes to cover the screws with drywall joint compound.

sound is the stud. (Locating studs this way takes some practice.)

Drywall Needs Careful Support

❏ Some people recommend placing drywall screws at intervals closer than every 16", but there's a catch-22: The more screws you use, the more support you'll get—and the more work you'll have to do to cover them. There is a way around this problem. Instead of placing screws closer together, get more support by staying with 16" intervals but using two screws instead of one at each spot. For every location at which you choose to anchor the board with one screw, add a second an inch or so away. You double the support but add hardly any labor or material for covering the screws. A potential pitfall in this technique is that if you do a clumsy job, it's easy to tear up the paper and crumble the board. So if you try this, be sure to do it carefully and cleanly.

Ceiling Work: Help from a Deadman

❏ When you're working overhead, drywall is heavy and awkward. But two people can hang drywall from a ceiling comfortably if they use a "deadman." Start with a board that's 6" x 3'. Nail the center of the board to the end of a 2 x 4 that is at least as high as the ceiling you are trying to reach, so that the 2 x 4 is perpendicular to the board. Trim the 2 x 4 so that the height of the deadman, when upright, exactly matches the height of the new ceiling. Next, have one person stand on a stepladder and hold one end of a piece of drywall in place. The other person should then position the deadman so that it elevates the other end of the drywall and holds it in place. Once the deadman is up, the second person is free to help the first screw the drywall in place.

A "deadman" helps hold drywall in place while you work on a ceiling.

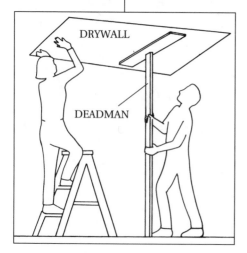

DRYWALL

DEADMAN

Ceiling Work: Going Solo

❏ If you prefer to work alone, you can rent a drywall jack, a device made expressly for hanging drywall on a ceiling. Center the sheet of drywall on the arms of the device and crank it almost to the ceiling. The jack is on casters, so you can move the sheet into position before you crank it all the way up and start screwing the drywall in place.

Joint Efforts

❏ To fill a joint between two sheets of drywall, use a 3"-wide putty knife to apply drywall joint compound in a strip all along the joint. Allow the compound to set slightly, but return to it while it is still plastic. Then, using the 3"-wide putty knife, press into the compound a fiber mesh tape that's made for this purpose. (Some people use paper tape, but the mesh tape is much easier to work with.) Go back over the whole thing to smooth off any compound that has come through the holes in the tape, creating as smooth and level a surface as possible.

After the joint has dried, apply a second coat of drywall joint compound with a 6"-wide finishing knife, so that the second coat overlaps the first by 2" or so on each side, creating a feather edge. (The objective is to obtain as smooth an application as possible with just the knife so that any final dressing is minimal.) Let this coat dry, then smooth the surface with medium-grit sandpaper.

Corner Beads Are Appropriate Accessories

❏ Use metal corner beads to form a protruding corner (on the end of a wall, for instance) that will look neat and withstand scrapes and blows. Corner beads are available anywhere drywall and drywall joint compound are sold—typically at hardware stores. Screw both edges through the drywall and into the corner studs. Apply drywall joint compound with a 9"-wide

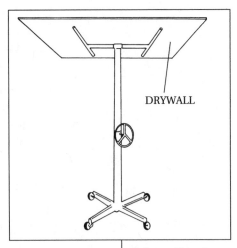

A drywall jack.

To fill a joint between two sheets of drywall, apply drywall joint compound, then fiber mesh tape and then an additional coat of drywall joint compound.

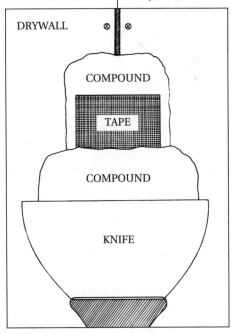

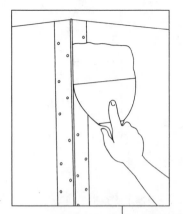

drywall knife to make a long, tapered joint extending about 8" from the corner bead out onto the drywall.

❑ The spongelike blocks with brown grit on the outside are also good for sanding drywall joint compound because they last a long time. Used wet, they also produce less dust than ordinary sandpaper.

❑ Be sure to wear a mask when sanding drywall joint compound—or anything else.

A metal corner bead provides a clean appearance and additional durability. Cover the corner bead with drywall joint compound.

BASIC WALL REPAIRS

Picture Perfect

❑ If you relocate a picture to a new wall, you can repair the old nail hole by putting spackling compound on a finger and forcing the filler into the hole. (On small jobs, spackling compound is easier to work with than drywall joint compound.) The spackling compound will harden, so you can paint over it. This is an easy way to repair any small defects in the surface of a wall or ceiling.

Patch Things Up

❑ When using patching plaster to fill large holes in old plaster, here's a way to make your work easier. Add about 1 tablespoon of white vinegar to every 2 quarts of plaster when you mix the plaster. The vinegar delays hardening, so you'll be able to smooth the patch more easily.

❑ You can repair large cracks and holes in plaster by stuffing wadded newspaper in them, then applying drywall joint compound over the surface.

❑ If you're confronted with drywall that has a hole no bigger than the size of your fist, you can repair it easily. Cover the hole with duct tape, then apply a layer or two of drywall joint compound over the tape.

SACKETT'S CHOICE

INVENTOR AUGUST SACKETT is commonly credited with having created modern drywall in 1902. His creation, a dense gypsum-and-paper sandwich board, has become the wall material of choice among modern builders and remodelers. (It's also called gypsum board, gyp-board, plasterboard, and Sheetrock.) Sold in 8', 12' and 16' sheets, drywall provides a fast, relatively inexpensive way to create a durable, flat wall surface. A special water-resistant (W/R) form of drywall is available for bathrooms and other high-moisture areas.

HANGING IN THERE

A VARIETY OF HARDWARE is available for hanging things on walls covered with plaster or drywall.

• The **standard picture hook** can bear a lot of weight. Two or more in combination can hold a picture weighing up to 100 pounds.

• A **nail or screw** driven through the drywall and into a stud is a simple and secure arrangement.

• If you need to drive a screw into drywall that doesn't fall on a stud, a **plastic sleeve** will hold light objects easily. Buy a sleeve designed to fit the size screw you intend to use. Drill a hole in the drywall just large enough for the sleeve and hammer it in. When you drive the screw into the sleeve, the sleeve will expand in the hole you drilled and hold tight in the wall.

A screw inserted into a plastic sleeve holds light objects in drywall without the support of a stud.

• A **toggle bolt** is a more heavy-duty option. Drill a hole in the drywall big enough to fit the "wings" of the toggle bolt when they are pinched down against the shaft of the bolt. Screw the bolt onto whatever you are trying to connect to the wall, then push the bolt into the

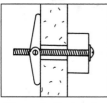

The nut of a toggle bolt has "wings" to provide additional support.

hole. Its wings will spread out again and hold against the back surface of the drywall once you have tightened it down.

• Another variation on this theme is the **molly bolt**. Drill a hole large enough for the bolt and drive the bolt in with a hammer so that its surface is snug against the drywall. Tighten the screw in the bolt so that the bolt's casing will expand behind the drywall and hold tight. Then remove the screw from the bolt, run it through whatever you are connecting to the wall, and tighten the screw in the bolt.

To install a molly bolt, first drill a hole (A) where you want the bolt to go. Drive the bolt in with a hammer (B), then tighten the screw in the bolt (C) to secure the bolt in the wall. Remove the screw, insert it through the object you are hanging, and tighten the screw (D).

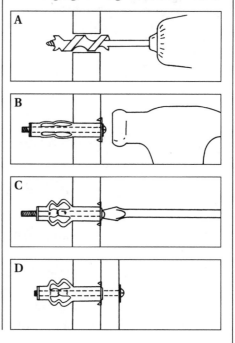

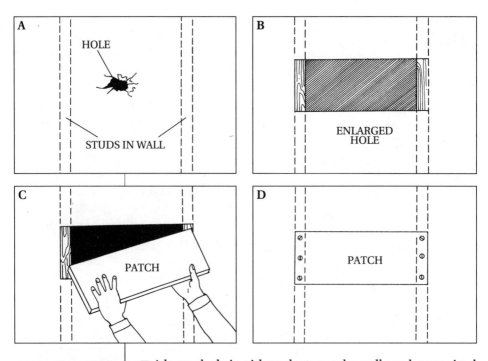

A	B
HOLE STUDS IN WALL	ENLARGED HOLE
C	D
PATCH	PATCH

To repair a sizable hole (A), first enlarge the hole into a rectangle that exposes two studs (B). Cut a patch to fit (C), then nail or screw it in place (D).

❏ A larger hole in either plaster or drywall can be repaired with a patch made out of drywall. To fasten the patch, you need to expose at least one stud in the wall—preferably two, to make the patch more secure. Using a utility knife, enlarge the existing hole until you reach a stud, then give the hole a rectangular shape. (If you're exposing two studs, this will make the hole at least 16" wide. Cutting the hole to a fairly regular shape makes it easier to cut a patch that fits.) Cut your drywall patch to match the shape of the enlarged hole. Use nails or drywall screws to fasten the drywall piece to the stud. Then fill the small space around the patch with drywall joint compound.

TONGUE-AND-GROOVE PANELING

See How It Stacks Up

❏ Before installing paneling, stack it in the room where it's to be used. Put boards between the layers of paneling to allow air to circulate. Leave the stack for at least 2 or 3 days—a week or more is better—to let the moisture in the paneling stabilize. This allows the paneling to shrink or expand to its final size *before* you install it. If you don't do this, you could be left with unsightly gaps if the paneling shrinks after installation, or fitting problems if it expands.

Keep the Shrinking from Showing

❑ Before putting up new tongue-and-groove paneling, decide how you want to stain it. Then stain the tongue of each board accordingly. Later, if a piece of paneling shrinks a little, the tongue that shows will be the same color as the rest of the paneling and thus will be less obvious.

Cut Paneling Down to Size

❑ After the paneling has been sitting for at least a couple of days, you can proceed with the installation. Measure the height of the room in several places. If the variation

PAINT YOUR WAGON

THE WORD *wainscot* literally means "wagon planking," which makes sense. If you're standing in a wagon, the wooden sides come up only so far—just like, well, wainscoting.

MAKE SURE YOUR PANEL FLOATS

THE DECORATIVE raised paneling found in colonial doors and walls appears to be constructed of solid wood, but the panels actually sit loosely in their frames. This construction allows them to move slightly as the frames contract and expand with the seasons and the varying moisture levels in the room, thus preventing panels from cracking.

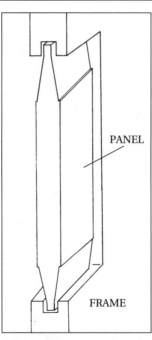

PANEL

FRAME

Decorative wood panels must fit loosely in their frames to allow the wood to expand and contract without cracking.

One of the biggest mistakes made in duplicating or recreating raised panels is focusing on the appearance and not the construction. The results are good for a time, but when the weather changes and the wood has no room to expand, the cracks start. To avoid this, construct the panel so it "floats" in its grooves (making sure the fit is not too tight). And don't glue the panel in place. When the humidity level in your house changes, you'll be glad you took the extra time.

is small enough that the ceiling molding will cover it, you can cut all the pieces of paneling to one length at the same time. If not, you'll have a more tedious job: cutting pieces individually to fit the different parts of the room.

BARN BOARDS

Allow a Little Rough Stuff in the House

❏ Clean old beams and barn boards thoroughly before you use them in your home. Scrub them with a stiff, dry wire brush (no water), then apply a coat of turpentine with a paintbrush. The turpentine acts as a preservative, and it's much less expensive than commercial equivalents. It will darken the wood somewhat until it soaks in, but eventually the wood will return to its original color.

Color Coordination

❏ If you're nailing up rough paneling such as barn boards, paint the wall behind it a color that approximately

The Resurrection of the Beat-up Beams

I ONCE DESIGNED A HOUSE for a couple who wanted a 26' living room—long enough to let them see the view in two different directions. To support that long a span, I needed three big beams. I remembered some old 10" x 12" beams that I'd used to move houses. They were pretty beat-up, but I thought of a simple way to clean them.

A Word from Earl

First I rented a floor sander. Then I laid the three beams side by side on some level ground and ran the sander up and down the three beams at once, as you would a floor. After I finished one side, I rolled all the beams to the next side. The sander didn't take all the dents out of the beams, but after I'd stained them, they looked properly "antique." You can use the same technique with smaller beams.

matches the paneling. Any gaps between the boards will be much less obvious.

❏ To make a good gray stain for decorative barn boards, combine 1 gallon of week-old coffee with 1 cup of salt. The salt makes the stain gray. If your week-old coffee grows mold, just skim the mold off the top before mixing your stain.

❏ You can also stain barn boards by wetting the area you want to color and rubbing in wood ashes until you get the shade you desire.

Perfect Protection

❏ You can protect barn boards or any other rough-finish paneling from the drying effects of a wood stove by applying a coat of satin finish urethane, sanding lightly and then applying a second coat of urethane.

❏ Another protective finish for barn boards is a mixture of equal parts boiled linseed oil and turpentine. Apply the mixture with a paintbrush.

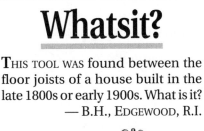

Whatsit?

THIS TOOL WAS found between the floor joists of a house built in the late 1800s or early 1900s. What is it?
— B.H., EDGEWOOD, R.I.

This is called a Lancashire tail vise, made in England for the watch, toy and jeweler's trades. To use it, you would hold the "tail" in your hand and put fine work in the jaws of the vise.

PREFINISHED PANELING

The Perfect Fit

❏ The first step in installing prefinished paneling is to place a piece against the wall and make sure it's plumb (absolutely straight up and down). If it isn't, you must scribe it to fit. To do that, hold the paneling with one side as close as possible to the corner of the wall but positioned so the panel is plumb. (You may need to lift a bottom corner to make the panel plumb; test for plumb with a level or plumb bob.)

Have a partner hold the paneling in position. Adjust the width of a scribing compass to the maximum width between the wall and the edge of the paneling. Then move the scribing compass along the edge of the wall. You want

Use a plumb bob to position your panel (left). Then scribe the panel (right) to fit the uneven corner.

the compass pencil to mark on the paneling a line that's parallel to the edge of the wall. When the line is done, remove the paneling from the wall and, with a coping saw or a power saber saw, cut the paneling along the line. If you install that piece of paneling first, then fit successive pieces to it, all the paneling will be straight and plumb.

❏ To cut holes in paneling for electrical switches and outlets, first cover the edges of the outlet with carpenter's chalk. Position your paneling as it will be mounted and strike it once with your palm in the general vicinity of the outlet. When you remove the paneling, you'll see the outline of the box on the back. Within that outline, drill a hole through the paneling to give yourself a starting place, then cut along the chalk outline with a saber saw.

The Application

❏ Prefinished plywood paneling in 4' x 7' or 4' x 8' sheets can be nailed or held in place with adhesive. Adhesive for paneling comes in tubes and is dispensed from a caulking gun.

Whatsit?

CAN YOU TELL ME what this implement is and its use? It's all wood with a metal tip on the plunger.
—R.W., PALOS VERDES ESTATES, CALIF.

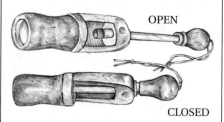

OPEN

CLOSED

This is a bottle cork depressor. First you soak the cork in water. Then you place this gizmo on the mouth of the bottle, raise the plunger and put the cork into the opening below the plunger. Jamming the plunger down compresses the cork enough so that it goes into the bottle easily and then expands to make a tight seal.

❑ Ideally, it's better to install sheets of paneling over a wall surface such as drywall rather than attach them directly to the studs. The existing wall gives rigidity to the paneling. At 12" intervals from floor to ceiling, apply horizontal lines of paneling adhesive to the back of the paneling, then mount the paneling. The adhesive will hold the paneling tight to the drywall, and you won't need to use any nails at all.

❑ If you decide to skip the drywall and use nails instead of adhesive, you'll need to nail through the grooves of the paneling and into the studs. If you start at a corner and measure 16" horizontally, you can generally count on hitting both a paneling groove and a stud. (In modern construction, studs are always placed 16" apart.)

❑ To nail paneling in place, start at the top and work down the wall and across the pieces, nailing every 6" along the edges. Then, working your way down the wall, nail through the grooves and along the studs so that the nails are about 12" apart (measuring vertically).

A Camouflage Operation

❑ After installing each piece of paneling, camouflage potential unsightly gaps with this trick: Using a wide felt-tip marker, draw a black line on the stud where the piece of paneling ends, following the edge of the piece. Even if the next piece doesn't fit quite tight to the previous one, the light color of the stud behind them will not show.

❑ If you prefer to nail your paneling in place instead of using adhesive, consider buying nails in the appropriate color to match your paneling. Nails in a wide range of colors are available anywhere prefinished paneling is sold and at most hardware stores.

NO KNOB IS AN OLD, OLD KNOB

EARLY DOORKNOBS in America were not really knobs but latches made of wood and, later, wrought iron. With the onset of the Industrial Revolution, new technologies made a wide variety of doorknobs readily available, from porcelain to cut glass to brass. Between 1870 and 1920, more than 2,500 different designs were produced.

Since door hardware was one of the easy things to modernize in a house, over the years many early homes were refitted with later-style knobs (many of which have become collectibles). If you're concerned with historical authenticity and you own a colonial or Greek Revival house, make sure your doors have latches, not knobs.

MOLDING

The One-Person Approach to Molding

❑ Working alone can be awkward when you're installing molding, trim or other long pieces of stock. To anchor one end of a piece of molding while you nail the other end in place, try this technique. First, tack a nail into a spot that will be covered by the molding. Loop a piece of string around one end of the molding and hang that loop on the nail to anchor the piece. Then you can work with the other end more easily.

WALLPAPER

Choices, Choices

❑ It's best to choose medium-weight wallpaper. Heavy paper will tear under its own weight while being installed in a room with a high ceiling. Lightweight paper tears more easily in general. Unfortunately, medium-weight paper, which is most popular, is usually more expensive than either of these two.

WALLPAPER: THE GREAT PRETENDER

A S SOON AS country people could afford wallpaper, they covered up their stenciling. And if stenciling and wall murals were often poor people's versions of wallpaper, wallpaper itself originally substituted for woven tapestry hangings found in the homes of European nobility prior to the seventeenth century.

Some wallpaper was produced here in the colonies by the mid-eighteenth century, but premier papers came from England, and the very best came from France. English paper stainers, as they were called, tended to favor monochromatic color schemes, especially in shades of blue, but French papers were known for their vivid colors. A favorite color scheme of French wallpapers used a background of greenish blue as a foil for vibrant oranges and metallic highlights produced by gold, silver or mica.

At first, wallpaper was hung with tacks; pasting came later. Borders made of separate pieces of paper have long been popular because they cover up ragged edges.

The Wallpaper Wouldn't Stay Stuck

ONCE WHEN I SHOWED UP to lay a new floor for a woman who was having her kitchen remodeled, I could see that she was in a bad mood when she met me at the door. As soon as we walked into the kitchen, I understood why. There were strips of wallpaper lying all over the floor. She told me that they had been falling off all night and that her paperhanger had papered the room only the day before. Apparently, the kitchen walls had been finished with enamel paint, so there was no surface to which the wallpaper paste could adhere. The room would have to be papered all over again with new paper, and she was planning to have it out with the paperhanger that morning.

A Word from Earl

I decided I'd better postpone my flooring job to another day.

If you're confronted with a problem like this, here's the solution: Sand the painted walls to kill the shine and provide a surface to which the paste will stick. Or wash the walls with a solution of TSP (or any other product containing trisodium phosphate) and warm water to reduce the gloss, then rinse and dry before applying the wallpaper.

❑ If you're a beginner, choose a small room or just one wall for your first wallpapering project. Avoid complex rooms such as bathrooms and kitchens until you build up some confidence.

Dye Lots Are Different

❑ Purchase enough rolls of wallpaper to complete the job the first time around, as colors can vary from one dye lot to another. Follow your shopkeeper's advice in determining the quantity you'll need. If you choose a large pattern or one that repeats infrequently, you'll need more wallpaper than if you choose a small pattern that repeats frequently.

❏ If you underestimate the amount of wallpaper you'll need and have to finish the job with paper that has a different run number, put the odd dye lot on a separate wall.

Before You Start

❏ Do not paper over existing wallpaper. Remove all the old material and make sure the surface is smooth before you begin applying the new covering. This will ensure a neat, professional-looking job.

❏ Before you begin to hang wallpaper, unroll the paper and inspect it for flaws. Reroll it with the back side out to relieve the curl and make it easier to handle later.

Historic Preservation

❏ When renovating an old house, you're likely to uncover layers of old wallpaper, sometimes dating back to the original. To preserve that record for future generations, pick a spot that won't be seen (behind a cupboard or in the cellar stairwell, for instance) and leave a small area that shows those successive peeled-back layers.

Hanging Wallpaper: The Execution

❏ Don't wait until you've finished the job to remove any excess wallpaper paste from the woodwork, ceiling or pa-

---

Four Hands Are Better Than Two

I'VE DONE A LOT OF WALLPAPERING by myself, but when two people work together, they can finish the job in less than half the time—and enjoy it a lot more.

I used to hang wallpaper with my brother. My job was to cut the wallpaper and apply the paste; his was to put up the paper and brush out the wrinkles. While he was applying one sheet, I'd drape the next over the top of an open door. That was where I had the advantage. If he wasn't paying attention, I'd get four or five sheets ahead of him before lunchtime. He'd have to hang those sheets before the paste dried—while I ate my lunch.

A Word from Earl

---

per itself. It's easier to do this while the paste is still wet. Also, you'll want to remove any excess paste before you gum up your brush with it.

❏ If you miss a bit of wallpaper paste, remove it with a wet rag after it has dried. (It will be tougher this way, but not impossible.)

❏ Bubbles sometimes appear when you're hanging wallpaper. Prick them with a pin and brush them out. If a bubble is thin and more than 1" long, you may need to slice it with a razor blade. You won't notice the cut when the paper is glued firmly to the wall.

Patchwork Makes Perfect

❏ Save wallpaper scraps for repairing stains or tears later. Make a patch by tearing (not cutting) a piece of the scrap slightly larger than the stain, then use wallpaper paste to apply it over the damaged area. Torn edges are thinner than cut ones, so a torn patch will fit tighter to the wall and blend in better.

CERAMIC TILES

Getting a Break

❏ If you're tiling only partway up a wall, it's easier to use only full tiles. If you have to fit your tiles in an exact space, use full tiles at the top and cut tiles at the base, where they'll be less conspicuous. Horizontally, you'll want to place cut tiles in the corners for the same reason.

❏ If you're going to be cutting a lot of tiles, rent a tile cutter from the store where you bought the tiles.

All Stuck Up

❏ Mastic is the adhesive used to install ceramic tiles. Use a toothed trowel to apply the mastic to the wall, covering an area no larger than you can tile in a few minutes. Place each tile about ¼" above where you want to position it and slide it down into place. Each tile has small bumpers on the sides. Position the tiles so that

Position partial wall tiles at floor level and in corners, where they will be less conspicuous.

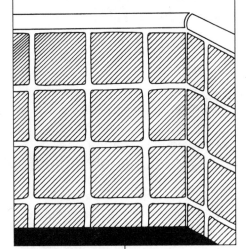

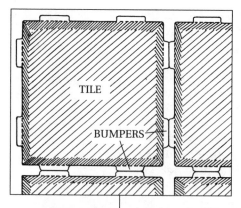

Bumpers on ceramic tiles keep spacing between them consistent.

the bumpers butt each other; that way the spacing between the tiles will be consistent.

❑ If you happen to get mastic on a tile surface, remove it right away before it dries. First, carefully scrape off as much residue as possible with a single-edge razor blade. Then, with paint thinner on a cloth, rub off the remaining mastic. Paint thinner is highly flammable, so after you're through using it to remove the mastic, let the cloth air out in the garage or outdoors until the paint thinner has evaporated. Then you can throw it away.

No-Grouse Grout

❑ To mix the grout that fills the cracks between ceramic tiles, put clean water in a pail and add the grout powder slowly, following the proportions given by the manufacturer and stirring in the powder until the mixture is the

LINCRUSTA ON YOUR WALLS: ODD BUT AUTHENTIC

E NGLISH ENTREPRENEUR Frederick Walton is responsible not only for giving us linoleum but also for inventing a thin, embossed linoleum offshoot called lincrusta. First manufactured in this country in 1883, lincrusta was a machine-made wall covering that could incorporate intricate patterns and imitations of other materials (the latter being a highly regarded Victorian trend).

In the American West, where wood was expensive, wainscoting-like lincrusta became the wall covering of choice. Middle-class homeowners everywhere delighted in the imitation of lavish, hand-tooled cordovan leather—a longtime hallmark of the wealthy. Hospital administrators chose the material to decorate the walls of their wards. Hygiene was just then coming into vogue, and lincrusta—impervious and washable—was billed as the sanitary choice. Also, as the advertisements truthfully claimed, it wouldn't warp, rot, fade or "be eaten by worms or white ants."

If you have this type of wall covering in your house, think twice about replacing it. It may be more historical than you think.

consistency of heavy cream. Grout powder is available from hardware stores.

❏ After applying grout with a trowel or putty knife, let it set up for 15 minutes before striking the joints (packing the grout in). Otherwise, you're likely to pull grout out of the joints.

❏ To strike the joints, run the narrow edge of an old toothbrush handle along them, pressing firmly. If necessary, apply more grout and strike the joints again. The idea is to pack as much grout in as possible.

❏ After striking the joints, use a damp sponge (almost dry) to smooth the grout into the joints and remove any excess grout from the tiles.

❏ Excess grout can also be removed with an old rubber spatula or squeegee. Just run the tool over the surface of the tiles.

❏ When you finish applying grout and striking the joints, let the project dry overnight. In the morning, you'll find a slight film remaining; you can remove this with a clean, dry cloth.

Replacement Tile: Chip Off the Old Block

❏ To replace a cracked tile, start by using a masonry or carbide-tip bit to drill a hole (any size) in the center of the damaged tile. With a glass cutter, score the tile diagonally from each corner to the center hole. Then, using a hammer and a cold chisel, chip away pieces of the tile, starting at the center and working out to the edges.

❏ Sometimes when you're replacing a wall tile, it will slide out of position before the glue dries. If you expect that this may be a problem, you can prevent it by putting small shims—wooden matchsticks or toothpicks—in the space under the tile to support it. Leave the tile like that overnight or until the mastic dries. Then you can regrout around it.

To remove a damaged tile, first drill and score it, then chip out the pieces.

SCORE LINES

GOTCHA!

THE VICTORIAN AGE was a great one for imitation. Inside the house, a variety of deceptive decorating techniques became popular, all designed to fool the eye. Popular *trompe l'oeil* (deceive the eye) finishes included marbling and wood graining—painted-on surfaces that imitated richer, more expensive materials.

There's been a resurgence of these decorating styles in recent years, so if you're redecorating a floor or wall, you might consider deceiving someone's eye. You can find the names of people who do this work by looking in the yellow pages under Interior Decorators and calling those folks for recommendations. Also ask local antiques shops, museums and home furnishing centers for recommendations.

Cut your stencil out of manila folder material (A). When you paint over the stencil (B), the design will show on the wall (C).

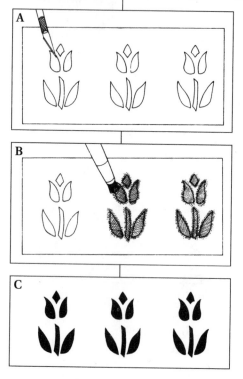

DECORATING TECHNIQUES

One-Step Plaster and Painting

❑ Not many people mix their own plaster these days, but if you're hiring a plasterer, an easy way to color a room without painting it is to have the plasterer add a little lime-fast colored cement powder (available from hardware stores) to the plaster. This is faster and easier than painting, and the effect will last a long time on low-use areas such as ceilings. The technique is good for walls, too. Tinting doesn't create a washable surface, though, so fingerprints and other stray marks will eventually have to be painted over.

Stencils: A Traditional Treatment

❑ Stenciling is an inexpensive, attractive, traditional way to decorate walls and floors. It's easy to create your own patterns. Work on scratch paper until you have a geometric or decorative design you like. The goal is to create a short series of fairly simple design elements that you can repeat along the edges of the wall or floor. Once you're satisfied with your design, use a pencil to copy it onto manila folder material, then cut it out with an X-Acto knife. Your stencil works just like the store-bought stencils you used as a child; the color of the design goes in the cutouts. Cover your pattern with boiled linseed oil and let it dry. Then varnish it to keep the paint from soaking in when you dab it over the stencil.

❏ For bigger stenciling jobs, cut your pattern from oak tag (available from art supply stores) instead of manila folder material. The oak tag is stiffer and will hold up better.

❏ If you're in a hurry when you're creating a stencil, you can coat the stencil with shellac instead of boiled linseed oil. Shellac is faster to use, but it won't last as long. (This technique is not appropriate in the unlikely event that you're stenciling with an alcohol-based paint.)

CEILINGS

When Paint and Plaster Part Company
❏ Early plaster ceilings were typically covered with whitewash—lime mixed with water. Later, calcimine was used.

CUT IT OUT!

STENCILING, the practice of painting over a cutout pattern, has been a popular decorating technique since colonial times. The earliest stenciled walls were probably only border designs that complemented the architectural detail of the room by outlining the woodwork. A little later, stencilers designed patterns that used vases of flowers, weeping willows, pairs of birds or, more rarely, the spread eagle, symbol of the young nation. It was probably in the first decade of the nineteenth century that overall stencil patterns were developed to imitate the imported French wallpapers that were beyond the reach of all but the wealthiest people.

Today you can find stenciling patterns in many magazines and pattern books. If you're choosing a stencil pattern for your house, don't be bound by tradition. Early homeowners looked to plenty of other places for inspiration: details in their woodwork or wallpaper, ornamental plants outside the home, the whimsy of imagination. You can turn to those same sources today to create patterns that are uniquely yours.

Layers of whitewash and calcimine usually aren't a problem (they can be removed with a vinegar solution), but if the layers become thick enough, they may start separating from the plaster. The only way to solve this problem is to strip the layers back down to the plaster. A single-edge razor blade is good for this.

❏ You can loosen any stubborn areas of old whitewash and calcimine on plaster with heat, which causes the whitewash-calcimine combination to expand faster than the plaster, breaking the bond between them. The type of electric heater normally used for stripping paint will do the job.

Maintaining the Suspense

❏ Consider installing a suspended ceiling in your basement. Although it will reduce precious headroom, a suspended ceiling is a great way to hide all the wires, joists and pipes and at the same time brighten the room considerably. Install lights flush with the ceiling or as panels

THOSE EARLY AMERICANS WERE EASILY UNHINGED

THE EARLIEST door hinges in America were large strap hinges made of leather, wood or iron. Many people treasure the aesthetics of those old hinges, but one advantage goes beyond how they look. The butt ends of the straps are curled into an eye that is hung over iron pegs (called pintles) attached to the doorjamb.

Strap hinge.

Thus the door can be easily removed simply by lifting the eyes over the tops of the pegs. (Removing doors with later H hinges is more complicated.)

Strap hinges are still a good choice today, especially for hanging large, heavy doors. Antiques shops often carry the old, handmade wrought-iron straps, but you can also find serviceable, less expensive machine-made hinges at hardware stores. Most original leather and wooden hinges have not survived.

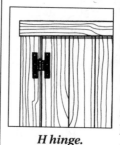

H hinge.

When the Plaster Came Tumbling Down

I**N THE OLD DAYS**, when trucks were new on the scene, just the impact of a truck hitting a pothole outside your house could knock a plaster ceiling loose. Whenever a ceiling came down in the local school, the officials would call my father to repair it because he could do it in one night. I was working for my father then, and we used to replace plaster ceilings with tin ones. We'd all work on one 4' x 8' platform that brought us within reach of the ceiling. My father and another man would install 2' x 4' sections of tin while I tried to paint the sections they had just put up before they advanced the staging. Many times we worked all night to get the job done.

A Word from Earl

It's still true that you shouldn't bother trying to replaster an old ceiling when it collapses. The easiest thing to do these days is to hang drywall instead.

in the ceiling. Should you need access to wires or pipes, you can simply remove the appropriate panels. Hanging a suspended ceiling isn't difficult. You can purchase all the necessary materials at a lumberyard.

❏ When you're cutting ceiling panels, a small bench saw will make the cleanest cuts. However, a utility knife is usually handier and will create less dust than a saw.

❏ Before you handle ceiling panels, wash your hands and dust them with talcum powder. This will prevent you from leaving fingerprints on the panels.

❏ To deal with marks on ceiling panels, try erasing them with an art gum eraser or hiding them with white chalk. (This works for ceiling tiles, too.) The chalk is also a good way to disguise a nick or dent in the panels.

Floors

THE LARGEST FLOOR I ever laid was in a shoe factory. The whole job had to be done between Saturday morning and Sunday noon, leaving time for the maintenance crew to reinstall the machinery before Monday morning.

I had two men bring the bundles of flooring up the elevator from the first floor and place them along the area where we would be working. A helper and I placed the flooring strips in position, driving them up tight to each other. Finally, two more men nailed the strips into place, speeding up the process by using special air-powered nail guns.

We worked 13 hours with breaks only for lunch and dinner, then another 13 hours to finish the floor about noon on Sunday. It was hard, constant work, and from time to time I glanced at a young man I had hired only a few days earlier. He insisted on using one of the nail guns the whole time, and soon the sweat was running in a stream off his forehead. But he wouldn't quit, and he wouldn't trade off for an easier job. He stuck with that nail gun until we were done.

After that one, most flooring jobs have seemed relatively easy to me and I'm sure that young man feels the same way. I've also found some ways to make the work easier.

This chapter gets into some of those techniques, both for installing floors and for maintaining and cleaning them once they're in place. Tips are included for refinishing hardwood floors, fixing squeaky floorboards and patching linoleum. There are plenty of hints for dealing with other kinds of flooring, too—including marble, slate, quarry tiles and concrete. And you'll find ideas for keeping scatter rugs from slipping and for making carpet runners last longer.

Also within this chapter, a whole section on carpets tells how to get rid of stains ranging from blood to bubble gum and from oil to orange juice. This section is fairly extensive so as to give you a lot of alternatives. You usually want to be able to treat stains with materials that you already have on hand. Besides, stain removal is always a trial-and-error process because two stains are rarely alike. So try one of these options and, if it doesn't work the first time, either repeat it or try another alternative. No matter what problems you have with your floors, you'll find some good solutions here.

IF YOU CAN'T FIND IT ...

... maybe you need to try another chapter. Check the index, or try these possibilities.

For Tips On ...	See the Chapters ...
Lumber	The Home Workshop
Nails	The Home Workshop
Sandpaper	The Home Workshop
Stains and finishes	Painting Inside and Out; Furniture

GENERALLY SPEAKING

Floors Are Last

❏ No matter where you're working, everything that's dropped or spilled ends up on the floor, and the constant moving of heavy saws and ladders can ding the floor, too. To minimize these kinds of damage in new construction or remodeling, don't install the floor until virtually everything else is done except painting the baseboards. Once the floor is down, be sure to use a protective covering until the work is complete.

INSTALLING WOOD FLOORS

Wooden Matches

❏ Matching the color of old, unpainted floorboards is tricky. One approach is to use the same species of wood as the original, then leave the new wood unfinished. It will stand out for a while, but over time it will darken to match the old boards around it.

❏ If you're restoring an old house in which the original floorboards were replaced at some point, the flooring in the attic might be the perfect material for bringing back the old wide-board look. You may well find that those boards were laid at the same time as the original floors downstairs, and since they've received little use over the years, they're likely to have a lot of life left in them.

❏ Before you put down a rug over part of a new pine floor, remember that sunlight will gradually darken the wood a few shades. A rug will mask the floor beneath it and create a light spot, like the spot underneath a picture on a wall. For an even tone, leave your new floors bare for a while, at least in

USE IT UP, WEAR IT OUT— OR TURN IT OVER

I N FRUGAL HOUSEHOLDS of earlier days, worn floorboards would often be pulled up and flipped over, adding a few more years to the floor's life. (You can confirm this today if you look up from the basement of an old house and find paint, whitewash or a worn surface on the underside of the floorboards.) Eventually, though, the boards themselves became too thin. Then they were either covered over with a new floor or swapped with the less-used floorboards in the attic. Sometimes, too, even the most frugal householders gave in and actually discarded the old floorboards altogether—or at least used them for some other purpose.

The Aborted Cover-up

A Word from Earl

I N 1970, A WOMAN HIRED ME to convert a 100-year-old barn into a weekend home. The barn was in tough shape—filled with rubbish, missing some of the barn boards and generally pretty far gone. After rebuilding the walls and roof, I started in on the floor. It was a wreck. Some of the floorboards were gone, and so were the old trapdoors. My plan was to patch the existing floor with old floorboards I'd salvaged from another building, then lay a new finish floor on top.

Once I'd given the floor a good cleaning and begun work, I changed my mind. I discovered that the wide pine planks were fastened to the joists with square wooden pegs. When I sanded the surface with a machine sander, the grain of the wood came through beautifully, and the detail of the pegs really stood out. When I was done applying three coats of varnish, the floor looked better than any new floor.

If you're fixing up an old house, be sure to look for the beauty underneath all the dust and dirt. First find out what you have, *then* decide if you want to cover it up.

summer. The room will be cooler, too, because you'll get the benefit of drafts that would otherwise be blocked by carpeting.

Joist Perfect

❏ Try to avoid using floor joists that have knots in them. Knots reduce the strength of the wood. If you must use a joist with a knot in it, position the knot at the top of the joist, where its weakness will be minimized.

Subflooring: A Little Undercover Work

❏ Never lay a finish floor directly on the floor joists. If you do, you'll lose both strength and beauty. A subfloor, which can be either plywood or planking, adds rigidity and eliminates the possibility of unsightly gaps showing in the finish floor.

INSTALLING WOOD FLOORS

FLOORS

❏ Board subflooring is best installed diagonally. Diagonal flooring makes your house more rigid, and you can nail a finish floor on top of it in either direction.

Hardwood: Laying It On

❏ Before laying hardwood flooring, you should unbundle it and leave it for 2 to 3 days in the room where it's going to be used. The temperature and moisture levels in the room will cause the flooring to shrink or expand before it's nailed into place.

❏ Aesthetically, wood flooring looks best when it's laid running parallel to the long dimension of a room. From a practical point of view, if you're working with a plywood subfloor, the finish floor can be laid either way, but it makes for a stronger floor if it's laid with the strips running perpendicular to the joists that support the floor.

Watch Your Step

IN THE LATE '60S, I WAS HELPING a do-it-yourselfer restore his colonial home. The wide pine floor in his living room was worn and split in many places, so he decided to pull up the existing floorboards, nail the good ones back down and replace the damaged ones with boards from other rooms.

I warned the man to be careful where he stepped on his subfloor, but he couldn't have taken my advice too seriously. When I went back to his house a week later, there were two holes in the living room floor. "That's where I went through," he said sheepishly as he pointed, "and that's where my wife went through."

A Word from Earl

If you're working on a colonial floor, remember that subfloors in those days were usually made of boards only ½" thick. When you're working on them, always step on the subfloor only where your weight will be supported by the floor joists.

When the Walls Are Irregular

❏ When laying a floor, start along the most irregular wall. It's easier to cut for that wall before laying floorboards that close you in.

❏ When installing floorboards next to a fireplace, use a scribe to fit the boards precisely. Rough-cut the boards first, then lay them so they're perpendicular to the edge of the fireplace hearth. Set the scribe to equal the widest gap between the hearth and the boards. Holding a pencil to the scribing compass, slowly trace a line on the floorboards that's parallel to the edge of the fireplace. Keep the scribing compass at a 90-degree angle to the plane of the wall. (This technique works for any other irregular feature, too.)

❏ Another way to install floorboards around an irregular feature is to work with a cardboard profile of the feature. In this case, instead of scribing directly on the floorboards, scribe your line on a piece of cardboard, then use the cardboard as a pattern for sawing the ends of the boards.

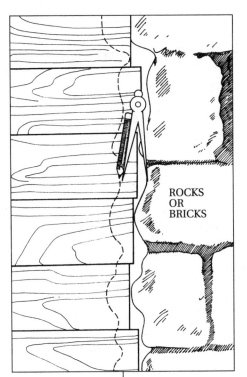

ROCKS OR BRICKS

Scribe floorboards to fit tightly around a hearth.

Keep It Straight

❏ Take some time to lay your first strip of finish flooring absolutely straight. This step is critical; if you get the first board straight, the rest of the boards will go down much more easily.

To do the job right, remove the baseboard from the wall. Don't trust the edge of the wall to be perfectly straight. Instead, measure out from the wall just a little more than one board's width. Snap a chalk line at that point.

Position the first piece of finish flooring between the wall and the chalk line, flush to the line. Nail it in place. Now replace the baseboard. If

IT'S NOT A TRAP— REALLY!

I T'S OFTEN SAID that a series of adjoining floorboards whose ends line up over a single joist are evidence of an old trapdoor. It's not likely. Only in recent years has it become fashionable to stagger the end joints of boards too short to cross a room. In the old days, it was the custom to line up all the ends, forming what was called a beaking joint.

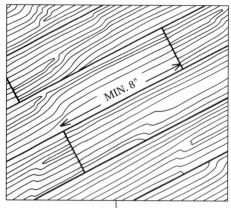

Make sure that the end joints of your floor strips are staggered.

the baseboard doesn't conceal any irregularities between the flooring and the wall, you'll need to scribe another floorboard to fit snugly between the first board and the wall.

Placement Is Important

❑ A strip floor is made up of strips of wood—usually oak, maple or hard pine—roughly 3" wide, laid tongue-and-groove fashion. Strip floors look best and maintain more rigidity if the end joint of each piece of finish flooring is at least 8" from the end joints of adjacent strips.

Get the Strength, Keep the Beauty

❑ Always nail finish flooring at an angle through the tongue and into the subfloor. This is the only place you can nail the floorboard without marring its surface or damaging its tongue. Set the nail head so that the tongue will fit properly into the groove of the next board. Placing nails every foot or so will make your floor rigid.

❑ To avoid denting the floorboards as you fit them into place, carry with you a scrap piece of flooring that's about 2" long. Insert the groove of the scrap piece into the tongue of the strip on which you're working. Hit your hammer on this scrap piece instead of the good flooring. This will let you drive the flooring tight without denting it.

❑ The easiest and most effective way to set nail heads below the surface of flooring is to use a nail set—a short, pointed punch made of metal and available from hardware stores. Lay the nail set *on its side* along the tongue of the strip. Position it so the nail head is in the middle of the nail set, then

ROUGH, TOUGH AND JUST FINE, THANK YOU

IN DECIDING WHAT wood to buy for flooring, remember that the more "finished" the wood, the more expensive it will be. For reasons of cost and convenience, plywood has become the subflooring material of choice for most of today's builders. Boards used for subfloors are usually rough, random-width hemlock or spruce without edging (lapping or grooving) or dressing (planing); those are the cheapest strong boards you'll find at the mill. Because the subfloor will be covered, it doesn't matter whether the joints are lapped or grooved or that the surface is rough. Strength, not appearance, is what's important.

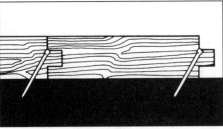
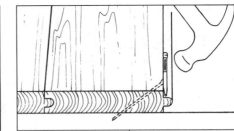

pound the nail set with your hammer. The blow will simultaneously tighten the piece of flooring against the others and set the nail below the surface of the wood.

Wood over Concrete: Prepare Yourself

❏ Strip flooring can be laid over concrete if you prepare the surface first. You'll need 3' lengths of 2 x 4s, called screeds, to nail the finish flooring into. The screeds must be pressure-treated lumber so that if any moisture comes up through the floor, it won't rot the screeds. You'll also

Nail tongue-and-groove flooring at an angle through the tongue and into the subfloor. Set nail heads easily by laying the nail set on its side and hammering.

The Saliva Solution

M Y FATHER TAUGHT ME what to do when you miss with your hammer and accidentally put a dent in the floor you're laying. Just put some saliva on your fingertip and place it on the dimple. Later put some more on. Keep it up until the wood has swelled back into place. For some reason, saliva works a lot better than water.

I always figured that people didn't want to see me spitting on the new floors I was installing for them, so I used to cover my spit with a scrap piece of flooring until the dent disappeared. My father, however, confident in the knowledge that he was doing what was best, would never hide it. He'd just

A Word from Earl

throw a little sawdust on the spit to make sure no one slipped. A customer of his once observed with a smile that my father wouldn't have been able to lay a floor at all if he hadn't had some spit and sawdust.

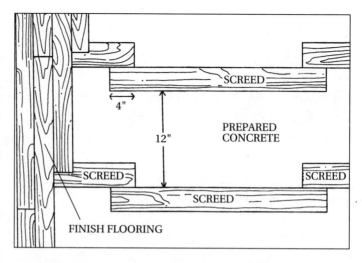

When you install a wood floor over concrete, each strip of flooring rests on two screeds. Position the screeds so that the rows are approximately 12" apart and each screed overlaps the one beside it by at least 4".

SCREED

4"

PREPARED
CONCRETE

12"

SCREED

SCREED

SCREED

SCREED

FINISH FLOORING

need asphalt primer and asphalt mastic, both of which are available from hardware stores.

To prepare a concrete floor before installing wooden flooring over it, apply a coat of asphalt primer to the concrete with an old paintbrush or a trowel. Follow the instructions on the can.

When the primer is dry, use a trowel to apply asphalt mastic (made for this purpose) to the concrete. Place the mastic where the screeds will lie. Stagger the screeds on top of the mastic in rows, about 12" apart, perpendicular to the direction in which you want to lay your finish flooring. Embed each screed in the mastic with the 4" side down; overlap the ends by about 4" (see illustration). Now lay the finish flooring, making sure that the weight of each strip is borne by at least two screeds. Sand and finish as desired.

❑ If you're installing strip flooring over a concrete basement floor that has no vapor barrier underneath it, you may want to provide a vapor barrier to keep moisture out of your cellar. In this case, your screeds could be two sets of 1 x 4s stacked on top of each other, with a vapor barrier such as 4-mil poly-

WHAT'S A LITTLE ROT AMONG FRIENDS?

WHEN INSPECTING the joists beneath the floors of an old house, keep in mind that pre-Victorian houses were built with hand-hewn or hand-sawn timbers that were almost always more substantial than the lighter, mass-produced boards common from the mid-1800s on. Insects or moisture may have caused rot on the surface of those joists, but there's likely to be plenty of good wood holding up your floors—and no need to replace it. Even if your penknife sinks a good 2" into the joist, if the full joist measures 6" x 6", you still have more solid wood left than many new houses start out with today.

STAIRCASE ARITHMETIC

WHEN PLANNING a staircase, keep these points in mind:
• A comfortable staircase has a riser that is no higher than 7½" and a tread no narrower than 9". A common tread width today is 11½".
• The higher the risers, the narrower the treads. The sum of two risers plus one tread should be 25" to 27".
• You'll need to plan on one more riser than tread.
• The bottom riser must be narrower than the others by the thickness of a tread.
• The top of the stringer must meet the landing in such a way that the distance from the top tread to the floor of the landing is the same height as the riser.

---

ethylene (plastic sheeting) sandwiched between the two layers of screeds.

STAIRS

Step-by-Step Instructions for Staircase Building

❏ The sequence of stair assembly is this: First, put up the stringers. Second, nail on the risers. Third, put on the skirtboards—the baseboards, cut to fit the stair steps—tight against the risers. Finally, put on the treads, starting at the bottom so you can reach behind the risers and nail them to the treads as you work your way up the stairs.

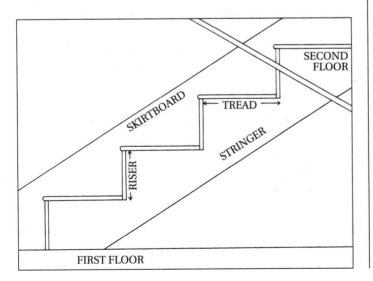

SECOND FLOOR

SKIRTBOARD

← TREAD →

STRINGER

RISER

FIRST FLOOR

When building a staircase, install the stringers, risers, skirtboards and treads—in that order.

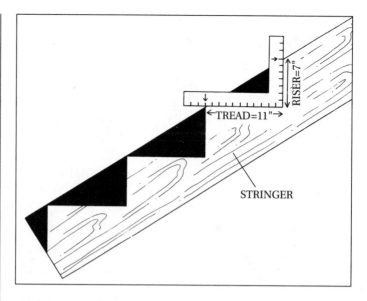

❏ It's not hard to mark the stringer (the support to which the risers and treads are nailed) for your staircase once you've determined the dimensions of your risers and treads. Use a framing square, which has inches marked on it. Lay the square on the board for the stringer, positioning the square according to the riser and tread dimensions. Mark the cuts you'll need to make, then slide your framing square to the next position, keeping the riser and tread dimensions at its edge. Repeat the process until you've marked the full length of the stringer.

❏ If you want additional support for your staircase, nail the triangles of wood you cut out of the stringer to a 2 x 4 to form a center stringer.

Save the Treads for Last

❏ When you're building a house, standard procedure should be to tack scrap boards onto the staircase for treads until the rest of the house is finished and the floors laid. Then the staircase can be finished properly. This avoids unnecessary wear and tear on the final treads.

Whatsit?

WE HAVEN'T BEEN able to figure out what this tool was used for. Can you tell us? The prongs are about 16" long and flexible. The handle is 5¼" long.
— D.R., CAMP HILL, PA.
This is a cheese curd whipper, made around 1880. It was used to help break up the curd to release the whey, which was finally expelled when the cheese felt the pressure of the press.

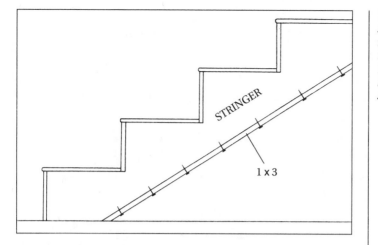

To shore up a staircase with too much bounce in the steps, nail a 1 x 3 into the bottom of each stringer.

Too Much Spring in Your Step

❏ If your basement stairs tend to spring up and down when you walk on them, you can reinforce them by nailing 1" x 3" strips of wood along the bottom edges (not the side) of the stringers. Stagger the nails about 1' apart to avoid splitting the strips.

FINISHING WOOD FLOORS

Get Down to Bare Wood

❏ If you don't want to sand an old floor, you can use paint remover and steel wool to strip it by hand. This is a lot of work, but hand-stripping is a preferred method for people who want to retain the most natural appearance of an old floor. Before undertaking this, cover up; it's a good idea to wear rubber gloves and a long-sleeved shirt. Use an old paintbrush to apply water-soluble paint remover to a small section of the floor at a time. (Don't apply the remover to an area greater than what you can reach.) Let it sit for 10 to 15 minutes, then rub the floor with coarse steel wool. Be sure to test the stripping product on an inconspicuous spot to make sure it doesn't have any adverse effects.

❏ Always do your hand-stripping in a season when you can leave the windows open for plenty of ventilation. Maximum ventilation is very important for both health and safety reasons.

The Case of the Missing Fingernails

A WOMAN ONCE WANTED me to strip her hall floors to bare wood and refinish them with clear varnish. It was the toughest stripping job I've ever done.

She wouldn't allow me to use a scraper or a sander because she didn't want to risk damaging the floors in any way. So I had to remove the finish with chemical varnish remover. The job was especially tricky because the floorboards ran sideways in the narrow hallways, and I had to be careful not to spatter any stripper on the baseboards.

A Word from Earl

In the end, the chemical stripper removed the finish all right, but it also took off my fingernails. (Lye was a primary ingredient in old chemical strippers.) The steel wool I used in combination with the stripper wore through any gloves I put on.

Today steel wool is still tough on your skin, but at least you can use it with water-soluble strippers. When you're shopping for a chemical stripper, read the label carefully and be sure to choose a water-soluble type. It will save the environment *and* your fingernails—although it's still advisable to wear gloves.

❏ You can strip some finishes off old floors with a solution of 1 cup of TSP (or any other product containing trisodium phosphate) mixed with 2 gallons of boiling water. Apply the solution with a mop and let it soak in for 20 minutes. Then wipe it up with rags. (There's no need to rinse.)

A Bleach Job

❏ Often an old floor that's stained can be bleached to a natural color with liquid household (5 percent) bleach. (Stains are unpredictable, so test the bleach on an inconspicuous area first to be sure you don't get an adverse reaction.) Remove the finish as described above, mop on the bleach and let it stand for 5 minutes. Then mop it up with water. Let the floor dry for several days. Smooth out "hairs" (slightly raised grain) with extra-fine steel wool or fine sandpaper, then vacuum to pick up the dust.

After You Strip

❑ To finish a hand-stripped floor, burnish it with superfine steel wool and leave it at that. Or sand it with very fine sandpaper, vacuum up the dust and apply whatever finish you prefer.

True Grit: Sanding Your Floors

❑ If you don't want to go to all the work of hand-stripping an old floor, you can sand it instead. Using a power sander is the easiest approach. Before you use a power sander, check the entire floor for protruding nail heads. If you find any, use a hammer and nail set to set the nails below the surface. If you don't, the sander will grind the heads off the nails. The nails will then be more obvious than ever. Setting the nails also reduces the risk of tearing the sandpaper, which is expensive.

❑ In power sanding, the first pass always should be made with coarse paper, holding the sander at a 45° angle to the direction of the boards. This levels the floor. The second pass should be with medium-grade sandpaper, again at a 45° angle. The third and final pass should be with fine sandpaper and with the grain of the wood; this will remove any scratches from the 45° passes.

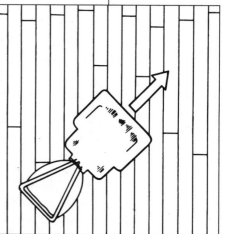

❑ You can't reach some places—such as corners, thresholds and the areas under radiators—with a power sander. Use a sharp paint scraper to remove the old finish in these areas, then sand by hand with 100-grit sandpaper.

❑ When sanding by hand, always sand with the grain of the wood, especially when using coarse sandpaper. Otherwise, you'll scratch or mar the surface.

The first two passes with a power floor sander should be at a 45° angle to the strips, as shown. The third and final pass should be with the grain.

The Chamber Pot That Left Its Mark

A Word from Earl

I WAS HELPING REMODEL an old house for some new owners, and they wanted the old oak floors, which were very dark, cleaned up. We started sanding in the bedroom, and the floor was coming out nicely until we began working on the section that had been under the bed. In six or eight places where the chamber pot had been left, there was a blue-black stain. Water stains in oak are very noticeable and penetrate deep into the wood. There's no way to get them out.

We had the whole room sanded when the owners saw the stains. When I explained that the old stains couldn't be removed, they said, "Stain it dark again."

Sometimes the most important part of refinishing is knowing when you're licked.

❏ Always feather the edges of the area you are sanding—gradually using a lighter touch toward the edges—to soften or eliminate any line between sanded and unsanded parts of the floor.

❏ Think twice before you sand softwood floors yourself. A beginner is likely to gouge the wood with the sander. If you're not sure of your abilities, it's better to hire a pro.

The Final Touch: Penetrating Finishes

❏ You may want to consider a penetrating finish (a wax or oil) for your floor. Unlike varnish, lacquer and shellac, a penetrating finish sinks down into the wood. It's clear, relatively easy to apply and resists alcohol, water, heat and scratching.

❏ If you decide to use a penetrating finish, be careful about choosing the color. These materials generally dry darker than you think they will. It's a good idea to test any finish on a scrap piece of wood or an inconspicuous area to be sure you're getting the color you want.

❏ If you want to be authentic, copy the technique of the old-timers. Those folks routinely finished their floors with boiled linseed oil, following instructions that sound like a nursery rhyme: Put it on once a day for a week, then once a week for a month, then once a month for a year, then once a year for the rest of your life.

❏ If you prefer, you can use tung oil, following the same instructions as for boiled linseed oil. Or use anything labeled "penetrating resin finish." These finishes are more work to maintain than polyurethane, but some people like them better.

❏ Before applying any penetrating finish, thoroughly clean the floor. Then pour the finish on the floor or sop it on with a rag. Keep the floor wet for about half an hour, then wipe off *all* the liquid that remains on the surface. Before this first coat has dried completely (within about 3 hours), sop on another coat and repeat the process.

Polyurethane: Tough Stuff

❏ Polyurethane is a tough, natural-looking finish for wood floors. As with any finish, you should prepare the floor by cleaning off all dirt and dust. Then apply the polyurethane

HISTORIANS STRIP LIGHTLY

WHEN YOU'RE restoring an old house or researching its history, you'll find that old floors often hold many secrets—if you know how to read the clues. In bedrooms, for instance, wear marks below the paint can help you determine traffic patterns or the location of an earlier owner's bed. Burn marks on a floor might indicate the presence of a bricked-over fireplace. Closet floors and the areas beneath baseboards or cupboards often show what the floor was like before it was painted or covered with linoleum. And removing layers of paint one at a time can show the "paint history" of the floor, sometimes even revealing stenciled patterns.

Most of these bits of history will be lost if you use a heavy-duty sanding machine with coarse sandpaper. If you're interested in the history of your home, you'll want to use gentler stripping methods, even though they take more time.

THE FINISH LINE

INTERIOR FINISHES come in two broad categories: penetrating and surface. Penetrating finishes, which can be either dull or satin (shinier), include waxes and oils. Waxes remain very light in color over a long period of time. They are popular for light-colored paneling and other woodwork. But waxes—especially spray waxes—will build up if you apply too many thick coats.

Oil finishes are usually derived from tung or linseed oil. They're easy to apply (wipe them on with a rag, then wipe off the excess), give long-lasting protection and add tone to unstained wood. Boiled linseed oil has major drawbacks, however; it darkens with age and offers little resistance to alcohol, water or mildew.

The three kinds of surface finishes are varnish (including polyurethane), lacquer and shellac. Of these, varnish is the most widely used among homeowners. It's durable, easy to clean and easy to apply, and it won't change color over time. Surface finishes are normally gloss or semigloss—the choice is one of strictly personal preference.

with a brush or roller. Wait until the first coat is dry (in moist or cold conditions, this can take a full 24 hours), then sand it by hand with 220-grit sandpaper. Vacuum up the dust. Repeat this process for a second coat, then put on a third and final coat. Don't sand after the last coat.

❏ As a rule, high-gloss floor finishes are tougher and harder than those that have a satin sheen or low luster, and they tend to repel water better. But they will show scratches if people walk on them with dirty or sandy shoes, and the scratches will be more noticeable than in a satin finish. If you prefer the appearance of a satin finish but are worried about how it will hold up to normal foot traffic, try this: Put down two coats of glossy polyurethane, then a final coat of satin. Your floor will have a harder surface, and you'll still have the finish you desire.

❏ If you're looking for extra protection for a hardwood floor in a high-traffic area such as a kitchen, apply an extra coat of a urethane varnish.

❏ If you have a polyurethane finish on a floor that gets moderate traffic, you can generally plan on its lasting 3 to

4 years before it starts to look dingy. Usually, at that time, you'll need to sand the floor just enough to create a surface for fresh finish to adhere to. (You don't need to remove the old finish completely.) Then apply a new coat of finish.

❑ You don't need to wax over a urethane-finished wood floor. To remove dirt and stains, simply clean the floor regularly with a mop dipped in a solution of 1 cup of white vinegar and 10 quarts of water. If your floor is particularly dirty, increase the amount of vinegar; use up to 1 pint of vinegar to 10 quarts of water for very heavy dirt.

❑ If you prefer to wax a polyurethaned or shellacked wood floor, fold 1 teaspoon of paste wax into a pad of either 00 or 000 steel wool and rub. The steel wool will smooth the floor's surface, and the wax will not only serve as a lubricant during the process but also add a soft gloss with good protection.

❑ You can use the same wax-and-steel-wool technique to hide a scratch in a polyurethaned floor.

When Waxing Wanes

❑ To remove wax from a polyurethaned floor, dampen a cloth with paint thinner or turpentine and wipe the cloth over the floor. Then wipe up the wax with a clean, dry cloth. Work on a small area at a time, wiping the wax up as you go. (Otherwise, the wax will readhere as the solvent evaporates.) Standard wax removers work equally well, but this method is less expensive.

Paint: Color It Durable

❑ If you decide to paint your wood floor, choose an alkyd-resin type. This is a good finish for floors that get a lot of traffic.

Whatsit?

WE FOUND THIS OBJECT under our family-owned general merchandise store in the woods of Texas. The store dates back to 1870. The item is made out of metal. It's 9" high, and the bowl diameter is 2½". Do you know what it is?

— B.C., NEW BRAUNFELS, TEX.

This appears to be a cruse lamp, an early form of lighting. Grease or fat was put in the pan, and a wick was laid in the groove with one end in the grease. The other end was lit to provide feeble light. (A disadvantage was that the grease would sometimes seep up the wick and drip on the floor.) To convert it to a wall lamp, the hanger would be driven into a timber.

VICTORIANS DIDN'T LIKE BLEACHED BLONDES

THERE ARE two kinds of shellac: orange and white (or clear). The orange type colored the oak floors of the Victorian era; it's very rarely used today. White shellac has been bleached and gives a more natural finish to wood.

❏ If you paint your floor, add an extra coat or two in especially high-traffic areas before applying the final coat overall.

Should You Shellac?

❏ Shellac was a popular floor finish in the late nineteenth century, but modern homeowners may not have the patience for the maintenance and shortcomings that go with it. Before making up your mind, consider the practical advantages of shellac. First, you don't have to strip your floors down to bare wood when you need to add another coat; a new layer of shellac softens an old one and bonds to it. Shellac is also forgiving and will go on a floor that isn't hospital clean (although every effort should be made to clean the floor before applying any finish). It also dries dust free in half an hour or less and gives a lovely color to wood.

❏ Fresh shellac is relatively cheap, so it's wise to avoid using any that was left over from previous jobs. Shellac up to six months old is no problem, but older shellac darkens and creates drying problems. Look at the expiration date on the can before you buy it, and don't buy too much at a time.

❏ A shellac finish will not stand up to water and alcohol abuse, but if spills are wiped up quickly, the clouding they cause will usually disappear. You can rub a trouble spot with denatured alcohol, then apply fresh shellac.

❏ Either liquid or paste wax can be used on a shellacked floor. Polish it with an electric floor polisher. On new work, apply two coats of wax an hour or so apart, polishing after each coat. From then on, whenever the old coat wears thin, apply a new coat right on top of the old.

MAINTAINING WOOD FLOORS

Quick Fixes

❏ If a knot comes loose from the flooring you've laid, just glue it back in place with carpenter's glue.

❏ If you lose a knot that's come loose, fill the hole with wood putty and stain the area to look like a knot.

❏ If your wide floorboards shrink in width, here's a way to fill the cracks between them. At your local paint store, pick up a can of powdered glue—Durham's Water Putty, for instance—as well as dry earth colors that match the floorboards as closely as possible.

Back at home, soak old newspaper thoroughly in water, pound it into a pulp and squeeze it out. You'll need enough pulp to fill all the cracks.

Mix the powdered glue with water until the mixture is the consistency of light cream. Add it to the pulp, mixing it in well, then mix in the dry earth colors. (The mixture must be colored at this point; it won't take a stain once it has dried.)

Experiment with the earth colors on a small batch of pulp first to match the floor color as closely as possible. You don't have to wait until the pulp dries to double-check the color; the color won't change as it dries.

Fill the cracks with the mixture and smooth with a putty knife. If you do a good job of smoothing it, you won't have to sand it later.

❏ To fill scratches in a wood floor, apply shoe polish paste in a matching color. Just spread it on the scratch and rub it in with a damp cloth.

A Not-So-Quick Fix

❏ Sometimes wide pine floorboards cup or warp. This is caused by a combination of two things: dampness in the cellar below and the warm sun shining on the floor from above, drawing the moisture up into the boards. The only way to prevent wide floorboards from cupping and warping is to get the moisture out of your cellar.

The Squeaky Board Gets the Talcum Powder

❏ A quick way to stop wood floors from squeaking is to dust talcum powder into the cracks where the squeak is.

Whatsit?

COULD YOU TELL US what this tool is? It's 11½" long and has two sharp metal prongs at one end and a curved piece of metal at the other. The handle is wooden.

— J.S., MORRIS, CONN.

This is called a corn-husking peg. It was used to strip the husks from the ears of corn. The metal pin did the shucking, and the metal shield protected the hand from the rough husks.

To silence a squeaky tongue-and-groove joint, drive a nail into the joint (A), placing it an angle (B) to make it more secure. Afterward, set the nail head below the surface of the floor (C).

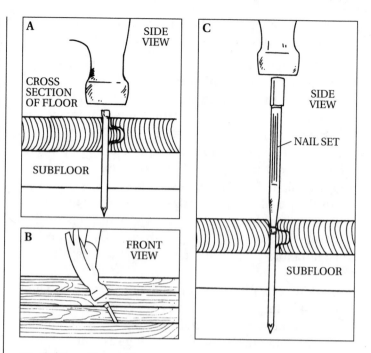

Nail That Squeak

❑ A more permanent solution for squeaky floors is to drive finish nails at an angle into the cracks between flooring pieces. The nails will go through the tongue of the floor pieces and into the subfloor, generally stopping the squeak. If you set the nails just under the surface of the wood, they won't be noticed.

❑ The same principles apply to squeaky stairs. If you can get at the back of them, you can repair them by driving nails from underneath through the riser and into the tread at an angle; this will make them hold better. Or sprinkle talcum powder into the noisy joint between tread and riser.

Cleanup Time

❑ Waxed wood floors should be wiped almost every day with a dry mop. Don't put any oil on the mop; oil will soften the wax. Any section of the floor that gets a lot of wear will need a new coat of wax more often than the rest of the floor. Apply wax only after cleaning.

❑ If the felt pads on your floor polisher are gummed up with wax, place them between four thicknesses of paper towels and press the towels lightly with a warm iron. Within a minute or so, the towels will absorb all the wax from the pads.

❑ To remove candle wax from a floor, scrape off what you can, then place a blotter or paper bag over the wax and hold a warm iron on it until the paper draws in the wax. Or use a blow dryer instead of an iron.

❑ To get scuff marks off a floor, mop the floor with a solution of ¼ cup of TSP (or other product containing trisodium phosphate) and 2 gallons of hot water. This should work on any hardwood floor.

❑ To remove those blackish spots on the finish of a strip floor, pour on a little nonsudsing ammonia, then rub with fine steel wool.

❑ To get rid of a urine odor in a shellacked hardwood floor, dust the floor with baking soda, let it stand for a few hours and vacuum up the baking soda. Repeat if necessary.

VINYL AND LINOLEUM

Neatness Counts

❑ To keep a linoleum or vinyl floor clean, vacuum or dust mop it often. That way you'll pick up loose dirt before it scratches the surface.

❑ Don't use a rubber- or foam-backed mat or rug on a linoleum or vinyl floor. Rubber and foam can cause discoloration.

❑ Add 1 tablespoon of vinegar to a pail of rinse water when cleaning a no-wax floor. This will prevent soap buildup and will keep the floor from looking dull.

FLOORS

Whatsit?

I HAVE NO IDEA what this tool was used for. The overall length is 22", but I think the wooden handle is a replacement; the original handle may have been longer. The two side arms are of spring steel. When you pull the two jaws apart, you arm the four-pronged trigger mechanism in the center. Lightly touching the pronged trigger against an object causes the jaws to snap shut rapidly. Other than the two sharp prongs on each jaw, there are no cutting edges. Stamped into the metal neck is "Norland's Lion Made in USA." What is it, and what was its use?
— W.P., EAST HAMPTON, CONN.

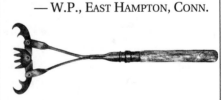

This is an implement used to spear fish or eels. When opened and struck down on the back of an eel, the spear would snap shut, and the fish could be pulled from the water.

FLAX FLOOR FACTS

THE WORD *linoleum* is a combination of the Latin *linum* (flax) and *oleum* (oil), because it was those ingredients that Englishman Frederick Walton combined in 1864 to make a revolutionary floor covering.

Walton covered fabric with oxidized linseed oil, spread it with chopped cork and other colored fillers, pressed the whole mess onto burlap and voilà!—something durable and water and stain resistant that looked nice on the kitchen floor.

Linoleum producers today begin by mixing linseed oil and oxygen in a tank, where oxidation turns the oil into a rubbery material. Gums and heat are added, further strengthening the substance. After a few days of strengthening, the linoleum cement is mixed with colors and filler material, such as sawdust. A machine then presses the mixture into burlap-backed sheets. Sometimes, to create a design on the new sheet, inks are applied in a stenciled pattern. Plain linoleum is often called battleship linoleum because of its use in Navy ships.

Linoleum reached its peak of popularity in the 1940s. Thereafter, it began to be replaced by more durable waterproof vinyl flooring. Don't throw out that half a roll of old stuff in the barn, though. Some collectors will pay top dollar for vintage specimens. (Imagine.)

❏ If you'd rather avoid commercial floor wax removers, you can mix your own alternative. Combine 1 cup of laundry detergent, ¾ cup of ammonia and 1 gallon of warm water. Apply with a mop.

❏ Sometimes adhesives are put down to keep carpets from skidding as you walk on them. If you have adhesive left on your floor after you remove carpeting, pour boiling water on the adhesive. Let the water work into the adhesive for a couple of minutes, then scrape with a putty knife. Wear heavy rubber gloves to avoid being burned, and work on only a small area at a time.

❏ Turpentine or kerosene will remove stubborn marks from linoleum. Rub the solvent into the linoleum, then wipe up all that you can, removing the mark at the same time. The rest of the solvent will evaporate quickly, but you'll probably want to keep a window open to dissipate the smell.

Perfect Patches and Other Repairs

❏ *Never sand old vinyl or linoleum flooring* or the backing or lining felt of such flooring. These products may contain asbestos fibers that are not readily identifiable. Avoid creating dust, and make sure to wear a mask when working with these materials if you think they may be old. Inhalation of asbestos dust is a serious health hazard.

❏ To flatten a tile on which the edges have started to curl up, try this trick. Warm the tile with an iron or blow dryer, applying just enough heat to soften the adhesive underneath. Lift up the edges of the tile and dab adhesive under the curled edges. Press the edges back into place and weight the tile down flat for several hours, or until the adhesive dries.

❏ To patch a damaged area of continuous vinyl or linoleum flooring, tape your new piece of flooring over the damaged area. Cut through both layers of the floor (the new patch and the old flooring material) well outside the damaged area to create a patch that will fit perfectly. Remove the new piece and pry up the damaged piece of

When you patch a damaged section of flooring (A), start by taping a new piece of flooring over the damaged area and cutting through both the new and the old flooring (B). Pry up the damaged section, clean the floor underneath and apply linoleum cement to the floor (C). Then install the patch (D).

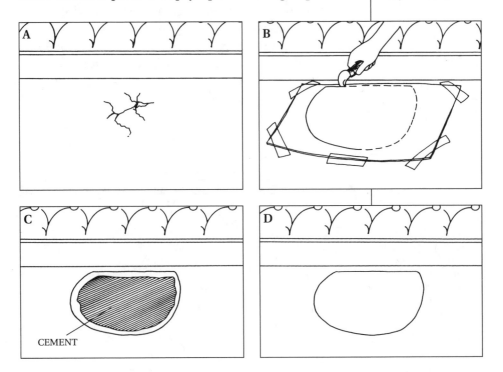

CEMENT

flooring. Clean the floor underneath the tile as best you can with a putty knife. Apply a thin coat of linoleum cement to the floor, keeping the cement ½" from the edge of the patch; you don't want it to ooze up through the cracks. Press the patch into place. You can walk on it right away.

Starting Over

❏ If you want to lay a new tile floor and don't want to go to the bother of removing the old one, here's an alternative. First, level the surface of the old floor; fill in the low spots with a leveling compound such as Top-n-Bond, available from hardware or flooring supply stores. Cover the entire floor with an underlay—a smooth, stable, clean surface such as Masonite or ¼" plywood. Nail the underlay down every 4" with ribbed underlay nails. (Be sure the nails are long enough to reach most of the way through the subfloor.) Then lay the new tile floor directly on top of the underlay.

❏ To remove old linoleum from floors, insert a putty knife at one edge and pry off all you can. To get off the felt and adhesive that are left, mix together ½ cup of white vinegar and 1 gallon of hot water. Using an old paintbrush, apply the mixture to the old adhesive. Put on enough so that it soaks in and softens the adhesive. Wait 10 minutes, then scrape off the adhesive with a putty knife. If necessary, repeat the process. If you're at all uncertain about

When you lay a new tile floor over an old one, begin by filling in any low spots. Nail a new underlay over the whole thing, then install the new tiles on top of the underlay.

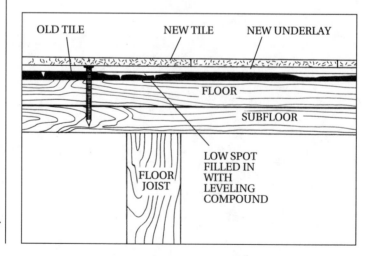

OLD TILE   NEW TILE   NEW UNDERLAY

FLOOR

SUBFLOOR

FLOOR JOIST

LOW SPOT FILLED IN WITH LEVELING COMPOUND

the age of the flooring, be sure to take the precautions listed earlier; there's always a potential health hazard in working with old linoleum, which may contain asbestos.

❑ One way to remove old asphalt or vinyl floor tiles is the freeze-and-chip method. (Remember that if the tiles are old, you should be sure to take extra precautions to avoid breathing in the asbestos they may contain.) For this technique, put dry ice in a wooden frame of your own construction. Place the ice and frame over a tiled area until the tiles freeze, then chip the tiles off with a flat chisel or putty knife. Move the frame to the next area and repeat the process.

❑ An alternative method for removing old asphalt or vinyl floor tiles is the heat-and-lift technique. For this procedure, which most people find easier than the freeze-and-chip approach, warm a small area with an iron or blow dryer. Then work the tiles off the floor with a broad-bladed putty knife. Repeat the process for the rest of the tiles.

❑ After removing old tiles, always scrape off any dried remnants of adhesive left on the subfloor. Make sure all loose material is removed before new tiles are laid.

CARPETING

Before You Touch the Carpet . . .

❑ Before laying wall-to-wall carpet on a rough floor, put down an underlay of ¼"-thick plywood. Or use a ³⁄₁₆" hardboard such as Masonite. If the floor is weak, use ½" or ¾" plywood. Nail the underlay down every 4" with ribbed underlay nails. (Make sure the nails are long enough to reach most of the way through the subfloor.)

For Stair Runners That Last Longer

❑ When laying a stair runner, calculate the length you'll need as if you had two more treads than you really do. When you lay the runner, fold half of that extra material under the top tread and half under the bottom tread. That way, when the edges of the treads get worn, you can just shift the placement of the runner.

Nonskid Scatter Rugs

❏ To keep scatter rugs from sliding, sew or glue to the bottom a few of those rubber rings that are designed to be used with glass canning jars.

Removing Furniture Dents: The Cold Approach

❏ It's easy to correct the dents that furniture leaves in carpets. Just place an ice cube in each dent and allow it to melt overnight. While the carpet is still a little damp, use your fingers to fluff up the fibers. If the dents are very deep, repeat the process. Once you've finished, avoid putting the furniture back in the exact spots where the dents were.

IT GIVES NEW MEANING TO "SANDING YOUR FLOOR"

UNTIL THE nineteenth century, the floors in most houses were made of random-width white pine boards butted together. In general, the widest boards were used in utility rooms such as the kitchen. Narrower, more uniform-width boards were used in formal rooms. Early floors typically weren't painted; they were covered with carpets or canvas floor cloths, or they were sprinkled with fine sand. When the sand got dirty, it was simply swept up and discarded, and a new layer of sand was put down. It was also common to paint the floors with a mixture of sand and lye, which left a whitish finish. (The abrasiveness of the sand kept the floorboards free of splinters, too.)

By around 1830, narrower floorboards were becoming fashionable, in spruce and hard pitch pine as well as white pine. Any softwood floors that were laid toward the middle of the century or later were likely to have been intended as an underlay for carpeting. (Many people have gone to great lengths to refinish and expose floors that were originally meant to be covered.)

Hardwood floors are a product of the Industrial Revolution, when the increased use of water-powered planers made it practical to mill hardwoods such as birch and maple. Oak flooring didn't become popular until very late in the nineteenth century.

Removing Furniture Dents: The Hot Approach

❏ You can also use a small steam iron to get rid of dents in carpets. Steam the area for a minute or two, then fluff up the fibers with a comb. If the carpet is synthetic, avoid touching the hot iron to the carpet fibers; the carpet could melt under intense heat.

Toward Brighter Carpets

❏ To bring out the color in a rug, dip a broom in a mixture of 1 cup of white vinegar and 1 gallon of water, then brush the rug with the broom. No need to rinse.

Shampoo the Carpet, Not the Furniture

❏ Before shampooing a carpet, put plastic sandwich bags on the legs of all furniture that's too big or heavy to move. This keeps the legs from getting wet and marking the carpet.

Baking Soda: The Odor Eater

❏ To absorb carpet odors, sprinkle the smelly area with baking soda, wait 15 minutes and vacuum. For problem odors, let the baking soda remain overnight, then vacuum. Use this approach only on dry carpets, and be sure to test a small, hidden area for color fastness before applying baking soda to the entire carpet.

The Basics of Carpet Stain Removal

❏ When you're buying carpeting, it's helpful to know that rugs made of synthetic fibers—nylon, acrylic, polyester or polypropylene—stain less easily than those made of natural fibers because they aren't as absorbent. Keep this in mind when choosing your carpet.

❏ It sounds obvious, but too many people forget: Whenever you spill something on a rug or carpet, wipe up the spill as soon as possible. That way, it's less likely to stain.

Whatsit?

MY WIFE INHERITED this tool from her great-grandfather. Can you help us identify it?
— L.D., PHILLIPSBURG, N.J.

This was used to repair wire fences. You could pry a staple loose with the long prong, then grab the wire with the pincers and lock them around the fence post to tighten the wire before hammering the staple back in. The long prong served an additional purpose: When you had to put the tool down momentarily, you could stick the prong in the ground so you wouldn't lose the tool in the grass.

❑ Don't apply any cleaning solution to a carpet without testing it on an inconspicuous spot or a piece of scrap first to check the results. Put a few drops of the solution on the carpet, then hold a paper towel against the treated area for 5 seconds. If the dye runs, it's time to give up on the do-it-yourself approach and call a professional cleaner.

❑ Even if your carpet is colorfast, stain removal can be a process of trial and error. If a certain solution doesn't work in the time allotted, apply it again for a little while longer. If the solution still doesn't work, try a different one.

❑ Be careful not to make the problem worse when you're trying to remove a stain from a carpet. When applying a liquid to treat the stain, always use the smallest amount that will do the job. (You can always apply more if necessary.) If you apply too much liquid, it will soak the carpet backing and possibly ruin the finish on the floor underneath.

❑ Avoid rubbing a stain; blot it instead. This keeps the stain from spreading.

Water-Based Stains: Whipping Up a Solution

❑ Most water-soluble stains can be removed from carpets if you attack them while they're still fresh. Apply a solution of ¼ cup of a mild dishwashing liquid, 1 quart of warm water and 1 tablespoon of white vinegar. With an eggbeater, whip the solution into a stiff foam. Apply the foam with a soft brush, rubbing gently. Scrape away the soiled foam with a dull knife, then wipe off the residue with a damp sponge. Rinse the stain with a little cool water on a sponge. Then blot with paper towels.

No More Oily Mess

❑ Your best bet for removing oily stains from carpeting is a cleaning fluid such as Energine (available from hardware stores). Check the label on the rug to see if the cleaner is safe for your fiber. Or test a little fluid on an inconspicuous area. If the label or test says it's safe, dampen a sponge with the fluid and apply it to the stain. Blot with paper towels. Repeat as long as there is an improvement. Finally, apply a mild solution of dishwashing liquid and water, then blot again.

❑ Here's another technique for getting oil stains out of carpeting. Cover the stain with flour. Let it sit for 24 hours, then brush it up. Keep repeating the process with fresh flour until all the oil has been absorbed.

Get the Grease Out

❏ To remove a set-in grease stain from carpeting, dip a bar of Lava soap (available from hardware stores) in warm water and rub it on the spot. Rinse well. If any of the soap remains in the carpet, the soapy area will remain lighter in color when the carpet dries.

The Job I Did in Miniature

FOR A WHILE I WAS IN BUSINESS for myself laying linoleum floors and countertops. During that time, the most complicated job I did was for a woman who wanted all the floors in her house covered with inlaid linoleum. I took my collection of linoleum scrap pieces to her house. We'd go into a room together, and she'd pick out a piece of linoleum to cover the center of the floor. Then she'd pick out different pieces for feature strips and the border. The border and the feature strips, which I had to cut ⅜" wide, followed the contours of the room.

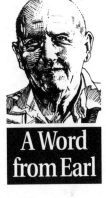

A Word from Earl

We went through every room in the house that way, laying out miniature floors using different scraps. Even the closets had feature strips in them.

Today most people put down plain linoleum or vinyl patterns— and then only in the kitchen or bathroom. If you want to be creative, take some time coming up with a design and be sure you're comfortable with it before you start laying down the linoleum. You don't want to change your mind after the whole job is done.

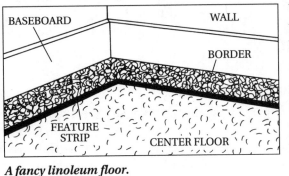

A fancy linoleum floor.

BASEBOARD · WALL · BORDER · FEATURE STRIP · CENTER FLOOR

❑ Another way to remove a set-in grease stain is to apply a few drops of turpentine, soak that up with cornmeal or kitty litter and then vacuum. Follow up by dampening a cloth with a cleaning fluid such as Energine (available from hardware stores) and blotting the remaining spot. No need to rinse.

Shaving Cream for Juice Stains

❑ Shaving cream will remove fruit juice stains, but you need to be careful to apply just a little, or you'll have trouble getting the cream out of the rug. Spray just enough cream onto your hand to cover the stain. Apply the cream to the stain and allow it to sit for a minute or two. Blot the cream with a sponge dampened with water or club soda. You may need to repeat the process to get out all the stain.

Don't Mess with an Oriental Rug

❑ Oriental rugs require special care because they're handmade. If you spill something on one, blot up the spill with white paper towels and flush the area with water and dishwashing liquid to keep the stain from setting. Then take the rug to a reputable cleaner immediately.

Ink Stains Are Not Invincible

❑ To remove ballpoint ink from carpeting, cover the affected area with salt. As the ink is absorbed, vacuum up the salt and repeat the process.

❑ You can also get ballpoint ink out of carpeting by blotting the ink with milk on a rag, then brushing the milk with an old toothbrush. Be sure to rinse the milk out of the rug thoroughly, or you'll just be replacing one stain with another.

Gum in Carpeting: Ice it Out

❑ To remove soft gum stuck in carpeting, rub the area with an ice cube, then scrape the gum with the dull edge of a knife. Remove any residue with a cleaning fluid such as Energine (avail-

Whatsit?

HERE ARE DRAWINGS of some pieces of pewterware. The tank hangs on a wall and has a candle holder on it. What are they?
— B.W., MEDUSA, N.Y.

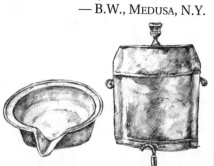

This is a valuable lavabo, used before lavatories were common. The underbasin sat on a stand, with the tank hung on the wall above it. A candle placed in the holder provided light for washing.

able from hardware stores) on a rag. The cleaning fluid will evaporate quickly. Rinse the area right away with a solution of dishwashing liquid and warm water. Dry with a fan or blow dryer.

No More Blood on the Rug

❏ To remove a bloodstain from carpeting, cover it with equal parts meat tenderizer and cold water. Allow the mixture to sit for half an hour, then sponge off with cool water.

❏ Another possibility for removing a bloodstain from carpeting is to sprinkle on salt, then cold water. Gently blot the area with a sponge, then wipe up the mixture.

Coffee: Spilling the Beans

❏ You can get coffee out of carpeting if you attack the stain while it's fresh. Blot up the excess coffee, then rub the stain with a mixture of 1 tablespoon of white vinegar, a squirt of mild dishwashing liquid and 1 cup of water.

When the Rug Becomes a Litter Box

❏ To get rid of pet mistakes on rugs, make a solution of 3 tablespoons of white vinegar and 1 quart of warm water. (A squirt of dishwashing liquid added to the solution also helps.) Dip a rag in this mixture and gently apply to the stained area. Blot up the mixture with thick rags. If the stain is near the wall, and if the culprit was a male cat, it's a good idea also to wash 18" up the wall. No need to rinse.

❏ To get the odor of cat urine out of a carpet, sprinkle baking soda on the area. Leave it on for several hours, then vacuum it up. If necessary, repeat the process with fresh baking soda.

❏ Another trick for getting the urine smell out of carpeting is to sponge the spot with club soda, then vinegar. You don't need to rinse.

❏ You can also get urine out of carpeting by sponging on a solution of 1 pint of water and 1 to 2 teaspoons of ammonia. Blot up any excess solution with rags.

If Your Shoes Take a Shine to Your Carpet

❏ Remove shoe polish marks on carpeting by applying a cleaning fluid such as Energine (available from hardware stores) with a rag. Then wash with a solution of dishwashing liquid and warm water. You won't need to rinse.

Rust Removal

❏ Rust stains on carpeting call for a mild solution of oxalic acid (available from hardware stores and drugstores) and water. *Use the oxalic acid with caution, and never leave it in a spot that's accessible to children; it's an active poison.* Put a few crystals in a glass and cover them with hot water. Let them dissolve in the water overnight. Then, wearing rubber gloves and eye protection, brush the solution on the stain. Let it sit for half an hour, then blot the area dry with a rag.

Salt Removes Soot

❏ You can use salt to remove soot from carpeting. Brush to mix the salt and soot, then vacuum. Repeat with fresh salt if necessary. Wash with a solution of dishwashing liquid and water, rinse and blot dry with an old towel.

MARBLE AND SLATE FLOORS

Marble Maintenance

❏ Most of the time, the best way to maintain a marble floor is to dust it with a soft broom or vacuum it. Occasionally, you should give it a thorough washing with a few squirts of dishwashing liquid in a pail of warm water. Rinse it well with warm water and wipe dry.

Create a Clean Slate

❏ To clean a slate floor, wipe it down with paint thinner or kerosene. The solvent will evaporate and the odor will dissipate quickly if you open your windows.

QUARRY TILES

Scoring, Spacing and Other Ideas

❏ Quarry tiles are hard to cut. For big jobs, you'll want an electric masonry saw. If you need to cut only a few, try scoring them first with a glass cutter and snapping them over the edge of a workbench.

❏ Quarry tiles are frequently laid ½" apart. You can space the tiles evenly if you insert ½" strips of wood between them as you lay them. As you finish setting each tile, remove the spacers to use with the next one.

❏ To clean quarry tiles, apply a solution of TSP (or other product containing trisodium phosphate) and water. Mix the solution according to the instructions for masonry on the TSP container.

CONCRETE FLOORS

Seal Well Before Painting

❏ Any concrete floor that is to be painted should first be sealed with a product especially made for concrete. After pouring a concrete floor or setting brick in cement, wait 3 weeks, then apply the sealant with a brush. Allow 1 day for it to dry. This lets the concrete dry properly and the lime work out, resulting in a fine white powder. Clean up this powder before you paint the floor. Vacuum up what you can, then scrub off the rest with water and a stiff brush.

A Concrete Cleaner

❏ Before painting old concrete, clean it with vinegar on a rag. There's no need to rinse.

Testing, Testing

❏ Before laying tiles on a concrete floor, test for dampness. Tightly tape a piece of bright tin, rubber mat, plastic sheet or even aluminum foil to the floor for at least 24 hours. (The test piece can be any size that's handy.) Then look for water droplets on the surface and dampness underneath. If you find dampness underneath your tester, you have a seepage problem. Tile won't stick to wet concrete, so don't try to lay the tiles until you've taken care of the seepage. Droplets on the surface of your tester are an indication that moisture in the room is condensing on the cold concrete floor. If you don't take steps to correct this, the condensation will really be evident on the surface of your tile floor.

Whatsit?

ON A RECENT TRIP to Florida, I came across this article buried in the sand on a deserted beach. It is made of brass and is in excellent condition. An old-timer said it looks like a candle trimmer and snuffer. Could you please identify it for me? No name or company appears on the object.
— B.A., MIDDLETOWN, CALIF.

The object you found is a candle trimmer and snuffer. The wicks of candles today are consumed by the flame, but the wicks of candles made before 1800 needed trimming to pick off the charred remains. This snuffer worked like a pair of scissors, cutting off the old wick and shoving it into the box in one motion. The short legs let it sit on its brass tray on the sideboard in the dining room when not in use.

The Linoleum Wouldn't Stay Stuck

AFTER I HAD LAID a linoleum floor in a kitchen, the owner called to complain that giant blisters had formed underneath the floor. I went right over, concerned that I'd done something wrong.

When I slit open one of the blisters, I discovered that the adhesive was wet. That was the clue I needed to solve the puzzle. I went down into the cellar, and, as I expected, I found a big puddle of water standing on the cellar floor. The sun was coming in the kitchen windows, hitting the kitchen floor and drawing the moisture up from the cellar. The moisture could make it through the floorboards but not through the linoleum—thus the blisters.

A Word from Earl

I told the owner that he needed to ventilate his cellar now that he had a linoleum floor above it. He doubted that the moisture was the source of the problem, so I made him a deal: "I'll make screens for your cellar windows," I said. "If you ventilate your cellar properly for one week and those blisters aren't gone, you don't have to pay me."

Once the cellar windows had been open for a few days, the puddle evaporated, the blisters disappeared, and I got my check.

Never underestimate the importance of a dry cellar.

❑ If tiles are insulated from cold concrete, moisture will be less likely to condense on the surface. To insulate tiles partially before you lay them on a concrete floor, mop onto the floor a thin coat of the asphalt that you use to adhere the tiles. Then immediately lay 15-pound saturated roofing felt in the asphalt, butting the joints together. Apply another coat of asphalt over the roofing felt and lay the tiles.

Warming Up

❑ To warm up a concrete basement floor, lay a sponge-rubber-based indoor-outdoor carpet. (This solution is appropriate only if there are no moisture problems in the cellar.)

Cleaning Solutions

❏ Before sweeping a large concrete floor or patio, sprinkle slightly damp coffee grounds on the surface. They will keep the dust down and pick up the dirt.

❏ To get dried raw egg off a concrete floor, scrub the egg with a scrub brush while pouring on boiling water. Wear heavy rubber gloves for this process and be very careful to avoid burning yourself.

❏ To clean grease and oil from a concrete floor, sprinkle TSP (or other product containing trisodium phosphate) over the area, add a little hot water to make a thin paste and scrub vigorously with a stiff bristle brush. Allow the paste to sit for 20 minutes, then rinse with water. Repeat the process if necessary.

❏ If the oil spill on a concrete floor is a small one, you can treat it by covering it with a prewash spray designed for fabric stains. Let the cleaner sit for a few minutes, then sprinkle on a cleanser such as Comet. Scrub with a stiff brush or broom, then rinse with the hose.

❏ Oil on concrete can also be removed by soaking the stain with paint thinner for 20 minutes or so. Then scrub with a stiff bristle brush as you add more paint thinner. Cover the stain immediately with fresh kitty litter or dry sawdust. As soon as the litter or sawdust has absorbed the oil, vacuum it up. Repeat with fresh kitty litter or sawdust until most of the oil has been absorbed.

❏ If any residual stain is left on your concrete floor after one of the above approaches, you can get out the last of it with a solution of 1 cup of laundry detergent, 1 cup of household (5 percent) bleach and 1 gallon of cold water. Be sure the concrete is dry, then scrub the solution into the stain. When the stain is gone, rinse off the solution with the hose.

❏ Remove superficial rust stains from concrete with 4 ounces of oxalic acid (available at hardware stores) dissolved in 1 quart of hot water. *Oxalic acid is a strong poison; keep it out of the reach of children.* Brush the solution on the stains and let it dry. Repeat if the stains remain. Oxalic acid is expensive, but you use only a little at a time.

CONCRETE FLOORS

Furniture

How to salvage the best from Grandma's attic.

WHEN MY WIFE'S UNCLE DIED, we cleaned his house and arranged for the furniture to be sold at auction. The house was in pretty tough shape, so there were several pieces that the auctioneer wouldn't take. One such piece was a common side table with a drawer. We found it in the cellar covered with coal dust. All the joints in the table and drawer had become unglued because of the dampness in the cellar. "What should we do with this?" my wife asked me. I decided to take the table back to my shop and work on it when I got a chance.

I didn't get around to working on the table for several years. Finally, I washed, sanded and reglued all the pieces. I straightened the warped top and stained the whole piece. Then the table sat in my shop for another year before I found time to put a coat of varnish on it and place it in our living room. In the end, the piece that we'd almost sent to the dump turned out to be a nice little antique—so nice, in fact, that I recently sold it to an auctioneer.

The moral of the story is that if you have the space, it's worth holding on to pieces of furniture that have some inherent value—regardless of their condition. When you find time to work on them, you'll be rewarded.

In this chapter, you'll discover simple tricks for removing candle wax from wooden furniture, cleaning the caning of an old chair and covering surface scratches in finished wood. You'll also find ingenious tricks for removing the glop created by chemical strippers and for cleaning up the particles left when you rub down a piece with steel wool. You'll learn how to remove the last of the old glue when you want to disassemble a chair and reglue it—and how to make a simple clamp to hold the pieces in place while the new glue dries. You'll even find out how to keep a rocking chair from walking.

IF YOU CAN'T FIND IT . . .

. . . maybe you need to try another chapter. Check the index, or try these possibilities.

For Information On . . .	See the Chapters . . .
Animal pests in summer furniture	Pets and Pests
Cleaning furniture	Cleaning Around the House
Finishes and stains	Floors; Painting Inside and Out
Odors in upholstered furniture	Stains and Odors
Outdoor furniture	The Great Outdoors
Powder-post beetles in furniture	Pets and Pests
Stains on furniture	Stains and Odors

CLEANING WOODEN FURNITURE

Polish: The Big Buildup

❏ You create a dust trap when you apply an oil-based polish to a piece of furniture, so use polish sparingly. It's fine to polish a piece right after refinishing it and every few months thereafter, as long as you buff the piece well to remove as much of the oily residue as possible. In between applications of polish, simply dust with a clean rag.

❏ If you have a problem with built-up polish, you can solve it by rubbing the piece with turpentine and a clean rag at least twice. Keep changing the part of the rag you're

ANTIQUES: SPOT THE FAKES

Y<small>OU'RE IN</small> an antiques store, and you have your wallet out. Suddenly you begin to sweat. Just how "antique" is the piece you're about to buy? Experts have written volumes on this subject; telling a genuine antique from a fake is a tricky business. At least, however, you should know how to spot a blatant forgery. To do this, you need to answer these questions: Was it made by hand? Has it seen many years of use? Has it been repaired? If the answer to the first two questions is yes, it's probably an antique. A positive response to the third question may also mean it's old, but a piece that's been repaired is less valuable than an intact original.

The first thing to investigate is whether the piece was made by hand. Since World War II, most furniture has been made by machine, so if it's handmade, it's more likely that it's old. Here are some ways you can tell:

• *Check the parts you don't usually see.* If the back of the piece or the bottoms of the drawers are finished, it's probably fairly new. These areas would have been left unfinished on an old piece. Also, a plywood back suggests that the piece was made after 1900.

• *Look at the saw marks in those same areas.* Machine-made saw marks will run straight across the board if made by a band saw or in an arc if made by a circular saw. If the saw marks on the edges and ends of these boards are angled slightly, it's more likely that the boards were cut with a handsaw.

• *Check under the piece.* If the glue blocks used in the corners for additional strength are crude or hand-carved, the piece was probably handmade.

• *Inspect the joints.* Dovetail joints that were cut by hand will be

using and change rags if necessary. If you're not sure you have removed all the excess in two passes, go over the piece again.

Wax in the Hinges

❏ Wax buildup in furniture hinges may eventually interfere with the working of the hinges. To prevent this, try "painting" turpentine onto the hinges with an artist's brush to remove the old wax, being careful not to get turpentine on the wood. Wipe the hinges clean with a damp cloth afterward.

❏ Another method of removing wax buildup in furniture hinges is to scrub the hinges with a small piece of a steel

---

sized and spaced irregularly, and you won't find many on a drawer; sawing them by hand was a lot of work. Also look for score marks. It was standard practice for the craftsman to mark old dovetails with a gauge that had a sharp point, so the presence of such marks suggests a handmade piece.

If the piece passes all these tests, you need to determine whether it's been around for a while. Does the piece look as if it's been used for 200 years? These are the next steps in your investigation:

• *Check for roundness.* Measure the diameter of a round tabletop twice—with and against the grain of the wood. On an antique, the measurement across the grain will be less than that with the grain because the wood will have shrunk across the grain over time, regardless of how the piece was finished. Turned legs and dowels can be measured for roundness as well.

• *Take another look at the back*

and compare it to the inside. Bare wood that's exposed to the air turns darker as it ages, so the unfinished back of an old bureau will have darkened over the years. The wood in the drawer compartment, however, should look almost new.

Is it still looking old? If so, it's time for the final tests—the search for repairs:

• *Look at that back one more time.* In the old days, the backboard—the panel on the back of a piece of furniture—was usually very wide and made of pine or poplar. If the edges of these boards are not the same color as the face, they are substitutes made of newer wood and added later.

• *If you're buying a chair, inspect the bottoms of the legs.* Antique chairs should have scratches there from years of sliding and scuffing on wood floors, but they shouldn't have new wood or lathe marks, which suggest you're looking at a replaced or repaired leg.

---

wool soap pad. Be careful not to rub the wood. Follow up by wiping the hinges clean with a damp cloth.

Brighten Up!

❑ To clean wooden furniture that has become dull and discolored over the years, try a solution of equal parts mineral oil, turpentine and white vinegar. Rub the mixture on with a sponge, then wipe it off with a clean cloth. Stir or shake the solution while you're working, as these materials have a tendency to separate.

Creative Ways to Remove Candle Wax

❑ To remove candle wax that's stuck on wooden furniture, you need to apply a little heat. First, carefully scrape off as much wax as you can without scraping the wood. Use a blow dryer to warm the remaining wax, but be careful not to get the wax too hot, or it will adhere even more strongly to the wood. Blot the wax with a paper towel once it softens. Repeat until all the wax has been removed.

❑ Here's an alternative way to clean candle wax drips from furniture. Again, start by carefully scraping off what wax you can without marring the wood. Then put three or four layers of paper towels or brown paper bags over the wax. Hold a hot iron over the spot, but don't touch the iron to the paper; you could scar the finish on the piece. Once the wax is hot enough to melt, the paper will absorb it. You may need to repeat this process several times.

Get the Flannel off the Table

❑ If the flannel backing from a tablecloth sticks to a table, remove the flannel from the tabletop by applying mayonnaise liberally to the area. Let it soak in for 1 hour, then wipe it off with paper towels or a soft cloth.

Stains: The Easy Answers

❑ To remove white marks from wooden furniture, try rubbing on a little toothpaste (not the gel type) with your finger.

A SOFA BY ANY OTHER NAME

A *SOFA* IS A LONG PIECE of furniture used for sitting that is entirely covered with upholstery. A *davenport* is an overstuffed sofa with upholstered arms and back, often convertible into a bed. (A small writing desk is also called a davenport.) A *divan* is a large, low couch with no back or arms.

HOW TO KEEP OLD DESKTOPS ON A ROLL

OLD ROLLTOP DESKS are charming, but unfortunately their tambours (rolltops) wear out occasionally. The simplest and least expensive way to repair a tambour is to reglue the wooden slats onto a window shade.

First, remove the tambour from the desk. Strip the slats off the old cloth backing and sand off any glue left on the slats. Make note of the space, if any, between the slats on the tambour, as you will want to place them the same distance apart on the new material. If you're planning to refinish the desk, now is the time to refinish the slats.

Get a piece of window-shade material at least as wide as the slats are long and long enough to hold all the slats. Unless you have a large table, the floor is the best place to assemble the slats. Lay the shade material out flat and apply a 3" band of white glue that runs the width of the material. Place the slats on the glue, pressing them down with your hand to make sure all of the wood is in contact with the material. Apply another band of glue and add more slats, keeping the same spacing as in the original. When all the slats are on, let the material and slats dry overnight. Cut off any excess material and install the tambour in the desk.

❏ To make another minor abrasive for removing white stains from wooden furniture, combine 1 tablespoon of salad oil with enough cigarette ashes to make a thick paste. With a soft cloth, rub the paste into the stain. Wipe off with a clean cloth.

❏ Sometimes you can remove white stains from wooden furniture by applying baking soda with a damp cloth.

Stains: The Tough Stuff

❏ When moisture stains on oak furniture appear dark, they are hard to remove because they have penetrated into the finish and stained the wood itself. To get at this kind of stain, you need to apply paint remover or another appropriate solvent to remove the finish. Then apply a solution of equal parts household (5 percent) bleach and water. If the stain is large, brush on the bleach solution; otherwise, apply it with a rag. Keep the solution confined to the area of the stain, and leave it on until it dries. If the solution doesn't do it, try straight bleach.

❑ There's one further step you can take if bleach doesn't remove a deep stain in furniture. Buy some oxalic acid at a drugstore or hardware store. Oxalic acid is fairly expensive, but sometimes it's the only thing that will work. *Use it with great care, and always keep it out of the reach of children.* Stir the crystals into hot water until you can't dissolve any more of them. Remove the finish and apply the solution the same way you applied the bleach. Leave it on until it dries. Really tough stains will require multiple applications of oxalic acid.

Kill the Crayon Marks

❑ Remove crayon marks from furniture by rubbing mayonnaise on them. Let it sit for a minute or so, then wipe with a damp cloth.

❑ Some crayon marks can be removed with dry laundry starch (available at grocery stores) mixed with water according to the package directions. Apply the starch with a clean paintbrush. Let it dry, then rub it off with a clean, dry cloth.

REPAIRING WOODEN FURNITURE

Surface Scratches

❑ Small defects and scratches in the finish of a piece of furniture can be rubbed out fairly easily. Apply a few drops of a light oil, such as salad oil, then a little pumice (available at paint stores and hardware stores). With a piece of old felt held on a wooden block (much as you'd hold sandpaper on a sanding block), rub the oil and pumice into the finish. The defect should disappear.

❑ Scratches in old wooden furniture can sometimes be concealed with a paste of instant coffee and water. (This is a quick-and-dirty technique; it's not recommended for priceless heirlooms.) Put some instant coffee in a small bowl, then sprinkle just enough water on the coffee to make a thick paste. Rub the mixture into the scratches.

❑ Some scratches in wooden furniture can be hidden by rubbing them with a wax crayon that matches the color of the finish. Smooth the spot by rubbing with your finger.

❑ An old-time way of filling surface scratches in wooden furniture is also worth trying. Just rub the scratches with a piece of walnut meat, then polish with a soft rag.

Know When to Say No

❑ A poor job of repairing a piece of furniture will do more damage than good. Consider your abilities carefully before you undertake a repair. It might be wiser to have a professional do the work.

How to Tighten a Rope Bed

A WORD from Earl

ALTHOUGH ROPE BEDS are hardly ever used anymore, I still get letters from time to time asking for the best way to tighten the rope supports for the mattress on one of these old beds.

To tighten a rope bed, you need a rope wrench and a wooden wedge small enough to fit in the rope holes. It's easy to make a rope wrench (see the Whatsit on the facing page). The old ones were sometimes made of cast iron, but you can use wood.

To apply the wrench, start at a side rail, in the spot where the rope comes through the first hole after leaving the knotted end. Tighten the rope by winding it on the wrench. When this first section is tight, push the wedge into the hole to bind the rope at that point. Then move the wrench to the other rail and tighten the next section. Work your way all around the bed in this way. (To make the process easier, an alternative technique is to use two wedges and leapfrog them as you go.) When all the ropes are tight and the wedge is in the last hole, tie a new knot to keep the rope tight. The process is much like tightening a shoelace; you just keep pulling on one length at a time.

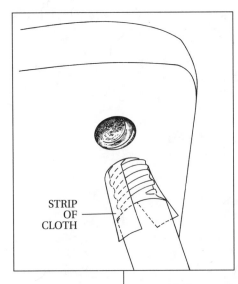

STRIP
OF
CLOTH

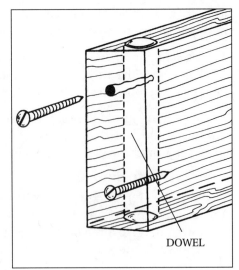

DOWEL

Avoid Loose Living

❏ Legs that screw into a piece of furniture, such as a desk or table, sometimes become loose. The first step in correcting this is to remove the offending leg and hang a ½"-wide strip of old sheet over the top of the leg's threaded end. While holding on to the ends of the cloth, screw the leg back into place. If the leg is still too loose, remove it and try again, this time using a strip of cloth 1" wide. Once you've determined the size strip you need to hold the leg, repeat the process with the other legs. When all the legs are secured, cut back the cloth to remove any excess.

❏ It's pretty well known that screws don't hold well in end grain, but occasionally you'll find a piece of furniture in which the manufacturer missed that principle. The hardware on the end of a bed rail, for example, can yank the screws right out. To solve a problem like this, drill a hole on the bottom edge up through the rail and tap a dowel into the hole. This gives those screws some nice cross-grain hardwood to bite into.

Flute the Dowels

❏ Dowel joinery—useful for bed frames and the legs of tables and chairs—works better if you chamfer the ends and flute the sides of the dowel. To do this, lightly sand a couple of flat faces on the dowel. Or crimp the dowel with

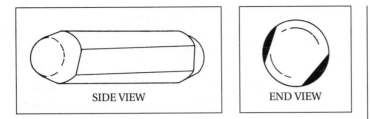

SIDE VIEW | END VIEW

Chamfer the ends and flute the sides of dowel plugs in joints.

the toothed part of a pair of pliers. Either technique allows excess glue to ooze out. Without this relief of the hydrostatic pressure, you can't squeeze your boards together.

Tabletops: Go Straight

❏ Here's a way to remedy warped table boards. Remove each board from the table and place it on supports (boxes or blocks) with the concave side up and the ends just resting on the supports. Place dampened towels on the boards and an electric heater underneath. Leave at least 18" of space between the heater and the boards. Keep the towels damp and the heat on. Make sure the towels are not wet enough to drip on the heater, but do not allow them to dry out completely. To avoid any chance of a fire, do not leave this setup unattended for an extended period of time.

The time it takes to straighten the boards will depend on the kind of wood involved and how badly they're warped. The trade-off here is that the dampness can damage the finish on the boards, so you may need to refinish them after they are straightened.

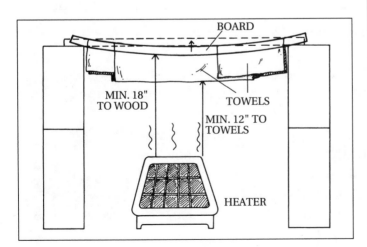

BOARD

MIN. 18" TO WOOD

TOWELS

MIN. 12" TO TOWELS

HEATER

When treating a warped board, be sure that the electric heater is a safe distance (at least 12") from the towels.

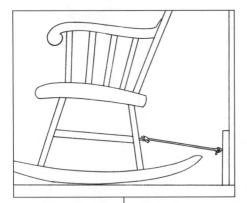

Rock, Don't Walk

❑ A rocking chair will "walk" forward or from side to side when one rocker is smaller or more worn than the other. The best way to correct this is to turn the chair over and plane the bottom of the larger rocker to match the size of the smaller one. A temporary solution to the walking problem is to fasten one screw eye to the back of the chair's bottom rung and another to the baseboard directly behind the rocker; then tie a piece of stout cord between the eyes to keep the chair from advancing while you rock.

Coming Unglued

❑ When you want to disassemble a chair and reglue it, it may be difficult to take the chair apart. Try knocking the pieces apart with a wooden mallet, which won't damage the rungs and legs the way a steel hammer will. Or wrap cloth or cardboard around the pieces before striking them with a standard hammer.

❑ If you're trying to disassemble a chair for regluing and the joints are stubborn, lay the chair on its side and brush warm vinegar around the rungs at the joints. If you prefer a more focused way to apply the vinegar, put it in a

The Tabletops Kept Warping

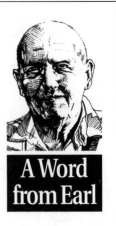

A RETIREE WHO WAS MAKING and selling pine tables wrote me with a problem. The boards on his tabletops were always warping. When I wrote back, I asked whether he was sealing the bottom as well as the top of the tabletops. He wasn't. So moisture could get in one side of the pine boards, but not the other. His tabletops didn't warp once he started to varnish both sides of the planks.

A Word from Earl

small, clean oilcan and squeeze the can to apply the vinegar to just the right spot. Wait a minute or two and apply more. The vinegar should dissolve the glue without damaging the finish.

❏ If you're having trouble removing a spindle from the point where the back meets the seat of a chair, turn the chair over and drill a small hole through the seat to get at the joint with the spindle. Fill the hole with warm vinegar and wait for it to soften the glue. Then gently pull the pieces apart.

To remove a stubborn chair spindle, drill through the chair seat and get access to the spindle joint.

Repairs with Glue: Sticky Situations

❏ Yellow carpenter's glue is best for regluing a chair. Available at hardware stores, it sets up hard and fast. Assemble the pieces immediately after applying the glue.

❏ If a chair rung is too small for its hole, don't just fill the space with more glue. Instead, try inserting a bit of steel wool into the hole to create a tighter fit. Then reglue the rung in place.

AMERICANS JUST KEEP ROCKING AND ROLLING

IN THE ARCHAIC SENSE, the word *furniture* described any outfit—the trappings of a horse, the rigging of a ship or the appliances of a printing shop, for instance. Today the word is used more narrowly to refer to the movable objects that decorate and serve our homes and offices.

In colonial times, furniture of the well-to-do was almost always brought over from Europe, but it wasn't long before America was making its own mark on the world furniture market—thanks in large part to the excellent types of wood found here and to American ingenuity. The bureau was an American combination of two European articles known as the chest of drawers and the dressing table. The upright folding bed was an American invention. But America's most distinctive contributions were the rolltop desk and that icon of hospitality and leisure, the rocking chair.

❏ If a glue joint comes apart, you must clean off the old adhesive before regluing. To do this, brush on hot vinegar with an old toothbrush. This will usually do the trick.

❏ When you're regluing chair rungs, it doesn't matter in what order you replace them. But it *is* important to get the right rung in the right slot, as the four rungs may not all be the same length. To be sure each piece is in its correct place, as you take the chair apart, mark each end of each rung according to which leg it fits into. Also mark the top or bottom of each leg. In addition, at the end of each rung, make a line on the top so that you will get the same part on top when you reassemble the chair. This is particularly important if the rungs are worn or are not finished on the underside.

The Chairs with Broken Backs

I ONCE HAD TO FIX a set of antique high-back dining room chairs. It was one of the toughest furniture repair jobs I've ever faced. The chairs were all cracked on the short wooden supports that connected the upholstered seats and backs. At some point, powder-post beetles had tunneled about and weakened the wood. The backs then cracked when the children of the house leaned back in the chairs. To repair the damage, I had to remove the upholstery in places and screw iron braces onto the cracked supports. After all that, the hardest part of the repair was filling the damaged areas of the wood so that no repair could be detected.  This would have been relatively easy to do earlier, but since the family had used the chairs for years after the backs were cracked, the wood around the cracks was extensively damaged, and that made the job difficult.

A Word from Earl

If you can't repair a broken piece of furniture right away, at least put it in storage until you can fix it. Using the piece while it is broken will make the repair that much more difficult when you finally get around to it.

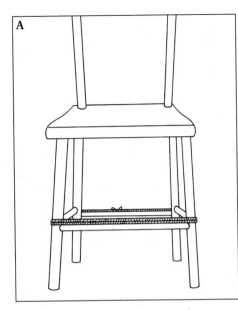

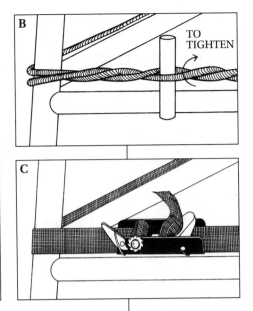

□ When gluing the legs of a chair, you'll need a simple clamp to hold the pieces in place while the glue dries. It's easy to fashion a tourniquet clamp out of a piece of rope and a stick. Wrap the rope around the leg structure twice and tie it. Then insert a stick between the two rounds of rope and twist it until the desired tightness is achieved. Lock the stick in place by bracing it against a rung.

□ Alternatively, you can use a web or strap clamp, made of a piece of webbing and available at hardware stores. Wrap the loop of webbing around the frame of the chair and tighten. A ratchet keeps the webbing from slipping loose as you tighten it.

□ Before you finish any furniture, make sure no glue remains on the surface of the wood. The glue will protect the wood from stains and oils, so that part won't appear the same color as the rest of the piece. The best time to clean off excess glue is before it's dry. Assuming you're using water-soluble carpenter's glue, wipe it off with a wet cloth; the water will help dissolve the glue. Then dry the wood thoroughly and sand the piece before applying a finish.

Venerable Veneer

□ To remove veneer, apply warm vinegar with a small paintbrush. Brush some vinegar on an edge of the veneer or on a joint between two pieces. Wait a few minutes,

For a makeshift tourniquet clamp, tie a rope around the legs of a chair being glued (A), then place a stick between the rounds of rope and twist it to tighten the rope (B). Or use a web clamp (C) from a hardware store.

DOVETAILS: THE BEST JOINT IN TOWN

OVER THE PAST 3 or 4 millennia, the only significant change in dovetail joints has been the attitude of the people who make them. Egyptian woodworkers used an exposed (or through) dovetail, in which the joint shows on both exterior surfaces. Gradually, more sophisticated woodworkers developed lapped, double-lapped and mitered dovetails, in which the joints are increasingly well hidden. Over the past quarter century or so, there has been a move back to exposed dovetails. Something that works as well as the dovetail joint doesn't leave much room for improvement.

This venerable method of joining boards at a right angle is an elegant combination of strength, beauty and simplicity. The interlocking wedges of the tails and pins allow the joint to be assembled or disassembled in one direction only. The large gluing area ensures that once the glue dries, it won't come apart without a destructive degree of persuasion. A skilled home handyman equipped with a modern, high-speed router and the latest fancy jig can make dovetail joints almost as good as those of a moderately skilled craftsman.

DOVETAIL JOINT

SIDE OF DRAWER

KNOB

FRONT OF DRAWER

The interlocking wedges of dovetail joints provide a high degree of strength.

then pry up the veneer at that point, working carefully to get as much of it at once as you can. Apply more vinegar under the lifted part, wait a few minutes more, and pry up some more. Eventually, you should be able to remove all the veneer.

❑ When a piece of veneer has come off and you want to put it back in place, lay it on a flat surface and, with a cabinet scraper, scrape the old glue off right down to the wood. Coat the place where the veneer goes with a good white wood glue. Replace the veneer. If the surface is flat, place weights on top to hold the veneer until the glue has set. If you're working with a curved surface, use a bag of sand to clamp it in place.

REFINISHING WOODEN FURNITURE

The Finish or Just the Beginning?

❏ If a piece of furniture is dull or dark, you may be able to improve its appearance more easily than you think. Often a washing, a light sanding, and a new coat of finish can bring such a piece back to respectability with a lot less effort than a full-blown stripping and refinishing job.

A Shower Will Help

❏ Before you refinish a really dirty piece of furniture, be sure to hose it clean, or sponge it with warm water to remove the dirt. You want to clean it without saturating it. For this, water pressure is better than water saturation.

Off with the Old

❏ When stripping old finish, you need to identify what it is. If the piece you're working with is an old one, the fin-

---

FINISHING CHOICES

YOU'VE JUST BOUGHT an old walnut table at an auction. The finish is in terrible shape: cracked, alligatored and dirty. You clean it off and remove the old finish. Now you have to decide what to use to refinish it. Here are your choices.

Varnish is a mixture of resins, solvents and drying agents. Many different resins and drying agents are used, with each type of varnish tailored to a particular job. Varnish creates a durable finish, acceptable even for outdoors, but its lengthy drying time (typically 6 to 8 hours) diminishes its appeal.

Shellac is a type of varnish called a spirit varnish. It is made with the sticky secretions of Indian and Burmese insects dissolved in alcohol. Shellac's tone creates a very warm finish. It dries quickly but requires several coats, with sanding between coats. Retouching shellac is easy, as each layer adheres to the one before. However, shellac can whiten when exposed to water, so it is not a good choice for a tabletop.

Lacquer is another spirit varnish. This is a good choice for a table, as it dries to a waterproof finish. If you want to apply it with a brush rather than a clean cloth, be sure to buy a brushable satin lacquer for best results.

Polyurethane is a petroleum product that creates an extremely durable finish. Polyurethane is an excellent choice for floors and heavily used surfaces. It lacks the warm tone you get with a natural-based finish such as shellac, some other varnishes and lacquer.

Whatsit?

HERE IS AN ILLUSTRATION of a tool we got from my father's workshop. Unfortunately, we have no idea what it was used for, but it appears to be some kind of shaving tool. Do you have any idea what it is?

— C.C., WESTBROOK, CONN.

This is a butteris, a farrier's tool for trimming a horse's hoof before putting on the shoe. The farrier would take the horse's foot between his knees, then press down on the handle end of the tool with his shoulder, forcing the sharp blade to trim the sole of the hoof.

An "alligator" finish, as on these raised door panels, is a sign of either old paint or improper bonding between paint layers.

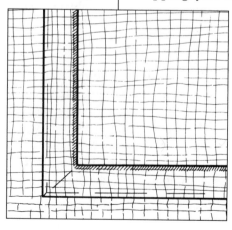

ish is probably not varnish, as varnish wasn't perfected until the late nineteenth century. Even then, it was used sparingly because it took a week to dry. Polyurethane can be ruled out, too, as it is a mid-twentieth-century invention. The finish on an old table is probably either shellac or lacquer.

❑ Every finish has a solvent. For liquid (as opposed to dried) varnish, it's likely to be turpentine; for shellac, denatured alcohol; for lacquer, lacquer thinner.

A Close Shave

❑ When stripping furniture, try this trick. After you've applied the stripper and it has lifted the finish, the instructions say to wipe up the glop with rags or steel wool. Forget that; it always seems to smear the mess around. Instead, dump a bunch of planer shavings on the surface and scrub with a cloth. The shavings won't scratch the piece; but they will scrape and hold the dissolved paint.

Old Strippers Are Still Active

❑ If you use a commercial paint stripper on an old piece of furniture, don't throw away the paste after the first stripping; you can use it again. The stripper is active as long as it's fluid, no matter how viscous it is.

See You Later, Alligator

❑ Sometimes the paint on old furniture or woodwork develops an "alligator" finish. If the alligatoring extends all the way down to bare wood, it's a sign of old, thick paint that has lost its flexibility. To cure this, you'll need to remove all the paint, then start over, applying both primer and a top coat. If the alligatoring appears only on the surface layer, it usually means the top coat didn't bond properly to the coat underneath it, possibly because of differences in the types of paint used for the two layers. Sand and scrape off as much of the top layer as you can. Then, before applying fresh primer and a top coat, sand the glossy undercoat to dull it.

Sanding: Don't Go against the Grain

❑ Never sand wood against the grain if you are going to stain or varnish it. Even the finest cross-grain scratches will show up when you apply the finish.

Ragtime

❑ When using an oil finish such as Watco, use wool rags to apply the product and cotton to wipe it down. The wool will hold a lot more, and the cotton will absorb more.

Lighten Up

❑ Refinishing with a lighter stain than the original is a risky venture. (Sometimes it's impossible to remove all the old, darker stain from the wood grain.) If you want to try it, remove as much of the old stain as possible with a water-

CREATING YE OLDE ALLIGATOR FINISH

O VER TIME, old furniture and woodwork used to develop an "alligator" finish—a mosaiclike cracking of the paint that looks something like the surface of a very old painting. This happened because the wood was covered with several incompatible coats of paint. Old paints were mixed with varying degrees of oil, leading them to dry at different rates. Eventually, this difference in drying rates would cause the top coat to crack.

Usually you'll find yourself stripping examples of this phenomenon *off* your furniture. However, if you strive for an old look for a particular piece, you can create this effect intentionally. Brush on a coat of latex paint, then follow it immediately with a coat of oil-based paint before the latex has a chance to dry. (You can use the same color for both paints or different colors for a contrasting effect.) The two paints will dry at different rates, causing the oil-based coat to crack. To be sure of getting exactly the effect you want, it's a good idea to experiment on scrap wood or a hidden part of the furniture before you begin painting in earnest.

MAPLE: TIGERS AND BIRD'S EYES

CABINETMAKERS and furniture makers in the Northeast have always prized tiger and bird's-eye maple. These figured woods are hard to find, and even harder to work, but a tiger maple tabletop or a highboy with bird's-eye maple drawer fronts gives a craftsman a chance to show off his best stuff without having to open his mouth.

Tiger maple displays a series of parallel stripes running perpendicular to the length of the board. The curly effect of tiger maple is caused by the wood fibers growing in a sinuous, wavy pattern. Some say it's caused by a recessive gene, some say it's the result of the tree swaying in the wind, and some say it's the weight of the tree distorting the grain. As these fibers intersect with the surface of a board, we see an alternating pattern of side grain and partial end grain. Properly finished—which is to say polished within an inch of its life—tiger maple has a striking three-dimensional appearance.

Bird's-eye maple displays randomly scattered "eyes," the result of tiny local depressions that develop in the surface of the tree as it grows. One theory holds that these are caused by some kind of microorganism that interferes with the cambium (the growth layer) of the tree.

The irregular grain of these woods calls for razor-sharp tools, a deft touch and great patience. The results can be quietly spectacular.

---

soluble paint remover. Then stir ¼ cup of household (5 percent) bleach into 1 quart of water. Brush on the solution, working on only a small area at a time. Let it soak in, then wash the surface well and dry it before starting on the next section. Keep bleaching until the wood won't lighten any more. Wear rubber gloves and eye protection while doing this, and always make sure you have plenty of ventilation while working with these substances.

Putty in Your Hands

❑ Use wood putty to fill large cracks and holes in a tabletop or table leaves. Buy the putty in powdered form and mix it with water according to the manufacturer's instructions. Pack the putty into the cracks and holes with a putty knife, leaving the surface as smooth as possible. Let the putty dry and harden, then sand it flush with the top of the wood and finish it to match the wood. (Powdered wood putty will absorb stain when you apply it. If you plan to use a premixed putty to repair a piece of furniture, read the label carefully before you buy the putty. Some premixed putties, such as Plastic Wood, don't absorb stain when you apply it.)

We Have Met the Enemy, and It Is Dust

❏ Dust is the enemy of wet polyurethane and varnish. A good layer of dust in a coat of polyurethane will make the finish feel like sandpaper. To avoid this problem, apply any finish in a work area that's as free from dust as possible. It's best to apply it at a time when you haven't been in the room long—before you've stirred up the dust.

Polyurethane: Nothing but the Best

❏ Of all the choices for wood finishes, polyurethane has the highest resistance to scratches, dents, ordinary chemicals and water. However, it's so hard that it tends to show scratches, much as glass does. For the best results, don't buy cheap brands of polyurethane.

The Varnished Truth

❏ When applying varnish to furniture, always thin the first coat with a little turpentine—3 tablespoons for every pint of varnish. The wood will more readily absorb the turpentine-thinned coat, thus improving the bond between varnish and wood. As in painting, this bond is essential to the entire job.

❏ Stir a can of varnish gently; never shake it. Otherwise, air bubbles will form, and they will show up in your work.

Give the Coat a Good Brushing

❏ When applying varnish, brush it on in line with the grain of the wood. Then brush the same coat across the grain. To finish the coat, brush in the direction of the grain again. That's three brushings per coat, which will give you a smooth finish.

DEATH OF A ROOM

IN THE 1800s, every house, however humble, had a parlor, a room furnished for sitting and visiting with guests and family. The parlor also was the room where the deceased were placed and mourning (a long, elaborate process) was observed—hence the term *funeral parlor*. During World War I, when so many families lost loved ones, mourning was almost universal. In England, it was decided that to boost morale, lengthy mourning periods should no longer be observed. Mourning became somewhat unfashionable. In America, an editor of a popular women's magazine decided that the parlor, with its association with drabness and death, should have a new name. His suggestion? The living room. It caught on.

The Frames Were Right— and So Was the Price

A Word from Earl

I USED TO BELONG to an art association in my town. We met every week to show our paintings and discuss them. I always made frames for my paintings; sometimes I made the frame before I finished the painting. The art association president approached me once and asked me about my frames. I told her that I made them out of a combination of standard moldings available at a lumberyard, since big, fancy moldings from a frame shop were expensive. She asked me to consider making frames for the other artists.

I drew up patterns for 18 different frame designs, but I never gave them to the art association president. I could foresee that I'd be making frames for the rest of my life if I showed the association members those patterns. I used the patterns many years later, however, when I was working at *Yankee* Magazine. The company archivist wanted to frame a lot of the original paintings used as artwork in the early issues of the magazine.

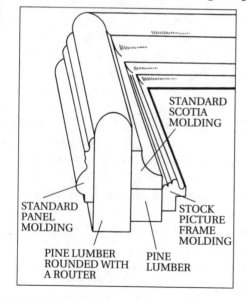

STANDARD SCOTIA MOLDING

STANDARD PANEL MOLDING

STOCK PICTURE FRAME MOLDING

PINE LUMBER ROUNDED WITH A ROUTER

PINE LUMBER

She asked me if I knew any way to frame the paintings inexpensively, and I volunteered my standard molding method. In all, I made 40 frames for her. "It's surprising how much a frame adds to a painting," she declared when she saw them all. Even the paintings that were of marginal quality looked great in the frames.

Design your own picture frame from stock moldings and lumber.

Don't Forget Your Overcoat

❏ In all, three coats of varnish are usually enough for any piece of furniture. The first soaks in and seals the wood. The second fills in all remaining pockets in the surface of the wood. The third and final coat gives the finish its gloss and smoothness.

Tacky Is Good

❏ Between coats of varnish, sand lightly with fine sandpaper (220 grit or finer) and go over the surface with a tack cloth to remove all dust. You can buy a tack cloth, but why spend the money when you can make one yourself? Just take a lint-free cloth such as cheesecloth or an old sheet that has been washed many times. Soak it in water and wring it dry. Then spatter varnish lightly on it. Fold the cloth and wring it to distribute the varnish. Store the cloth in a glass jar to keep it from drying out. Renew it by sprinkling with a little water and wringing it out.

Special Attractions

❏ If you use steel wool to rub down a piece after varnishing, you'll want to get all the steel particles off before applying another coat of varnish. Wrap a magnet in a piece of cloth (to avoid scratching the finish and allow easy removal of the filings from the magnet) and slide it over the piece to remove these particles.

Boiled Linseed Oil: Back to Basics

❏ For an inexpensive and quick natural wood finish, mix together 2 parts boiled linseed oil and 1 part turpentine. Brush it on and leave it overnight. Repeat this process the next day. On the third day, use a rag to wipe off any excess oil. As the linseed oil soaks into

FURNITURE

Whatsit?

WE FOUND THIS OBJECT in the wall of our 1850 farmhouse. It's 4" in diameter and almost 4" high. It has a weighted base (2 pounds), a glass-lined reservoir and bristles on the top. It looks as though it's made of pewter. The wording on the side is "Hudson's Patent. April 27, 1938" in raised letters. What is it? — H.P., TURNER, MAINE

This appears to be an inkstand. The bottom contained the ink and the small holes held the quill pens, which could be cleaned by wiping them across the brush.

the wood, it helps to preserve it. Later, if the wood starts to look dry and dull, apply another coat.

Dark Stains: Give Them a Little Time

❏ Before applying a dark oil stain, thin it with a little boiled linseed oil. The oil adds to the time it takes for wood to absorb the stain, giving you more time for blending and wiping.

❏ Here's a way to get a really rich finish without spending too much time or money. Mix 1 part boiled linseed oil, 3 parts polyurethane and 2 parts turpentine. Flow it on the piece, pouring on just enough so that it pools up and soaks in, but not so much that you have a lot of excess finish. Over the course of several hours, keep wiping off the finish just as it starts to get tacky, then flow on some more. Finally, apply the mixture with 600-grit wet/dry sandpaper, rubbing hard. To finish, buff and polish vigorously by hand with a clean rag. You'll end up with a hard, durable finish, natural in color.

Get Shellacked

❏ For a hard maple finish on any light wood, apply two or three coats of equal parts white shellac and denatured alcohol. After the last coat, apply one or two coats of clear varnish. (Do not try to substitute polyurethane for varnish;

A MOVING TALE

THE WORST PART of accumulating furniture is moving it to a new house. Ben Franklin wrote that "three removes are as bad as a fire," and after hauling down the seventeenth box of I-have-no-idea-why-we-save-this-stuff, kindling a little blaze may sound like a good idea.

The tradition makers have been hard at work to help make this traumatic time easier. They say for good luck you should follow these rules: Place in the new house a new broom, a loaf of bread, a used box of salt and water; move while the moon is on the increase; use something old in building the new house. Don't move on a Friday or a Saturday (yeah, sure) or on a rainy day (double yeah, sure), don't move downstairs in the building you already live in and don't enter your new house for the first time through the back door. Hmmm . . . with a big enough bonfire, maybe the old place will be roomy enough so you can stay put.

WHAT DID OUR FOREFATHERS BED ON?

Today's synthetic and innerspring mattresses make up just a fraction of what this country has slept on over the years. In early days many Native Americans slept between fur robes. The first settlers built wooden platforms that they covered with leaves, hay and furs. Spruce boughs were a common bedding material in the northern colonies. Eventually, platforms and floors gave way to rope, which, crisscrossed within a frame and pulled tight, provided a softer support for crude mattresses filled with leaves and hair.

As America became more prosperous, hair mattresses eventually were replaced with feather mattresses, which brought full circle the whole question of bedding. Feather mattresses, it turns out, had been around for years, although they hadn't been widely available in America. They can be traced back as far as ancient Rome, where many considered the introduction of feather beds a sign of a nation going soft. Some sages, in fact, predicted that the luxury would inevitably lead to the fall of the Roman Empire.

---

it won't stick to shellac.) Before each new coat of shellac or varnish, sand lightly and dust off the piece.

Special Effects

❏ A "pickled-pine" finish is like a white, translucent stain, which some people prefer for the old-time look it gives a piece. To achieve a pickled-pine finish, apply a coat of white paint to bare pine wood and immediately wipe it off, leaving the pores of the wood filled with white. Let the piece dry overnight, then sand lightly to further clean the flat areas. To complete the job, dust off the piece and apply varnish or lacquer.

LEATHER FURNITURE

Dress-Up Time

❏ To keep leather furniture supple, apply a good leather dressing (such as neat's-foot oil or saddle soap) with a soft cloth. Let it sit for 2 hours or so, then wipe off any excess. If you want a glossy finish, apply a neutral shoe polish and buff.

AN AMERICAN STYLE

MISSION FURNITURE (also called mission oak, arts-and-crafts or craftsman-style furniture), common from around the turn of the century to the 1920s, is enjoying a resurgence in popularity. The style was a back-to-basics reaction to the Victorian era's excessive decoration, impersonal machine production and penchant for making everything look European. Gustave Stickley, one of the people who got the style going in this country, wanted to create furnishings "essentially cheerful and durable and appropriate for the kind of life I believe the American public desires." Mission designs are squarish, sturdy and straightforward, with functional features. The dovetails, keys and mortise-and-tenon joinery are the only decoration. (Frank Lloyd Wright's "form follows function" dictum was influenced by the Mission ideal.) The style was much copied and elaborated upon until the end of World War I, when doughboys returning home to America brought with them a new vision of Europe—the stylish designs they had seen there that came to be called art deco.

Un-Make Your Mark

❑ Marks, spots and stains on leather furniture can sometimes be treated with petroleum jelly. Spread it on about ⅛" thick and leave it on overnight or until the spot disappears. Wipe up the petroleum jelly with paper towels when you're done.

Table Manners

❑ Clean a leather tabletop by sponging on a solution of equal parts lemon juice and warm water. Then wipe the tabletop dry.

❑ To patch a small hole in a leather tabletop, melt a little piece of a wax crayon of the appropriate color and fill the hole. Smooth the crayon with your finger while the wax is still warm.

CHAIR RESTORATION

Arcane Solutions

❑ To clean cane seats, wash them with hot water and dishwashing liquid, then rinse and let dry.

❏ Cane seats that have become stretched can be tightened by soaking the cane with hot water. Use a sponge and soak the material well. As the cane dries, it will shrink tight. Do not soak the spline around the rim of the cane, however, as it might come loose if it gets too wet.

❏ If you are going to both refinish and recane a chair, the job will be much easier if you do the refinishing first.

❏ Before recaning a chair, be sure that the groove for the spline is well cleaned. Chip out the larger pieces of old spline with a chisel. Then scrub the groove with vinegar on an old toothbrush to remove all the glue.

❏ To preserve new cane seats, apply two coats of equal parts white shellac and denatured alcohol. The shellac will soak into the cane and preserve it. Then brush on a coat of clear varnish to keep the cane clean and tight. Coat the underside also, or it will absorb moisture and stretch out of shape.

Save a Seat

❏ Although you can still commonly find chairs that had tacked-on seats rather than holes for caning or grooves for prewoven cane, replacement composition seats are hard to find. A simple replacement is ⅛"-thick Masonite. Bevel the edges to make each seat fit in the chair. Fasten the seats with large-headed, fancy upholsterer's tacks.

Wicker: The Light Touch

❏ To lighten unfinished wicker that has become discolored, use a paintbrush to apply a solution of ¼ cup of household (5 percent) bleach and 1 quart of water. (Wear rubber gloves for this.) You can also use borax and water in the same proportions. If you want a finish, wait until the wicker is dry, then spray it with clear satin urethane varnish or lacquer.

TOP: *A caned chair seat in need of repair.* BOTTOM: *Masonite is a simple replacement for a composition chair seat.*

Heating and Cooling

Getting to the right temperature takes more than just a lot of hot air.

ᴮACK IN THE 1930s, I got a job digging a cellar under a cottage on a local lake. The owner lived in Boston and stayed there only on summer weekends, but he wanted to come up in the winter also.

Part of my job was to install an oil-burning hot-air furnace in the cellar as a way to heat the cottage. I put a thermostat on the wall in the first-floor hall and set it at 70°F. All the owner had to do was turn on the power switch when he came in the cottage later that day.

At 11:00 that night, my phone rang. It was the owner of the cottage. He said it was so hot in the cottage that he and his guests had been forced outside. They had taken their chairs to the porch and were sitting out there. He wanted to know how he could turn down the heat.

I told him where the thermostat was and asked him to check its setting. When he came back to the phone, he said it was set at 90°F. Apparently, his guests, not knowing what a thermostat was, had been fiddling with it. I explained to the owner, who had never seen a thermostat before, how it worked.

Today everyone knows what a thermostat is, but there's a lot more to heating and cooling your house. This chapter tells you how to keep your house warm for the lowest possible cost and the least possible effort—all without compromising safety. You'll find simple tips for fixing banging radiators, avoiding chimney fires and keeping wood fires burning longer. Here are great ideas for easier, more efficient ways to cut and stack firewood, low-tech methods for humidifying your house and drying your clothes, and super shortcuts for buttoning up the house for the winter. And for the warmer months, this chapter offers great ideas for keeping your home cool with a minimum of fuss and expense.

POSITIONING THE HOUSE

Get Oriented

❏ If you live in a cold region, it's smart to orient your new home to get the most sun in the winter. Face your house south and install a lot of windows on that side.

❏ It's smart to make the roof overhang your house on the south side. The overhang will shade your house from the hot sun in summer, when the sun is high in the sky. In win-

IF YOU CAN'T FIND IT . . .

. . . maybe you need to try another chapter. Check the index, or try these possibilities.

For More On . . .	*See the Chapter . . .*
Heating a summer cottage	The Summer House
Masonry	Maintaining the Exterior

ter, when the sun is low on the horizon, the sun will stream into your windows and warm the house.

Build Your Home into the Land

❏ There's no better energy conservation measure than building your home partially into the surrounding land.

CENTRAL HEATING

Furnace Fundamentals

❏ If you're installing a furnace in the basement, especially if it's a wood or coal furnace, the best location for it is in the center of the room. As the heat radiates from the furnace, it will rise to warm the floor above it. Centering the furnace maximizes the size of the heated area above it.

❏ Furnaces should be checked and cleaned each year by a professional. Improved efficiency will lead to fuel savings that will more than cover the cleaning cost.

❏ If your new house is airtight for energy efficiency, your furnace should draw air for combustion through a duct to the outside. As the furnace fuel burns, the process creates a suction that brings in more air. In a tight house, if you don't have a duct to the outside, that air is drawn from inside the house, and the resulting vacuum can draw potentially dangerous gases such as carbon monoxide back down the flue and into the house.

Registers: Let the Heat Rise

❏ One way to heat your upstairs easily is to install open ceiling registers between your first and second floors. Heat will rise to the second floor through the registers, and cool air will return down the stairs. The air circulation will keep the second floor warmer.

Stop the Big Bang

❏ Sometimes hot-air furnace ducts make a loud noise after the furnace

---

TREE CHEERS

TREES ARE ONE of the best energy bargains for your home. Trees on the south side of your house will shade it in the summer (saving 10 to 50 percent on air-conditioning), then drop their leaves in the fall and let the sun warm the house in the winter. A windbreak of evergreens on the north side can help cut your heating bill. Trees also filter out dust from the air, put moisture back in and replace carbon dioxide with oxygen. In fact, an acre of trees can absorb 2.6 tons of carbon dioxide—as much as you create by driving a car 26,000 miles.

WHY NORTHERN ROOFS ARE DARKER THAN SOUTHERN ONES

WHEN MOST old houses were built, they were poorly insulated by today's standards—which is not to say the builders were blind to the need for insulation. Although good insulating materials weren't available, the builders incorporated many low-tech elements into their designs, which helped keep the house warm in winter and cool in summer. Many of these ideas are worth remembering today. They include:

- *Dark-colored roofs* in extreme northern areas, light-colored roofs down south
- *Covered porches* that allow the low winter sun (but not the high summer sun) to shine into the house
- *Vented gables* to create insulating air spaces under the roof
- *Closets built under eaves* to act as a temperature break
- *Few, if any, windows* on a house's northern (cold) side

Siting was important, too. Unlike many of today's houses, which are positioned to maximize the view, early houses were set in the lee of a hill or backed up to woods, sheltered from the wind.

---

has shut off. This happens because, as the metal cools, the panels of the duct work contract. To find the source of the problem, wait until the furnace shuts off, then inspect the duct work immediately.

Check the largest panel first, then the smaller ones, with the goal of either hearing or seeing the metal move. When you've identified the offending panel, use sheet-metal screws to fasten a 1"-wide metal strip, oriented diagonally, to it. The metal strip will keep the panel from expanding and contracting so much and so rapidly. (This tip

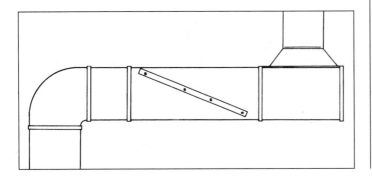

To correct a loud banging when the furnace shuts off, locate the offending panel in the duct work and screw a metal strip onto that panel in a diagonal position.

assumes that your duct work is readily accessible. If it's concealed, you'll need to decide whether correcting the noise is worth demolishing the wall or ceiling that's hiding the offending panel.)

❑ Sometimes, if you're bothered by a noisy single-pipe steam-heating system or a radiator that just doesn't heat, all you have to do is raise the air-vent end of the offending radiator. Each radiator on this kind of system needs to have a noticeable tilt back toward the supply-valve end (where the pipe connects to the radiator) so that condensed steam can drain back toward the boiler. Check the

The Man with the Smoke-Filled Rooms

A READER OF MY "PLAIN TALK" column wrote to say that whenever he used the fireplace on the first floor of his house, smoke filled the cellar and came up the stairs. How was the smoke getting into the cellar?

I responded by asking how many flues were in his chimney. Although flues are designed as exhaust pipes for your house, air can be sucked down them as well. It turns out there were two—one for the fireplace and one for the furnace. Both came out the top of the chimney side by side and at the same height.

A Word from Earl

The fireplace, needing air, was drawing that air from outside, down the furnace flue and up the cellar stairs. But because the two flues were so close together, instead of drawing fresh air down the flue, the fireplace was drawing back its own smoke. The man must have lived in a very well insulated house.

An outside air duct installed near the fireplace took care of the problem. Another solution would have been to extend one of the flues so that the two would no longer be the same height. If you look at photos of the rooftops in England, you'll notice that the various flues come out of the chimneys at different heights. That way, the smoke from one flue can dissipate before it's sucked down another.

HEATING CENTRAL, HERE

CENTRAL HEATING systems burn fuel in a furnace and distribute the resulting heat through the house, either by blowing hot air through ducts or pumping hot water through pipes. Generally, temperature levels in the house are controlled by a thermostat, and the furnace is able to function for a long period of time without refueling—unlike stoves and furnaces that burn wood or coal.

The most commonly used central heating fuels are oil and propane gas, both of which are readily available almost everywhere in the United States. The relative costs of oil and natural gas vary according to the area of the country in which you live.

If you're considering the purchase of an older house, talk to the owner about having the furnace tuned and tested for efficiency. Some old units are only 40 percent efficient, as opposed to the 80 percent efficiency of some newer ones. Also, many old installations are oversize, putting out much more heat than the house requires (and even more than the same house would require if it were well insulated).

If you decide to install a new central heating system for which the house was not designed, it's often cheaper to adapt to forced hot water than to hot air; the installer has to cut only small holes for pipes rather than large openings for ducts and grills. Most hot-water systems also use the furnace to heat domestic hot water. They're not quite as efficient as a separate system in terms of operation, but using them saves the cost of another installation. Perhaps the major drawback to forced hot water is that if the furnace goes out in winter, replacing burst pipes is expensive.

problem radiator with a level to make sure it's sloping in the right direction. If it isn't, insert shims at the base, on the end opposite the spot where the pipe connects, to adjust the slope.

Rules for Radiators

❏ If you're replacing your old radiators with a more modern system, don't discard the radiators or sell them for scrap. They'll fetch a fancy price on the restoration market. Ironically, it sometimes seems that the older and less efficient the radiator, the better the price.

❏ When selecting or building an enclosure for a radiator, be sure to provide two things: circulation and reflection.

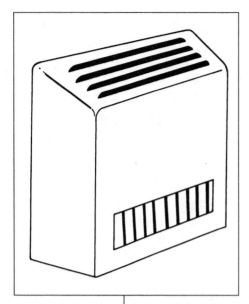

A radiator enclosure.

Cold air should come in at the bottom of the enclosure and be reflected off the back to the open grillwork at the top or front of the enclosure. You can design and build a radiator cover yourself; just fashion the grillwork out of any material that's open enough to allow the heat to escape into the room. But it's easier to buy prefabricated metal radiator covers from a mail-order company that specializes in their construction.

❑ When choosing radiator enclosures, always select covers with angles that deflect heat toward the middle of the room.

❑ To improve heating efficiency and prevent heat loss through the wall, place a heat shield behind each radiator. Ask at your hardware or heating supply store for a fire-safety-approved heat shield. Mounting instructions come with the shield.

❑ If you want to spend a little more time and less money, you can create your own heat shield. Just fasten aluminum foil or aluminum-faced insulation board to the wall behind the radiator.

Get into Hot Water

❑ If you currently have electric heat and want to increase the value of your house and lower your heating costs, consider installing a new forced hot-water heating system. Depending on where you live and the current economic situation, a new forced hot-water system might raise your home's selling price by a few thousand dollars more than it costs you. Check with local real estate agents and a heating contractor to find out whether this would be a wise investment.

❑ When planning for hot-water heat, figure on a generous number of baseboard heating units and radiators. The more heating units you have, the lower the water temperature necessary to heat the house. More units mean less fuel and less wear on your boiler.

□ If you're planning for a hot-water system, hire a plumber to run one main line around the house, under the floor. Then run one loop up into each room. Install a thermostat on each loop. This arrangement will allow you to keep each room at an appropriate temperature.

□ If a radiator in a hot-water heating system is noisy or doesn't heat well, it may have air in it. Using a wrench, turn the valve in the top of the radiator until air starts to escape. This is called bleeding the air from the valve. When water starts to spit out, you'll know all the air is gone.

ENERGY SAVERS

Bathing and Showering

□ To save on energy and hot water, make it a practice to take quick showers rather than baths.

□ When you do take a bath, leave the water in the tub after you get out. If you let it sit until it reaches room temperature, it will add a little warmth to the house and help humidify it.

CHIMNEYS

The Fine Art of Chimney Construction

□ Instead of building an exterior chimney, try locating your chimney inside the house. The chimney will retain heat from stove and fireplace fires and reflect that heat back into the living space if it's inside. Also, creosote builds up when the gases from your fire don't have enough momentum to escape from the chimney before they cool. A chimney on the outside of your house is colder than one on the inside. The exhaust from your fire will cool more quickly in an exterior chimney, and the potential for creosote buildup will be greater.

Whatsit?

I BOUGHT THIS OBJECT at an auction 12 years ago. The round bottom holds oil, and a wick comes in the middle. The tank on the back, which holds water, says "rain water" on the side. The tank is connected to the wick area by two pipes, one larger than the other. No one seems to know what it was used for. Can you help?
— R.S., FENTON, MICH.

This looks like a brooder stove used in the raising of chickens. The device would turn water into vapor and provide a moist heat.
By sticking with rainwater, the user prevented calcium from building up in the pipes.

❏ As a rule of thumb, the thickness of the concrete foundation on which a chimney sits should be ¹⁄₂₆ the height of the chimney. If a chimney is 26' high, its base should be 1' thick.

❏ Plan your chimney so that it extends at least 3' above the highest point where it passes though the roof and 2' above any part of the roof within 10', measured horizontally. This is sometimes called the 3-2-10 rule. If the top of the chimney is too close to your roof, air that travels over the roof will slide down the chimney and ruin the draft.

THE ANATOMY
OF A CHIMNEY

SIDE VIEW

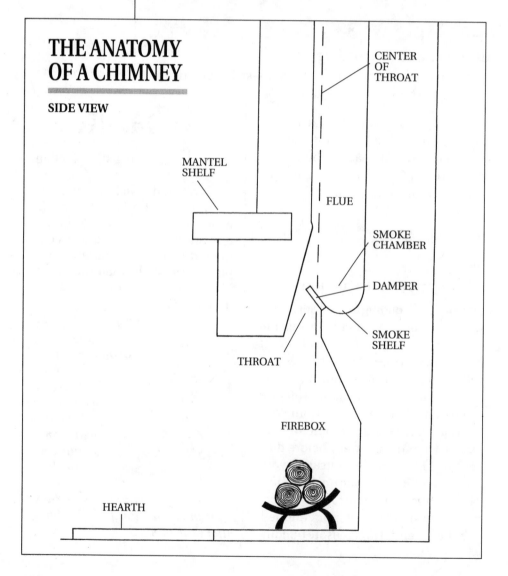

CENTER OF THROAT

MANTEL SHELF

FLUE

SMOKE CHAMBER

DAMPER

SMOKE SHELF

THROAT

FIREBOX

HEARTH

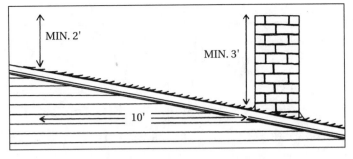

Follow the "3-2-10 rule" when you plan the height of your chimney.

Also, elevating the chimney above the roof helps minimize the chance of a spark igniting a fire on the roof.

Prescriptions for the Flue

❑ A flue is a lined smokestack inside a chimney. You can have more than one flue in a chimney, but don't connect more than one heating unit (a stove on one floor and a furnace on another, for instance) to the same flue. Doing so ruins the draft for both units.

❑ If your wood stove requires an 8"-diameter stovepipe, the chimney flue to which it hooks up should be 8" wide.

Flue Tile Efforts

❑ If you're building or repairing a chimney, you'll be working with hollow sections of round or square clay flue tile, stacked one on top of another and cemented together. The flue tile will need room to expand both horizontally and vertically. Leave an inch or two of space between the outside of the tile face and the inside of the chimney wall, then stuff that space with fiberglass insulation—packed loosely to allow for the tiles' expansion. Also leave a space at the top of the tile. Caulk this area with flexible caulking so you have a weathertight seal and still have room for the tile to expand.

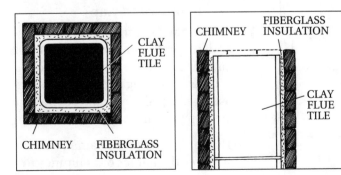

LEFT: *An overhead view of a chimney.* RIGHT: *A cross section of the chimney from the side.*

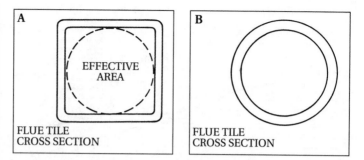

FLUE TILE
CROSS SECTION

FLUE TILE
CROSS SECTION

RIGHT: *For a fireplace with an opening 36" x 36" (1,296 square inches), install a square flue tile (A) with an opening of 130 square inches (¹⁄₁₀ the size of the fireplace opening). Or use a round flue tile (B) with an opening of 108 square inches (¹⁄₁₂ the size of the fireplace opening).*

BELOW: *You can use insulated stovepipe to exhaust a wood stove.*

❑ If your fireplace is not too large, consider installing a round flue. Round flue tiles, though not commonly available in large sizes, are more efficient than square ones. In a square flue, the effective area is the area of an inscribed circle. A square flue should have an opening ¹⁄₁₀ the size of the fireplace opening. In a round flue, the entire area is effective, so it needs to have an opening only ¹⁄₁₂ the size of the fireplace opening.

The Cheap Chimney

❑ If you're looking for a cheap, easy-to-install chimney for a cabin or outbuilding, consider using insulated stovepipe. *For safety's sake, be sure to follow the manufacturer's specifications and clean the stovepipe often.* To keep cleaning easy, run the pipe straight up, all the way from the stove to the chimney cap (which sits on top of the stovepipe if there's no other chimney). Connect the pipe to the stove with a T joint, capping it on the bottom.

Chimneys: To Cap or Not to Cap?

❑ If you have a problem with the mortar deteriorating on your chimney, it may be caused by rain falling into the chimney, resulting in excess moisture that damages the mortar. To prevent this, cap the chimney.

❑ Capping can make cleaning difficult and force the flames of a chimney fire

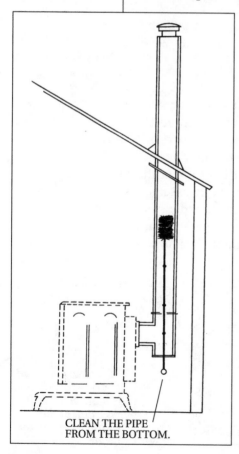

CLEAN THE PIPE FROM THE BOTTOM.

down toward the roof, so install a chimney cap *only* if you have severe water or downdraft problems. A cap can't correct a poorly built or misproportioned fireplace.

❏ If you install a chimney cap, make sure it's closed on two sides, forcing wind to move through it in a constant direction, and have it built as high as possible to allow more ease in cleaning the chimney.

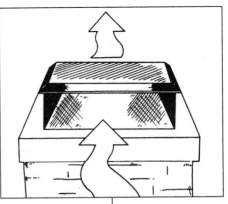

When the wind moves through a chimney cap in a constant direction, the draft is more even.

Mortar Sins and Other Problems

❏ Even if you correct a moisture problem by installing a chimney cap, if the mortar between the bricks is crumbling, the chimney will need to be pointed (freshly mortared). Scrape out all the loose mortar from the outside of the joints. Then mix up masonry cement by combining 3 parts sand, 1 part cement and enough water to make it a workable consistency. Apply this new mortar to the joints with a trowel.

❏ If the bricks in your chimney are not the best or are starting to crumble from age, seal the outsides with a clear masonry sealer, applied with a paintbrush. Preventing the bricks from absorbing rainwater will extend their life.

❏ If the bricks you're laying seem to be drying out the mortar too fast, dip them in a bucket of water before setting them. If your bricks are so soft and porous that they dry the mortar out extremely quickly, you may need to soak them for 2 to 3 minutes.

❏ After pointing or repointing a chimney, clean any excess cement or mortar off the bricks with a sponge or stiff bristle brush dipped in muriatic acid (available from hardware stores and, in many areas, pool supply stores). Be

DON'T TRY TO USE THEM AS PLANTERS

HAVE YOU EVER wondered about those decorative terra-cotta pots you sometimes see at the top of chimneys? Chimney pots are sometimes used to improve the draft, keep weather out and add architectural interest. In some cases, they act as a substitute for decaying or rotten masonry. They were popular in the United States during the nineteenth century, but today they're more commonly found in Europe.

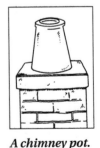

A chimney pot.

Whatsit?

I'VE DISPLAYED THIS tool at several shows hoping to find out what it was used for. No one has been able to give a satisfactory answer. It's 16½" long, including the handles, and made of solid brass, highly polished from use. The handles are stained from heavy use. I'm counting on you for the answer.

— N.L., MIDDLETOWN, OHIO

In my column, "Plain Talk," I admitted I had no idea what this was, and I asked our readers for help. I received many letters identifying it as, among other things, a drawshave (drawknife), a steam-valve wrench or a tool to strip bark from logs. Someone suggested it was designed to help two men carry a railroad rail. Someone else thought it was used to repair a flywheel on a small engine. A 12-year-old girl thought it might be a bottle opener.

Then I received two more letters, one from John W. Lock and the other from Robert Walters. Both men have some of these and both gave me the same answer. This is a beaming tool and was used to scrape the interior membranes and flesh from hides during tanning. Burnishing and softening of the hide could be done with the same tool. A leather casing was placed over the crescent part of the tool while doing the work.

sure to wear gloves and avoid getting the acid on your skin or clothes.

Bricks: Premature Aging

❏ To make interior brickwork look older, brush on boiled linseed oil. (Boiled linseed oil is available from paint and hardware stores. *Don't* try to make your own by boiling plain linseed oil.) Let it sit for a couple of hours, then scrub off any excess oil with rags. Oily rags are flammable, so spread them out to dry in a well-ventilated place before disposing of them.

Add a Flue Liner

❏ Old chimneys were built without flue liners. The mason simply applied a layer of plaster to the inside of the chimney as he built it. If you have an old chimney that's in need of repair, consider adding a flue liner instead of rebuilding the chimney. The former approach is much less expensive than the latter. Also, if your chimney has no liner, adding one will strengthen the chimney and provide some insulation.

❏ Don't expect a flue liner to prevent creosote buildup. The creosote will simply form on the walls of the liner.

❏ Depending on how frequently you use your chimney and how hot a fire you burn, you may want to use a stainless steel liner in your old unlined chimney. To install the liner, hook the sections together and lower them down the chimney. Stainless steel liners will burn out in time, so they're most effective if you don't have a lot of very hot fires.

If you want to reline a chimney that isn't straight, poured concrete is about the only material you can use. Old houses frequently have corbeled chimneys, where the mason moved part of the chimney a few inches to dodge a rafter. Before pouring a concrete flue liner, the contractor will stuff a giant balloon down the chimney as a form for the concrete. This balloon and the concrete can bend with the chimney. Metal flue liners will accommodate some bends, but poured liners are more versatile.

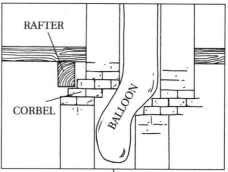

When a concrete flue liner is poured, a giant balloon serves as a form for the flue inside the chimney.

If your chimney is used for a stove and you're considering relining it with poured concrete, be sure to double-check the size of the flue before proceeding. A poured concrete liner should be at least 1" thick all around, and the remaining flue area should be no smaller than about 40 square inches. (For a round flue, that translates to about 7" in diameter.) Make sure your flue is large enough to meet these requirements. If it's not and the liner consumes too much space in the chimney, the draft will be cut back, causing smoke to escape into the room.

If you have a poured-concrete flue liner installed in a chimney that leads to a fireplace, make sure that the concrete is stopped at the bottom of the flue and does not fill up the chimney's smoke shelf. (You can make an exception if you have a wood stove hooked up into your fireplace and don't plan to use the fireplace without the wood stove again.)

Creeping Creosote

Avoid burning wood at a low temperature. Even dry wood burned at a

Whatsit?

CAN YOU TELL ME what this cast-iron item is? A number of antiques collectors haven't been able to name it or tell its use.
— W.O., WASHINGTON, N.H.

This is a jelly maker's stand. Placed on the hearth, it held two kettles. Fruit would be placed in one kettle to cook, then strained through a cloth placed over the second kettle. The strained juices in the second kettle would then be used to make jelly.

low temperature will produce more creosote than green wood burned fast and hot. (Much of the heat generated by burning green wood, however, is used to evaporate the moisture in the wood, not heat the house.) If your stove creates too much heat for the space around it, don't always damper it down to a slow burn. If you burn wood every day, once a week let it burn hot and crack open a window or two to make the room more comfortable.

Inspection Time

❏ Even if you use your chimney only for a central heating system, be sure to clean it. Soot can build up in the chimney, and birds may nest in it during the summer.

❏ Clean your chimney prior to each heating season and when inspection reveals a buildup of ¼" or more of creosote. A chimney positioned on the exterior of a house will

The Demolition Crew Tackles a Chimney

I HAD A CUSTOMER WHO WANTED to expand his kitchen. The problem was that a good-size chimney, not used anymore, was positioned in the space he wanted to expand into. He wouldn't hire someone for the job until that person could assure him that there would be no dust in the house resulting from the chimney's demolition. My approach convinced him.

A Word from Earl

I cut one side out of the chimney in the basement, making a hole about 1' wide and 4' high. Then I put a man on top of the chimney with a sledgehammer and orders to knock the brick into the flue as he worked his way down through the house. Meanwhile, another man drew the loose brick out the opening in the cellar. At each floor level, I used a vacuum cleaner to take up the dust and dirt in that section.

It's not a method I recommend for amateurs, but if you have a chimney that's getting in the way of renovations, you might ask your contractor about this approach.

generally require cleaning more fre-quently than one on the inside. If you use your chimney daily, check it every 2 months until you become familiar with how often it should be cleaned.

❑ When inspecting a chimney, check for leaks as well as creosote buildup. You'll know your chimney is in trouble if you see smoke leaking out between the bricks. Another bad sign is when you look up your chimney and see light from sources other than the top. To check your chimney for leaks, block off the cap, light a small fire and watch where the smoke comes out. Those are the spots that need repair. Once you've diagnosed the problem, call a mason to do the work.

❑ An easy way to examine a flue is to hold a small mirror underneath it at a 45° angle. If you have a clean-out door in your chimney, you'll find that door at the base of the chimney, in the cel-lar. Open it to gain access to the flue. If you have a stove and no clean-out door, you'll need to take down the stovepipe to get at the flue.

❑ It's best to examine your flue on a sunny day, when the maximum amount of light is in your chimney.

Chimney Sweeps

❑ It's easy to clean your own chimney—if you don't mind getting dirty. You can find an appropriate-size chimney brush at a hardware or wood stove store. Lay a drop cloth in your fireplace or at the base of your chimney to catch the falling creosote. Push the brush up the chimney, scrubbing back and forth as you go. One method to try is 2' up, 1' back. The brush comes with flexible nylon rods; add these to the handle to extend your reach as you push the brush farther up the chimney. Immediately after you finish, clean up all the creosote you've knocked loose be-fore you track it through the house.

FLUE ATTACKS

SOOT AND CREOSOTE are different materials. Soot is ashes that have left the stove or fireplace. A dry substance that forms on the inside of stovepipes and chimney flues, it's dirty but harmless. Cre-osote is wood tar that is distilled when wood is burned. It can condense inside your chimney, where it appears shiny and hard. Creosote is much more danger-ous than soot because it's flam-mable. Burning wood very slowly and burning green wood are the two major causes of creosote buildup. And creosote buildup is a major cause of chimney fires.

❏ You can also clean a chimney by climbing up on the roof and pushing the brush down the chimney, if that's more convenient and your chimney has no cap.

❏ Another way to clean your chimney is to use a small fir tree. Go up on the roof and drop a rope down the chimney. Then go inside the house and tie the rope to the stump of the fir tree. Go back onto the roof and pull the tree up the chimney. Then drop the rope back down into the chimney, go inside the house and haul the tree back down. (Or work with a partner and save yourself several trips to the roof and back.)

You Can Prevent House Fires

❏ If your wood stove is close to a wall, here's an easy way to protect the wall from catching on fire. Attach a sheet of ¼"-thick masonry board to the wall behind the stove. (A 4' x 4' sheet will be adequate for any of the common wood stoves.) Leave a 2" air space between the wall and the sheet of fireproofing to provide ventilation and keep the wall cool. Cut 2"-long sections of copper pipe (approximately one for every square foot of board) and position them as shown in the illustration. These will act as

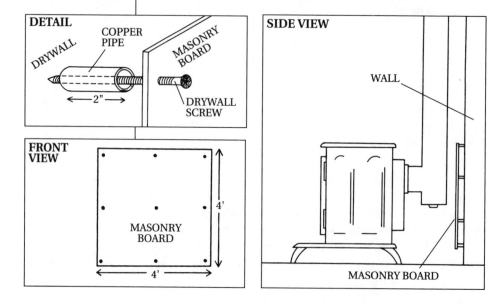

Chimney Fire

A Word from Earl

T HE FIRST THING YOU SHOULD DO when you know your chimney is on fire is call for help. Once a chimney fire starts to roar, there's nothing you can do on your own to stop it. I remember one chimney fire that broke out on an Easter Sunday when I was growing up. Flames were shooting out of our chimney by the time the firemen, who came directly from church in their best clothes, arrived at our house. My father sent me up into the attic to see whether the fire was going to break out. Bricks were cracking and popping from the heat. The firemen put the fire out in no time, but the chimney was ruined. We had to rebuild a good portion of it.

If you're aware of a fire before it really takes off (if your neighbor notices the smoke, for instance), you can do a couple of things while you're waiting for the fire department to arrive. (Never do these things *instead of* calling the fire department.) First, close all the drafts on your stove or fireplace. Take care not to get burned. Next, the fire chief in my town recommends (unofficially) throwing a cup of water on the coals in your stove. The idea is that the water will evaporate immediately, and the steam produced will choke the fire—and choking it is your only hope.

spacers. Predrill holes in the board, then place 4½" drywall screws in those holes and through the pipe, then tighten the screws into the wall.

❏ The intense heat from a chimney fire is likely to crack the bricks in the chimney, making it easy for the fire to ignite any woodwork that's in contact with it. For this reason, keep all structural members at least 2" from a chimney.

If Your Chimney Catches Fire
❏ The old-timers used to say that if your chimney caught fire, you should allow the fire to burn itself out. Don't lis-

ten to them. If you have a chimney fire, call the fire department immediately.

❏ After the fire department has extinguished a chimney fire, wait until things cool down, then clean your chimney thoroughly before using it again. The fire may not have consumed all combustible material in the chimney.

FIREPLACES

Building Basics

❏ In planning a fireplace, figure the depth at 18" from front to back. Make the opening at least 30" high and, if you want it to take a 24" log (usually a convenient size), 30" wide.

❏ Also in planning a fireplace, make the volume of the smoke chamber—the area above the damper and below the flue—one-half the volume of the firebox.

❏ You may want to use firebricks—baked yellow bricks that can withstand greater temperatures than normal red bricks—in parts of your fireplace where they will not be obvious. It's not uncommon for the back and two sides of a fireplace to be built out of firebricks, with just the front (exposed) side faced in red bricks.

Firebricks are less attractive than normal red bricks, but they're more durable. Use them on the back and sides of your fireplace, and save the red bricks for the facing.

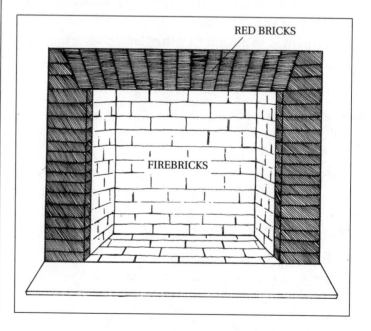

RED BRICKS

FIREBRICKS

Improving on Mother Nature

A Word from Earl

A CUSTOMER OF MY FATHER'S wanted a stone fireplace built in his cottage. My father hired a mason to build the fireplace, but he asked me to lay out the stones. Using some stones from an old wall on my own property, I laid out the hearth, mantel and lintel.

Unfortunately, stones rarely come with 90° corners and in the exact lengths you want. I had a beautiful keystone for the lintel, but making matching pieces on either side of it required a stone to be split in half. A couple of other stones needed to be cut to make square corners for the hearth and lintel. I showed the mason which ones to cut and went back to my carpentry work.

The owner of the cottage stopped the mason when she saw he was going to cut some stones. She told him that I had laid them out and that they were to be arranged just that way. The mason couldn't convince her that they had to be cut to fit right. She called my father, and he called me to go straighten things out.

When the mason explained the situation to me, I went into the cottage and suggested that the owner visit her neighbor, as it would be an hour or so before I got the mason going again. While the mason started cutting the stones as I had instructed, I went outside and built a little fire out of pine needles and twigs—and a couple of old asphalt shingles to make it smoke.

When the mason brought me a cut stone, I held it over the fire and smoked up the cut edge. Then I pulled moss from another stone and rubbed it into the smoked edge. When I had the stones all doctored up, it was impossible to tell that they had been cut. The mason replaced the stones on the floor where I had first laid them out. When the owner came back and looked them over, she said, "I knew Earl had the right stones. Now go ahead and lay them up."

Remember: Nature isn't always perfect. Don't be afraid to improve on it once in a while.

KEEPING YOUR BACK TO THE FIRE

M ETAL FIREBACKS originally were designed to hide the backs of fireplaces once the bricks had started to crumble. They also served to reflect more heat into the room. Firebacks are still manufactured and available from several mail-order companies. If you want to cover up cracked bricks or simply like the old-time appearance of these devices, you might want to look into ordering one.

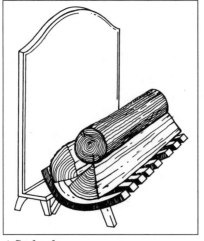

A fireback.

Fire Control

❏ Don't try to burn wood in your fireplace on andirons that are too high. Firewood will burn better and provide more heat when burned on andirons with 3" legs. These are low enough that the hot coals that fall through the andirons can still preheat the firewood that's sitting on top of them. Also, the lower you keep your fire, the more heat will go into the room before it escapes up the chimney. And low andirons make it easier to place wood in a fireplace.

❏ To start a draft going in a fireplace, light a crumpled piece of newspaper and hold it at the top of the fireplace for a few seconds before lighting the log fire. That will start to warm the air in the chimney, creating an updraft.

❏ If wood in your fireplace burns too quickly and all your heat goes up the chimney, your draft is too great. You can compensate for this by closing the damper slightly.

❏ If your fireplace doesn't have a damper, you can help regulate the draft as you build your fire. Pile ashes on the floor of the fireplace, as well as under and on the sides of the logs. You might also consider hiring someone to install a damper.

❏ If you burn newspaper logs, soaking the paper in water before rolling it lets you roll the paper into a tighter log, which will burn more slowly. If the logs burn too slowly for you, soak only about 4" of each end and don't roll them so tight. Use only black-and-white newsprint for this; colored inks used for comic pages and most magazines can emit poisonous fumes when burned.

Sometimes You Shouldn't Clean Up

❏ Don't make the common mistake of removing the ashes from your fireplace too often. Let them build up to 1" to

1½" from the base of the andirons. This will allow enough draft room between the wood and the hot coals that will fall on top of the ashes, but it will also insulate the bottom of the hot coals, thereby throwing more heat up against the wood. And it will protect the bricks on the floor of your fireplace from cracking when directly exposed to hot fires.

Sometimes You Should

❏ At the other extreme, don't allow ashes to fill the space under the grate completely while a hot fire is burning on top. Air needs to circulate under the grate to keep the underside cool, or the grate will burn out.

WOOD STOVES

Big Stove or Small?

❏ Are you trying to choose between one large wood stove and two smaller ones? Usually one large one works better. It takes larger chunks of wood, can burn longer fires and cuts maintenance and cleaning time in half. In some cases, though, such as in a ranch-style house, two stoves are necessary because the heat from one won't circulate throughout the house.

❏ On the other hand, don't go overboard and get a stove that's too big for the space you're heating. If the stove is too large, it won't have the opportunity to burn at a high enough combustion rate, and creosote will collect in the chimney. A smaller stove operating at a higher burn rate will provide better efficiency. Choose the smallest single stove that can adequately heat the space.

Backup Heat

❏ If you burn wood and need automatic heat backup when you're away, have a heating contractor take a hot-water loop off your domestic hot-water heater and run it through a fan-

WOOD ASHES FOR YOUR GARDEN

THE ASHES FROM wood fires contain everything in the wood minus water and carbohydrates, and they're very useful in the garden. The potassium in wood ashes encourages strong stems in plants, and the phosphorus encourages root growth. Spread over root crops such as carrots and beets, wood ashes discourage root maggots. Spread over vegetables, they deter slugs. Don't put ashes on a compost pile, though. The moisture in the pile will leach out the ashes' nutrients.

coil unit mounted on or in your living room wall. It won't heat the whole house, but it will help keep the temperature up until you get back home.

The Slow Burn

❏ If you're using a new cast-iron stove, light only small fires for the first week or two to season the metal and reduce the risk of cracking the cast iron.

❏ It's a good idea to line the bottom of a wood-burning stove with an inch or two of sand or ashes. That will reduce the heat reaching the stove bottom and extend its life.

❏ If you're building a fire that you want to last all night, it pays to know that one large log will last two to three times longer than the same volume of smaller logs.

❏ If you want a long-lasting fire, carefully choose the wood you're going to burn. The best woods for this purpose include hornbeam, hickory, white oak, rock elm and apple.

Careful Additions

❏ When you start the stove from scratch or revive it in the morning, use small pieces of wood to get a fast, hot, roaring fire going. Then add larger blocks of wood and turn down the draft. This helps prevent creosote buildup.

❏ To prevent a backflash or puff of smoke from coming into the room when you open the stove door to add firewood, first open the damper for a minute or two to provide more air to the fire. Then open the door slowly.

❏ Never put a piece of wood with ice or snow on it into a wood stove. The thermal shock can crack the iron. Leaving an ice-covered piece leaning against the stove to melt can also cause damage. Instead, let firewood thaw in

KEEP THE HOME FIRES BOILING

Wood doesn't just burn. There are actually three distinct phases to the process. First, the remaining water vapor in the wood must be heated to steam and boiled off before much flame can exist. Next, the flammable oils in wood (turpentine in a pine tree, for instance) are vaporized and burned. This is what creates the tongues of flame you see above a fire. The oils don't burn cleanly, either, and are responsible for the creosote buildup in your chimney. In the last burning stage, the coals combust. Since they are nearly pure carbon, they burn with little or no visible smoke or flame.

a mudroom or on the hearth (but not touching the stove) before burning it.

Humidify While You Heat

❑ Humidity helps keep wood and furniture from drying out. To add humidity to the air, place a kettle of water on the wood stove. Be careful not to let the kettle boil dry.

❑ If you don't heat with wood, you can add humidity to a room by placing containers of water on the radiators or near the air vents.

Top-of-the-Stove Room Fresheners

❑ To add a fresh scent to the room as you humidify it, place a small bough of balsam fir, a few cinnamon sticks or a handful of whole cloves in the pot of water on top of the wood stove.

❑ If you'd like to revive an old custom, try burning fresh potato peelings on top of the fireplace or wood stove logs to keep the chimney clean; some folks also use citrus fruit rinds. These techniques are not guaranteed chimney cleaners, but they are a good way to recycle peelings or rinds and produce a pleasant fragrance.

Clothes Drying: Save Energy, Money and Space

❑ For a cheap, energy-efficient way to dry clothes, place drying racks near the wood stove or wood furnace. (Don't place them *too* near, though; you want to dry the clothes, not burn them.) To save space, hang the rack overhead and attach a rope and pulley. That will allow you to lift the rack out of the way after you've hung clothes on it. If you have a grate for heating upstairs rooms, place a rack near the grate, too.

Keep Your Stove in Shape

❑ To increase efficiency, seal the joints in old cast-iron stoves once a year. You

Whatsit?

I'VE BEEN TRYING to find out what this is for some time. It couldn't have been used to carry anything, since it opens on the upstroke.

— M.S., FORT PLAIN, N.Y.

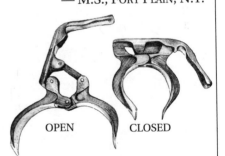

OPEN   CLOSED

This tool was used to open an auto tire wide enough to reach in and patch a hole or tear. Of course, the tire had to be taken off the rim beforehand. Today patching is done without all this work.

NO WONDER GEORGE CHOPPED DOWN THAT CHERRY TREE

THE FIRST AMERICAN heating fuel was wood. A typical colonist built a home with a large central chimney that had a fireplace on each face. The flues lacked any sort of damper, and it's estimated that 90 percent of the heat escaped up the chimney. No wonder people in harsher climates burned firewood at a rate of 4 to 5 cords per person per year! They spent a lot of time keeping the woodbox full.

can make stove cement inexpensively by mixing 2 parts wood ashes and 1 part table salt, then adding just enough water to make a thick paste. With a putty knife or trowel, apply this mixture to the seams inside the stove. (Newer stoves are still manufactured in sections but are less likely to have problems with cracking seams.)

❏ Before repainting a wood stove, go over it lightly with a wire brush. Then dust the stove with a rag moistened with paint thinner; this removes any dust without creating rust. When it's dry, spray-paint the stove with enamel stove paint, which is made to withstand high temperatures. The paint is available from wood stove and hardware stores.

❏ As an alternative to repainting a wood stove, you can restore it with traditional stove black applied with a rag. Stove black is available from wood stove and hardware stores.

❏ Before storing a stove for any length of time, wipe it with kerosene to prevent rust from forming. Be sure to store the stove in a dry place.

FIREWOOD

The Perfect Cut

❏ Some people prefer to cut their firewood in the spring, when the leaves on the trees have just come out. If you're a believer in this approach, wait several weeks after felling the tree before you limb it and cut it into firewood. During that time, the leaves will draw the water out from the wood. That will give you a head start on drying the wood and make it lighter to transport.

❏ Most people prefer another approach to cutting firewood: Fell the trees between late fall and early spring, when the wood is a lot drier to start with, then limb them and cut them to firewood lengths immediately. Most of the moisture in wood exits through the end grain. Cutting promptly means that you're creating more surfaces through which the moisture can escape.

❑ When possible, select dead or dying trees to cut for firewood. (This is good forest management, too.) Check a tree when the leaves are still on. If it's healthy, the top will have strong branches covered with leaves, and the bark will be smooth and of one color. Decay in the top branches and bark separating from the wood are signs of decline.

❑ Need a rule of thumb for estimating how much wood you can cut in a given area? In fairly good timberland, you should be able to cut 1 cord of wood for every 4 square rods. (Four square rods is a square of land measuring 33' on each side.)

WHICH WOODS BURN BEST

IF YOU NEED firewood fast, cut *ash.* Unseasoned, it burns better than any other wood. Seasoned, it's excellent.

White birch burns fast but not very hot. It's good for a quick fire to take off the chill in spring or fall. Or use it with slower-burning woods to keep them going. Strip off the bark and use it for a fire starter; there's nothing like it.

Beech, yellow birch and gray birch are tough to split and a little slow to dry, but they burn well and give plenty of heat.

Elm is best when it's cut in the dead of winter and dried for at least 2 years. But it's murder to split, it barely burns, and there's not much heat in it. Use elm only as a last resort.

Hornbeam, also called iron-wood, burns hot and lasts longer than any other wood. It's scarce, though. Don't cut live trees, but harvest any dead ones you find and save the wood for when you really need to hold a fire.

Oak makes excellent firewood but needs to be well seasoned. It sometimes sizzles and spits even after a year under cover.

Red maple is easy to cut and split and relatively easy to dry. It doesn't burn particularly hot, though.

Sugar maple dries slowly and splits hard, but it burns hot and lasts a long time.

WOODPILES: MEASURE FOR MEASURE

A CORD OF WOOD measures 4' high, 8' long and 4' deep when stacked. A *face cord* isn't a specific volume of wood. It is 4' high and 8' long when stacked. Its depth is simply the width of a log.

Stacked in a "beehive," your woodpile will stand more securely, and the individual pieces will be better protected from the weather.

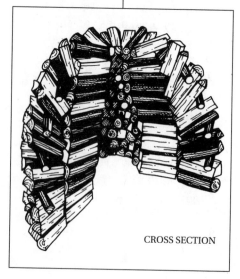

CROSS SECTION

Stacking Up

❑ If you can, stack your firewood where you cut it and leave it until it's dry. Why carry all that water back to the house if you don't need to?

❑ Avoid stacking firewood against a wooden building, as wood in direct contact with a building will encourage the building to rot.

❑ Stack your wood in a way that permits the air to circulate through it. If you stack your wood densely, it will dry very slowly.

❑ Long rows of stacked firewood are likely to tip over. What's worse is that successive rows of firewood can fall like dominoes. If you stack your firewood in rows, criss-crossing the ends of the rows will provide some stability.

❑ Another effective way of stacking a woodpile is to pile your wood up in a heap like an old-fashioned beehive. Lay two concentric circles of wood on the ground, leaving an 18" to 24" hole in the middle. This hole will act as a chimney, letting more air flow through the wood so it will dry faster. Build up the pile layer by layer, keeping the wood sloped toward the center. Around the outside ring of the pile, lay small pieces of wood perpendicular to the other pieces every few rows. This will keep the wood sloping toward the center so it won't fall out of the pile. A pile about 6' high will hold almost a cord of wood. As you get toward the top, close in the center hole so it won't fill up with snow.

❑ If the beehive technique of stacking firewood strikes you as too complex, here's an alternative. Get some used wooden pallets from any company that ships products. Lay the pallets flat on the ground, and they'll provide a good base for stacking firewood. They

Getting Firewood into the Basement Fast

I USED TO BRING MY FIREWOOD into the house by loading my pickup at the woodshed, driving it over the lawn to the basement door and wheeling the wood in a handcart down a step or two and into the basement.

Then I got smart. I cut a 2'-square hole in the floor of my garage, which is attached to the house on the first floor. Then I cut another hole to match in my foundation wall. I dug away the dirt between the holes to make a chute and lined the chute with concrete. To keep out the cold, I built an insulated plywood door for the hole in the foundation wall. Now I can unload the firewood from my pickup directly into my basement through the chute.

You don't need an attached garage to make a firewood chute. Just cut a hole in your foundation wall. But first make sure you won't be creating any structural or drainage problems.

keep the wood away from the moisture of the ground and allow air to circulate below the stack for ventilation.

❏ Here's another way to use wooden pallets to manage your woodpile. In addition to using a pallet as a base, use two more as end supports. For this approach, you'll also need four metal fence posts, each 4' to 6' long. (Fence posts are generally available at garden supply stores.)

Old pallets lend support to the end of a woodpile.

At one end of the woodpile, set a pallet on the ground next to the spot where you want to stand it on end. Place the fence posts in the ground about 6" in from either end of the pallet. Pound each post into the ground so that the metal "tag" is buried (that will put the base of each post about 1' deep), then simply turn the pallet on edge and slip it over the posts. Repeat for the other end of your woodpile.

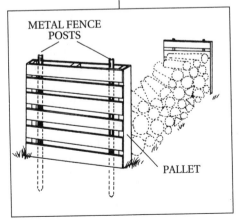

METAL FENCE POSTS

PALLET

This structure can easily be removed in spring. Even left out in the open, the pallets should last for several years, as they're usually made of hardwood. Any extra pallets can easily be cut into kindling.

❏ When you bring wood into your house, you're likely to bring in moisture and insects, too. Ideally, store the wood for your wood stove or fireplace outside the house and bring it in only a day or two before you plan to burn it—or even the same day.

❏ If you store wood in the cellar, pour a concrete floor first. This will make for easy cleanup.

What Not to Burn

❏ Don't bother to burn wet or green wood. Aside from the creosote problem it causes, it takes a lot of heat to boil the moisture out of wood, and that heat isn't recoverable.

❏ Pine isn't a good wood for burning; it creates excessive creosote buildup. If you must use it, burn only a stick or two at a time, and always at the same time as hardwood.

❏ Don't burn scraps of pressure-treated wood. This wood is treated with chromated copper arsenate (CCA), which is extremely toxic when burned.

Special Effects from Pinecones

❏ You can get some benefit from your pine trees without burning pine logs. Melt down your leftover candle stubs and dip pinecones in the wax. They make great fire starters for the fireplace or wood stove and also look nice piled up in a box or basket. (You can also start fires with pinecones that have not been waxed.)

❏ Here's another way to create special effects when burning pinecones. Dry the cones, then soak them for 24 hours in a solution of 1 pound of Epsom salts (available from drugstores) and 1 gallon of water. Let the cones dry before burning them. When you put them on the fire, they'll produce a rainbow of colors in the flames.

New and Improved

❏ You may want to consider heating with coal rather than wood. Coal used to be very messy, but when wood stoves came back, improvements were made in coal stoves, too. Today coal is readily available, clean, highly efficient and inexpensive.

❏ If you decide to burn coal, buy anthracite coal, which is sprayed with oil to keep down the dust and allow the burn to start more easily. Bituminous coal, which is not sprayed, is softer and dirtier; it's used mostly for industrial purposes.

❏ If you heat with coal, you'll probably want to buy nut-size pieces—1½" to 2" in diameter. This is the size most popular with homeowners because it is easy to handle and burns well in coal stoves. Other common sizes of coal—

In Days of Coal

MY MOTHER'S FATHER MADE his living delivering coal to homes and mills. Because it was handy, my mother preferred using coal rather than wood. We burned it in both the kitchen stove and the hot-air furnace in the cellar. I used to be sent down cellar to put more coal in the furnace and was always reminded at least twice to be sure to punch a hole in it. After I threw a few shovelfuls of coal on the fire, I'd take a long poker and make a hole in the pile of new coal. The hole provided a means of escape for the gases from the coal burning underneath. If I forgot, the gases would build up, there would be a minor explosion, and the smell of the coal fire would permeate the house.

A Word from Earl

    Burning coal is trickier and produces a few more potentially dangerous gases than burning wood. So when you build a fire in a coal stove, don't forget the hole. Otherwise, you'll get a pretty loud reminder.

Whatsit?

I HAVEN'T BEEN ABLE to figure out what this implement was used for. It's made of cast iron, and the words on the top of the lid read, "Enterprise Mfg. Co., No. 33. Pat. July 4, 93." Do you know what it is? — J.S., ATHOL, MASS.

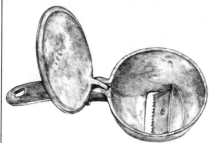

This is an ice shaver or shredder, used when ice was delivered in large cakes. A person who needed ice for a drink would drag this shaver across the ice cake, and it would shave off slivers to fill the cup. Then the ice would be dumped into a glass or pitcher.

large chunks and pea-size pieces—are used primarily in industry.

Get Started, Keep Going

❏ Heating with coal doesn't mean you won't ever need wood again. To start a coal fire, get a good hot fire going with hardwood kindling. Then add a shovelful or two of coal. When this coal has begun to burn, add more coal. It will usually take about 10 minutes for the wood fire to get hot enough to ignite the coal, so be sure to use enough kindling to last that long. Leave any dampers open for a good 10 minutes or so to get rid of the gases. Anthracite coal will not light unless it has a bottom draft.

❏ It can be a chore lighting a coal fire in the morning, so it's easier—and warmer!—if you keep the fire going all night. First, turn down all the drafts on your coal stove. Then throw a few shovelfuls of coal onto the fire, being careful not to smother it with the new coal. To let the gases escape from the existing fire, leave a small hole in the layer of coal you're adding. The fire will burn slowly until morning.

Ashes to Ashes

❏ Coal creates a fair amount of ashes (two to three times as much as a comparable amount of wood), so be sure to clean the ashes from the stove regularly. If your stove has a small ashpan, you may have to empty the pan once a day.

PORTABLE HEATERS

Handle with Care

❏ Portable electric heaters should be used with great caution. Don't use old electric heaters if the wiring appears at all worn.

☐ Make sure all flammable objects are clear of an electric heater before using it.

☐ Electric heaters can use a sizable amount of electricity. It's common to blow a fuse or trip a circuit breaker if you use one on the same circuit with another appliance. If you can, try to plug your heater into an outlet that's not supporting a heavy load already. Make sure the current (fuse) rating can support the heater.

Kerosene: Proceed with Caution

☐ Kerosene heaters are especially dangerous and are illegal in many areas. If you must use one, look for a heater that has these safety features: an automatic shutoff device that is triggered whenever the heater is jarred or tipped over; guards or grills to protect people from touching the hot surfaces; a tamperproof wick adjustment mechanism to ensure that the wick burns cleanly and evenly and isn't subject to sudden flare-up. Also make sure that the label says that the heater is Underwriters Laboratories (UL) listed or tested and approved by the Kerosene Heater Association. Their tests are stringent.

Other Choices

☐ Liquefied petroleum gas (LPG) space heaters make a good backup system for wood stoves. If you use one of these, be sure to vent it to the outdoors and place the vent at least 2' away from a window that opens. (You don't want the exhaust coming back in the house.)

☐ Don't be alarmed by that strange smell when a space heater first fires up. If the heater isn't used for a spell, dust settles on it and then cooks off during the first few minutes of use.

☐ Before you decide on an unvented oil- or kerosene-fired heater to provide supplemental heat in your living room, consider this: Even the most modern units generate about 1 gallon of moisture for each gallon of fuel

THE BACK-DOOR APPROACH

OLD YANKEES NEVER used the front door in winter. They used the back door, more often than not walking into a mudroom or back hall that had a door, kept closed, separating it from the rest of the house. Not only was that back room useful in preventing gales of wind from surging through the house every time the outside door was opened, but it also was a handy place to keep a shovel and a bucket of sand. That way, the owners could keep at least one entry to the house open and safe.

burned. The cost of repairing the condensation damage may be greater than the savings in heating dollars.

Basic Warm-Ups

❏ Maximize the effect of passive solar heat in winter. Keep all the curtains and shades open during the day on the side of the house where the sun comes in. (This is all day on the south side, morning on the east and afternoon on the west.) The warmth from the sun warms the floor and furniture. After sundown, close all the shades and drapes.

❏ If you have the old type of storm windows that need to be installed each winter, it can get confusing figuring out which window goes where. To avoid this, use a screwdriver, a hammer and Roman numerals to mark each window frame. Tapping the screwdriver lightly with the hammer, indent the blade in the wood just enough to make any number needed. Then make corresponding marks in an inconspicuous part of the appropriate windowsill. Even if you repaint later, your marks will remain intact.

❏ Before winter arrives, make sure registers and convectors are open, unblocked by furniture and rugs. Keep furniture from blocking off the flow of air to and from radiators.

❏ For some additional winter heat and humidity, disconnect the exhaust to your clothes dryer and put a nylon stocking over the machine's air outlet. The nylon will trap lint while releasing hot air and humidity into the house. (Be careful not to direct the hot air onto a wall or other potentially flammable object, and make sure you're not creating a moisture problem.)

ON A CLEAR DAY, YOU CAN SEE THE HEAT LOSS

B E CAREFUL WHEN talking about R-values and insulation in your house's windows. Although the window-making industry has made some real advances in keeping the cold air out, it has done relatively little to make windows better at keeping the hot air in. Old, standard single-pane windows had an insulating value of about R-2. The best of the new ones provide about R-4—double the performance of the old panes. But that's still not much to brag about when you consider that a new window is likely to be placed in a wall with an R-value close to R-19.

Dodge the Draft

❏ Stone foundations can be drafty when winter winds blow. In the fall, place a row of hay bales or bags of leaves snugly around the outside of the foundation; these will conserve heat come winter. It's critical that your "banking" doesn't come in contact with the house's wood siding. If it touches the siding, it will conduct and trap moisture, damaging the wood.

The Message in the Mail Slot

HOUSES WERE NOT SO WELL insulated years ago. This actually had its advantages; they could breathe, letting stoves and fireplaces get their air through cracks and loose windows and doors.

I once built a large house for a man who, when he kept feeling a draft from this door or that window, asked me to install more weather strip. I kept telling him he was making the house too tight, creating potential health and safety hazards, but he wanted to eliminate all the drafts. Finally, he told me that when he walked by the front door, he could feel a draft. I had to put more weather strip on the door.

A Word from Earl

Not long after that, he called me at 11:00 one night and said that something was very wrong with his house. The mail slot in his front door was wide open and he was getting a draft from it. Each time he closed it, it would fly open again. I asked him if his fireplace was going, and he said it was. I told him to crack a window in the living room and then check on the mail slot. Sure enough, it was closed. His house was so tight that his fireplace was starved for air. After that, I installed a duct to bring fresh air to his fireplace.

If you live in a house that's especially well insulated and you want to operate a fireplace or wood stove, you must install a duct to furnish air for the fire. The air that escapes up your chimney must come from somewhere.

❏ A small crack under a board or at the sill line of a house can cause significant heat loss. Before winter arrives, inspect all around your sills and seal all cracks or holes with a caulking gun and flexible caulk. Flexible caulk remains pliable even at very low temperatures.

❏ To repair big holes at the sill line or holes in hard-to-reach places, use expandable foam, available from hardware stores and sold in a pressurized can. Squirted into a hole, it expands and hardens to fill the spot.

Heat Loss from the Ground Up

❏ If you live in an older house, drafts may come up through cracks in the wood floors and even through your room-size rugs. To avoid this and create a useful vapor barrier, roll back all large rugs and lay down 4-mil polyethylene (plastic sheeting, available in rolls from hardware stores). In each instance, cut the polyethylene a few inches smaller than the rug. After installing the polyethylene, replace the rug. The room will be warmer, and the rug will hide your new insulator.

❏ You can put 4-mil polyethylene under wall-to-wall carpeting, too. But don't try this under scatter rugs; the plastic will make them slip around.

❏ Perhaps the greatest source of heat loss in some homes is the sill plate, where the house meets the foundation. To prevent this, stuff fiberglass insulation between the joist ends and along the sill plate parallel to the joists.

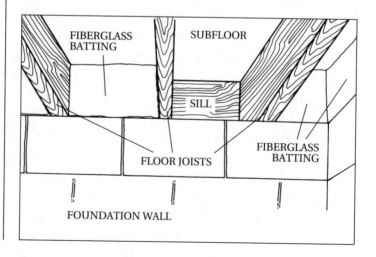

Insulate the sill plate as thoroughly as you can.

The Day I Got Rid of a Ghost

A Word from Earl

A NEW HOMEOWNER HIRED ME to lay hardwood floors in a second-floor apartment. He and his family had already moved in on the first floor. One day he told me that his wife had been hearing someone moaning every once in a while. She had told him that if he didn't find where it was coming from, she was moving out. It seems the previous owner had died in the house, and the wife of the new owner feared that the house was haunted. The husband had heard the moaning, too, but he couldn't identify its source.

I went downstairs, and, sure enough, I could hear the moaning. It seemed to be loudest in the kitchen. I listened for a while and observed that the moaning stopped when the wind died down. After examining the windows in the room, I noticed that the weather strip on one window was not tight to the sill at one end. When the wind blew, the thin metal strip would vibrate and create a moaning sound. Bending it out a little with a screwdriver stopped the moaning.

If you're bothered by ghostly moans in a new house, conduct a brief inspection tour before you call in an exorcist.

Plug the Leaks

❏ In many homes, plenty of heat is lost through switch and outlet holes. To stop a lot of leaking, remove the switch plates and seal behind the hardware with canned foam insulation, available from hardware stores. It's easy to remove the dried foam if you ever need to work on the outlet or switch later.

Strip Joints

❏ Weather strip is an obvious but effective tool for sealing in heat. If you're not sure what kind to use around your windows, try the ropelike coils of semisoft putty. They're easy to use and inexpensive. Around doors, install felt weather strip, which is very durable.

❏ Silicone caulk is more expensive than most other types, but it's the best type to use for weatherproofing because it stays flexible at just about any temperature. Most other caulks get hard and crack. Use silicone caulk around windows, along sill lines, between the cracks of a log cabin— virtually anywhere you need weatherproofing.

VENTILATION AND INSULATION

Venting: A Good Trade

❏ To reduce indoor pollution from insulation, plywood glues, gas stoves and oil-fired furnaces in a highly insulated house, it's a good idea to ventilate the home during the day or install a heat exchanger. A heat exchanger will transfer the heat from the warm indoor air you are exhausting to the cold fresh air you are bringing in. It's more energy efficient than opening a window.

❏ To provide appropriate ventilation in a house with a gable roof, install louvers in both ends of the roof, letting attic heat escape in the summer and moisture out in the winter. Most people make louvers too small, not realiz-

INSULATION: A WARM AND WONDERFUL IDEA

EARLY INSULATION wasn't very successful. The insulating value of crumpled newspaper was almost nil, and newsprint was hard to come by. Sawdust, wheat chaff and corncobs were more readily available but also more likely to foster wood rot and nests of vermin. Aged manure was occasionally used—in truly desperate situations. Soft brick infilling was sometimes laid up between the walls, and in some cases, backplastering was applied to the inside of exterior sheathing before the interior walls were plastered. These two methods worked a little better than other types of insulation.

By the early twentieth century, more insulation materials were being tried, with some degree of success. Mineral wool and shredded cellulose were the most common materials, along with a commercial product called Cabot's Insulated Blankets—woven eelgrass mats stitched between layers of kraft paper. It wasn't until the post–World War II housing boom that the use of fiberglass insulation became widespread.

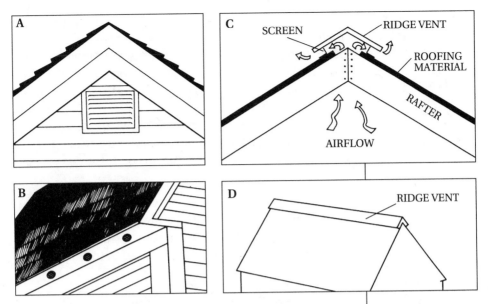

A

C
SCREEN   RIDGE VENT
          ROOFING
          MATERIAL
          RAFTER
AIRFLOW

B

D
          RIDGE VENT

ing that the openings lose half their ventilating area when they're covered with screens and slats. Install louvers as high as you can on the gable so that the air at the peak of the roof can escape.

❑ Be sure to install vents under the eaves, too. These vents work with the louvers in getting rid of heat and moisture. And consider installing ridge vents that run the length of the roof. The idea is to keep cold air circulating through your attic.

❑ Make sure your house has adequate ventilation above the insulation in the attic. Remember that heat isn't doing you any good in your attic. Once it has escaped the heated portion of your house, you want it gone. Heat escaping slowly through the roof will melt any snow on it and form an ice dam. And moisture stuck under your roof can lead to rotting timbers. Your roof's only purpose is to keep the elements off your house; you don't want it to keep heat and moisture in.

❑ In any basement crawl space, be sure to install at least two vents, and locate them on opposite walls. One vent on every wall is better.

The Great Vapor Barrier

❑ If you don't have vapor barriers in your walls, the water vapor in the air of your warm room is likely to enter

Position attic louvers (A) as close to the peak of the roof as possible. Vents installed under the eaves (B) let cool air into your attic. When a roof is capped with a ridge vent (C, D), the roofing material stops short of the peak. Hot air escapes from the attic through the gap in the roofing material. Small screens in the vent keep bugs out.

the walls and condense in the stud space between the walls and the exterior siding. This can cause paint to peel down to bare wood on the outside of your house. To prevent this problem, install a good vapor barrier in each outside wall, on the warm side of the insulation. This can be the vapor barrier that comes with blanket insulation, or you can use 4-mil polyethylene (plastic sheeting). Install the polyethylene vapor barriers inside each exterior wall. The best placement usually is on the studs just under the drywall.

❑ You can insulate an exterior wall with batts of insulation even if they have no built-in vapor barriers. Simply place the batts between the studs, then staple a clear plastic vapor barrier over all the studding before you install your drywall.

You can increase the insulating performance of your walls by adding 1" of air space between your insulation and drywall.

❑ As a rule of thumb, the vapor barrier in any insulation always goes on the side toward the warmest room, as the warm air contains the most moisture. This is particularly important when you're working in a basement or attic area.

❑ Besides serving as a vapor barrier, the foil part of an insulation batt is designed to reflect heat back into a room. It's most effective when there's at least 1" of air space between the foil and the drywall. To achieve this, install the insulation between the studs, then extend the flap on the insulation and staple it (the flap) to the studs. Nail 1" x 2" strapping on the face of the studs, driving the nails through the flap on the insulation. Then hang the drywall.

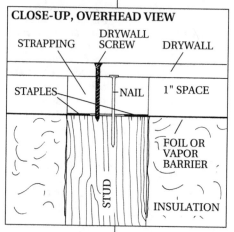

CLOSE-UP, OVERHEAD VIEW

STRAPPING / DRYWALL SCREW / DRYWALL / STAPLES / NAIL / 1" SPACE / FOIL OR VAPOR BARRIER / STUD / INSULATION

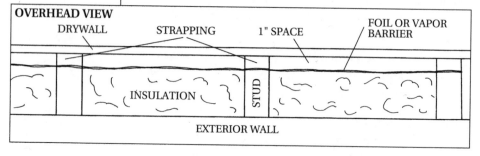

OVERHEAD VIEW

DRYWALL / STRAPPING / 1" SPACE / FOIL OR VAPOR BARRIER / INSULATION / STUD / EXTERIOR WALL

Proper Placement

❏ In the floor of a heated room with an unheated space below it, install the vapor barrier between the subfloor and the finish floor.

❏ An alternative is to install the insulation in the ceiling of the colder room below and nail chicken wire across the joists to keep the insulation in place. In the case of a room with an unheated space above it, the vapor barrier should be positioned between the ceiling and the ceiling joists.

❏ Surface condensation in a crawl space shows that a vapor barrier is needed to keep out the excessive moisture. To make an inexpensive vapor barrier, install a complete seal of 4-mil polyethylene (plastic sheeting) on the floor. Carry it up the walls and any posts or chimney bases about 6". (It's not necessary to secure the plastic to those surfaces; simply stand a few bricks against the wall to hold the plastic in place.) Overlap all seams 6" and anchor the plastic at seams and walls with bricks or stones. Don't crawl on the film; any holes you make in it will make the vapor barrier less effective.

A SANDWICH THAT'S HAZARDOUS TO YOUR HEALTH

POLYSTYRENE FOAM has become a popular insulation material in recent years. It is found, among other places, in stresskin "sandwich" panels. There are two methods of producing the foam, both of which are associated with some environmental concerns. Better than polystyrene from an environmental standpoint is rigid fiberglass—a material that has been available for some time in the United States for insulating foundations and is now being marketed for insulation in other parts of the home.

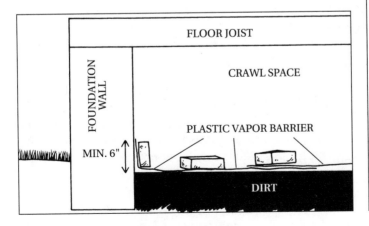

FLOOR JOIST

FOUNDATION WALL

CRAWL SPACE

MIN. 6"

PLASTIC VAPOR BARRIER

DIRT

If you use sheets of plastic as a vapor barrier in a crawl space, anchor the plastic with bricks or stones and continue the plastic at least 6" up the wall.

Insulation: The Fourth "R"

❑ In buying insulation, it's helpful to know that the R-value stands for the thermal resistance of the material. One type of insulation may be thicker or thinner than another, but if they have the same R-value, they'll do the same job.

❑ If the winters are hard where you live, try to have an R-value of at least R-33 in the ceiling and R-19 in the walls. As long as your house is properly ventilated, you can't have too much insulation.

❑ The attic floor is an important and easy place to add insulation. Nine-inch-thick fiberglass batts are about right for most houses, although you may use rolls of thicker material. Lay the insulation between the attic floorboards and the ceiling of the room below. A lot of heat is commonly lost through the roof, so if you're going to insulate only one part of your home, this is the place to do it.

❑ Another good alternative is to blow a layer of fiberglass insulation onto the attic floor. This is particularly effective because the insulation is seamless.

❑ If the rafters in your attic show signs of wetness in the cold weather, check the attic floor insulation to make sure you have a vapor barrier between the insulation and the ceiling below. If there isn't any barrier, draw the existing insulation back and install a blanket insulation that has a vapor barrier on it. Lay the batts between the joists with the vapor barrier facing the ceiling below. Then place the loose fill on top of this blanket.

❑ Black stains showing on ceilings only under the joists are caused by the joists' being colder than the ceiling sections between them. Warm, moist air in the room below picks up dust, and since the area below the joists is colder than the ceiling area between them, the moisture condenses on the coldest areas first and leaves the dust

---

Whatsit?

WHILE CLEANING out our attic, I found this item. It's 12" long, the rings move freely, and the center is jointed. What is it?

— E.B., NEW CANAAN, CONN.

This is a jointed-mouth standard team bit. It goes into a horse's mouth, and the reins hitch onto the large rings.

---

that causes the stain. To remedy this situation, lay blanket insulation across the tops of the joists. This will make them warm enough to help prevent the stains. Lowering the humidity in the room by increasing the ventilation will also help.

Look to the Window

❏ In windows that have sash weights, you can sometimes feel a draft coming from the pulley holes. You can't do anything to insulate the cavity in which the weights move, but you can stuff the area below the weights with fiberglass insulation. Also, check the outside of the window for cracks between the siding and casing, and seal them with caulk.

COOLING

Windows: An Open-and-Shut Case

❏ Think twice before opening a window when it's hot outside; doing so can let more hot air into your house. Instead, try this simple technique during the next heat wave. Keep all the windows closed and the shades drawn during the day. Then open all the windows at night, when the air has cooled off. In the morning, close the windows and pull the shades before the air warms up again.

❏ When you do open the windows to enjoy a breeze or the cool night air, try to take advantage of cross ventilation. When you open one window on the side of your house with the prevailing winds, open another on the opposite side of the house. The draft created should help cool things down.

Fans Can Be Fabulous

❏ When you use an electric fan to cool off in hot weather, don't direct it at yourself; all that does is surround you with

---

STORM WINDOWS: CONDENSATION IS GOOD

THE AIR SPACE between the storm window and the inside window does the insulating, so a tight fit is essential. For this reason, old wooden storms (though a chore to put on and take off) are usually superior to more modern aluminum combination windows. Aluminum expands and contracts with changing temperatures, eventually losing its once-tight fit. A good storm sash is custom-made for each window opening, and even after many years, it will fit tightly.

A sign of a tight-fitting storm sash is fog or condensation on the inside glazing. If there's never condensation, it means one of two things (probably the latter): an exceptionally tight-fitting inside window or excessive infiltration between the storm sash and the window casing.

more hot air. Instead, set the fan in a window on the sunny side of the house, blowing out. Then open another window on the opposite (cool) side of the house. The fan will blow hot air out and draw cool air in.

❑ Consider installing a ceiling fan to circulate the air in your home. These fans are not very expensive, and they're simple to install if the wiring is already in place. You may be able to take advantage of wiring that was installed for overhead lighting and install a fan instead of a light fixture. (If you're unsure about electrical work, hire an electrician for this.)

❑ Don't install a ceiling fan in a room with a low ceiling. The blades of the fan should be at least 1' from the ceil-

AIR-CONDITIONING: AN ANCIENT IDEA

BACK AROUND 2000 B.C., the Egyptians were the coolest. They were the first people to figure out a way to produce ice in a dry, temperate climate. Their method was simple but ingenious. Around dusk, the women would place water in shallow clay trays on a bed of straw. Evaporation from the water's surface and the damp sides of the tray, combined with the drop in the nighttime temperature, caused ice to form in the tray (even though the temperature didn't come close to freezing). The Egyptians knew a key natural principle: Cooling occurs through the process of evaporation. And with such low humidity, those trays of water were enough to cause quite a temperature drop where the action was taking place.

A thousand years later, the Babylonians hit on the same idea and expanded on it. Some of the smarter ones discovered that if they sprayed the floors and walls of their rooms with water shortly before sundown, the resulting evaporation would be enough to create some relief from the oppressive heat, effectively creating the world's first air-conditioning system.

The term *air-conditioning* wasn't coined until 1907, when a physicist named Stuart Cramer presented a paper on humidity before a meeting of the American Cotton Manufacturers Association. When the first consumer models came off the line a few years later, the term, which by then had become common within the industry, began to establish itself as part of the American consciousness (and, later, part of the American dream).

ing, so the fan has a sufficient supply of air, and at least 8' from the floor, so that a person inadvertently reaching over his or her head while standing won't be struck by the blades.

❏ During hot weather, get in the habit of using the fan over your stove whenever you cook, not just when the food being cooked is creating lots of steam. The stove produces heat whenever it's in use, and the fan will blow at least some of that heat outside.

❏ When you use the fan over your stove, be sure to open a window elsewhere in the house, too. This will give the fan a greater supply of air to blow, so it will be more effective.

Use Your Home's Natural Cooling Potential

❏ Your cellar is a natural air conditioner for your home. Open the door to the cellar or basement and use a fan to draw the cool air into the upper floors. Warm air will circulate into the cellar, which will help keep moist air from condensing there.

❏ If you have a hot-air heating system, you can use it to cool your house in the summer. Just turn off the furnace and run only the fan. This will take cool air from the basement and distribute it through the house.

❏ In the winter, close your fireplace damper when the fireplace is not in use so your heat doesn't go up the chimney. In the summer, when you want the heat to go up the chimney, open your fireplace damper.

A FAN-TASTIC IDEA

THE ELECTRIC FAN was invented by Dr. Schuyler Watts Wheeler in 1882, when he had the revolutionary idea of mounting a propeller on the shaft of an electric motor. In 1904, apparently believing the maxim "better late than never," the Franklin Institute awarded Wheeler the prestigious John Scott Medal, thereby proving that the institute was a big fan of his work.

Maintaining the Exterior

Vines on the brickwork, moss on the roof— it's a jungle out there.

During the Hurricane of 1938, a large buttonwood tree blew over onto my parents' house. The house was groaning under the tree's weight, so my brother and I went out in the middle of the storm to cut it up with a two-man saw.

The power of the hurricane was amazing. All the chimneys in our neighborhood had blown off. When we looked up the street, we saw a whole grove of tall pines snapping off 10' up from the ground and flying away. Looking in the other direction, we watched as the wind tore rows of slate off a roof and fired the tiles into the sky like machine-gun bullets.

The next morning, I noticed that the wind had driven slivers of slate deep into the telephone poles outside our house. We were lucky we hadn't been killed by the flying debris.

I doubt I'll ever see another storm as powerful as the Hurricane of 1938. But the forces of nature are always at work on the exterior of your home. Only if you keep the shell of your house in shape—from the peak of the roof to the floor of the cellar—can you win the war against the elements.

To help you in that effort, this chapter offers some time-tested battle plans. Here are ideas for getting mildew off the siding and moss off the roof, matching new shingles to weathered ones and dealing with dry rot. You'll find a creative suggestion for making your new brickwork blend in with the old and learn how to get hardened concrete off your best shovel—so you'll be all set to start your *next* project.

CLAPBOARD SIDING

Replacing a Clapboard

❏ To replace a damaged clapboard, pry it up with a wood chisel or thin bar and remove the nails along the bottom edge. Next, carefully pry up the clapboard above the one you want to replace and remove the nails on *its* bottom edge. Draw out the damaged clapboard and slide in a new one cut to fit. Then renail along the bottom edges of

IF YOU CAN'T FIND IT ...

... maybe you need to try another chapter. Check the index, or try these possibilities.

For Tips On ...	*See the Chapter ...*
Chimneys	Heating and Cooling
Concrete	The Great Outdoors
Doors	Basic Household Repairs and Maintenance
Insulation	Heating and Cooling
Masonry	Heating and Cooling
Painting	Painting Inside and Out
Ventilation	Heating and Cooling
Weather strip	Heating and Cooling
Windows	Basic Household Repairs and Maintenance

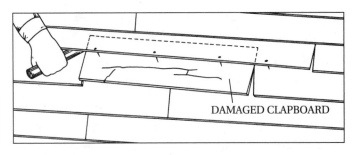

Loosen the clapboard above the one you want to remove.

DAMAGED CLAPBOARD

both the new clapboard and the old one above it with 3d to 5d hot-dip galvanized wire box nails.

What to Do about Mildew

❏ If the painted exterior of your house has developed mildew, you can get rid of it with a TSP solution. Combine ½ cup of TSP (or another product containing trisodium phosphate), 1 quart of household (5 percent) bleach and ¼ cup of dishwashing liquid. *Be sure the dishwashing liquid doesn't contain ammonia, which creates lethal fumes when combined with bleach.* Add enough warm water to make 1 gallon of solution. Apply the solution with a rag or scrub brush. When the mildew is gone, rinse the siding with a hose.

❏ Before repainting mildewed clapboards, sterilize the area to discourage mildew from forming again. Make a solution of equal parts household (5 percent) bleach and warm water. *This is a powerful solution, so handle it with care. Wear gloves, goggles and old clothes, and keep the mixture away from children and pets.* Cover any nearby plants to protect them from the mixture while you're using it. Scrub the solution into the affected area with a medium-soft brush, then rinse it off with plenty of water. After the area has dried, prime it, then paint it to match the rest of the house.

Skirtboards: All Dressed Up

❏ On an older house with clapboard siding, you'll usually find a skirtboard

---

KEEPING UP WITH THE WASHINGTONS

OURS IS NOT the first generation to care about what the neighbors think. One example of early homeowner vanity can be seen today on old houses and barns that still have their original siding. It was a common practice in early America to place clapboards on the side (or sides) of the building facing the road and cover the back with less expensive wooden shingles. Passersby looking at the building would see only the clapboards and think the homeowner a person of good taste and means.

---

where the siding meets the foundation. The top of the board is usually beveled to shed water. Skirtboards are frequently omitted on new clapboard-sided houses for reasons of economy, but if you want to add them, just remove the bottom two rows of clapboards and replace them with pine lumber of the appropriate width.

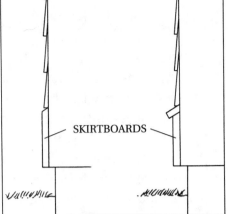

❏ If you're installing a skirtboard, you may want to add a second piece to act as a beveled roof over the skirtboard. This piece directs any water that's streaming down the siding away from the foundation. It's also a nice decorative touch.

A skirtboard (left) is positioned at the bottom of the siding. A slightly fancier version (right) adds a second piece as a beveled roof to direct water away from the foundation.

SHINGLE SIDING

Cedar Can Be Swell(ed)

❏ Most wooden shingles used for siding are made of either red or white cedar. Red cedar shingles—which are better finished, more expensive and red in color—are used most commonly on homes. When laying red cedar shingles, leave a ⅛" to ³⁄₁₆" gap between shingles as you nail them. Since the shingles have been dried, they will swell with moisture when exposed to the elements, and this will make them buckle if they're laid tight.

❏ If you're using white cedar shingles, lay them tight to each other. They haven't been dried and are loaded with moisture, so they will shrink with time.

❏ In deciding between red and white cedar shingles, you may be drawn to the attractive color of white cedar. Initially white, these shingles will weather to a nice gray if left untreated. However, because they are crudely finished, white cedar shingles tend to curl. If you can afford red cedar shingles, you'll probably be happier with them.

Uneven Shakes

❏ Cedar shakes are shinglelike coverings that are very rough and irregular in shape. If you use them to roof your house, nail them up as close together as possible. Their irregularity will leave space for expansion and contraction.

Wasps and Eaves Go Together

IF YOU'VE EVER WORKED on a big roofing or siding project, you know that wasps and bees can be a menace in those areas.

One time my brother and I were nailing asphalt shingles onto an old barn. The air outside the barn was thick with wasps. We tried to ignore them, but you can stand them hovering around you only so long. My brother got a can of insect repellent and started spraying it around liberally. The wasps were put off, but we were discouraged to see that the insect repellent, when it landed on the gray asphalt shingles, turned them black. We had to replace a good number of the shingles.

A Word from Earl

On another occasion, two of my father's men were supposed to be installing clapboards on the side of a barn. When he went to check on them, he found them standing around swatting at wasps that kept coming out of a hole high up on the side of the barn. Whenever the men started to nail a clapboard, the wasps would come after them.

My father was not easily put off. He went to a nearby manure pile, grabbed a fistful of manure and threw it at the hole. His shot was right on target and plugged the hole tight. Then he told his men to get back to work.

You have to be prepared to deal with wasps and bees when you work on the exterior of your house. If these pests get to be too much for you, call it quits for the day. Then go back at night, when the occupants are less active, and attack the nest with a carbon dioxide fire extinguisher or an insecticide made specifically for wasps.

Cedar Shingles: The Graying of America

❏ Whether cedar shingles are red or white, when damaged they have to be replaced. It may take years before the new shingles weather to match the color of the old ones. To make them blend in at once, mix up a solution of 1 pound of baking soda and ½ gallon of water. Spray or brush the mixture on the new shingles, and they'll turn gray in a few hours.

Make a Perfect Match . . . with Linseed Oil

❏ Here's another way to match new red or white cedar shingles with old ones on a house exterior. First, purchase burnt umber—not the powdered kind, but the type that's already mixed in oil—in the smallest quantity you can buy. Or buy some lampblack. (Burnt umber will give you a brown stain; lampblack will create a gray color. Burnt umber can be found at art supply stores and lampblack at masonry supply stores.) Mix equal parts boiled linseed oil and turpentine. Add a few drops of the burnt umber or a small amount of lampblack until you get the shade you want. Spray or brush the mixture on the shingles.

Always Be True

❏ When you're nailing wooden shingles on as siding, make this simple guide to help keep your rows true. Take a long, straight piece of 1" x 3" pine and nail a thin piece of 3" x 6" aluminum on each end. Use several nails so that the aluminum is well attached.

As you lay shingles, always work from the bottom up. For the first row, place the guide against the side of the house, so that the top edge of the 1 x 3 forms the base on which the row will be placed. Tack through the two pieces of aluminum to secure the guide in its place. Use only one nail in each piece of aluminum, and place the nail at the very edge of it. Pound the nail all the way in, so its head won't stick out under a shingle later in the process.

Stand all your shingles on the guide to be sure they're positioned evenly, then nail them in place. When you're ready to move on to the next row, give each end of the guide a downward blow with your hammer. The aluminum will tear where you nailed it, and the guide will come free. Working up the side of the house, repeat the process for each successive row. Position the guide so that each new row of shingles overlaps the row below.

This guide, which helps you nail shingles in straight rows, is easy to tack up and pull down.

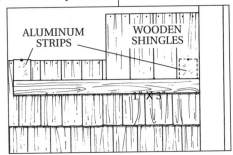

ALUMINUM STRIPS

WOODEN SHINGLES

1" X 3"

BRICK

A Different Mortar

❏ Mortar for laying cement blocks or bricks is finer than the concrete you use in big jobs such as a foundation or walkway. Use 1 part mortar cement to 3 parts mortar sand. The mortar cement has lime in it; mortar sand is finer than the sand used in most concrete.

Imitation Aging

❏ To match the mortar used with old bricks, experiment with light and dark cements and various colors of sand. Light mortar cement and fine sand will result in the lightest color.

❏ To encourage the aged look of exterior brick and stone masonry, encourage the bacteria that create mold on the surface. To do this, spray on liquid cow manure (wash it off with water after a few days), beer or a commercial product such as Miracle-Gro. In a short while, the surface will start to look slightly mottled. Repeat the process to stimulate more bacteria growth. Bacteria will grow fastest in shady areas.

Pass the Freezer Test

❏ Exterior bricks—special bricks that can withstand repeated freeze-thaw cycles—are also recommended for outside masonry work. If you aren't sure whether the bricks you have are the exterior type, soak one or two in water and put them in the freezer overnight. Repeat this a few times. If the bricks don't crack, they're safe to use on the outside of the house.

A Vine Thing

❏ It's not a good idea to encourage vines to grow on exterior walls—particularly brick walls, and most particularly brick walls in poor condition. If the masonry isn't in good shape, the roots, pads and suckers of vines can dislodge the mortar, thus loosening the bricks. This is particularly problematic as the vines get heavier.

❏ To remove vines from the outside walls of your house, cut off as much of the plants as you can. Let the remaining tendrils dry for a couple of weeks, then sponge a solution of ¼ cup of TSP (or another product containing trisodium phosphate) and 2 gallons of water onto the walls and the

PEOPLE WHO LIVE IN BRICK HOUSES MIGHT PREFER STONE

A STONE OR BRICK home is the product of many hours of loving, patient labor. Few such homes are built today, so to own one is to own a piece of history. But history has its price, and owning an old brick or stone home can be an expensive nightmare. Before you decide to buy such a house, look at it with these questions in mind.

• *Is the mortar sound?* Mortar typically requires repointing (replacing or refreshing) every 20 to 30 years. If you can easily scrape out pieces of mortar with a knife, repointing is needed.

• *Are the bricks sound?* Stones will last almost forever, at least in human terms. Bricks will not. Older bricks have a dense outside surface and softer center. As the outside surface weathers away, deterioration accelerates. If there are many badly weathered bricks, extensive repairs may be required.

• *Are the walls cracked?* Small, somewhat random hairline cracks are common. If found in the mortar, such cracks signal the need for repointing. In the bricks, small cracks suggest some aging but typically not serious trouble. Large cracks, especially ones extending continuously through many courses of bricks, may signal a serious structural problem that deserves further investigation.

• *Are the window and door openings square?* Structurally, the best stone or brick house would have no windows or doors. But who would, or could, live in it? The lintels (supporting members above these openings) often deteriorate more rapidly than the surrounding masonry. As they do, sagging occurs, the walls crack, windows and doors don't open, and repairs are needed.

• *Are there integral chimneys?* Stone and brick homes often have chimneys built into the structural wall system. When this is the case, any repairs, rehabilitation or maintenance may be difficult.

• *Are there any bulges in the walls?* The chief enemy of brick and stone masonry is moisture. As the mortar ages, water can penetrate into the walls and freeze. Then portions of the walls can be torn apart by the internal forces. Extended neglect will allow this condition to occur. Catching up with the needed repairs can be complex.

Stone and brick homes aren't maintenance free. Although they may not need painting (except for the wood trim), they do require other work. It pays (literally) to know what you're getting into.

remaining bits of vine. Once the tendrils soften, scrub them off with a stiff scrub brush. Suckers that are left to rot and oxidize can become nearly impossible to remove.

BRICKS ARE ANCIENT HISTORY

TO HOLD A BRICK is to hold the oldest manufactured building material known to man, a product made in much the same way as the blocks that were slapped together from mud and dried in the sun as early as 4000 B.C. By the time the colonists brought the process to America, most bricks were molded while wet, then fired for hardening. Sand was typically used to keep the clay from sticking to the mold during the firing process.

Less common were water-struck bricks, which were made from molds that were first dipped in water. Though somewhat more expensive, water-struck bricks were desirable among those who could afford them because they were better looking and had a smoother surface.

Old bricks were smaller than their modern counterparts, and the color within each brick varied more than it does today because of the varying temperatures in different parts of the kiln.

STUCCO

New and Improved Stucco

❑ Stucco is simply a concrete mixture that you apply as siding. To give the mixture more body and make it easier to work with, add hydrated lime. Mix 1 part portland cement, 3 parts sand and $\frac{1}{10}$ part hydrated lime. You can buy hydrated lime wherever you buy your cement.

Basic Application

❑ Stucco can be used as siding when spread over hardware cloth (a heavy-duty wire-screen material). One-half-inch hardware cloth nailed to the frame of the house works well. Apply coats of stucco about ⅜" thick until you reach the desired thickness. (You'll probably need to apply a total of three coats.) Each undercoat of stucco should be left with a rough surface so that the subsequent layer will adhere to it.

THIS DEFINITION HOLDS WATER

WHAT'S THE DIFFERENCE between cement and concrete? Cement is a binder used with aggregate (sand or gravel) to make mortar or concrete. Portland cement (named for its similarity to limestone found on the Isle of Portland, England) is, these days, the most commonly used type of cement. You can have cement without concrete, but you can't have concrete without cement.

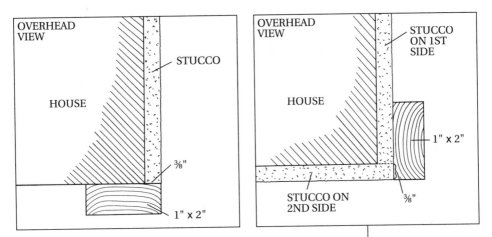

OVERHEAD VIEW

HOUSE

STUCCO

⅜"

1" x 2"

OVERHEAD VIEW

HOUSE

STUCCO ON 1ST SIDE

1" x 2"

STUCCO ON 2ND SIDE

⅜"

❑ To make a good square corner when applying stucco, hold a piece of 1" x 2" strapping against the side adjacent to the one on which you're working. Extend it out ⅜" from the surface of the wall and secure it with a few nails. Butt the stucco against the strapping and leave it to harden for a day or two. Then hold the strapping against the new stucco and bring the stucco on the adjacent wall out to it. That will give you a well-defined corner.

When you stucco a corner, hold a piece of 1" x 2" strapping against the side next to the one on which you're working. Butt the stucco to the strapping (left). After the stucco has dried, repeat the process on the adjacent side (right).

VINYL AND ALUMINUM SIDING

The Vinyl Approach

❑ If you're thinking of investing in vinyl siding, here are some important sales points to consider. Solid or rigid vinyl siding comes in many colors and styles, but clapboards are the most popular and affordable style. Like aluminum siding, vinyl doesn't rust, rot or peel, and it does resist denting. But vinyl siding has an advantage over aluminum siding in that its color isn't just a surface finish; it actually permeates the material. In terms of maintenance, vinyl siding just needs an annual hosing off, and stains can be removed with either abrasive or nonabrasive cleaners.

❑ Don't install vinyl siding during periods when temperatures are likely to drop below freezing. At low temperatures, the vinyl can become brittle and crack when nailed.

❑ Never lay pieces of vinyl siding tightly together. Leave a gap of about 1/32" for expansion and contraction. Also, avoid nailing siding too tightly to the house. This will cause the siding to buckle and create an unsightly appearance.

Corrosion by the Sea

❏ Think twice about choosing aluminum siding if you live by the sea; corrosion is a problem in such areas. And no matter where you live, if you're considering aluminum siding, you should be aware that the baked-on finish won't last forever. It will fade and lose its gloss with time.

Cover-Ups Won't Solve Your Problems

❏ Think twice before installing *any* artificial siding if the paint on your house is constantly peeling. This is a sign of excess moisture. Artificial siding may hide moisture or rot problems for years, but then repairs will be expensive.

Aluminum: All Washed Up

❏ Clean aluminum siding once a year with a strong spray from a hose. If some spots remain, sponge them off with a solution of ¼ cup of dishwashing liquid and 2 gallons of water. Avoid abrasive cleansers, which might damage the finish.

❏ Washing aluminum siding with a strong detergent solution will improve a faded, weathered look, but the color may not be uniform after the siding dries. To be safe, wash only a small section first. If the color is consistent after this area has dried, it should be safe to wash the rest of the house the same way.

❏ To make a basic solution for washing aluminum siding, combine ⅓ cup of laundry detergent, ⅔ cup of TSP (or another product containing trisodium phosphate), 1 quart of household (5 percent) bleach and 3 quarts of water. Wash the siding with this solution, then immediately rinse it off with a hose.

EARLY BUILDERS SET THEIR SITES DIFFERENTLY

EARLY HOME BUILDERS thought differently about siting their homes than many of us do today. They were more concerned about maximizing drainage and minimizing sun and wind damage than they were with wide-sweeping views or waterfront vistas.

It's interesting to look at old houses in the country and see how similarly they all sit on their sites. More often than not, there's a natural windbreak of some kind to the north of the house. A gable end of the house faces due south (so that the sun won't beat down on the roof during the hottest part of the day). And there's a natural slope away from the foundation on at least three—and often all four—sides. The slopes carry water away from the foundation, reducing the freeze-thaw effect and the chance for shifting over time.

❏ You can paint aluminum siding, but wash it first to remove the dirt and loose pigment and provide a surface that will bond with the paint.

DECKS AND RAMPS

Aren't You Glad You Didn't Cut Geometry Class?

❏ In laying out the locations of posts for an outbuilding or a deck, high school geometry is invaluable. Use the classic 3-4-5 triangle formula to determine the right angles. Position the corner posts in their approximate locations, then run taut pieces of string between them. Starting from one post, measure 3' along the string to the right of that post; tie a small rag to the string at that point. Then measure 4' along the string to the left of the post; tie another small rag at that point. Keeping one post-to-post string constant, adjust the other one until the distance between the rags measures exactly 5'. At that point, you have a 90° corner. Repeat for the other corners.

On Deck

❏ Use a brush when applying a wood preservative such as Cuprinol to a deck. You can do the job with a mop, but you'll waste less sealer with a brush.

❏ Any deck with a penetrating finish— wood preservative (such as Cuprinol), stain or oil—should be treated at least once every 5 years. Penetrating finishes don't create a surface film as paint does. Paint chips and peels, but penetrating finishes just wear out. And as the penetrating finish wears out, a portion of the wood fiber is exposed to ultraviolet rays and the elements, resulting in weathering.

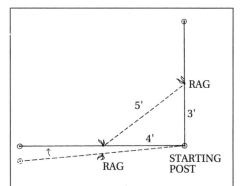

Use the 3-4-5 triangle formula to find the right angles for the corners of an outbuilding or deck.

Whatsit?

WE HAVE NO IDEA what this is. It's made of iron, and the V is flattened and sharp. Do you know what it is?   — E.S., KEENE, N.H.

This is a hay-spade knife, used to cut out sections of hay from the haystack. Before hay was baled, it would get tightly packed, and a hay saw or hay knife was needed to cut out enough to feed the stock each day. The farmer would drive the tool into the haystack, then place his foot on the step to force the tool in farther, thus cutting out the amount wanted. This tool also was used to cut the tops off pumpkins when they were used as food for farm animals.

The Job with the Moving Foundation

I WAS DOING SOME WORK for a woman who wanted a porch built onto her weekend house. While we were excavating for the footings and concrete slab, she had a utility shed delivered. She had it set up about 10' from my job, in an area on a slope. To level the shed, the people who assembled it put posts under the back and let the front sit on the ground.

A Word from Earl

The woman was disappointed that they hadn't leveled the ground on which the shed was sitting. The shed had no floor, and standing on the uneven ground inside it was an awkward proposition. I told the woman that I would take care of the problem. Using the stone from the excavation we were doing, we extended the walls under the utility shed so they touched the ground. Then we used extra soil from the excavation project to make a level dirt floor for the shed. My job was made easier because I didn't have to truck the stone and soil away, and the fact that the shed was now perfectly level pleased the woman to no end.

Disposing of rocks and dirt is very labor-intensive. It pays to find a way to use the excess rocks and dirt from one project in another on the same site.

❑ If you're pouring concrete to support a deck, porch or toolshed or another small structure, you may be able to get free building material from your local carpet dealer. Leftover cardboard rug-winding cores can serve as small Sonotubes—the heavy-duty cardboard tubes into which you pour concrete for foundations. Just peel the cardboard off after the cement has hardened. Before using the carpet cores for this purpose, you might want to oil the insides to make it easier to peel them off later.

Ramps: Get the Angle Right

❑ If you need to build a ramp, don't make it too steep. A comfortable slope is a rise of 1" for every 1' of ramp.

GUTTERS

Big Roofs Mean Big Runoff

❏ For a roof up to 750 square feet, plan on a 4" gutter. A roof area between 750 and 1,500 square feet needs a 5" gutter. Any roof over 1,500 square feet ought to have a 6" gutter.

Care and Cleaning

❏ Clean your wooden gutters at least once a year. Let them dry, then apply a generous coat of raw linseed oil to the insides. (The oil can be applied full strength or thinned with turpentine. Add as much turpentine as you like, up to the point where you have equal parts turpentine and oil.) This treatment prevents moisture saturation but allows the wood to breathe out moisture following wet weather.

WHEN IT COMES TO GUTTERS, LOOSEN UP

MANY HOMEOWNERS have poor luck with gutters, because the tendency today is to tuck them up close to the last row of shingles—so as to catch every last drop of water. The problem is that when they're so placed, they catch snow and ice as well.

Old-time roofers knew better, which is why century-old installations still go through winter after winter without damage. Their secret was really no secret at all: They simply placed the gutter (or eaves trough, as it was sometimes called) low enough on the facia so that snow and ice coming off the roof would slide by harmlessly and not take the gutter with it. If you're installing gutters, plan for an inch or more of clearance under that imaginary line that extends along the plane of the roof, and your installation will last as long as the work of the old-timers.

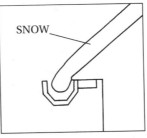

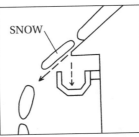

A gutter that is too high (top) catches the snow and ice. A gutter placed below the imaginary extension of the roofline (bottom) will catch water but allow snow and ice to slide by.

The Day I Was Accused of Witchcraft

A WOMAN CALLED ME because every time it rained hard, the water backed up in her downspouts and flooded the area around her house. I thought her dry wells might be the problem. As water comes down a downspout, it needs to go into a dry well—a pit or hole in the ground (usually, but not always, lined with loose-fitting stone or block) that allows you to get rid of liquids such as gutter runoff by letting them percolate into the surrounding soil. It sounded to me as though this woman's dry wells had become clogged with leaves and sediment that had come down her gutters over time. Consequently, they couldn't absorb the water quickly enough when it rained hard.

A Word from Earl

Each of the downspouts on the house emptied into a clay elbow that led to the dry well. I told one of my crew to run a snake down one of those elbows, and he was doing this when the woman came out to talk with me. I could hear the snake moving under the spot where I was standing. I shuffled along the grass on top of the snake until I heard it hit the end of the dry well. About then, the woman stopped talking. "Dig right here," I told my helper. The woman looked at me, surprised, and asked, "Earl, are you a water witch?" I had to laugh, then I explained how I'd known where the dry well was.

We cleaned out the dry well and set up a system to prevent more leaves and sediment from filling it up again. I cut the downspouts off a few inches above the clay collars that were sunk in the ground. Then I inserted pieces of heavy screen in the tops of the collars. When a leaf came down a spout, it would catch on the screen and be thrown aside by the continuing blast of rainwater.

You can avoid similar problems by using screens to catch leaves before they fill up your dry wells.

Put Away That Paintbrush

❑ Don't paint the insides of wooden gutters, as that makes them dry out. The dry wood will crack, allowing water to leak into the house.

SCREENS AND STORMS

Cure Corrosion

❑ To remove corrosion from aluminum screens and storms, rub the affected area with steel wool dipped in paint thinner.

❑ You can also remove corrosion from an aluminum screen by rubbing it with aluminum jelly, a product made for this purpose. Look for it at hardware stores, and follow the directions on the container.

THE WINDOW: A WONDERFUL INVENTION

THE ORIGIN of the word *window* can be traced to two Scandinavian terms, *vindr* and *auga,* meaning "wind" and "eye." The openings cut into the solid Norse houses were just that: eyes to let the wind in for ventilation. English carpenters borrowed the term and shortened it from "wind's eye" to "window." It wasn't until years later that it became common to cover such openings with glass.

CAULK IT UP TO PROGRESS

BUILDING SUPPLY stores now offer more types of caulking and sealants than ever before. Although the variety can be useful, it can also be confusing. Here's a guide to some of the choices.

Butyl rubber caulking has been on the market since the 1950s and is still a low-cost, all-purpose workhorse. It's stringy to apply and not flexible enough for demanding applications (such as expansion joints), but it's acceptable for projects such as caulking between woodwork and aluminum storm window frames.

Latex caulking also appeared in the 1950s. It's commonly used in residential work because it cleans up with water and adheres to damp surfaces, and you can usually paint over it. It's not ideal for demanding jobs but, like butyl rubber, is acceptable for caulking around storm window and door frames. It's generally in the same price range as butyl rubber.

Silicone caulking is a more recent development and a more expensive one, but it's an excellent sealant that stays flexible for a very long time. It's a little more demanding to work with than other caulking (surfaces must be very clean, and some woods won't accept it), but it's very commonly used these days by professionals and homeowners alike.

A NUTTY IDEA

EARLY SETTLERS felt that placing an acorn on the windowsill would keep a house from being struck by lightning. This hearkens back to the old Norse story that Thor, the god of thunder and lightning, was also the protector of oak trees. Judging from the number of oak trees that get hit in thunderstorms, lightning rods are probably a better bet.

It's the Pits

❏ Pitting cannot be removed from aluminum, but it can be camouflaged to make doors or window casings look better. Make a ball of aluminum foil and scrub it back and forth across the pitting. Little bits of the foil will catch in the pits.

❏ If you have old aluminum windows that are pitted and scarred, it's best to sand them with medium-grit sandpaper before painting. Be careful to keep the sandpaper away from the glass. After sanding, wash with a solution of ¼ cup of TSP (or another product containing trisodium phosphate) and 1 gallon of water. Once the windows are dry, apply a metal primer, then a coat of latex house paint.

STEPS AND SHUTTERS

Front Steps: Avoid the Force Play

❏ The top step outside an exterior door should be at least 3' from front to back, allowing room for the door to swing open without forcing the visitor to back off the step.

Shutters Can Come Unhinged

Round-head screws are best for securing shutters in place. When you go to remove the shutter after multiple applications of paint, you won't be able to locate a flat-head screw.

❏ Shutters are installed today purely for decorative reasons, so if you don't care about authenticity, you can save a little time and mount them without hinges. Just screw the top and bottom into the trim around the window. On the outer edge of the shutter (the one away from the window), install a spacer to keep the shutter parallel to the wall. Place a block of wood between the shutter and the wall, then insert a long

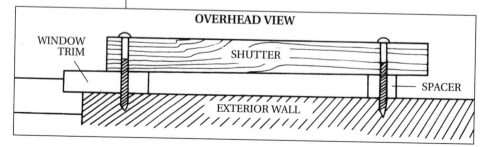

OVERHEAD VIEW

WINDOW TRIM — SHUTTER — SPACER — EXTERIOR WALL

stainless steel or brass screw through the shutter and wood into the wall. Or install decorative S hooks to keep the shutters in place.

ROOFS

The Layered Look

❏ You can lay a new roof of asphalt shingles over one existing layer, but not more than one. Too many layers of shingles add a lot of weight to the roof and may cause it to sag or cave in. Multiple layers also make for a lumpy job.

In the South, Color It Cool

❏ If you're choosing new asphalt shingles for a roof, keep in mind that dark colors absorb the sun's heat; light colors reduce heat gain.

The Curling Shingle: A Pressing Problem

❏ If your asphalt shingles curl in the heat or flap in the wind, apply a quarter-size spot of roofing cement under each problem shingle and press against it for about 10 seconds. (If your roof is steeply pitched and it's dangerous to walk on it, consider hiring a professional roofer to help you.) For maximum adhesion, readhere problem shingles on a warm, sunny day. But if the temperature is above 75°F, wait for a cooler day. Walking on the shingles in that kind of heat could damage them.

Asphalt: Making the Cut

❏ When cutting asphalt shingles, dip your utility knife in turpentine. This will keep the shingles from binding when you cut.

❏ It's best to cut an asphalt shingle through the back to the front. Your knife blade will dull less quickly because it will have less contact with the shingle's mineralized face.

Whatsit?

I saw this stone in the remains of a late eighteenth-century Welsh settlement in Connecticut. The stone is approximately 4' x 2' x 2', with the grooves about ⅜" deep. Do you know what it was used for?
— J.P., Baltic, Conn.

Before modern detergents were invented, a housewife had to make her own washing aids. A barrel, with open top and bottom, was placed on a sloping stone such as this one out in back of the woodshed. A layer of straw or small twigs was packed in the bottom, and a piece of muslin covered the twigs. The barrel was filled with wood ashes, and water was poured over the ashes now and then. The stone had a groove dug in it that enclosed the barrel and drained to the edge, forming a spout. A small iron pot was placed under the spout to catch the alkaline solution—lye—that drained from the bottom of the barrel. This lye was mixed with fat from the kitchen to make a soft brown soap to use on washday.

Up on the Roof

I**T'S EASY TO GET SCARED** when you're working on a roof. When I first began roofing work, I was assigned to patch a large, sloping roof. To get to the spot that needed to be repaired, I had to climb one ladder to a narrow parapet, walk this parapet for 20' or so and then climb up to the main roof on another ladder. Walking across that parapet really disturbed me.

A Word from Earl

I worked on that roof all day. I even ate my lunch, which I had brought up with me, on the roof. But at quitting time, when I started down, I couldn't bring myself to walk back across the parapet. I was marooned. I tried and tried to walk across it, but I finally gave up and sat down to wait for someone to miss me. Eventually, the boss came and got me down with a long ladder. All the time I had been working on the roof, subconsciously I had been thinking about walking that parapet again and had convinced myself that I couldn't do it without falling.

Years later, I was directing some men working on a large, flat roof only 10' off the ground. At noon, when we climbed down off the roof to eat lunch, I noticed that one man was missing. When he didn't appear after 15 minutes, I went looking for him.

I found him up on the roof, trying to get the courage to climb down. He would swing one foot around onto the ladder, but he couldn't bring himself to take the other foot off the roof. I went up the ladder and helped him onto it and down to the ground. He admitted having a fear of heights but said he'd hoped to overcome it by climbing again.

Don't be ashamed if you're ever stricken by fear on a roof. It's just your body's instinct for self-preservation at work.

Off with the Dead Wood

❏ Before you can install new cedar shingles (either white or red) on a roof, you must remove the old roofing material and pull out or drive in all nails.

A Flat-Out Lie

❏ Wooden shingles more than 8" wide are likely to cup. If you split them in two with a utility knife before you nail them down, they'll lie flatter.

Staining Made Simple

❏ The best time to stain pine or spruce roofing shingles (often used by people restoring old homes) is before they are installed. Dip each shingle in a bucket of stain and set it aside to dry. When using this method, it pays to set up a trough or rack to recover the runoff stain so you can reuse it.

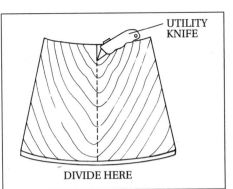

Draw the utility knife along the grain of the shingle to split it.

Wash Off the Dead Stuff

❏ Dead leaves and needles on a shingled roof hold water and hasten the deterioration of the shingles. Be sure to sweep or hose them off in both spring and fall.

Moss: A High-Pressure Situation

❏ Moss or fungus on a roof can penetrate shingles and, if heavy, even work them loose from the roof. Before things reach that stage, remove moss and fungus with a pressure washing. You can rent equipment for this (try a store that rents wallpaper steamers), but it's probably better to hire a professional.

❏ To prevent more moss from forming, mix up a solution of 2 capfuls of household (5 percent) bleach and 1 gallon of water. Apply it to the shingles with a sponge. If you have a serious moss problem, you may need to repeat this process every 3 years or so.

If Your Chimney Leaves Its Mark

❏ To remove creosote marks from asphalt roof shingles, try scrubbing the stains with a stiff brush dipped in a solution of ¼ cup of TSP (or another product containing trisodium phos-

DON'T LET YOUR ROOF BE A COMPASS

Most Boy Scouts and Girl Scouts learn this rule of thumb when hiking away from the trail: Moss grows on the north sides of rocks and trees. The same logic holds true for roofs, and it's for the same reason.

Moss, mildew and other fungi thrive in damp, shady areas. The sun rarely hits the north side of a house's roof. Quaint-looking moss- and mildew-covered roofing shingles aren't likely to last very long, so your routine maintenance should include removing those fungi.

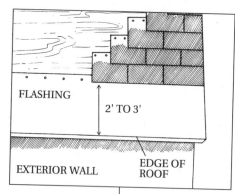

FLASHING

2' TO 3'

EXTERIOR WALL   EDGE OF
                 ROOF

Snow and ice tend to slide off exposed metal flashing along the roof edge.

phate) and 2 gallons of water. Rinse well after the scrubbing.

Flash!

❏ To help the snow and ice slide off the roof and prevent ice dams from forming, consider installing metal flashing—a band of sheet metal made for roof edges—on the eaves of your house. Be sure to use galvanized metal or aluminum, or you'll be in for some rust problems. Nail the flashing up first, then work up the roof with your shingles from there. Snow and ice will be less likely to stick to the flashing than to your roofing material, and the result will be fewer ice dams. Flashing is available from hardware stores.

Look before It Leaks

❏ To avoid situations that may result in a leaky roof, inspect your roof in the spring for winter damage. Check for cracks in gutters and downspouts and for curled, torn or blistered shingles. If repairs are needed, see that they're done right away.

❏ In the autumn, make the same inspection, then clean out all the gutters and downspouts as well.

Break the Ice

❏ An ice dam can form whenever you have a good amount of snow on your roof. If you let ice and snow build up too much, the roof may begin to leak. To prevent this, keep a ladder and hatchet handy and break up any ice buildup as soon as it begins. (Use only the blunt end of the hatchet; you don't want to damage your roof.)

Slate: Breaking Up Is Easy to Do

❏ Generally speaking, if you have a slate roof, leave your roof work to a professional. An experienced roofer

A LESSON ON SLATE

TODAY SLATE ROOFING is a design decision rather than a practical one, but historically there were practical reasons for using slate:

• A hot coal from a wood stove landing on a slate roof wouldn't set the house on fire.

• After the initial burst of a rainstorm washed away sediment, the rainwater that spilled over slate eaves and into a barrel could be filtered for drinking.

• The colonial homestead was a source of family pride. Therefore, a roof that would last 100 years was worth paying for.

A MAN'S HARD LUCK

WHEN POOR François Mansart died in 1666, he had no inkling that his scheme for letting light and air into the attic (and, some say, dodging French building codes) would be all the rage 200 years later across the Atlantic. The steep-sided, shallow-topped mansard roof struck Americans' Victorian fancy so hard that a writer of the day reported, "The French roof is in great request . . . no man who wants a fashionable house will be without it." The ex-citement lasted until the mid-1880s, when it became fashionable to call this roof a horrid, boxy monstrosity. Both opinions are still around today.

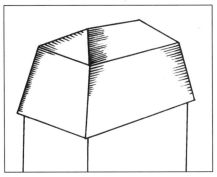

A mansard roof.

has the know-how and the proper tools to do the job without breaking the fragile tiles.

❏ You can handle one part of slate roof maintenance yourself. From the ground, inspect the roof every year in the spring and fall, checking for missing, cracked or loose tiles. A pair of binoculars will help you get a closer look.

❏ If you have a slate roof, warn any worker who has to get up on the roof that it's made of slate. Advise him or her to avoid walking directly on the roof and suggest laying a ladder on the roof and walking on it. This will distribute the person's weight enough to avoid breaking the slate. Immediately after anyone has been up there, inspect your roof from the ground to see if any of the tiles have cracked or become loose.

Proper Storage

❏ Always store slate tiles on edge, like a stack of phonograph records. There's less chance of breakage.

A SQUARE DEAL

A SQUARE OF SHINGLES will cover 100 square feet of surface. For asphalt shingles, three bundles (each containing twenty-two 3'-long shingles) make up a square. For wooden shingles, usually four bundles make up a square. (The number of wooden shingles in a bundle varies because the shingles are not all the same width.)

DRY ROT

When Your Wood Turns to Sponge

❏ If you can easily push a knife blade into the wood of a beam in your house, that wood has dry rot and should be replaced. Dry rot is caused by a fungus that forms when wood is dry one day and excessively wet the next. It ultimately reduces wood to a spongelike material that's weightless and without strength—and that's no good for supporting a house.

❏ The best way to prevent dry rot is to deal with your home's moisture problems. In the meantime, when you replace the rotted wood, treat the new lumber with a penetrating water repellent or wood preservative such as Cuprinol on all faces before installing it.

❏ A stopgap measure when you discover dry rot is to paint the area with boiled linseed oil. Let it sit overnight, then apply a second coat. The oil won't strengthen the existing wood, but it will help keep out further moisture. This isn't a long-term solution, but it will help keep the dry rot from getting worse if you discover it early and know that you won't be able to replace the timber right away.

A SQUARE PEG IN A ROUND HOLE

WE'VE ALL HEARD the expression "like a square peg in a round hole," which has come to mean something that doesn't quite fit in. Originally, though, the phrase referred to something done right: the pegging of a post-and-beam frame.

Although most framing timbers were made of softwood, the pegs were always hardwood, oak being the most common. A rough square peg would be split out with a froe (an old-time cleaving tool), then the peg would be tapered to a point and driven into slightly offset holes with a wooden mallet. Square or 8-sided pegs allowed room for swelling. The action of the pegs pulling the holes into line gave the joint its tightness. A round, exactly sized peg would likely split the joinery if it swelled. The best timber framers, by the way, are the Amish, whose pegged joints are often so tight that a single sheet of paper cannot be slid into them.

THE FOUNDATION

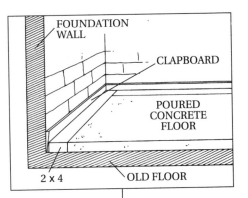

Make Your Own Moat

❏ If you have water leaking into a cellar that has a concrete floor, pour a few more inches of concrete on the floor, leaving drainage space around the edge to create a moat effect. One way to create that moat is to place 2 x 4s around the perimeter of the floor before pouring the new concrete. If the walls are block or concrete, also place a clapboard on edge between each 2 x 4 and the wall; this will make it easier to remove the 2 x 4s later. If the foundation walls are rough stone, wedges work better between the 2 x 4s and stone. Let the concrete set up for a day or so, then remove the 2 x 4s. Make sure the moat drains in one direction—toward a sump—where you can put a pump if necessary.

A "moat" around the floor of a leaking cellar will help the water to drain. Set 2 x 4s around the edge of the floor, then pour a fresh concrete floor and allow it to harden. Once the concrete is dry, remove the 2 x 4s.

It Will Stand and Deliver

❏ Water coming through cracks in the concrete floor of a basement is the result of hydrostatic pressure in the basement. The water level in the ground around the building is higher than the concrete floor. To lessen this pressure before it makes the floor heave, put in a standpipe—a 4"-diameter pipe cemented into a hole in the floor. The top of the pipe should be above grade—that is, above the level of the ground outside the foundation. The water

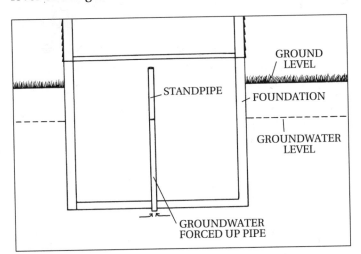

A standpipe relieves the pressure from groundwater on your cellar walls and floor.

pressure in the ground will push the water up inside the pipe instead of through your foundation floor and walls.

No More Bouquets at the Doorstep

❏ Don't plant flower beds right next to your house. They make dams that hold water close to the foundation instead of encouraging it to run off.

WORKING WITH CONCRETE

Mix It Up

❏ You can mix concrete by hand in a wheelbarrow, but be careful to mix it well. If you're planning to mix more

The Cellar Had a Major Leak

BACK IN THE EARLY '50s, I was doing some work for the owner of a large store. One day he started telling me about the problems he'd had with his cellar floor. I asked him to show me exactly what he was talking about, so he took me down there. It was quite a sight. Hydrostatic pressure had caused the concrete floor to heave up in the center, and water was streaming through the cracks.

A Word from Earl

I told him that I could make the space usable by building a platform over the existing floor. He had me begin on a 20' x 20' area. I started at the highest point of the floor and laid bricks and blocks in the surrounding area to create a level foundation for the platform. Then I placed 2" x 4" joists on the bricks and blocks and had my men lay a floor of matched fir on top of the joists. The water flowed continuously under the floor and into sumps at the four corners.

Before I had that section completed, the owner came down and had me do another 20' x 20' section. By the time I left, we'd floored half the basement, and the owner was moving his extra inventory into the space. He was one happy man.

It just goes to show that no basement or cellar is too wet to be put to use.

than a few wheelbarrows of concrete, you're better off renting a small gas-powered cement mixer from a rental company.

❑ When mixing concrete, add only enough water to the sand and cement to make the mixture plastic and workable. If you add too much water, you'll compromise the strength of the concrete.

It's Getting Darker . . .

❑ If you want to darken your concrete, add lampblack to it. One pound of lampblack for every 100-pound bag of cement will result in a medium-gray shade. You can buy lampblack in powdered form at a masonry supply store or a good paint store.

For Smoother Walls, Do Some Spade Work

❑ As you pour concrete into a form (the wooden mold that holds the concrete until it dries), you need to "spade" it to make sure it settles properly. To spade the concrete, use a lawn edger or, on smaller jobs, a ¾"-thick piece of strapping.

If you're working with a form that's more than 6" deep, pour 6" of concrete into the form. Work your spading tool up and down in the wet concrete, then pour another 6" of concrete and repeat the spading process. Agitating the concrete allows you to pack it tightly and push the coarse aggregate away from the form. The fine grains of aggregate will be left near the form, creating a smooth surface when the concrete is dry and the form is removed.

Sometimes It's Good to Carry a Torch

❑ If concrete has dried on your hoe, shovel or wheelbarrow, don't panic. Heat the metal with a torch. The concrete won't expand as quickly as the metal, and the unwanted material will fall right off.

Whatsit?

CAN YOU IDENTIFY this old tool? My wife inherited it from her great-grandfather, who had a furniture and cabinetmaking shop in Easton, Pennsylvania, at the end of the nineteenth century.
— L.D., PHILLIPSBURG, N.J.

This is an antique pipe wrench. Before the invention of the adjustable pipe wrench as we know it, a plumber had to get by with this oversize pair of pliers.

The Great Outdoors

How to get rid of stumps, prepare the garden and make a nifty rope swing.

MY WIFE, MY SON AND I worked for 4 years on nights and weekends preparing the site for our current house. We did most of the work ourselves, all of it by hand. The driveway alone took 3 years to build. It's 1,000 feet long and rises in a steep pitch at the end.

Most people can't understand why we chose to do by hand work that is usually done with heavy equipment. Well, we weren't in a hurry. Doing the work ourselves saved money. And working outside together was a pleasure. It was a great opportunity for me to spend time with my boy.

But most important, the impact on the land was kept to a minimum. Early on, I hired a man with a bulldozer to help me clear the driveway, but he hadn't worked an hour before I sent him home. My driveway winds through the forest, tall trees just inches from its edges. It was simple to navigate around those trees with a wheelbarrow, but it would have been impossible for the bulldozer to spare them.

332

What's more, I could see that I'd need to spend many hours cleaning up the mess that the bulldozer would leave.

As it was, we were able to work very efficiently. We transferred the dirt from the uphill side of the drive to the downhill side to make a level road. The pace of our handwork gave us time to read the land and to think about what we really wanted.

There's no question that you can work outdoors more quickly and powerfully with heavy equipment than with hand tools. But it's surprising what you can accomplish on your own—and it's rewarding, too. That's why most of these tips emphasize things you can do on your land with a minimal amount of equipment.

In this chapter, you'll find ideas for fertilizing your outdoor plants without stooping over the soil, encouraging lilacs and discouraging bamboo, and providing good foot and car traction in winter snow. Here are tips for removing stubborn stumps from your property, dealing with frozen car locks and simplifying springtime bird feeder cleanup. And when you've finished all the chores and tended to all the emergencies and you finally have a minute for some

IF YOU CAN'T FIND IT . . .

. . . maybe you need to try another chapter. Check the index, or try these possibilities.

fun, be sure to come back to these pages one more time—for instructions on how to make a simple rope swing for the backyard.

GETTING STARTED

Help Is on the Way

❑ When you're planning to build a structure or do some landscaping, don't neglect two good resources: the Soil Conservation Service and the Cooperative Extension Service. A representative of the Soil Conservation Service will come out to your site and draw up a plan to provide good drainage and prevent erosion. The Cooperative Extension Service will give you advice and literature on a wealth of topics, which can help you decide which trees to cut down or where best to locate your gardens and landscaping. In most cases, fees are nominal or nonexistent. To locate these services, call directory assistance for your county seat and ask for listings under county services. Or call the closest branch of your state university system.

Plan Ahead for Proper Drainage

❑ Drains and ditches that overflow into cold, shady areas may freeze in winter. When laying out your drainage

DRIVEWAYS: NO DRAIN, NO GAIN

GOOD GRAVEL DRIVEWAYS are unobtrusive, but bad ones get your attention every time. Rain and melting snow cause much of the trouble, abetted by poor materials and design. The proper construction of a driveway depends on soil type and siting, but there's one guiding principle that all good driveways follow: They have proper drainage.

If you plan to have a driveway built or repaired, make sure you don't skimp on what's needed to do the job right, be it the gravel base, the ditching, the culverts, the crown in the center of the driveway or the bluestone layer on top. (Bluestone is gravel that has been run through a rock crusher. Consisting of particles ranging from acorn size to rock dust, it compacts into a tough, durable surface.) Whip your driveway into shape one time, and you should be able to ignore it most of the time.

LAWN ORDER

I S IT SMARTER to bag up your lawn clippings or leave them be? Or should you get one of those mulch-o-matic gizmo blades for your lawn mower? The experts say that as the grass clippings decompose, they provide up to one-half the nitrogen your lawn needs. Ironically, chemical fertilizers stymie this process by slowing down the earthworms, bacteria and microorganisms that break down the clippings. Then a thick layer of thatch builds up, strangling the grass. So if you fertilize chemically, you have to collect the grass.

A much smarter approach is to leave the clippings and feed your lawn with organic fertilizers such as compost, limestone, blood meal, bone meal and wood ashes, which don't discourage the decomposers. Any gadget that chops the grass finer will probably help speed this breakdown, but you can accomplish the same thing yourself by cutting the grass more often, making sure you never take off more than half the top growth at one time.

---

plans, make sure you won't mind an iceberg in that shady spot.

❑ To prevent erosion, a driveway generally needs a ditch along the uphill side to prevent water from collecting in the driveway. If there's no easy way to run water away from your driveway, consider having one or more culverts (drains under the driveway) installed.

❑ To ensure proper drainage, make sure any concrete drive, porch or deck slopes at least ⅜" per linear foot.

LAWN CARE

Time to Rake

❑ In the spring, give your lawn a good brisk raking, then reseed any bare spots. Lightly mulch reseeded areas with peat moss or grass clippings.

The Hansel and Gretel Method

❑ When you're seeding grass by hand, how do you know what spots you've missed? Mix fine sawdust in with your seed; you'll be able to see the sawdust where you've spread the mixture.

LAWN CARE   335

Everything's Coming Up Clover

❏ If your lawn is troubled by summer dry spells, add clover seed in the spring. Follow instructions on the seed package. When the clover becomes established, it will help keep your lawn green during hot, dry weather.

The Well-Dressed Lawn

❏ Apply a top dressing of loam and peat moss to improve the overall quality of your lawn. Once the grass is more than a couple of inches high, spread on ½" to 1" of the loam-and-peat-moss mixture.

❏ When you lime and fertilize your lawn, apply half the dosage in one direction and the other half in the opposite direction. This greatly reduces the likelihood of missing any strips or corners.

❏ Never fertilize a lawn when the grass is wet or even damp. If you do, the fertilizer will burn the grass.

❏ Don't fertilize new grass with standard lawn fertilizer, which is high in nitrogen. The roots need to become established before top growth is encouraged. While the grass is young, use 5-10-10 or some other low-nitrogen fertilizer, and then only in modest doses (following package instructions) 2 to 3 months after the lawn is planted.

Into Every Lawn, a Little Rain Must Fall

❏ Frequent light watering of a lawn will cause the grass roots to remain at a shallow level. Except in the case of new lawns, it's better to water only occasionally (once a week during dry spells) but very deeply.

Create a pointed edge on a 2 x 4 and use it to make an effective but unobtrusive drainage ditch for your lawn.

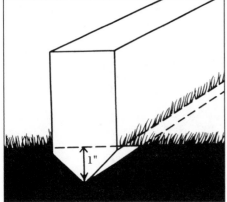

❏ If shallow puddles form in your lawn during a period of heavy spring rains, you may be able to drain the puddles by making a small indentation in the lawn.

Take a 4' length of 2 x 4 and, with a power saw, cut the base of the board to form a pointed "ridge" that runs the full length of the board along the 2" dimension. Make two cuts at 45° angles along the entire length of the 2 x 4. Lay the freshly cut edge of the board on the

The Lawn Needs No Clipping

I HAVE A LOW STONE WALL that surrounds my lawn, and I hate trimming the grass along it. One day I got smart and embedded a line of bricks along the wall. I sank the bricks into the lawn so that they were flush with the surface. Their 4" width is just enough so that, when I mow, I can keep one wheel of the mower on the grass and one on the brick. The bricks prevent grass from growing right next to the stone wall, so there's no need to trim.

A Word from Earl

If you're as tired of trimming as I was, try this trick.

ground, with the board headed in the direction you want the water to drain. To create the drain, pound the board 1 or 2 inches into the ground. Pick up the board and lay it with the newly cut edge on the ground again, lining it up so that it continues the path for your drain. Pound it in again. Repeat the process as many times as is necessary.

Water will run along the indentation made by the board, but the drain won't be readily visible. You'll have no problem mowing over it either. The indentation will eventually fill in, so you will need to repeat the process each year.

A Time to Sow

❑ Make time in the fall to sow new grass where there has been excessive wear or damage. There's less danger of disease and weed competition in autumn than in spring, and given adequate water, the rejuvenated lawn will establish itself before winter.

The Beaten Path

❑ When the ground freezes, it puts a hold on many gardening activities but provides opportunities for others. Take advantage of this time to truck loads of manure out to your garden. Avoid repeated traffic over one area, however, which may cause some damage to the grass.

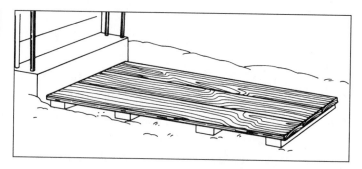

A boardwalk will keep you from wearing down your lawn in winter. Use short crosspieces to support the walkway so the larger boards don't rest directly on the lawn.

❏ Regular foot traffic over a lawn in winter will damage the grass, causing bare spots that won't fill in readily in spring. To prevent this, install a boardwalk, which will absorb some of the pressure and reduce damage. To form a boardwalk, set boards lengthwise on short crosspieces (such as 2 x 4s) so that the boards don't rest directly on the ground. If you want to be especially good to your lawn, reposition the boardwalk slightly from time to time so that the crosspieces do not lie in the same place all winter.

❏ When driving a vehicle over soft ground leaves tire tracks in the lawn, don't fill them in with dirt. Eventually, the compacted earth will rise again, and you'll have a high spot. Furthermore, the grass will grow differently where it has been compressed. Rather, insert a spading fork at an angle on the edge of the compressed area, loosening the underlying soil and prying the turf up to its original level. At first there may still be a slight depression, but it will soon disappear.

For Lawns with Acid Indigestion

❏ Moss or sorrel in lawns is a sign of poor drainage and acidity. You can improve the situation by aerating the lawn and spreading lime on it.

WALKWAYS AND PATIOS

Sow Little Thyme

❏ Consider planting thyme between the stones of a walkway. It will yield a pleasing fragrance whenever you pass over it.

If the Walkway Is a Weedway

❏ To kill small quantities of weeds or moss in walks or patio cracks, douse them with boiling water.

EARL PROULX'S YANKEE HOME HINTS

❑ You can also attack moss with a solution of household (5 percent) bleach and hot water. Adjust the strength of the solution according to the seriousness of the problem and be sure to wear gloves to avoid getting the bleach on your skin. A very strong solution would be equal parts bleach and water; you won't need anything stronger than that. Apply with a stiff bristle brush to scrub off all the moss you can.

The Right Way to Split Granite

❑ You may have a nice piece of split granite on your property that would make a great doorstep—except it's too

Where There's a Will, There's a Crowbar

A Word from Earl

THERE'S AN OLD CELLAR HOLE on my property lined with big, beautiful pieces of granite. I decided to use some of the granite as stone steps from the lawn up to the patio, but the stones were very heavy. Generally speaking, 1 cubic foot of rock usually weighs somewhere around 100 pounds, so the stones I'd selected probably weighed more than 300 pounds each. That's a lot of weight, and I spent some time considering the best way to handle them.

In the end, I used my truck to drag the stones up my driveway to the lawn. Laying the bottom step on the ground was easy enough. Then I leaned a plank against it and used the crowbar to slide the second step up it and into place. On the third step, I introduced some small sections of pipe as rollers. As I advanced the stone up the planking, which I had lengthened, I wedged a small rock under the last roller to keep the stone from sliding backward. To position the fourth and final step, I extended the ramp, using numerous planks and supports, until it was almost 50 feet long. It took quite a while to maneuver the stone (on rollers) up the ramp, but I finally got it in place.

It's amazing what you can do when you take full advantage of the leverage that a crowbar can offer.

WHY STONE WALLS ARE FOR WEIGHT LIFTERS

IF YOU'RE PLANNING to do any stone wall or foundation work, be prepared for the physical labor involved. A little decorative stone wall about 3' high, 2' wide and 20' long will weigh some 5 tons or more and include about 1,000 average-size stones. If you have to bring the stones in from somewhere else, there's also loading and unloading to be done, and then the trial and error of finding the right stone to lay. By the time that little 20' wall is finished, the builder may well have lifted close to 20 tons of rock.

Given all this, make sure you're in good physical condition before you start, lift with your legs instead of your back and try to use your brains more than your brawn. Levers, winches, chains, ramps, wheelbarrows, carts and trucks all have a place in rock work. They are, so to speak, worth their weight in stone.

long. You can split granite cleanly and easily if you know what you're doing. Mark on the rock with a crayon where you want the granite to split. Wearing eye protection in case small pieces of granite fly, drop a sledgehammer at any point on the line. Hold the hammer over your head (not over one shoulder) and drop it down straight for a straight cut; the split will follow the angle of your swing. Hard blows won't break the granite. Just continue to drop the sledgehammer up and down the line. The stone should split in a matter of minutes.

Keep Flagstone in Its Place

❏ If you want to secure a flagstone walk with more than sand, mix 1 part dry portland cement and 5 parts sand (the type you normally use to fill the joints between stones). Pack the mixture down into the joints and sprinkle it with a little water. The filler will set hard enough so it won't wash away.

Concrete: Divide and Conquer

❏ When pouring a concrete walk, every 3' or so make divisions about half as deep as the concrete. A mason has a special tool called a jointer or groover to make this cut, but you can use almost anything—a small stick or the edge of your trowel, for instance—as long as you drag the tool along the side of a board to create a straight edge. The cuts provide a place for the concrete to crack from expansion, contraction or frost pressure. If you don't make the divisions in your walk, unsightly cracks are likely to develop.

No Half-Baked Bricks

❏ When building a walk or patio from bricks, use bricks that are weatherproof. These bricks have been baked longer and have a hard surface that won't absorb water. You can identify a hard brick by its size (hard bricks are usually a little smaller than soft ones) and by the sound it makes when tapped with a hammer (a hard brick will ring, whereas a soft brick will produce a dull thud). Soft bricks won't last as long as hard ones in a walk or patio. They'll also absorb water over time and freeze and crack in the winter.

TREAD SOFTLY AND CARRY A BIG TAPE MEASURE

EVERY NOW AND THEN, someone comes along who is so good at what he or she does that he or she changes the terminology for the whole field. Frederick Law Olmsted was like that. When he was chosen to design New York's Central Park in 1858, it was clear that he was more than what was then called a landscape gardener; he was a landscape architect. Olmsted went on to increase his fame by designing the U.S. Capitol grounds, the 1893 World's Columbian Exposition, and the Boston park system.

When you're landscaping a set of steps on your own grounds, you might want to use Olmsted's law: $2R + T = 27"$. Olmsted found that if twice the riser height plus the tread length equals 27", you have a comfortable step. Others have suggested striving for 25" or 26", but Olmsted's equation is particularly credible. After all, Law was the man's middle name.

According to the rule, the tread width plus twice the riser height should equal 27". Steps with 12" treads and 7½" risers, for instance, are comfortable for the average person.

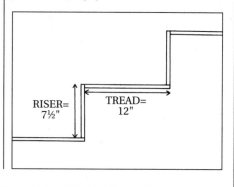

OUTDOOR FURNITURE

Prevent Furniture Marks on Your Clothes

❑ To prevent aluminum furniture from marking clothes, clean the furniture by wiping it with paint thinner on a cloth pad. Then place the furniture outdoors and spray on a coat or two of clear lacquer.

❑ A simpler but less permanent way to prevent aluminum furniture from marking clothes is to apply a coat of paste wax on the furniture. Buff the wax until the aluminum shines, and it will not mark your clothes when you sit on the furniture again.

Prep before You Paint

❑ Before painting aluminum outdoor furniture, scrub the piece with coarse steel wool and file down any bumps. Wipe the piece down to remove any dust, then brush or spray on a coat of metal primer. Apply one or two coats of an alkyd enamel spray paint.

Whatsit?

W E'RE MYSTIFIED by this object. It is made of wood with wooden pegs and is 30" long, 14" wide and about 1" thick. Do you know what it was used for?

— D.W., CHELMSFORD, MASS.

This was used to start plants in the spring. After the gardener prepared a flat with soil and smoothed the top, he or she would grip this object with both hands (one handle of this one is broken) and press it into the soil. When this handy tool was removed, there would be the perfect spacing and depth of holes for dropping in seeds.

GARDEN PREPARATION

Stake Out Your Territory

❑ Pound short, heavy stakes in the corners of your garden beds. That way, next time you're dragging a hose around the garden, it will come up against the stakes rather than mowing down all your seedlings.

Newspaper Cover-Ups for Freshly Sown Seeds

❑ Vegetable seeds need warmth to germinate but don't need light until after the sprouts have emerged. If you can check your garden every day, you can try placing newspaper or plastic over newly sown areas. (Don't use magazines and advertising supplements. They're often printed with colored inks containing heavy metals, which can leach into the soil.) Remove these cov-

EARL PROULX'S YANKEE HOME HINTS

erings immediately when signs of life appear. You can use the plastic later to mulch garden rows or cover fallow sections of the garden.

Mulching: Save That Moisture

❏ To protect your garden from drought, be sure to apply mulch, which saves moisture by lowering the rate of evaporation. Fresh grass clippings make excellent garden mulch. Spread the clippings so they're about 1" thick, but don't bunch them too heavily around young plants, as the grass can burn tender stalks.

To Air Is Humus

❏ Mulching your garden can also reduce or eliminate the need for weeding, but if this technique is to be effective, the soil needs air. If you don't cultivate your garden, at least agitate the soil with a weeder or spading fork from time to time.

Fertility Treatments

❏ Give your garden a boost with manure tea. Put a few shovelfuls of cow manure in a 30- to 50-gallon drum of water and allow it to steep for a few days. Stir the mixture occasionally during the steeping period, then once again just before you use it. Apply the tea by pouring it evenly from a bucket. (You can buy used metal or plastic drums from local factories after they've emptied them of raw materials. Or substitute a large trash can for the drum.)

❏ If you'd like to avoid a lot of stooping when fertilizing your plants, pour the fertilizer down a length of pipe to the base of the plant, where it will do the most good.

That Acid, Burning Sensation

❏ Don't apply any manure or compost that's not thoroughly decomposed to the early garden. Such treatments can do more harm than good by burning seedlings and attracting flies that introduce root maggots.

DIRTY BUSINESS

AS A GENERAL RULE, whether you're seeding a lawn or planting a garden, good soil means deep soil.

When using a tiller or plow, turn over a good 10" to 12" of soil, not just the surface layer. And if you have topsoil brought in, don't just set it over the poorer soil and put the seeds in it. Mix it in with 4" to 6" of the soil underneath.

Remember, the deeper the soil, the deeper the roots will go, allowing the plants to take in more water and nutrients on their own. A beautiful layer of 2" topsoil looks rich, but once the grass seed has taken, it will be a shallow lawn, dependent on its owner for nourishment.

❏ Even if you happen to have some manure that is de-composed, don't put a pile of it directly on the garden un-less you can spread it right away. An unspread pile of ma-nure can create excessive nitrogen and acidity in the area where it sits.

Time to Retire

❏ Old tires are becoming increasingly difficult to dispose of. You can avoid paying a stiff fee at your local landfill by simply incorporating your used tires into the garden as small, circular raised beds. Tires are particularly good for melons or other plants that want warm soil; the black rubber serves as a good solar collector. Also, once filled with dirt, the inside of the tire ceases to be a haven for breeding mosquitoes.

SHRUBS, BUSHES AND TREES

Don't Shock Those Shrubs

❏ Don't remove winter protection from shrubbery too early or on a bright, sunny day. It's better to wait for an overcast day. Abrupt exposure to bright light can damage

---

The Gum That Isn't

SPRUCE GUM IS REALLY just pitch that you can find built up in the crook of a spruce tree branch. It was quite popular when I was growing up, and you can still find it today. Just cut it off with a knife and pop it in your mouth.

You can still buy spruce gum in some drug-stores in Maine, too. To keep it from sticking to the box, the manufacturers roll it in cornstarch. When old-time chewers wanted to save the spruce gum they found, they used to roll it in sugar.

I never liked spruce gum. It takes a lot of rolling around in your mouth before you can enjoy chew-ing it. My father and brother swore by it, but I only swore at it.

**A Word
from Earl**

bark and foliage and make the plant more vulnerable to disease and insect infestation.

Prudent Pruning

❏ Trim hedges often. For most species, frequent trimming produces more compact growth.

❏ Prune evergreen trees and bushes at least 2 months before summer dry spells, so the pruned branches have time to recover.

For the Love of Lilacs

❏ To improve the flowering of lilacs, keep the grass from growing around them. A 16" to 24" circle of landscape cloth placed around the bushes and covered with bark or stone will keep the grass down.

❏ After your lilac bush has finished blooming, spread some lime and well-rotted manure around the base. Trim the bush to shape it and remove suckers at the same time.

Dropping Dead

❏ Remove dead flowers from rhododendrons carefully; next year's buds are just under the old heads.

❏ It's a good idea to dispose of any rose leaves that have dropped to the ground; they may be infested with black spot or other diseases. It's okay to burn the leaves, but don't add them to the compost pile, as they can reintroduce diseases into the garden.

A Fruitful Idea

❏ Sprinkle wood ashes around berries and fruit trees. The potash will enhance the sweetness of the fruit.

COMPOST

Hold That Compost

❏ Tomatoes love rich, composted soil, so here's a way to boost your tomato

Whatsit?

WE BOUGHT THIS article at an auction. Can you tell us what it's called and what it's used for?
— P.C., YORK BEACH, MAINE

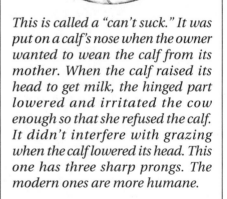

This is called a "can't suck." It was put on a calf's nose when the owner wanted to wean the calf from its mother. When the calf raised its head to get milk, the hinged part lowered and irritated the cow enough so that she refused the calf. It didn't interfere with grazing when the calf lowered its head. This one has three sharp prongs. The modern ones are more humane.

Desperation Was the Mother of This Invention

A Word from Earl

M Y NEIGHBOR HAS INVENTED a clever system for disposing of all the leaves he rakes up every fall, and it can work for you, too.

You start with an old sheet or a piece of plastic that is 5' square. Staple 6' lengths of wood strapping to two opposite edges of the sheet, leaving 6" of strapping hanging on either side. With the help of a partner, you can use this "stretcher" to carry leaves.

There's no need to rake the leaves onto the stretcher. Just drape the stretcher over a leaf pile, push the handles down toward the ground and bring them together under the pile. When you lift the handles (keeping them together), you'll find that the stretcher has enclosed a load of leaves. Simply carry it away and dump it.

The only hitch with this system is that it takes two people to make it work. I'm still looking for a volunteer to help me test it in my yard.

---

yield. First, erect a wire-fence compost enclosure about 3' in diameter and 4' high. Fill it with grass cuttings and leaves and set tomato plants around its perimeter. The compost constantly feeds the growing plants, and the wire fence gives them a framework to climb on.

❑ For a quick compost container, arrange wooden pallets into a box shape and wire them together. Pallets are widely used in shipping and can usually be found anywhere large trucks deliver. Sometimes companies give them away. Pallet manufacturers sell used ones for a nominal price. For specific sources of pallets, look in the yellow pages under Pallets and Skids.

One Good Turn Deserves Another

❑ During dry periods, water your compost frequently so that it will remain active. With a shovel or pitchfork, turn it about once a month to provide the proper balance of air and water.

Shred the Evidence

❑ To give the composting process a head start, shred leaves before composting them. If you don't own a shredder, fill a large barrel (or even your garbage can) half full of dried leaves and run your string grass trimmer in the barrel. In just a few minutes, a half barrel of leaves will be shredded to the point where they're just right for composting.

PLANT CONTAINERS

Wood Planters: Everyone Needs a Stable Home

❑ Ceramic planter pots collect more heat than wooden ones, but they also subject the plant's roots to greater temperature fluctuations. For a more stable environment, choose wood, which will most often result in superior growth and flowering.

Clay Pots Need a Good Soaking

❑ Soak clay pots in water for 2 to 3 hours before using them to repot plants. Otherwise, when you water your newly potted plants, the pots are likely to absorb the water.

BULBS

Keep Your Bulbs Cool and Dry

❑ If you dig up tulips or other bulbs for storage, keep them in a place that's cool and dry and where they'll be well protected from freezing. Many garages and cellars do not meet these standards.

Rules of (Green) Thumb

❑ As a rule of thumb, plant flower bulbs to a depth that is at least three times their diameter. A bulb that is 1" in diameter should be planted 3" deep.

❑ Place a small stake or other marker where you've planted new bulbs in the fall. This will be helpful in the spring, when your cleanup activity might otherwise disturb the area.

Whatsit?

WE HAVE NO IDEA what this tool is. The head measures 5" on each side, and the handle is 16½" long. What is it?
— W.R., MURPHYSBORO, ILL.

This is a ship scraper, used for scraping down the deck planking and removing excess pitch from joints in planking after they have been caulked. The length of the handle was cut to suit the hands of the shipwright who used it.

❏ Don't use manure fertilizer with bulbs. It can encourage bulb rot or disease. Instead, apply a sprinkling of bone meal.

CUT FLOWERS

Everlastings—or Nearly So

❏ Whenever possible, pick flowers in the late afternoon. They have a greater sugar content then and will last longer than ones picked earlier in the day.

❏ Cut flowers can be kept fresh longer if you put them in a vase containing a solution of 2 tablespoons of vinegar, 3 tablespoons of sugar and 1 quart of water.

❏ Avoid putting fresh cut flowers next to fruits and vegetables. The ethylene gas discharged by the vegetables can kill the flowers overnight.

Dried Flowers Like the Dark

❏ To dry flowers, cut them at or just before their peak of bloom. Be sure to leave the stems long. Remove the foliage and hang the flowers upside down in a dry, dark place for several weeks, or until they're dry.

WOODLOTS: LET THERE BE LIGHT

THINNING A WOODLOT is a healthy exercise for both owner and forest. Left to their own devices, trees fill in the forest floor, competing for what little sunlight comes down through the canopy. This slows growth and results in small trees that are all about the same age. Thinning the woodlot helps let in more light and encourages the strong trees to become even stronger, while simultaneously giving you the benefits of firewood, fence posts and a view through to that stone wall you never knew was there.

Your county extension forester (check with the Cooperative Extension Service) can help determine which trees are best culled. Ideally, your woodlot will emerge with three distinct generations of trees: mature trees providing a high, leafy canopy; middle-aged trees with good size and health that will replace the dying or harvested mature trees; and young trees that get enough sunlight to continue growing, eventually replacing the older trees above them.

Why My Mother Always Ran Out of Ginger

BACK BEFORE THE DAYS OF GATORADE, farmers used to drink switchel when mowing hay. It refreshed them after they'd been working in the intense heat. My father used to make a batch on a hot day. He'd mix 1 gallon of water, 2½ cups of sugar, 1 cup of dark molasses, ½ cup of white or cider vinegar and 2 teaspoons of ground ginger. Switchel is very sweet and has a strong gingery taste. My mother always complained that when it got hot, she couldn't keep ginger in the house.

A Word from Earl

FALL CLEANUP

Time for a Transfer

❏ In the fall, be sure to transfer any boxed fertilizers or garden chemicals to plastic containers, as their original cardboard packaging may deteriorate over the winter. Don't forget to label the new containers.

❏ Check the garden shed in the fall and remove any aerosols, liquids or other items that might freeze. Otherwise, the contents are likely to be unusable in the spring.

Only the Good Die Young

❏ Fungi, viruses, insects and nematodes will live in garden debris through the winter. To prevent this, rake the garden clean of decaying vegetable stalks, fallen foliage and old mulch each fall. Remove all this debris from the garden and burn it, compost it (allowing the high temperatures of the compost to kill the pests) or set it some distance away from the garden.

BAMBOO

Don't Be Bamboozled

❏ To get rid of bamboo, dig it up, taking care to get the entire root clump. Don't dump the bamboo anywhere near its old home. Plant grass in the area so that any left-over shoots will be mowed down regularly.

❏ If you have a patch of bamboo that you want to get rid of, here's how. Cut the stalks about 1' above the ground and clear away the cuttings. Fill a plastic pail roughly one-quarter full of rock salt. Fill the rest of the pail with boiling water and stir well. Pour the hot mixture into the hollow stalks. Wait a week, then dig out the bamboo stalks and roots. You may need to repeat the process. It's tough to dig out a complete bamboo root, but this way you know you've killed the plant.

ELSEWHERE AROUND THE YARD

Run It Up the Flagpole

❏ If the rope breaks on your flagpole and the flagpole is strong enough to support your weight, you can replace the rope without taking down the pole. Stand a ladder tight against the pole and, as you climb, tie the ladder to the pole with short ropes every few feet. This is still a balancing act and isn't recommended for acrophobes, but the rope keeps the ladder tight to the pole until you reach the pulley.

MY, THEY WERE POLITE

O NE OF THE TRADITIONAL devices for reducing erosion in a driveway or road is a mound near the crest of a hill that sheds water to both sides. This mound is known in some places as a "thank-you-ma'am," a reference to the days when people traveled in horse-drawn coaches. Upon crossing the mound, the coachman's head would invariably dip forward, as if saying "thank you" to his passengers.

Basic Bird Feeder Cleanup

❏ Are you tired of cleaning up all the sunflower-seed husks left under your bird feeder each spring? Try this simple solution. When you set the bird feeder out in the fall, place a sheet of nylon netting under the feeder and anchor it with a few rocks. (The sheet of netting should be larger than the feeder, of course, so that it will catch all the stray husks dropped by the birds.) If you live in the North, snow will cover the netting for most of the winter. In the spring, just gather up the netting to clean up the husks.

A Little Swing Music, Please

❏ A tall backyard tree with a big branch is a lovely place for a rope swing, but

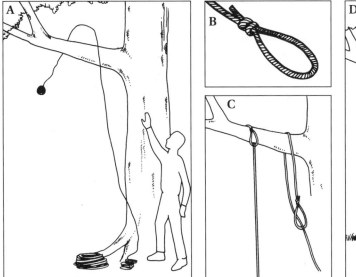

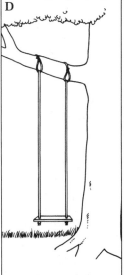

what if you don't have a ladder tall enough to reach the branch?

Start with a ball of twine and the rope you want to use for the swing. Measure the distance from the ground to the branch you're using, then double that measurement. Cut both the twine and the rope to that doubled measurement. Tie an apple or a tennis ball to one end of the twine and throw it over the branch.

Untie the apple and tie the twine to one end of your rope, then pull on the twine until the rope is over the branch and back down to the ground. Untie the twine and set it aside.

Tie a strong loop in one end of the rope and pass the other end through it. Now pull on the free end of the rope until the knot is up tight against the branch. If you wish, repeat with a second rope and attach a seat at the base.

❏ It's hard to remove water from the inside of a tire swing without splashing water all over yourself. You can avoid this problem by punching holes in the bottom of the tire so the water can drain out.

Pallet-able Storage

❏ Place some wooden pallets flat on the ground, hammer some heavy staples partway into the sides, and you'll have a handy tarp tie-down for storing things under cover. Sta-

When you hang your rope swing, toss the apple with the end of the twine over the branch where the swing will hang (A). After you follow the twine with rope, tie a loop in the rope (B) and pull the knot tight to the branch. Repeat for the second side of the swing (C). When you attach the seat (D), make sure the swing is level.

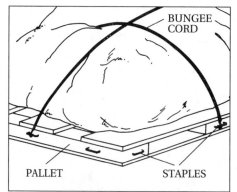

BUNGEE CORD

PALLET   STAPLES

It may be hard to hammer staples into hardwood pallets, but they're sure to hold.

Close-up of heavy-duty staple

ples that are ¾" wide work nicely for this; they're available from hardware stores.

If Good Fences Make Good Neighbors . . .

❏ When you're choosing fence post material, it's useful to know that cedar lasts longer than other commonly available woods.

❏ When installing fence posts, be sure to taper or round off the top of each post to shed water and reduce the risk of checking (splitting the ends of the wood).

❏ The standard post-hole digger has two handles that you pull apart to grip the dirt in the bottom of your hole. The top of the hole has to be wide enough for you to pull these handles apart, which makes for a lot of unnecessary digging.

If you're installing a lot of fence posts, consider investing in a different type of post-hole digger that lets you dig a hole straight down. It looks and works like a regular shovel, but when you tip a lever, the blade of the shovel cocks into a perpendicular position so that you can remove the earth from the bottom of the hole. Look for this tool at garden supply stores.

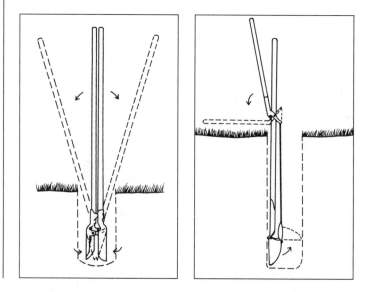

LEFT: *A standard post-hole digger.* RIGHT: *A shovel-style post-hole digger.*

The Right Way to Dig to China

I N THE LATE 1930s, a woman hired another fellow and me to put in a well for her. A dowser had told her where she could find water 20' down, so that's where we set to work.

A Word from Earl

If you're going to dig a deep hole by hand, you need a way to get the earth out of and away from the hole, so we figured out a way to do that. On the surface of the ground, we dug the hole 20' wide—much wider than the well would be. The idea was to dig down about 5', then narrow the hole by 4', leaving a 2' shelf that the person in the bottom of the hole could throw dirt up to. The other person would stand on the shelf and shovel the dirt up and out of the hole. We'd keep stepping the hole down and in until we reached the desired depth.

At the end of the first day of digging, the owner came home and saw what we had accomplished. There was a hole 20' wide and 3½' deep. She wasn't impressed. Come to find out, there'd been a misunderstanding. She'd wanted a well *drilled*, not dug.

I never got to apply the shelf principle to a hole 20' deep. But I've used it many times for holes deeper than 6' that I've had to dig by hand.

Using the shelf principle, the worker on the lower level lifts his dirt to the shelf above him. The worker on the higher level lifts the dirt to ground level.

❑ Always set fence posts on a couple of inches of crushed stone, then pour an additional 2" of stone around the posts before filling in with either soil or cement. This will allow for drainage at the base and deter rotting.

Bushwhacking

❑ When clearing smaller brush, consider pulling the brush out of the ground instead of cutting it down. Sometimes this is just as easy as cutting it, and if you get the roots, the brush won't come up again.

❑ In some areas, it's illegal to burn brush. If you're not going to dispose of brush once it's cut, leave it where it falls. If you gather it into a pile, it won't rot as quickly.

❑ When stacking brush for burning, arrange it compactly and all in the same direction. This will make the fuel dense enough to create a better fire.

❑ Avoid adding plywood or pressure-treated wood to your burn pile. The fumes from these materials can be toxic.

❑ Also be on the lookout for vines growing around branches. Such vines could be poison ivy, which is not easily recognized without its leaves. Be careful not to get these vines mixed in with your brush pile; inhaling the smoke from burning poison ivy can be fatal.

Don't Be Stumped

❑ The easiest and fastest way to get rid of stumps is to get a company that deals in tree work to chip the stumps out with a machine. You can then use the chips as mulch on flower beds.

❑ If you're planning to dig out a stump and you happen to have a pig on your property, you're in luck. Fence the pig in with the stump and sprinkle corn around the roots of the stump. The pig will dig around the roots until it has

BEFORE STONEWALLING WAS REDEFINED

STONE WALLS are a common feature throughout the Northeast and the mid-Atlantic states. The walls, many of them now surrounded by second- and third-growth forest, were built from rocks found in farmers' fields and pastures.

There are a few theories about the intended purpose of the stone walls. They were a convenient place to store the rocks that were continually getting in the way of the scythe and plow, they kept livestock from straying, and they marked boundaries between individual plots of land. No one can say for sure what the primary purpose was, but all three functions were served.

found every kernel of corn. After you've done this repeatedly, the pig will have exposed most of the roots for you.

STONE WALLS

How Firm a Foundation

❏ A dry (mortarless) stone wall needs a good foundation to make it resistant to frost heaves. Give it a base of crushed rock 6" thick and 1' or so below the surface of the ground. This will help to drain the area and keep shifting to a minimum.

❏ If you're building a mortared stone wall, build it up from a point below the frost line. In New England, that means 4' below ground level.

The Building-Block Approach

❏ When building or repairing a stone wall, use the same construction method as you would for a brick or block wall: one over two and two over one. If the stones overlap, the wall will be stronger.

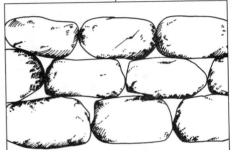

"One over two and two over one" is the oldest rule in masonry.

DRIVEWAYS

Don't Get the Stones Too Thick

❏ Don't put too much stone on a stone driveway. A deep bed of stones will be hard to walk and drive on, and footprints or tire tracks will show in it. Whether you use 1" stones or peastone, the walk or driveway will work and look best if it's only two stones deep.

The Sure Cure

❏ Don't use salt on a new concrete driveway before it has cured (about 6 months). If you rush things, the salt will corrode the concrete. To avoid this problem, pour your concrete driveway in the spring if possible. And if the 6 months aren't up when the first snowfall arrives, use sand on the driveway. It won't melt snow and ice, but it will give your car traction.

Concrete Fillings

❏ You can fill small cracks (no wider than ⅜") in concrete with a latex-based caulking that comes in a caulking cartridge. (Mortar Patch is one such product.) Wet the area around the crack, then apply the filler. If you don't wet the surrounding area first, the dry concrete will draw the moisture out of the filler, and you'll end up with a weak patch.

Seal the Deal

❏ If the concrete floor of your garage or driveway gets heavy traffic, seal it once a year to avoid pitting. Do the job on a day when the temperature is at least 70°F so the sealer will dry quickly.

First make sure the surface of the concrete is dry and swept clean of any dirt or debris. Then use a short-nap paint roller to spread the sealer over the surface.

A time-tested, inexpensive concrete floor sealer is a mixture of equal parts boiled linseed oil and turpentine. The turpentine makes the oil penetrate more deeply into the concrete and allows it to spread more easily. The boiled linseed oil forms a film that keeps out water and winter salts.

To give a concrete floor additional protection, apply a second coat of turpentine and boiled linseed oil, again in equal parts, 24 hours after the first one. This mixture is much cheaper than commercial products available for this purpose.

Basic Black

❏ To remove an oil stain from a black-top driveway, spread TSP (or another product containing trisodium phosphate) on the stain and sprinkle hot water on top. Scrub hard with a stiff bristle brush. Let the cleaner sit for half an hour or so, then rinse with a hose.

SNOW AND ICE

Give the Wind a Break

❏ Snow can make the wind visible. Watch the snow during a winter storm to see where you might consider planting a hedge, either to act as a break

---

Whatsit?

I FOUND THIS ITEM in the barn of my old home. It is made of iron and is about 5" long. What was it used for?   —R.S., SHARON, CONN.

This is an oxbow key. One of these was needed on each end of each bow where the bow projected through the yoke. There were holes in the ends of the bows to fit the keys. A key would be put through a hole and turned a quarter turn; this locked the bow in place. The locked bows kept the yoke in place on the oxen's necks.

against drifting snow or to reduce drafts in the house or barn.

❑ If you do decide on a hedge fence, it's useful to know that pine, cedar, Japanese barberry, arborvitae, spruce and hemlock are especially well suited for hedge fences. Any of these plants can protect against wind and snow as well as provide privacy.

Frozen Locks: You'll See the Light

❑ During the winter, carry a small butane cigarette lighter to heat car or house keys and thus thaw frozen locks. *With your gloves on,* heat the key to the offending lock and gently insert it into the lock. If it sticks and won't go in all the way, use the lighter again to heat the part of the key that is still out. That should free the lock and the key.

Create Traction, but Keep It Safe

❑ Sprinkle wood ashes over icy walks and driveways to add traction, but make sure the ashes are completely cooled before spreading. Hot ashes can melt tire rubber and the bottoms of boots. And be careful about using ashes on walks leading into the house; tracked in, they can make a mess.

❑ Keep a bucket of sand or kitty litter outside the door (and another in the trunk of the car) to spread for traction.

Simple Hand Warmers

❑ To keep your hands warm in winter when you're doing a job that prevents you from wearing gloves, rub a little baby oil or beeswax on them. This closes the pores so the cold air can't get in.

DON'T SELL THAT SNOWSUIT BEFORE YOU MOVE

I F YOU'RE MOVING to another part of the country, don't assume that you can predict the climate solely from the area's latitude. Wind patterns, moisture levels and elevation all play a part. The U.S. Department of Agriculture has divided the country into distinct climatic zones that reveal some real surprises. The zone that includes New England (Zone 4), for instance, also includes parts of northern New Mexico.

The Summer House

It's summertime, and the living should be easy.

ONE OF MY FIRST JOBS was helping my father maintain a number of summer cottages on a lake near our house. My whole family would help close up the cottages after Labor Day each year, when the summer people had left. We'd spend the days washing windows, painting boats, covering the furniture and removing docks. It was a lot of work.

There was also an easier side to those summers, though. One woman who owned a cottage hired me to chauffeur her guests around the lake in her big mahogany motorboat whenever she hosted a party in the evening. I can't remember how often that was, but it wasn't often enough for me. I loved taking care of that boat. (Of course, I had to take it out for a spin from time to time—just to be sure everything was working.) As jobs went, it couldn't be beat.

I learned early on how hard it is to keep up a summer house. But the time I spent driving that wonderful boat around that beautiful lake gave me a good idea why owning a summer house is appealing nonetheless. Here are some ideas that will let you spend more time enjoying your cottage and less time maintaining it.

In this chapter, you'll find great ideas for keeping sand out of the house and leeches off your feet, restoring wooden canoes and refreshing food that's gone stale in a damp cottage. Here are suggestions for letting nature clean your dirty barbecue grill and using a pulley technique to reel your boat in from its mooring. Finally, when it's time to close up the summer house, turn to these pages once again for tips on draining pipes and keeping out mice and burglars alike.

IF YOU CAN'T FIND IT ...

... maybe you need to try another chapter. Check the index, or try these possibilities.

LIGHTING

Keep the Lantern Burning

❏ Some summer cottages still depend on light from kerosene lamps. To keep these lamps operating properly, be sure to burn only kerosene or oil sold especially for oil lamps.

❏ When burning a kerosene lamp, make sure you have at least 18" of air space above the chimney. Otherwise, the heat rising from the chimney can be enough to catch something on fire.

❏ Soak a new wick in vinegar and let it dry thoroughly before inserting it in a kerosene lamp. The wick will burn more cleanly and efficiently as a result.

❏ Pinch the burned area off the wick of a kerosene lamp when the lamp is cold. Cutting it with scissors wastes wick unnecessarily.

❏ If a kerosene lamp smokes a lot, try adding 2 to 3 tablespoons of salt to the kerosene.

Candles: Beeswax Is Better

❏ Candlelight is a warm way to light a summer camp or cabin. When choosing candles for your cottage, look for beeswax ones. They are widely available, tend to drip less than paraffin candles, won't smoke and hold their shape well during hot spells. A 12" beeswax candle will burn for 10 to 12 hours—several hours longer than a paraffin candle of the same size. But the nicest advantage may be the scent. Beeswax, whether it's burning or not, has a lovely honey-vanilla fragrance.

Keep Candles in Shape

❏ It's important not to store or place candles near excessive heat, such as

SHEDDING SOME LIGHT ON CANDLES

A 12" HOUSEHOLD paraffin candle will burn for 7 to 8 hours. Even better are the emergency candles designed for lengthy blackouts. Molded under 1,600 pounds of pressure, these stubby microcrystalline paraffin candles will burn for 50 hours or more.

Candle power is good for more than blackouts, though. Scented with citronella or some other insect repellent, a burning candle raises a defense against mosquitoes. A small candle under a kettle heats up a fondue pot or stewpot. Sulfur candles are used to fumigate; perfumed candles burn like incense. And there's no denying the romance that candles add to an evening meal. More candles are burned in this country's restaurants than in homes, and most candles in the home are burned at the dinner table.

near a sunny window. If the heat bends them, they'll burn too fast and drip more than usual.

❏ If your candles warp, immerse them in a pan of warm water to make them pliable enough for straightening.

BOATS AND CANOES

Boats Shouldn't Be Grounded

❏ Be sure to store your wooden canoe or rowboat up off the ground. Overturning the boat on blocks or sawhorses works well. If the wood comes in contact with the ground, it's very likely to absorb moisture and rot.

Painting: Start with a Clean Canvas

❏ When a canoe is used in a body of water that's also home to motorboats, it's likely to accumulate a slight coating of oil. Before repainting a wood-and-canvas canoe, wash the canoe with dishwasher detergent and warm water to remove any traces of motor oil. Then lightly sand all existing paint until the shine is gone, so the new paint will have a good basis for bonding.

❏ Bare canvas or worn areas will need special treatment. For these sections, pick up urethane floor enamel at a hardware store, thin it with 3 to 4 teaspoons of paint thinner per quart of enamel and apply it as a first coat in problem areas, following the instructions on the can. Then give the entire canoe another coat of the same paint, this time undiluted. If this coat doesn't cover the canoe evenly, you may need to apply an additional coat.

Weathering Heights

❏ After many years, the varnished wood interior of a wood-and-canvas

Whatsit?

THIS ILLUSTRATION shows an iron object my son found while digging in an old dump site. It's about 10½" long overall. The ring is 3½" in diameter and will allow the 3¼" plunger to pass completely through it. What is it?
— W.C.M., HARVARD, MASS.

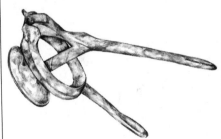

This is a potato ricer, but the perforated cup is missing. The cup was 3½" in diameter and fit into the ring. If you put boiled potatoes in the cup and pressed down on the handle, out would come riced potatoes. Or you could use it to drain berries, make cranberry sauce without the skins or separate fruit juice from the pulp. Ricers are still made and are sold in some country stores.

canoe will show signs of weathering. To restore it, don't remove the varnish completely. Instead, sand any weathered areas and, where the varnish has worn off completely, sand down to the bare wood. Sand the rest of the woodwork only enough to dull the shine. This will allow the new varnish to stick to the old. When all the sanding is done, wipe off any dust and apply a coat of spar varnish (commonly used for marine applications and available from hardware stores).

Boat Repair: It May Not Be Worth It

❏ Joints that leak in an aluminum boat with aluminum rivets are very difficult to repair. You can try holding a heavy hammer against the rivet on the inside while a helper tightens the rivet from the outside with another hammer. Or use a caulking gun to apply any kind of waterproof caulking to try to stop the leak. But neither of these techniques is surefire; you may have to buy a new boat.

Moorings: The Clothesline Approach

❏ If you like to keep your small boat (up to 15') on a mooring but you hate having to swim or row out to it, set up a rope system to help you bring the boat back to the dock. The principle is the same as that of a pulley clothesline.

You need a loop of rope that goes from the dock through a ring attached to the mooring and back again. (Make sure the rope is tough enough to stand up to weather and abuse, and do not use this technique in an area where people—especially children—are likely to go swimming.) Anywhere on the rope, tie on a weather-resistant piece of hardware—an eye works well—to which you can attach

The clothesline approach to boat mooring requires plenty of room for the boat to swing around the float.

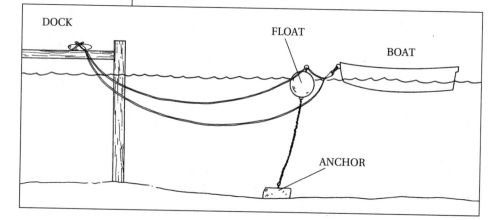

DOCK

FLOAT

BOAT

ANCHOR

the boat at its bow. When you finish using the boat, you can get off at the dock, clip the boat onto the eye, pull the boat out to the mooring and tie the rope to the dock.

If you make the loop long and leave it slack when you tie it, the rope will settle in the water, and boats will be able to pass over it safely. In coastal locations, remember to allow for tidal changes in the water level. The rope must have extra slack to make sure it lies well below water level at low tide.

DOCKS AND FLOATS

Don't Let Ice Destroy Your Dock

❏ A dock left in fresh water for the winter is likely to be destroyed by the pressure from ice if the lake freezes. You must remove your dock or get a submersible pump (sometimes called a bubbler) to circulate the water around it for the winter. If the water is moving rapidly enough, it won't freeze.

Use a Screw, Save a Swimming Suit

❏ When building a dock, the best choice for securing the decking is galvanized screws. They hold better than nails, and they won't work their way out over time—potentially saving you a torn bathing suit or two.

Keep Tradition Afloat

❏ Many rafts have been built over the years using Styrofoam for flotation. But Styrofoam is easily chipped or scraped, resulting in floating bits of debris that are both unsightly and unhealthy for birds and other wildlife that mistakenly feed on them. Instead, use empty, capped 55-gallon drums. Best of all are plastic drums, which are much lighter and less subject to rust than metal drums. Before using these, make sure they're completely clean so they won't pollute the water in which you place them.

Whatsit?

THE ITEM PICTURED below does not have any openings and is hollow. It measures 9½" wide and 23" long. It's circular in shape. Can you tell me what it is and what it was used for? — R.F., CANTERBURY, CONN.

This is a mooring used to anchor a boat offshore. An anchor of some sort would be tied to the bottom ring, and the boat would be tied to the large ring on the top. This would let the boat swing with the wind in a circle without hitting another boat or the shore.

IN THE WATER

The Great Sand-Off

❑ To keep bare feet from bringing beach sand into the cottage, leave a galvanized tub filled with water near the outside door and have people dip their feet in it before entering the house.

❑ Another way to minimize the amount of sand tracked into the cottage is to keep a number of pairs of inexpensive flip-flops or old sneakers on hand and have people put them on when getting out of the water. (Old sneakers are good to wear in the water, too, if the bottom is rocky or hard on the feet.)

Leeches: Break Off the Engagement

❑ If leeches attach themselves to you while you're in swimming, sprinkle salt on them. They'll soon be persuaded to let go.

No Fish Story

❑ To protect fishing rods, give them a coat of automobile wax once or twice each season.

FOOD, INDOORS AND OUT

Food Revival

❑ Summer cottages can be damp. If your crackers become stale and your cereal soggy, you can restore them to a state of crispness by placing them on a cookie sheet and heating them for a few minutes in a 350°F oven.

❑ Sugar can be softened by storing it in an airtight jar with a piece of grapefruit, orange or lemon rind. (The sugar won't absorb the citrus taste.) Replace the rind with another piece when it dries out. This method will also keep sugar from hardening in the first place.

❏ To revive cookies that have become hard and dry, place them in a closed tin with a piece of fresh bread.

All Fired Up

❏ The fastest, easiest and cheapest way to start a charcoal fire in a grill is with a 12" length of stovepipe. Starting at one end of the stovepipe and continuing for about 2", punch a few ½" holes in the pipe for ventilation. Crumple a sheet or two of newspaper on the grill, then stand the stovepipe on top of the paper, with the perforated end resting on the paper. Pour your charcoal through the stovepipe and onto the paper, then touch the paper with a match. In 5 minutes or so, lift off the stovepipe with tongs or pliers, and your fire will be well on its way.

Bid Adieu to Grease

❏ An easy way to clean the grill is to remove the grill top after it has cooled and place it cooking side down on the grass. Leave it overnight and let the dew do the work. In the morning, wipe with a damp paper towel.

PORCHES, NARROWLY DEFINED

W E'VE BEEN SAYING IT wrong for years. A porch is not a porch, at least not usually, and especially not if it wraps around, is screened in or is used for sleeping. The porches in our minds might actually be balconies or piazzas. Probably, though, they are verandas.

In the classic definition, porches are relatively narrow, vertical features associated with doors. They developed from defensive towers, city gates and temple entrances. A typical porch projects from a house, is open on the sides, is one story high and has a roof supported from the floor by pillars, columns, posts or piers. Traditionally, a porch's basic function was to protect visitors from the weather as they stood and waited outside the door.

Verandas are horizontal features attached to walls. They developed from barn sheds, market stalls and roofed passageways. These are the more elaborate affairs we associate with rocking, sipping lemonade and watching the tide come in. Of all the foreign names for "an open, roofed passageway attached to the side of the building," America picked *veranda,* an Indian term made fashionable during the British raj. Such was the prestige of British culture in Victorian America.

A Grill in an Instant

❑ Next time you're at the town landfill, look for old refrigerators with the grills still in them. As long as the grills are not vinyl coated, they're great for cooking over a charcoal fire (or for use as cookie cooling racks).

CLOSING UP

Natural Air Fresheners

❑ When closing up the summer house, place shallow pans of cider vinegar under the beds and in the closets. This will keep the rooms from smelling stale come spring.

❑ Also when closing up the cottage, put bowls of charcoal briquettes in each room and closet to absorb moisture and prevent mildew.

Mouseproofing

❑ Cover mattresses and other furniture with newspaper to keep off dust. Newspaper is better than sheets because

The House That Got Frostbite

SOME PEOPLE BUTTON UP too tightly when they close their summer houses for the winter. They close every interior door and draw every curtain. They're forgetting that the sun's warmth, if given a chance, will keep a house from turning into an ice cave in winter.

A Word from Earl

I once saw as much as an inch of frost on the walls of a summer house with all the interior doors shut. The house had a small moisture problem, and because the air in the house could not circulate, the rooms that never got any sun frosted up. The next winter, the owners left all the room and closet doors open, and the problem didn't recur.

If your summer house has a cellar, leave the door to it open. The air in the cellar, which will stay at ground temperature, will come up the stairs and help warm the house.

mice don't like the sound newspaper makes when they run on it.

❑ Old trunks can come in handy in a summer cottage. Pack your blankets in them for the winter to prevent damage from moths and rodents.

❑ Put all candles and matches in metal canisters with tight covers to keep them away from mice. It is possible for a mouse to light a match by gnawing on it, so unenclosed matches are a fire hazard.

❑ You can use dried peppermint leaves (available from health food stores and some grocery stores) to keep mice out of kitchen stove insulation. Crush the leaves and put them in golf ball–size bags made from old pantyhose. Place these bags in the stove when closing up for the winter. It's a good idea to leave a few bags under the beds and in the closets, too.

❑ Mice will winter in very small and very strange places. Make sure the pipes of your summer house don't become their lodging spots. After you drain the plumbing, tie pieces of cloth over the ends of all open pipes that are ¾" or more in diameter and over all holes of the same size from which plugs have been removed. Use cloth, not plastic. Cloth will allow water to drain through, while plastic will hold it in the pipe, allowing it to freeze and perhaps break something.

You Wouldn't Want to Handle the Cleanup

❑ Close fireplace and stovepipe dampers to keep out squirrels and birds that sometimes find their way down these openings and into the house.

SUMMER CLASSICS

I F YOU WERE wondering what the classic furniture of summer is, wonder no more. Traditionalists make sure their cottages are complete with these items:
- Adirondack chairs
- Hammocks made from hemp or cotton
- Wicker armchairs
- Oak rockers (with cane or rush seats and backs)
- Porch swings
- Cast-iron garden set (four chairs and a table)

VIDEBO GAMES

T HE TERM *GAZEBO*, for a small, open building for outdoor visiting, comes from the word *gaze* and the Latin future suffix *-ebo* (as in *videbo*, which means "I will see"). So, to be truly accurate, a good gazebo is situated so that you have something to gaze at while you're sitting in it. If your spouse is pestering you to build one, you may accurately respond, "Videbo."

❏ Any liquid containing water will freeze. Either remove the liquid or be sure there's room in the container for expansion of the frozen contents.

Plumbing: Prepare for the Deep Freeze

❏ When you close up a summer house in the fall, every drop of water must be drained from the water system. After you've shut off the water main, open all the faucets, including any outside spigots. When you get to the cellar, place large buckets under the faucets and bleed valves for the pipes, then open those faucets and bleed valves. Most of the water in your plumbing system will drain from the basement pipes, but be prepared to wait; these pipes can take a while to empty.

Pipe Cleaners

❏ Sometimes water pipes sag and don't drain well. The water left in the lines will freeze over the winter and split

The System Relied on Boy Power

WHEN YOU THINK OF a hand pump, you generally think of one that serves as the water source for one sink only—usually in the kitchen. But the house I grew up in had a hand-pumped plumbing system that also served the bathroom. The pump was at the kitchen sink, so you could pump water directly to the sink. But if you closed the faucet on the snout of the pump, the water would be directed to a reservoir in my bedroom. From there, the water was gravity-fed back down to a first-floor bathroom. My father hooked a weight on a string to a float in the reservoir. The weight hung on the wall in the kitchen and indicated the level of the water in the tank. My brother and I had to pump the tank full when it ran low.

**A Word
from Earl**

It's still possible to buy hand pumps designed for this application today. A hand-pumped plumbing system is ideal for cabins without power.

The Proper Position for an Outhouse

I'VE BUILT A LOT OF OUTHOUSES. Back before the invention of "Porta-potties," I had to build an outhouse every time the contracting firm I worked for took on a big road-building project for the state.

Only the crudest camps use outhouses today. The factors in positioning an outhouse, however, are the same as they have been for centuries. You want it near the house, downwind, out of sight, in a place that's easy to dig. One other factor: Make sure the path to it goes by your woodpile. When you're returning from the outhouse, you can bring in an armload of wood. Better yet, guests who are embarrassed about heading in that direction can pretend they just went out to get more wood. If you put your woodpile along the path to the outhouse, you'll never have an empty woodbox.

A Word from Earl

the pipes. If you have any doubts about how well your water pipes drain, use an air compressor to blow the water out of the lines. A short blast of air applied to the end of a pipe or fixture is usually sufficient.

❏ If you're dealing with a short pipe and a compressor isn't available, just blow hard at the end of the pipe or fixture. This should clear out any water.

❏ An alternative way to clear long pipes of water is to disconnect them at all low points and drain them well. Consider adding a fitting (a union, valve or bleeder, for instance). This will allow you to drain a long pipe more effectively.

❏ It used to be necessary to remove all sink, tub and basin traps to get the water out of them, but now it's easier and cheaper to pour in recreational vehicle (RV) antifreeze to drive out the water and prevent the traps from freezing. *Don't use automobile antifreeze; it's not environmentally friendly.* Nontoxic RV antifreeze designed for this purpose is available in the appropriate season from some general hardware stores (in summer communities, for instance), marine hardware stores and RV suppliers.

For toilet bowls and tanks, you'll need to remove as much water as possible with a small tin can, then sop up the rest with a sponge. Pour in enough antifreeze to replace the water and make a seal in the drain, keeping out sewer odors.

No Tanks

❑ Water tanks and water heaters must be drained before winter. Before you drain the water heater, be sure it's turned off at the circuit breaker, or if you have a fuse box, be sure the fuse is removed. Put a garden hose on each drain and place the other end of the hose outside. Let the water drain while you do other work.

Clutter in the Gutter

❑ Outside the cottage or camp, clean out gutters and remove any leaves or pine needles from low-sloped roofs and roof valleys. These materials will hold snow and ice and can cause leaks.

A single board with a V in the center makes a good brace for a door. Make sure the brace is positioned snugly, or it won't hold when forced.

Low-Tech Burglarproofing

❑ If you have sliding glass doors, cut a carefully measured piece of broomstick and fit it snugly into the track behind the door that opens. This will keep an intruder from forcing the door open.

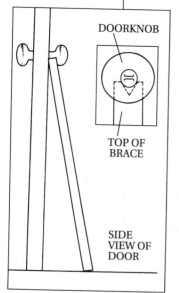

DOORKNOB

TOP OF BRACE

SIDE VIEW OF DOOR

❑ For a door that swings rather than slides, make a brace that will serve as a simple but foolproof door lock. Start with a single board (1" x 3" lumber works well). Cut a V in one end of the board. Measure the distance from the floor to the center of the doorknob. Cut the other end of the board off square at a length that is ½" to 1" longer than this length, as measured from the bottom of the V. Now slip the V under the doorknob and push the base of the board along the floor toward the door until it's snug. An intruder can't kick in the door when it's braced this way.

It Helps to Have Nosy Neighbors

❑ You can apply all these extra protections to other doors, but you won't be able to use them on the door by which you leave—so that door will be

Security and the Summer House

WHEN MY FAMILY AND I were hired to close up cottages on the lake near our home, we used to board up all the windows with heavy shutters to keep people from breaking in and stealing valuables. After the Great Depression began, however, we changed our strategy. Vagabonds started breaking into the cottages and living in them for weeks, unseen behind the shutters we had put up. So we switched to leaving the shutters off and the curtains open. That way, someone passing by the house could see if anyone was camped out inside.

A Word from Earl

And any robber looking for valuables wouldn't see any through the window. In the houses we maintained, we built secret compartments for silverware, antiques, guns and even liquor. But the best strategy for securing the valuable objects you keep in a summer house is the same now as it was then: Remove them from the house each winter.

the most vulnerable. As a safety measure, plan to leave from the door that's most easily seen from the road. It's best to have your most vulnerable entrance be the one that's also most visible to neighbors and passersby. Then if an intruder does try to break in, he or she is more likely to be spotted.

OPENING UP

How to Handle a Water Heater

❏ When you open up a cottage in the spring, remember that you drained the water heater the previous fall and you need to refill it now. Never turn on a water heater until the tank is full. Instead, after you've attempted to fill the tank and *before* you turn on the heater at the fuse box or circuit breaker, turn on a hot-water faucet. If water comes out of the faucet, the tank is full, and you can go ahead and turn on the heater. If no water comes out or you suspect the

The Party Needed to Warm Up

I ONCE DESIGNED AND BUILT a summer cottage for a man who liked to host big parties. I made the living room large, to accommodate the large numbers of guests he entertained, and built it with a cathedral ceiling.

One year the man decided he wanted to visit his cottage in the winter. We'd made no plans for a heating system when we built the house. There was no insulation in the cottage, and the only source of heat was the fireplace in the living room. I knew that the man wouldn't be able to heat that large room effectively with just the fireplace, so we decided to build a temporary room within the living room.

I set up a partition 16' from one wall. Then I spanned 2 x 4s from the partition to the wall and lay sheets of Homosote board on them to create a lower ceiling. (Homosote board is similar to drywall but not as strong, smooth or heavy.) This little room around the fireplace could be heated quite comfortably. From then on, I assembled the partition and ceiling every fall and took them down in the spring.

If children and pets are a threat to your screen door, fortify the door with strapping.

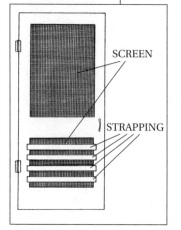

tank is not yet full, investigate further or call a plumber before turning on the heater. Otherwise, you'll burn out the heating element or crack the lining of the tank.

Keep Broiled Mice off the Menu

❏ Before using the stove for the first time each season, check it over thoroughly. Mice sometimes nest in the drawer at the bottom of the stove.

This Trick Is for Kids

❏ There's nothing like a screened door on a summer camp. If you have kids or dogs around, though, the screen will be in constant danger of being ripped. If your door has a large area of screen fairly close to the floor, within easy reach of kids and dogs, you can prevent them from pushing directly on the screen by screwing a couple of strips of wood or strapping across it.

Stuffed Fish: It's All in the Presentation

❑ To make that prize fish trophy look alive, dampen a cotton cloth with glass cleaner and wipe it gently over the fish.

❑ Use fingernail polish as an adhesive to repair a cracked fin on a stuffed fish.

How to Clean a Deer Head

❑ Dust collects in the fur of deer heads and moose heads, so you should vacuum them periodically. Use the furniture attachment on your vacuum cleaner and stroke the fur lightly. Don't go against the nap of the fur.

❑ Every 5 years, a moose or deer head should be washed. Sponge the fur with a mild solution of dishwashing liquid and warm water. Then rinse with warm water. Don't saturate the skin of the trophy. Leave the head outside to dry for a few days, brushing the fur occasionally to fluff it up.

❑ With a rag, apply a light coat of boiled linseed oil to improve the look of antlers.

WHEN SPRING CLEANING REALLY *MEANT* SOMETHING

BACK IN VICTORIAN TIMES, before the age of the air conditioner, houses of the well-to-do were "summerized" or "disrobed" before the hot weather set in.

Heavy curtains, draperies and other textiles were taken down and cleaned, then wrapped in linen and stored with tobacco leaves to protect them from insects. In their place went thin lace curtains that were cooler and allowed in more light.

Heavy carpets were pulled up and beaten clean, then rolled and stored, replaced by thin straw mats from China or India. Expensive furniture was covered with linen to prevent perspiration stains and fading from the sun.

The practice largely died out after World War II, but it's still followed today by some affluent families. Nowadays, though, the intent is not to make the house cooler and airier during the summer. It is to close the house for the summer, while the owners are away at the summer cottage.

Index

Cars *continued*
  dogs chasing, 64*i*
  dried bugs on windshields and headlights of, 31
  insulation, mouse damage to, 77
  odors in, 60
  pitch on, 30
  protecting while carrying ladders, 102
  scratches in finish of, 30
  stale cigarette smoke in, 60-61
  tar and tree sap on, 30
Casein paint, 146
Casing, door, 139*i*
Cast iron, 15-17
  cleaning, 16-17
  seasoning, 15-16
Castor oil, 14
Cat(s), 66-68
  bathing, 67
  digging in gardens, 77
  fleas, 68
  litter box odor, 66
  scratching post for, 66*i*-67
  trimming claws of, 67*i*
  urinating in the house, 67-68
  urine stains from, 47, 49
Caulking, 166-67
  cleaning, 33
  to prevent heat loss, 297-98
  types of, 321
Cedar
  chests, restoring fragrance of, 57
  clapboards, priming, 168
  fence posts, 352
  shakes, 309
  shingles, 309-11
    installing on roofs, 324-25
    installing as siding, 311*i*
    measuring area of, 327
    splitting, 325*i*
Ceiling(s)
  calcimine on, 147, 197-98
  cleaning, 199
  cobwebs on, 11
  drywall on, installing, 180*i*-81*i*
  fans, 304-5
  paint separating from plaster on, 197-98
  panels for, cutting, 199
  pebble-finish, painting, 162
  plaster
    coloring, 196
    coming off, 199
  stains on, 302-3
  suspended, 198-99
  whitewash on, 197-98
Cellars. *See* Basement(s)
Cement
  applying, 120

recipe for masonry, 273
vs. concrete, 314
Central heating, 264-69
  banging from, 264-66
  furnaces, 264
  hot-water systems, 268-69
  radiators, 267
  registers, 264
Ceramic tiles, 193-95
  adhesives for, 193-94
  grout for, 194-95
  partial tiles, 193
  replacing, 195
Chair(s). *See also* Furniture
  cane seats, 261*i*
  disassembly for regluing, 246-47*i*
  regluing, 247-49
  replacing seats, 261*i*
  restoring, 260-61*i*
  rocking, 246*i*, 247
  rungs, tightening, 247
Chalky exterior paint, 164
Charcoal-fire starter, 365
Charcoal fires, grills for, 366
Checking in lumber, 130*i*
Cheese curd whipper, 210*i*
Chests of drawers, mothball odor in, 55-57
Chimney(s), 269-80
  capping, 272-73*i*
  cleaning, 276-78*i*, 280
  creosote buildup in, 274, 275-76, 277
  demolishing, 276
  fires, 279-80
  flue liners for, 274-75*i*
  flues in, 271
  inspecting, 276-77
  kerosene lamp, cleaning, 21
  leaks in, 277
  mortar deterioration in, 272, 273
  parts of, 270*i*
  positioning of, 269, 270-71*i*, 279
  proportions of, 270
  repointing, 273-74
  soot in, 277
  stovepipe for, 272*i*
Chimney pots, 273*i*
China
  brown stains, 50-51
  cleaning, 26, 31
  coffee and tea stains, 50
  mice nesting odor, 59
Chipping hammer, welder's, 92*i*
Chisel(s)
  ice, 6*i*
  method of using, 108
  from old files, 120
  sharpening, 117
Chlorine bleach, lethal mixtures with, 6

Chocolate stains on fabric, 40
Chopping knife, triple-bladed, 112*i*
Chrome
  cleaning, 10-11, 29
  discoloration, 28
Cigarette odors, 60-61
Clamp(s)
  from old inner tubes, 102*i*
  tourniquet, 249*i*
  web, 249*i*
Clapboard siding
  history of, 308
  replacing, 307-8*i*
  types of, 167*i*
Clasps, window, 142*i*
Claws, trimming cats', 67*i*
Clay pots
  for plants, 347
  sharpening knives on, 117
Cleaning, 4-37
  air conditioner filters, 12-13
  aluminum, 14-15
    doors and windows, 33
    siding, 316
  animal hair
    on clothing, 29
    on upholstery, 36
  under appliances, 7-9, 11
  artificial flowers, 34
  ashes from coal stoves, 292
  barn boards, 186
  baskets, 34
  bathrooms, 27-28
  beams, 186
  under birdfeeders, 350
  bone objects, 33-34
  bottles, 17-18, 19
  bowls, wooden, 17
  brass, 21-23
  bronze, 21-23
  brooms, 31
  candle wax on wooden furniture, 240
  cane chair seats, 260
  cars, 29-31
  cast iron, 16-17
  caulking, 33
  ceilings, 11, 199
  ceramic tiles, 194, 195
  chimneys, 276-78*i*, 280
  china, 31
  chrome, 10-11, 29
  clothes, 29
  coffeepots, 14
  copper, 21-23
  countertops, 13
  crystal and glass, 17-21
  decanters, 17-18
  deer heads, 373
  dishwashers, 11, 22
  dog hair, 65
  drains, 13
  eyeglasses, 21
  fabrics for rags, 6-7

Fabric *continued*
  rust stains on, 40
  scorch marks on, 46
  shoe polish stains on, 46-47
  tar on, 45
  tea stains on, 40
  urine stains on, 47
  varnish stains on, 46
  yellow spots on, 43
Face cord, as unit of measure
  for wood, 288
Fake antiques, spotting, 238-39
Fans, 303-5
Farmer's anvil, 68*i*
Fence posts, 352, 354
Fences
  painting, 163
  to deter garden pests, 76-77*i*
Fertilizers, 336, 343
Files
  chalk on, 111
  reused as chisels, 120
  using, 111
  wood in, 114
Film
  on bathroom tiles, 27
  on car windshields, 30-31
  in wineglasses, 18
Fingernail polish on fabric, 45
Finish(es)
  for barn boards, 187
  for decks, 317
  floor, 214-18
  for furniture, 249, 257-58
  pickled pine, 259
  solvents for, 252
  types of, 251-52
Finishing wood floors, 211-18.
    See also Refinishing
  bleaching, 212-13
  with paint, 217-18
  with penetrating finishes,
    214-15
  with polyurethane, 215-17
  sanding, 213-14
  with shellac, 218
  stripping, 211-12
  wax removal, 217
Firebacks, 282*i*
Firebricks, 281*i*
Fire extinguisher stains on fabric, 42
Fireplace(s), 280-83
  air ducts for, 295
  andirons in, positioning, 282
  cleaning, 37, 282-83
  damper as means to cool
    house, 305
  drafts in, regulating, 282
  firebricks in, 281*i*
  flooring next to, installing,
    205*i*
  newspaper logs for, 282
  pinecones, burning, 290
  proportions of, 280

stone, 281
  in summer houses, 367
Fires
  charcoal, starting, 365
  chimney, 279-80
  stages of, 284
  in wood stoves, starting, 284
Firewood, 286-90
  bringing into the basement,
    289
  cutting, 286-87
  earwigs in, 91
  ice on, melting, 284-85
  measuring, 288
  needs for, estimating, 287
  stacking, 288*i*, 289*i*-90
  stages of burning, 284
  types of, 287
  woods to avoid, 290
Fishing rods, protecting, 364
Fish odors, 58
Fish, stuffed, 373
Fixtures, stains on kitchen and
  bath, 49-50
Flagged bristles in paintbrushes, 157*i*
Flagpoles, repairing, 350
Flagstone, securing in walkways, 340
Flannel stuck to wooden tables,
  240
Flashing for roofs, 326*i*
Flat-sawn clapboards, 167*i*
Flattening floor tiles, 223
Fleas, 68
Flies
  bottle, 88
  cluster, 89
Floats for summer houses, 363
Floor(s), 200-235
  candle wax on, 221
  cleaning
    concrete, 233, 235
    quarry tiles, 232-33
    slate, 232
    vinyl and linoleum, 221
    waxed wood, 220-21
  concrete, 233-35
    carpeted, 234
    leaks in basement, 329*i*,
      330
    rust stains on, 235
    sealing, 233, 356
  coverings, historic, 226
  drafts from, 296
  joists, 203
  linoleum, 221-24
    blisters in, 234
    laying, 224*i*
    marks on, 222
    patching, 223*i*-24
    patterns in, 229*i*
    removing, 224-25
    rugs on, 221
  marble, 232

new pine, 202-3
polishers, gummed-up pads
  in, 220-21
quarry tile, 232-33
subfloors, installing, 203-4
squeaks in, 219-20*i*
stenciling, 196-97
tiles
  over concrete, 233-34
  flattening, 223
  removing asphalt, 225
vinyl and linoleum, 221-25
  flattening, 223
  laying, 224*i*
  patching, 223*i*-24
  rugs on, 221
wood
  over concrete, 207-8*i*
  dents from nailing, 206,
    207
  finishing, 211-18
  installing, 202-9, 205*i*
  knots in, 218-19
  maintaining, 218-21
  nailing finish, 206-7*i*
  sanding, 213*i*-14
  scratches on, 216, 219
  scuff marks on, 221
  stains on, 41, 212-13, 214,
    221
  strip, 206*i*
  stripping, 211-12
  urine odors in, 221
Floorboards
  defects in, 219
  matching old, 202
  positioning for straightness,
    205-6
Flowers
  cleaning artificial, 34
  cut, 348
  drying, 348
Flues, chimney, 271
  liners for, 274-75
  positioning of, 266
  positioning of tiles for, 271*i*
  poured concrete liners for,
    275*i*
  round vs. square tiles for,
    272*i*
Fluting iron, 120*i*
Food
  bugs in, 91
  odors from burned, 57
  reviving stale, 364-65
  in summer houses, 364-65
Forks, cleaning silver, 25
Formula stains on fabric, 44
Foundations, 329-30
  insulating, 295-96
  protecting from winter
    drafts, 295
  termites in, 83
Frames, picture
  cleaning gilt, 26

Health hazards. *See also* Safety
  cleaning agents, 5-6
  oxalic acid, 232, 235
  painting without ventilation, 151
  plaster dust, 177
  sanding dust, 182
  sanding old vinyl or linoleum floors, 223
  sizing as, 148
Heat exchangers, 298
Heating, 263-303. *See also* Chimneys; Fireplaces; Firewood; Radiators; Wood stoves
  backup, 283-84
  chimneys, 269-80
  with coal, 291-92
  Colonial means of, 286
  evergreens as windbreak, 264
  fireplaces, 280-83
  firewood, 286-90
  flue liners, 274-75
  fuels for central, 267
  furnaces, 264
  hot-water, 268-69
  insulation, 299-303
  passive solar, 294
  portable heaters, 292-94
  preparing for winter, 294-98, 349, 363, 366-67
  radiators, 267-68
  summer houses, 372
  ventilation, 298-99
  wood stoves, 283-86
Heat shields
  for radiators, 268
  with wood stoves, 278*i*-79
Hedges, 345, 356-57
Hinges
  door, 139*i*, 140, 141
  history of, 198
  screws loose in, 140
  wax buildup in furniture, 239-40
Historical features of homes
  doorknobs, 189
  hinges, 198
  lath, 179*i*
  paint, original, 154
  preserving while sanding, 215
  wallpaper, 192
Hoes, sharpening, 116*i*, 117
Holes
  cutting in paneling, 188
  dogs digging, 64-65
  in foundations, 296
  large, digging, 353
  in plaster, 150, 182, 184*i*
  in tabletops and table leaves, 254-55, 260
  in walls from nails, 182
Hoof nippers, 26*i*

Hornets, 86
Hoses, storing garden, 99*i*, 124
Hot-air heating. *See* Heating
Hot-water heating, 268-69. *See also* Heating
Houseplants, bugs in, 91
Houses, summer. *See* Summer houses
Housewife's tool, 172*i*
Humidifying rooms, 269, 285, 294
Hyde molding scrapers, 147*i*

I

Ice chisel, 6*i*
Ice on firewood, melting, 284-85
Ice shaver, 292*i*
Identifying your tools, 116
Ink stains, 43, 48, 49, 230
Inkstand, 257*i*
Insect(s). *See also* Bug(s)
  bats as controls for, 74
  bites, 90
  blackflies, 89-90
  in fruit trees, 92
  in paint, 168-69
  stinging, 310
  stings, 86-88
Inspecting chimneys, 276-77
Insulation, 298, 302-3
  installing, 300*i*
  of sills, 296*i*
  types of, 301
  vapor barriers in, 299-302
Irons, cleaning, 13
Ironwork, cleaning, 152
Itching
  from insect bites, 90
  from skin irritations, 8
Ivory
  cleaning, 33-34
  identifying antique, 135

J

Jamb, door, 139*i*
Japanese woodworking saws, 106
Jars, stuck lids on, 133-34
Jelly maker's stand, 275*i*
Jewelry, cleaning, 26-27
Jig for cutting wood projects, 125*i*
Joinery, dowel, 244-45*i*
Jointed-mouth standard team bit, 302*i*
Joints
  dovetail, 250*i*
  drywall, 181*i*
Joists, floor, 203
Jugs, recycling plastic gallon, 136
Juice stains, 40, 230

K

Kerosene heaters, 293
Kerosene lamps, 360, 21
Keys broken in locks, 143
Kitchens
  ants in, 80-81
  bugs in flour and cereal, 91
  odors in, 57-58
  stains on fixtures of, 49-50
Knives
  hay-spade, 317*i*
  rust on, 25
  sharpening, 117*i*-18
Knots
  in floor joists, 203
  in lumber, 129, 130-31
  in wood floors, 218-19

L

Lace, cleaning, 29
Lacquer
  as finish, 216, 251
  thinner, storage of, 175
Ladders
  as dividers for storing stock, 97*i*
  for painting, 169
  protecting during transport, 102
Lamp(s)
  cleaning chimneys of, 21
  cruse, 217*i*
  kerosene, 360
Lancashire tail vice, 187*i*
Latches, door, 139*i*, 140-41*i*
Latch plate, 141*i*
Latex caulking, 321
Latex paint(s), 156
  cleanup from, 173
  stains on fabric, 46
  storage of, 175
  types of old, 146
Lath, to date a house, 179*i*
Laundry softener, 29
Lavabo, 230*i*
Lawns, 335-38
  ants in, 81
  clippings from mowing, 335
  drainage for, 336*i*-37
  fertilizing, 336
  moss in, 338
  seeding, 335
  trimming, avoiding, 337
  watering, 336
  winter boardwalks over, 338*i*
Lead paint, 147
Leaks
  in basements, 329*i*, 330
  in chimneys, 277
  in roofs, 370
Leather
  cleaning, 32, 43, 48-49
  furniture, 259-60
  odors from curing, 60

Nailing *continued*
  prefinished paneling, 189
Nail sets for installing hard-
      wood flooring, 206-7*i*
Neat's-foot oil, 14
Newspaper
  logs for fireplaces, 282
  stains on glassware, 52
Noisy heating systems, 264-67
Nominal size for lumber, 126
Nuts, rusted, 103-4

O

Oak furniture, stains on, 241-42
Odors
  in boots, 60
  burned food in ovens, 57
  carpet, 227
  in china, 59
  in closets, 55
  in drains, 58
  fish, 58
  in freezers, 57
  in leather, 60
  in litter box, 66
  in microwave ovens, 58
  mothball, 55-57
  mustiness, 53-55
  oil spills, 61
  onion on hands, 58
  in outhouses, 61
  paint, 160-61
  in pets, 58-59
  in refrigerators, 57
  in shoes, 60
  skunk, 65-66
  smoke, 60-61
  urine
    in carpets, 231
    on leather, 49
    in hardwood floors, 221
    in wooden utensils, 58
Oil
  on blacktop driveways, 356
  in carpets, 228-29
  on concrete floors, 235
  on leather, 48
  odor from spilling, 61
Oilcans, homemade, 121
Oil finishes, 214-15, 216, 258
Oil paint(s)
  skin on, 175
  stains on fabric, 46
  vs. latex, 156
Onion odors, 58
Opening summer houses, 371
Oriental rugs, stains in, 230
Outbuildings, positioning posts
      of, 317*i*
Outdoor furniture
  marks on clothes from, 342
  squirrels chewing on, 70
Outdoor(s), 332-57
  bamboo, 349-50

bird feeder cleanup, 350
brush, clearing, 354
bulbs, 347-48
bushes, 345
compost, 345-47
drainage, 334-35
driveways, 355-56
fall cleanup, 349
fences, 352, 353
flagpoles, 350
flowers, cut, 348
furniture, 342
gardens, 342-44
lawn care, 335-38
lilacs, 345
locks, frozen, 357
patios, 341
plant containers, 347
shrubs, 344-45
stone walls, 355
storage, 351
stumps, removing, 355
swings, 351
traction, winter, 357
trees, 345
walkways, 338-41
windbreaks, 356-57
Outhouses
  odors in, 61
  positioning, 369
Outlets, holes in paneling for,
      188
Ovens
  burned food odors in, 57
  cleaning, 9-10
Oxalic acid, 232, 235
Oxbow key, 356*i*

P

Padlocks, preventing rust on,
      102
Paint(s). *See also* Paintbrushes;
      Painting; Paint removal
  alligator finish in, 252*i*-53
  applying exterior, 169-71
  blisters on house exterior,
      164
  on brass, 23
  cans, drips on, 161, 169
  on ceilings, 197-98
  chalking exterior, 164
  cleanup, 172-74
  colors
    choosing, 152, 153, 154
    Colonial, 159
    identifying, 152
    original, determining, 154
    Victorian exterior, 168
    Victorian interior, 155
    for window sash, 171
  crayon marks on, 53
  disposing of, 174
  enamel, 154, 191

exterior
  mildew on, 308
  peeling, 300, 316
  on fabric, 46
  on glass, 20
  insects in, 168-69
  lead, 147
  metallic, imitation, 154-55
  mixing, 158-59, 160
  odors from, 160-61
  oil, skin on, 175
  oil vs. latex, 156
  old, identifying, 146
  primers, 167-68
  red, 169
  sand, 153-54
  scrapers, 164
  stains vs., 165
  station in workshop, 100
  storing, 174-75
  straining, 174*i*
  thinners, 173-74
  wallpapering over, 191
  water-based, 146
  for wood floors, 217
Paintbrushes, 156-57
  bent, 173
  hanging in water or solvent,
      172
  hardened, 172-73
  new, 157
  types of bristles, 156-57*i*
Painting, 144-75. *See also*
      Paint(s); Paintbrushes;
      Paint removal
  aluminum, 151, 171, 317, 342
  exterior, 163
  canoes, 361
  concrete floors, 233
  doors, 138
  drop cloths for, 157
  exterior
    order, 169-70
    preparing, 164-68
  fences, 163
  gutters, wooden, 321
  inaccessible places, 162
  interior, 161-63
  ladders for, 169
  metals, 151-52, 167
  pebble-finish ceilings, 162
  radiators, 155-56
  behind radiators, 162-63
  with rollers, 162-63
  stained wood, 152
  stairs, 161-62
  storm windows and doors,
      322
  stucco, 171
  ventilation for, 151
  walls, 148, 150-52, 162
  window sash, 157*i*-58
  wood floors, 218
  wood stoves, 286
  woodwork, masking for, 158

Rasps, cleaning, 114
Rat poisons, 78-79
Rattles in doors, 141
Recycling
  baby-food jars to store hardware, 99
  brooms as tool handles, 101
  buckets as stilts, 100-101*i*
  coffee cans to store hardware, 99
  dishwashing liquid container, 121
  down from comforters, 137
  energy saved by, 136
  files as chisels, 120
  funnels as twine holders, 98
  glass pane as furniture scraper, 120-21
  gloves, latex exam, 101
  hacksaw blades, 120
  homemade wrecking tool, 118*i*
  inner tube
    as garden-hose hanger, 99*i*-100
    as padlock rust protection, 102
  ladders as shop organizers, 97
  paint-thinner cans for hardware storage, 98-99
  refrigerator racks as grills, 366
  screening as wire wheels, 120
  solvents from stripping furniture, 252
  storage for, 136
Refinishing. *See also* Stripping
  colors of penetrating stains, 253-54
  fabric for rags, 253
  floors, 211-18
  furniture, 251-59
  glass as furniture scraper, 120-21
  pickled pine finish, 259
  with polyurethane, 255
  sanding furniture, 253
  with shellac, 258-59
  steel wool for, 257
  types of finishes, 251-52
  with varnish, 255
Reflector pans, cleaning, 10
Refrigerators
  cleaning, 9
  cockroaches under, 85
  odors in, 57
  rust on racks of, preventing, 9
Registers, ceiling, 264
Removing stumps, 354-55
Repairs and maintenance, basic, 132-43
  adhesives, basic, 134

brass, antique look for, 134-35
clothes-drying racks, 136
comforters, salvaging down from, 137
copper, antique look for, 135
countertops, 135-36
eyeglasses, tightening, 134
recyclables, storing, 136
stuck objects, 133-34
Repointing chimneys, 273-74
Resin finishes for wood floors, 215
Restoring original paint colors, 154
Rhododendrons, 345
Ridge vents, 299*i*
Rings in bathtubs, 27
Ripsaws, 107*i*
Risers, stair, 209*i*
Rocking chairs
  as American invention, 247
  walking, 246*i*
Rock(s). *See* Stone(s)
Rodents, attacking bulbs, 76
Rollers, paint, 162-63
Rolling pins, odors in, 58
Rolltop desks, 135, 241, 247
Roof(s), 323-27
  colors for heat gain or loss, 265, 323
  fear while working on, 324
  leaks in, 370
  mansard, 327*i*
  metal flashing for, 326*i*
  moss and mildew on, 325
  overhangs for shade, 263-64
  shingles, 323-25
  sizing gutters for, 319
  slate, 326-27
  vented gables in, 265
  ventilation for, 298-99*i*
Root maggots, 92
Rope(s)
  beds, 243
  broken on flagpoles, 350
  storing, 99
  wrench, 242*i*
Roses, 345
Rot, 208, 328
Rowboats, storing, 361
Rugs. *See also* Carpet(s)
  on new pine floors, 202-3
  slipping, 226
  stains in Oriental, 230
  vapor barriers beneath, 296
  on vinyl or linoleum floors, 221
Rust
  on carpets, 232
  on cast-iron pots and pans, 17
  on concrete floors, 235
  on countertops, 49

on fabric, 40
on hardware, 103-104
on padlocks, 102
prevention
  on garden tools, 124
  on handsaws, 113
  on wood stoves, 286
on slate sinks, 50
on stainless steel, 25
on tools, 114
on wood stoves, 37
R-values, 294, 302

S

Sachets, soap, 54
Safes, musty odors in, 55
Safety. *See also* Health hazards
  sharper tools for, 117
  when painting on ladders, 169
  when stripping wood floors, 211
  with wood stoves, 284-85
  in workshops, 95-96
Salt marks on boots and shoes, 49
Saltshaker tops, cleaning, 18-19
Sand
  paint, 153-54
  in summer houses, 364
Sandblasting, 148-49
Sanding
  curved surfaces, 122*i*
  drywall joint compound, 182
  furniture, 253
  vinyl or linoleum flooring, 223
  wood floors, 213*i*-14
Sandpaper, 122, 123
Sash, painting window, 157*i*-58
Sausage stuffer, 119*i*
Sawhorses, 125*i*-26*i*
Sawing metal, 131
Sawn lath, 179*i*
Saws
  bench, 199
  for cutting ceiling panels, 199
  history of, 96
  Japanese woodworking, 106
  maintaining, 113
  safety with, 95
  sharpening, 113
  types of wood, 107*i*
Saw set, 114*i*
Scatter rugs, slipping, 226
Scissors, rust on, 25
Scorch marks on fabric, 46
Scouring powder, baking soda as, 7
Scraper(s)
  glass as, 120-21
  Hyde molding, 147
  ship, 347*i*
Scraping, exterior, 164

Stucco
applying, 314-15*i*
bird damage to, 72
painting, 171
recipe for, 314
Stuck objects
door locks, 143
drawers, 137
jar lids, 133-34
keys broken in door locks,
143
nails, 103
screws, 103-4
sliding doors, 137
windows, 137
Studs, locating in walls, 178-80
Stuffed fish, cleaning, 373
Stumps, removing, 354-55
Subfloors, installing, 203-4
Submersible pumps, 363
Substitutions for household
cleaners, 29
Subterranean termites. *See* Ter-
mite(s)
Suede. *See* Leather
Sugar
auger, 162*i*
hard, 364
Suitcases, musty odors in, 54
Summer houses, 358-73
air fresheners in, 366
burglarproofing, 370-71
furniture for, 367
heating small areas of, 372
lighting for, 360-61
mildew in, 366
musty odors, preventing, 55
opening, 371-72
outhouses for, 369
pests in, 366-67, 372
preparing for winter, 363,
366-71
sand in, 364
water heaters in, 370, 371-72
Sunburns, 8
Surface finishes for wood
floors, 216
Suspended ceilings, 198-99
Swallows as insect controls, 89
Swamp shoe, 23*i*
Sweat stains on fabric, 41
Swelling in doors, 138-39
Swimmer's ear, 8
Swings, backyard, 350-51*i*
Switchel, 349
Switches, cutting holes in paneling for, 188

T

Tablecloths, yellow spots on,
43
Tabletops. *See also* Furniture
glass, preventing dust on, 14

leather
cleaning, 260
holes in, 260
marble, stains and water
marks on, 51
wooden
cracks and holes in, 254-55
flannel stuck to, 240
warped, 245*i*
Tack cloths, 257
Tambours for rolltop desks, repairing, 135, 241
Tangling, preventing
in stored plumb line, 111
in stored twine, 98
Tape residue on glass, 19-20
Tar
on cars, 30
on fabric, 45
on hands, 7
Tarnish, 22-23, 25
Teakettles, scale in, 23, 44
Tears in wallpaper, 193
Tea stains, 40, 50
Television screens, cleaning, 35
Termite(s), 82-84
shields, 87
vs. carpenter ants, 80*i*-81*i*
Testing
concrete floors for damp-
ness, 233
for mildew, 46
Textured paints, 153-54
"Thank-you-ma'ams," 350
Thermoses, cleaning, 32-33
Thinners, paint, 173-74
Ticks, in dogs' coats, 63
Tiger maple, 254
Tightening
cane chair seats, 261
eyeglasses, 134
furniture legs, 244*i*
rope beds, 243
Tiles. *See also* Linoleum floors;
Vinyl floors
bathroom, film on, 27
ceramic, 193-95
over concrete floors, 233-34
grout between, whitening,
27-28
leftovers as workbench tops,
124
quarry, 232
slate, storing, 327
Timber framing, 328
Tire(s)
as raised garden beds, 344
repair tool, 285*i*
swings, 351
Toaster ovens
cleaning windows of, 10
melted plastic on, 12
Tobacco odor, 60-61
Toggle bolts, 183*i*
Toilets, cleaning, 27, 28, 29

Tomatoes, improving yield of,
345-46
Tongue-and-groove paneling,
184-86
Tool(s). *See also* Power tools
basic components of work-
shop, 105
buying, 105-7
checking squareness of
squares, 115*i*-16
concrete dried on, 331
garden, 124
handles, from old brooms,
101
maintaining, 113-16
making, 118*i*-21
paint scrapers, 164
protecting, 113, 116
for removing finish, 213
for removing old plaster, 177
rust on, 113, 114
sharpening, 116*i*-18
storing, 97*i*, 98*i*
for stripping paint, 147
tile cutters, 193
using, 107-13
wood sticking on metal, 115
Toothpaste, substitutions for,
29
Tourniquet clamp, 249*i*
Towel holder, bartender's, 75*i*
Traction, for driveways and
walkways, 357
Trapdoors, 205
Trash, raccoons in, 68*i*-69
Treads, stair, 209*i*, 210
Tree sap on cars, 30
Trees damaged by mice, 77
Trimming grass, avoiding, 337
Triple-bladed chopping knife,
112*i*
Trisodium phosphate (TSP), 11
Trivet, fireplace, 48*i*
Trompe l'oeil, 196
Trucks. *See* Cars
Trunks
mothball odor in, 56-57
for storage in summer
houses, 367
TSP (trisodium phosphate), 11
Tubs. *See* Bathtubs
Tung oil as wood floor finish,
215, 216
Tuning cone, 140*i*
Twine, storing without tan-
gling, 98
Twisted boards, 129-30
Typewriters, cleaning, 35

U

Upholstery
animal hair on, 36
musty odors in, 54